W9-AFT-682

The Relevance of English
Teaching That Matters in Students' Lives

Edited by

ROBERT P. YAGELSKI
University at Albany, State University of New York

SCOTT A. LEONARD
Youngstown State University

National Council of Teachers of English
1111 W. Kenyon Road, Urbana, Illinois 61801-1096

Staff Editor: Tom Tiller
Interior Design: Jenny Jensen Greenleaf
Cover Design: Pat Mayer

NCTE Stock Number: 39892-3050

It is the policy of NCTE in its journals and other publications to provide a forum for the open discussion of ideas concerning the content and the teaching of English and the language arts. Publicity accorded to any particular point of view does not imply endorsement by the Executive Committee, the Board of Directors, or the membership at large, except in announcements of policy, where such endorsement is clearly specified.

Although every attempt is made to ensure accuracy at the time of publication, NCTE cannot guarantee that all published addresses for electronic mail or Web sites are current.

Library of Congress Cataloging-in-Publication Data
The relevance of English : teaching that matters in students' lives / edited by Robert P. Yagelski, Scott A. Leonard.
    p. cm. — (Refiguring English studies, ISSN 1073-9637)
Includes bibliographical references and index.
    ISBN 0-8141-3989-2 (pbk.)
  1. English philology—Study and teaching (Higher)—United States. 2. English philology—Study and teaching (Secondary)—United States. 3. English philology—Study and teaching (Higher)—Social aspects—United States. 4. English philology—Study and teaching (Secondary)—Social aspects— United States. I. Yagelski, Robert. II. Leonard, Scott A., 1958– III. Series.
    PE68 .U5 R38 2002
    420'.71'173—dc21
                                                    2002000866

For my parents, Ron and Joan Yagelski,
who enabled me to find relevance in my life.

RPY

For my parents, brothers, and sister,
for their faith, love, and encouragement.

SAL

CONTENTS

Contents

Contents

PREFACE

C urrent scholarly thinking would have us believe that we tell
stories to make sense of our lives—to give meaning to them.
We English teachers are particularly invested in this belief, for it
informs and gives purpose to so much of what we do and what
we ask our students to do. Surely, many of us would find it difficult, if not impossible, to do this often exhausting, complicated,
and underappreciated work of teaching English were it not for
the stories we tell of the importance of that work.

This volume is a collection of such stories: diverse and complex stories of the value and difficulty of teaching English. Together, these stories become part of the larger narrative of English
teaching that is always being written. In many ways, this narrative both complicates our work and comforts us as we confront
the many challenges of teaching. In this spirit, this volume is an
effort to contribute to the story of English teaching in the United
States at the dawn of a new millennium. It seeks to find purpose
in that large and ambitious project even as it questions that very
same project.

The voices in this volume represent an eclectic rather than
comprehensive group of teachers and scholars, some familiar,
some perhaps less so, who draw from their experiences in secondary and postsecondary English classrooms to examine the
question of the relevance of their work to the lives of their students. Some of the arguments that emerge from these stories will
be familiar to readers who teach English or who are concerned
about writing and reading instruction in our schools. At the same
time, some of the ideas about the relevance of English that emerge
from this volume will strike some readers as provocative or troubling. As the "Exchange" chapters that close each section of this
book suggest, there is much agreement among these writers about
the relevance of what they do as English teachers, but there is

also disagreement. Perhaps that is as it should be, since we English teachers have been arguing about our work with one another and with representatives of other segments of society from the very beginnings of the modern discipline of English in the nineteenth century. In the end, however, the contributors to this volume share an abiding faith that what we do is important, that it has value—that it is, finally, relevant. This volume, then, is a story of the relevance of English.

We believe that the beginning of a new millennium, which seems to coincide with profound social, economic, political, and technological change, provides an opportune moment to tell such a story, for it would seem that the change we are witnessing has undermined some of the stories we tell about our work and challenged us to tell new ones. But we know, too, that there are limits to these stories—indeed, to narrative in general. As Crispin Sartwell reminds us in *End of Story* (2000), there is genuine value in "retrieving meaning out of narratively articulated traditions" (such as, for example, the teaching of English), but the impulse to impose order through narrative, he believes, rests on a delusion (4). And he laments that this never-ending impulse to tell our stories—and our obsession with language in doing so—leaves us unable to appreciate vital moments in our lives that, in his view, escape linguistic articulation. This may seem an extreme and untenable view for those of us whose work and lives are so deeply wrapped up in language, who engage in the challenge of teaching English in the belief that language is central to being human. But Sartwell's complaints are worth remembering as we try to understand the relevance of teaching English, lest we find ourselves too willing to believe that the stories we tell about ourselves and our students represent *all* of what is true.

In this light, we hope that this volume contributes something important to what we know and believe about teaching English without promising more than that. We believe these stories represent important, insightful, and, ultimately, useful perspectives on the question of the relevance of English studies—a question every English teacher must wrestle with every day. But we know, too, that much is left unsaid—perhaps, as Sartwell believes, *unable* to be said—about the work we do. There is, we believe, value in leaving some things unsaid, just as there is value in the many ways in which the teaching of English is understood and conducted by the writers in this volume—and by their thousands of colleagues in classrooms throughout the United States.

Work Cited

Sartwell, Crispin. 2000. *End of Story: Toward an Annihilation of Language and History.* Albany: State University of New York Press.

ACKNOWLEDGMENTS

There is also a story to tell about how this book came to be, and if we were to tell that story, it would be populated with many characters who have been central to the development of the book. To thank them in these pages seems too feeble a way to express our gratitude and to acknowledge their contributions. We'll try anyway.

First, there would be no volume without the teachers who wrote the following chapters. Many of them worked under extremely tight deadlines, and some juggled large workloads to accommodate this project. All of them invested much time and energy in the project and, in the process, shared their ideas and voices with us. We cannot thank them enough for their commitment to this volume—and to the students they describe in their chapters. We hope this volume does justice to their efforts. We would especially like to thank Steve North for his early advice about the book and his encouragement of the project—long before he even knew he would be among the contributors; Kathleen Yancey for suggestions that helped give the project shape; Jim Sosnoski for advice and support that helped the project to grow; and Juanita Comfort for stepping in to help at a very late hour in the project's timetable.

We would also like to thank Michael Greer, formerly an editor with NCTE, who saw value in the idea for this book and encouraged the project in its earliest stages; his support got the project off the ground. Our gratitude as well to Kurt Austin and Zarina Hock, who took the project over and ably guided it through its later stages. Their confidence in us and their support for our work helped us to overcome innumerable obstacles and eventually to complete the project.

Finally, we would like to express our deepest gratitude to our loved ones, without whose support we would have had neither the time nor the energy to complete this book: Cheryl, Adam, and Aaron Yagelski; and Taylor Leonard and Christine Miletta. They, truly, are at the center of this project—and our lives—in ways we can never express in words.

The (Ir)relevance of English at the Turn of the Millennium

ROBERT P. YAGELSKI

University at Albany, State University of New York

Not long ago, looking in a bookstore sale bin, I came across a volume called *The Irrelevant English Teacher*. Written by J. Mitchell Morse, who is identified on the jacket as full professor of English at Temple University and "well-known Joyce scholar," and published in 1972, *The Irrelevant English Teacher* is clearly a product of its time. On the first page of the first chapter, which is called "The Case for Irrelevance," Morse refers to the Vietnam War and the Civil Rights movement, and in the following pages he mentions Stokely Carmichael, George Wallace, and H. Rap Brown. Not surprisingly, the book is cast in political terms, and in that first chapter Morse unabashedly identifies himself as a liberal. He also asserts that the best thing a teacher of English can do for liberalism is to ignore it. Morse's justification for such an assertion is that "as a teacher of literature, I think it is vitally important for my students to develop some sensitivity to literary values" (4). The lack of concern with such values by our society, he writes, "has had unfortunate effects on the whole quality of its life, including its moral quality and ultimately its political quality" (5). To put it simply, Morse argues that we English teachers serve society best when we teach its children to read carefully, speak articulately, and write clearly, because if they can do these things, then they can think clearly, too. And if they can do that, he says, they will be less susceptible to the kind of political demagoguery that he describes as characteristic of his era. "If the next generation continues its wordless descent into mere inarticulate feeling," he writes, "it will soon be politically helpless" (122). The real job of the English teacher is thus to help students become politically astute not by teaching politics but by teaching literature.

Despite its lack of our currently fashionable jargon about agency, cultural critique, and hegemony, Morse's argument is one we still hear in various guises today. I am thinking here of obvious public figures like William Bennett but also of scholars like James Battersby, who has argued against overtly (left-leaning) political pedagogies in the English classroom, and Maxine Hairston, who has made similar arguments in the context of the teaching of composition. Their assumptions about what English studies should be (and about how English should be taught) are not very different from Morse's. Indeed, the notion that the careful study of carefully selected literary works and intensive instruction in "clear" writing are good for students and necessary for society has been put forth by English professionals from the time in the late nineteenth century when the modern English department began to emerge from the remnants of classics and rhetoric departments. But what interests me most about Morse's obscure book is the fact that he squarely confronts the question of the relevance of academic English in the context of the political turmoil of his time and asserts unequivocally that English is perhaps the *most* relevant of academic pursuits. Indeed, he argues that English studies need not assert its relevance either by adopting overtly political pedagogies or by offering politically-oriented content. For Morse, the relevance of English is implicit and defined not in terms of applicability to current political controversies or particular job-related skills or even the specific interests of students; rather, relevance is a matter of fostering the timeless and universal values of clear thought and expression. These, he says, apply in all venues of social and political life and thus are always profoundly relevant.

By today's standards (and despite Morse's self-proclaimed liberal politics), many readers would likely characterize Morse's stance as "conservative" or "foundationalist." His argument suggests, for instance, that he would oppose the kind of first-year composition course that generated so much controversy at the University of Texas a decade ago with its focus on "difference" (see Brodkey 1994), as well as the kinds of "critical pedagogies" that have gained popularity in recent years. And yet Morse's central point—that we help foster politically aware and active minds among our students if we teach a certain kind of writing and reading—resembles the arguments set forth by Brodkey and by proponents of critical pedagogies. They too argue that what we teach ultimately serves our students well in the political and cultural arenas; that is, we're teaching them to be critically aware citizens who can read, write, speak, and think in ways that enable them to resist political domination or hegemony. That's essentially what Morse argued in 1972. And that seems to have become in some basic sense the primary justification we have for English studies: academic English is about making "good" citizens. As James Berlin put it in his book *Rhetorics, Poetics, and Cultures* (1996), "English studies has a special role in the democratic educational mission" (54); our primary objective, he says, is "developing a measure of facility in reading and writing practices so as to prepare students for public discourse in a democratic political community" (110). We teach the literacy that students must have in order to become active, participating citizens. That's why we're relevant.

The authors in this volume, an eclectic (though by no means comprehensive) collection of voices from secondary and postsecondary English education, wonder about the relevance of our English classes to the lives our students lead in a complex, rapidly changing, and increasingly technological world. It seems an appropriate moment to do so, as we begin a new millennium amid concern, both public and professional, that English as a discipline (indeed, institutionalized education in general) has not adequately responded to our students' needs as literate persons at a time of profound social, political, economic, and technological change. We have been witnessing unusually intense public debate about the secondary and postsecondary school English curriculum. For instance, the controversy about English 306 at the University of Texas at Austin became, for a brief time in the early 1990s, a national cause celebre among conservative activists and commentators concerned that the study of English has become too radical, too political, too ideological (as if the teaching and study of English—or any subject, for that matter—are ever apolitical or ideologically neutral). Just a few years later teachers and scholars in rhetoric and composition (including Brodkey herself) are debating the very usefulness of required first-year composition courses for college students, arguing for their "abolition" partly on the grounds that they support exploitation of teaching assistants and adjunct faculty; meanwhile, many politicians and school administrators demand more attention to writing and other "basic skills" in college curricula, even as some schools move to eliminate "remedial" writing programs. In the late 1990s, controversy erupted over a policy in the Oakland (California) school district that allowed teachers to treat a nonmainstream dialect of English called "Ebonics" as a second language. Many of the most vocal critics of the policy (including Black leaders like Jesse Jackson) argued that students of color who spoke "Ebonics" could never succeed in school or business if they didn't learn "standard" English. One clear implication of such criticisms is that the study of English is vitally important to students seeking academic and professional success. Many state education policymakers seem to agree, and the last five or six years have seen renewed efforts across the country to implement standardized tests intended to ensure that all students are learning to read and write well enough to "compete" in the global marketplace. My own state of New York recently implemented a new more "rigorous" English exam, which eventually all high school students will have to pass in order to receive a diploma. And as I was finishing this introduction, I received a message from a former student, now living in Alabama, who described her experiences in fighting the efforts of local conservative activists to ban all books by Judy Blume from her school district's curricula—one more local battle in the never-ending censorship war in which English teachers are often unwilling combatants.

All of these instances of controversy about the teaching of English seem to suggest that academic English is indeed relevant. Otherwise, who would bother to get involved in such intense battles? Our society continues to send us these obvious signals that it considers what we do important and relevant, and it does so in the context of social, cultural, economic, and technological change that seemed unimaginable even a decade or two ago. Yet our classrooms, our curricula, and the structure of our schools have remained largely unchanged for most of the past century, despite various pedagogical reform movements, volumes of empirical research on writing instruction, and more theoretical arguments than we can cram into an ever-increasing number of professional journals and scholarly books. Meanwhile, professional discussions about what English studies should be proliferate in our journals and books, at our conferences, and in mission statements that we attach to curriculum documents and committee reports. Surely we English professionals spend much more time and scholarly energy writing and talking about who we are and what we do than is the case for teachers and scholars in most other disciplines. (I sometimes wonder, for instance, how many papers presented at the annual convention of, say, mathematics educators or biologists or even psychologists are devoted to questions of "disciplinarity": What *is* biology? How do we define mathematics? Should we abolish psychology 101?) Maybe our endless self-examination is just a reflection of the condition of academic English as a "field" or "discipline" always in search of itself, always in need of defining its purpose and asserting its relevance. But perhaps one measure of the importance (or lack thereof) of this ongoing professional obsession with self-definition is this: not far away from the sale bin in the bookstore where I found Morse's *The Irrelevant English Teacher* was a shelf labeled "Summer Reading," heavy with familiar volumes to be purchased by high school students in order to complete their summer reading requirement for their impending English classes. I purchased my own summer reading books from a similar shelf in the early 1970s (about the time Morse's book was published); my two high-school-aged sons and their classmates—and millions of other high school students around the United States—do the same three decades later. Morse argued that such reading, under the tutelage of a skilled English teacher, is precisely what students need in order to become capable, critical citizens; Battersby and Bennett and others make the same sort of argument today. Yet I wonder how much more relevant to a fifteen- or sixteen-year-old's life is reading (and writing a "report" on) Sandra Cisneros's *The House on Mango Street* (a common title on today's summer reading lists) as compared to, say, *The Catcher in the Rye* (a book I was required to read). In an age of virtual realities, live television and Internet coverage of shootings at places like Littleton High School in Colorado, falling real wages for many segments of the population, the North American Free Trade Agreement ("NAFTA"), and burgeoning "e-commerce" activity, what purposes do our summer reading assignments—and our many time-honored literacy pedagogies—truly serve for our students? Do they indeed foster the kinds of literacy abilities that might enable our students to negotiate this often treacherous world?

This project began with a similar, though more forthright, question from a student I met on a visit to a high school near my home: "What's the point?" she wanted to know, after listening to my enthusiastic pitch about writing and reading and technology. She sounded like a typical bored high school junior posing that tired question that every English teacher has tried to answer at one point or another, but her challenge to me suggested that there was more to it than that. The more I considered her arguments about the irrelevance of most of what she was asked to do by her English teachers, the more they sounded like my own concerns about the teaching of writing and reading in secondary and postsecondary schools. And there was something disturbingly incongruous about my own part in this enterprise we call English studies: so much of what I spent my professional time doing seemed far removed from what that young woman seemed to want—and need—from her English teachers. In sharing this story with colleagues at other schools, I began to sense a vague but unsettling concern among other English practitioners that perhaps this young woman is right: When we consider our work in light of students' needs as literate persons in a complex and difficult world, there often seems little point to what we as English professionals do. Meanwhile, our professional work is often characterized by trends, what one of my colleagues has called "stargazing," and direct participation in the all-pervasive system of curriculum management driven by large-scale assessment and textbook marketing that we sometimes decry in scholarly articles, books, and conference talks. (I do not in any way exempt myself from these criticisms, since I have also been a participant in these activities.) I am not so naive as to think that these are simple matters. These same professional activities that often seem so counterproductive and even reactionary can also at times serve students' needs (as well as our own). "The system" that we sometimes wish to blame for these ills can enable as well as disempower; it is as complex as the activities of writing and reading themselves. Nevertheless, when I look at the work my own two high-school-age sons are asked to do by their English teachers; when I consider how mindless and meaningless much of it is and how removed it is from the day-to-day pressures they encounter as adolescents and the literacy challenges they face outside their classrooms; and when I compare their experiences in their classes to the experiences of the millions of other students, most of whom (our professional experience and research tell us) encounter the same sort of assignments—when I consider all this, I myself begin to wonder, What's the point?

A look back at the brief history of English studies reveals that we seem always to have been asking this question, though rarely do we seem to have reached anything approaching consensus on an answer to it. We may have come close around 1958. Then, in a kind of national panic over the successful Soviet launching of Sputnik, Congress passed the National Defense Education Act, which provided federal funds for education research, curriculum development, and teacher training under the assumption that effective education was essential to the preservation of America's stature as a superpower. Interestingly, that landmark legislation did not include English as one of the vital areas of study to be supported by federal funds, and that exclusion prompted English educators to make a case for their discipline as crucial to "the national interest." Three years later, the National Council of Teachers of English published *The National Interest and the Teaching of English,* which some commentators—see, for example, page 11 of Stephen North's *The Making of Knowledge in Composition* (1987)—credit with convincing Congress to include English as a vital subject of study in schools (which Congress subsequently did in several related pieces of legislation). It seems a watershed, if short-lived, moment in the history of English as an academic discipline, bringing together conservative, traditionalist, moderate, liberal, and progressive educators in a rare moment of relative agreement about the importance of the study of

English in American society. More than forty years after the passage of the NDEA, however, no such consensus seems to exist among English educators about the purpose of what they do beyond the rather general idea that we educate students for citizenry. As Richard Ohmann has pointed out in an insightful essay called "English After the USSR" (1995), the world Americans inhabit is no longer structured around the "master narrative" of the grand struggle between Marxism and capitalism, as it seemed to be in 1958 and through the 1960s, 1970s, and 1980s. Sputnik seems as distant as detente—no closer to the concerns of contemporary students than a brief paragraph in a yellowing history textbook. The binary world of U.S. vs. USSR has given way to a multicultural world that challenges teachers of English to justify their traditional approaches to teaching writing and reading. And the students of those teachers inhabit a world of geopolitical confusion, of "downsizing" and economic "restructuring," that can make Shakespeare seem about as important to them as Sputnik.

Amidst this apparent confusion, our professional journals are filled with discussions that map out what we *should* be doing as a profession even as accompanying pages of those same journals traverse ground as varied as literary study, professional and technical communications, critical pedagogy, cultural studies, linguistics, ethnography, philosophy, rhetorical history and theory, poetics, and grammar—to offer an incomplete list of "areas" we consider somehow to belong to or comprise English studies. Surely a map of our "field"—to the extent that we can call it such— would encompass varied terrain indeed, and its boundaries would be as uncertain as many of the alliances we seem to have created as we struggle for space within the changing environment of higher education. We debate the role of "theory" (whatever that means), the abolition of first-year composition, the shape (or existence) of the canon, in ways that reveal the complexity of our "field" and our uncertainty about it. In my former department I have witnessed political and ideological battles that might once have been described as "internecine" but that cannot lay claim to such a descriptor given the widely divergent understandings of "English studies" among the combatants. Those battles reflect similar tensions elsewhere. And if English educators seem unable to muster the kind of loose consensus about their field that their counterparts were able to find in the early days of the Cold War, contemporary students may have cause to worry about what their English teachers have to offer them. What's the point? Indeed.

The contributors to this volume offer a variety of answers to that question. Those answers are not concerned with scholarly arguments about how to *define* English as an academic discipline. Rather, their focus is squarely on students: What might the study of English mean to them? How does it meet (or fail to meet) their needs as literate beings in a world increasingly defined by literacy? How does the English classroom relate to the lives our students lead outside it? How *should* it relate to those lives? Collectively, the contributors' purpose is not to offer a definitive or comprehensive answer to such questions, nor even to paint a representative picture of current thinking about such matters in our field, but rather to present what they believe they have learned as English teachers and scholars in order to examine our roles in the lives of our students and to explore the relevance of our work as literacy educators. No doubt this effort will raise further questions.

Victor Villanueva, for instance, considers the role of academic English in the perpetuation of racism in American culture—and the potential of English as a course of study for combating racism. For Villanueva, there is no avoiding the issue of racism in our increasingly multicultural and multiethnic society, and thus we must confront it squarely in our classrooms. English classrooms in particular, Villanueva suggests, given their focus on language and story and culture, have a responsibility to address this matter. To what extent might we English teachers represent the "utopian hope" for the radical change that Villanueva seeks in our racialized discourses and our ways of dealing with racial difference? To what extent is that our job? Answers—and disagreements—abound. But for Villanueva, the relevance of what we English teachers do is a function of the extent to which we can find ways to make our pedagogies address this kind of difficult challenge that we face in our society generally.

Juanita Comfort takes up that challenge in the specific context of graduate study in English (reminding us, along with Stephen North, that English studies also encompasses advanced graduate study and professional preparation). For Comfort, the problems of racism and sexism emerge in the obstacles faced by women of color who struggle to gain acceptance in the academy even as they insist on retaining an identity that positions them at the margins of that academy. Like many of the authors in this volume, Comfort understands the power of language—and, in particular, written language—to construct identity and claim agency, but she helps us see an irony in the way that English studies, a discipline ostensibly concerned with that power of language, can be an oppressive space where language is used as a tool for exclusion rather than empowerment. Her calls for understanding within English studies of the differences represented by the women of color to whom she introduces us relates to Villanueva's desire to connect the English classroom to the larger social and cultural contexts within which we and our students live. And she reminds us that to make English "relevant" to our students is a complex and difficult challenge that may differ from one student to the next. Relevance in this field, Comfort eloquently insists, is as much about identity as it is about literacy.

Margaret Finders also addresses issues of difference as they emerge in English classrooms, though she expands the notion of "difference" to incorporate socioeconomic status and encourages us to consider it specifically within the context of adolescent peer culture. That culture, she argues, not only diverges in complex ways from many of the values implicit in our conventional secondary school curricula but also undermines many of our efforts as teachers to convey to students what we believe is most important about literacy. Finders wants us to see that the relevance of what we offer our students cannot be understood as separate from the culture they themselves construct and inhabit. Her perspective is not just another version of the view, often associated with 1960s liberalism, that we should incorporate popular culture into the English curriculum in the form of song lyrics and movies and such. Rather, Finders pushes us to see that students don't want to be patronized in that way; they want literacy instruction that makes a difference in their lives, that has material consequences for them, that challenges our own deeply held beliefs about literacy. And summer reading assignments don't seem to pass muster on that score.

Such questions about the relationship between English instruction and the culture at large run through many of the following chapters and make for a provocative framework for understanding the study of English. Gerald Graff examines what he sees as a mismatch between ways of arguing—and ways of thinking about argument and about discourse—that we value in school settings and ways of understanding the world that seem to characterize popular culture. This mismatch is at heart an epistemological matter, for it goes beyond discourse conventions to how we know and how we can say what we know. For Graff, any effort to make our curricula relevant to students, who do not leave culture at the door when they enter our classrooms, must take these epistemological issues into account. And he forces us to consider the possibility that what we offer students is really a version of *our own* ways of seeing the world that may have little relevance to the lives students lead. In a sense, Paula Mathieu and Jim Sosnoski address the same epistemological problem, but they focus directly on pedagogical practice. Like Graff, Mathieu and Sosnoski see a divergence between the ways of seeing the world that are valued in the classroom—in their case, a classroom characterized by a cultural studies pedagogy—and the ways of seeing that students bring to that classroom. They examine how this divergence plays out within a cultural studies approach to teaching English that, they argue, many students believe forces on them a kind of "moral imperative" and therefore should be resisted. However, Mathieu and Sosnoski make no bones about asserting that teachers adopting such an approach must overcome that resistance, because the view of the world that they offer students is one that they believe will serve students' needs as citizens in a complex, media-driven culture. Indeed, they believe that cultural studies can offer students what they need in order to negotiate a treacherous world of discourse. In this sense, theirs is an overtly political pedagogy that defines relevance in terms of a pedagogy's ability to give students a critical perspective on the culture they inhabit. Sarah Robbins offers a similar kind of pedagogy for middle-school students, one that draws on Paulo Freire's ideas about critical literacy and its relationship to students' lives outside the classroom. Although a number of critics have questioned the applicability of a Freirean pedagogy to the American classroom (indeed, Steve North, whose essay appears in Part I of this volume, has raised such questions; see his "Rhetoric"), Robbins holds firm to the notion, central to Freire's work, that literacy is about constructing the world and thus is unavoidably about ideology, regardless of cultural or socioeconomic context. Accordingly, Robbins describes a pedagogy intended to prepare students for participation in their communities as literate persons with a stake in making those communities egalitarian. All these writers may agree with J. Mitchell Morse that English studies is ultimately about preparing critically aware citizens, but they advocate overt attention to that project and they are not content to define it as the indirect result of the study of literature and "clear" writing.

Many of the contributors to this volume define relevance more specifically in terms of the lives of individual students trying to negotiate the challenges they face as people in a changing world. For Patricia Fox, Donald Tinney, Cristina Kirklighter, Juanita Comfort, and Kathleen Cheney, the English classroom is relevant only to the extent that it helps students meet those challenges as men and women, as adolescents and "nontraditional" students, as people of color and people displaced by economic developments over which they seem to have no control. For example, the women returning to school find in Fox's classroom a place where they can construct stories of their often difficult lives in order to make sense of those lives and claim agency in them—lives deeply and often directly affected by the larger cultural developments about which Graff and Mathieu and Sosnoski write. Kirklighter offers a similar space for her students, who tell different versions of the same compelling stories that Fox's students tell. For them, relevance arises from the effort to find meaning in such stories and to write new ones as well. Tinney's high school students, too, write—and read—stories about living life, about finding one's way through the confusion of contemporary culture. He casts his role as a keeper of such stories—stories that he believes his adolescent students need at a crucial moment in their lives as they struggle to make their lives meaningful to themselves and to understand how others find meaning in their lives. Cheney's students are often much older than Tinney's, yet they encounter the same obstacles and engage in the same struggles, often at unexpected but critical junctures in their lives. For all these teachers, despite obvious differences in their approaches to literacy instruction, English studies is about what it means to be human. In a sense, they all offer a traditional answer to the question of the relevance of English, but they do so in a decidedly contemporary context that may challenge our notions about our traditional pedagogies and curricula.

Many of Cheney's students, she tells us, come to her classroom after losing a job or despairing of making their current jobs meaningful. They come to her because of seemingly faraway events like the North American Free Trade Agreement or a corporate restructuring at their workplace. Such economic developments raise hard questions about what we, as English educators, can offer our students, who are subject to changes that don't seem explicable by rules that obtained in the postwar era described by Ohmann—rules that crumbled with the Berlin Wall in 1989. It is precisely such questions that concern Scott Leonard and, indirectly, Stephen North. Both wish to understand the relationship of English as a discipline to the economic and legal systems within which we live, and they seek relevance in that connection. Leonard's students will perhaps remind readers of Cheney's or Kirklighter's students, but he won't let us forget that his classroom exists within a capitalist system that is ultimately the reason many of his students sit before him. At the same time, he resists the idea that teaching English is a business. Relevance, for Leonard, cannot be measured in a kind of educational profit-and-loss statement, though he makes it clear that he sees institutionalized education doing just that. He clings to an idea that literacy—and literature—can somehow give students something more than a credential or a set of job-related skills. If not, then we can define our relevance only in economic terms after all. Which would be OK with North, who worries that notions about English as somehow transcendent of legal and economic realities can serve only to make our discipline *less* relevant to our students and to the society within which we work. North sees our work in contractual terms: we have a legal responsibility to prepare students as readers and writers for functional lives outside the academy—*not,* he makes clear, to perpetuate a discipline built upon our esoteric scholarly interests, a discipline that supports itself through exploitative economic practices. In a sense, Mark Reynolds takes up similar issues, for his sense of the relevance of what teachers of English do is tied directly to the economic realities of students' lives. But Reynolds focuses on the specific institution of the two-year college, arguing that that institution is much more responsive—and thus more relevant—to those realities and to students' needs as citizens and workers in a changing economic landscape than are the universities whose English departments North criticizes.

Implicit in the concerns raised by Reynolds and Leonard about the relationship between the English curriculum and the changing economy is the profound impact of new technologies. What, for instance, might new computer technologies that seem to be reshaping the workplace and our culture in general mean for English studies in the coming decades? If we have indeed entered what scholar Jay David Bolter (1991) calls the "late age of print," have we also entered a new era of English teaching, one defined by powerful new technologies for literacy? Ted Nellen, writing from the perspective of an experienced teacher who pioneered the use of computer technologies in a New York City high school, argues not only that teachers must incorporate these technologies into the English curriculum but, more provocatively, that evolving computer technologies should indeed be at the center of a radically reformed curriculum. Nellen sees the conventional English curriculum as essentially outdated and thus irrelevant to students' needs as literate persons, workers, and citizens in a culture that is currently being reshaped by rapidly developing computer-based communications technologies. Unlike many educators who worry that these developments compromise literacy, Nellen believes they represent new forms of literacy through which students can deepen their learning and expand their inquiry into their world. Nellen's vision will worry some readers who are skeptical of the kinds of claims he makes about the possibilities represented by these technologies. But he will perhaps force such readers to rethink their own assumptions not only about the ways in which English is relevant to students' lives but also about the nature of literacy and its place in the English curriculum.

Richard and Cynthia Selfe are acutely aware of some of the concerns that teachers harbor about technology, and they share a worry that educators can be swept up by their own enthusiasm for the kinds of possibilities that Nellen sees in the new computer technologies. For them, the fundamental goals of a humanist education retain value in our changing world and must drive our efforts to design technology-rich pedagogies. They see technological change as inevitable, but they wish to find ways to shape these inevitable changes brought on by technology so that technology not only serves students' needs but *reflects* our most deeply held hopes for a just and equitable society. This is an ambitious vision for English teachers, one that implicitly defines relevance in terms of the extent to which the teaching of English ultimately contributes to such a society. In a sense, they share J. Mitchell Morse's wish for a better society, but unlike Morse they define a proactive role for English teachers in building such a society.

Valerie Drye and Kathleen Yancey share with Richard and Cynthia Selfe that belief in a proactive role for teachers in contributing to the building of a better world through the teaching of English. There is no denying the idealism that drives their arguments, which may make some readers uncomfortable. Yet my sense, reinforced by my interactions with teachers at all levels of education, is that such idealism remains a driving force in the profession of English teaching—despite the discomforting skepticism and worry that I described above. Like so many teachers I have known, like so many student teachers who have come through my undergraduate classes, like so many teachers we have all read about and met, high school teacher Valerie Drye entered the profession because she believed she could "make a difference." Her motives may seem cliché, but she is neither insincere nor naive. In her very first year as a new "lateral-entry" teacher, having changed careers in midlife to become a teacher, Drye must struggle hard to stave off despair in the face of what she believes are counterproductive (and even harmful) but increasingly widespread state tests and curriculum guidelines. She doesn't lose sight of the place of her classroom in the sprawling bureaucracy of public education and the obstacles her students face as they themselves struggle to make their way through a seemingly irrelevant curriculum. She has no illusions about what she, individually, can do in such a system. Yet she refuses to believe that the curriculum alone defines her relevance to her students. For Drye, the importance of what English teachers offer students like hers cannot be manifested in test preparation; rather, she defines the relevance of what she does in terms of its effect on the ways in which her students make sense of their lives and the complex and often confusing world they are entering.

In the midst of the controversies within English studies that I described above, I have sensed a desire to reclaim the idealism and hope that kept Drye in the classroom for a second year. In discussions at gatherings like NCTE's annual convention, CCCC, and smaller conferences, I have heard versions of Drye's vision along with her frustration and anger and skepticism. In recent publications, like Hephzibah Roskelly and Kate Ronald's *Reason to Believe* (1998), I hear a desire to keep that vision at the center of what we do even as we struggle to understand ourselves in a time of change and even as we battle among ourselves to define our mission while confronting uncertain prospects for the future. Perhaps it is a response to the turn of the millennium, a collective need to step back and try to make sense of where we are. Or perhaps it is a refusal to let go of a hopeful vision that seems to run through the short history of the teaching of English. In part, we English teachers function through myths that we both inherit and help perpetuate, myths about possibilities for individuals and for communities. Kathleen Yancey draws on those myths as she shares her own vision—a hopeful though complex one—for English studies. Like many of the other contributors to this volume, Yancey defines relevance ultimately in terms of the effect we can have on our students' lives. But she recognizes that that effect cannot be separated neatly from the cultural contexts within which we work or from the battles we fight with each other about what we do. Some readers will resist her calls for a kind of professional pluralism, drawing perhaps on recent critiques of pluralism as hegemonic and ineffective in eradicating racism, sexism, classism, and other such ills from our society. But Yancey understands that the pluralism that has characterized American society is inextricably wrapped up in identity formation, in our conceptions of who we are as individuals and as members of many communities at once. That isn't likely to change, Yancey tells us, and that's not a bad thing, since there is a kind of strength in our diversity that can open up opportunities to reveal and examine and combat the kinds of problems that inevitably arise in a pluralistic culture—the kinds of problems that Villanueva describes in his chapter and Finders in hers. Yancey is no dreamer, but she sees that we cannot do this difficult work without a dream. And she's willing to admit that our collective and uncertain vision of what we do, problematic though it may be, is and perhaps *must be* an idealistic one.

That conflict will attend any efforts to realize such a vision is self-evident, and even as most of the writers in this volume share fundamental assumptions about teaching English, they often diverge in the way they understand specific issues and in their prescriptions for how to proceed from here. The Exchange sections that end each of the three main sections of this book represent an attempt to acknowledge this inevitable conflict and to suggest that the arguments and visions presented here are not so neat and finished as they tend to seem in a published volume. They are in flux and are sometimes tentative and uncertain, and the authors here continue to refine, rethink, challenge, and even change them. The Exchange texts are not intended to present all the possible objections or critiques of the chapters in each section of the book (nor even the main objections or critiques); rather, their purpose is to raise some productive questions and to extend the ideas presented in the chapters. And they are meant to remind us that our attempt to define the relevance of what we do as English teachers—to answer questions about the *point* of English studies—is unfinished and ongoing.

It is important to note here in conclusion that this volume was never intended to present a comprehensive vision for English studies, nor was it compiled as a kind of point/counterpoint statement encompassing the dominant competing visions of English at this seemingly critical time in the discipline's history. Rather, it was an effort to answer the question of the relevance of our work as English teachers by listening to the voices of various people who offer their own visions, experiences, perspectives, hopes, and doubts. Some of those voices will be recognizable to readers who follow scholarly and professional discussions about such matters. Others are voices that readers have never before heard in such discussions—voices of committed classroom teachers who struggle with the question of their relevance every day. Scott Leonard and I considered it crucial to include those voices in this volume, no matter how variegated the volume would therefore become. We believe the sometimes uneven and unfinished "feel" of this volume is entirely appropriate to the subject we have addressed in it, and we hope readers will find in that quality of the book provocative reasons to think in new and useful ways about the relevance of English teaching.

Works Cited

Battersby, James L. 1996. "The Inescapability of Humanism." *College English* 58 (September): 555–67.

Berlin, James A. 1996. *Rhetoric, Poetics, and Cultures: Refiguring College English Studies.* Urbana, Ill: National Council of Teachers of English.

Bolter, Jay David. 1991. *Writing Space: The Computer, Hypertext, and the History of Writing.* Hillsdale, N.J.: Lawrence Erlbaum Associates.

Brodkey, Linda. 1994. "Making a Federal Case Out of Difference: The Politics of Pedagogy, Publicity, and Postponement." Pp. 236–61 in *Writing Theory and Critical Theory,* ed. John Clifford and John Schilb. New York: Modern Language Association.

Hairston, Maxine. 1992. "Diversity, Ideology, and Teaching Writing." *College Composition and Communication* 43 (May): 179–93.

Morse, J. Mitchell. 1972. *The Irrelevant English Teacher.* Philadelphia: Temple University Press.

National Council of Teachers of English. 1961. *The National Interest and the Teaching of English: A Report on the Status of the Profession.* Champaign, Ill.: National Council of Teachers of English (Committee on National Interest).

North, Stephen M. 1987. *The Making of Knowledge in Composition: Portrait of an Emerging Field.* Upper Montclair, N.J.: Boynton/Cook.

———. 1991. "Rhetoric, Responsibility, and the 'Language of the Left.'" Pp. 127–36 in *Composition and Resistance,* ed. C. Mark Hurlbert and Michael Blitz. Portsmouth, N.H.: Boynton/Cook.

Ohmann, Richard. 1995. "English After the USSR." Pp. 226–37 in *After Political Correctness: The Humanities and Society in the 1990s,* ed. C. Newfield and R. Strickland. Boulder, Colo.: Westview Press.

Roskelly, Hephzibah, and Kate Ronald. 1998. *Reason to Believe: Romanticism, Pragmatism, and the Possibility of Teaching.* Albany, N.Y.: State University of New York Press.

PART I

CONTEXTS: AMERICAN CULTURE AND THE STUDY OF ENGLISH

CHAPTER ONE

The Academic Language Gap

GERALD GRAFF

University of Illinois at Chicago

R ecent curricular debates have opposed those who urge a return to teaching basic information and traditional texts against those who want to decenter the canon and foreground politics and critical thinking. Overlooked in the clash between competing conceptions of intellectual culture, however, is the deep ambivalence students often feel toward intellectual culture as such, regardless of which side gets to draw up the reading list. For this silent majority of students, either a return to a traditional curriculum or the triumph of a nontraditional one is likely to seem like the same old deadly "school stuff." It will not matter much whether traditionalists or revisionists win the curriculum war if these students remain deprived of the cultural capital that terms like "traditionalist" and "revisionist" confer.

To address educational problems at their root, then, we need to start with the enormous gulf that separates the culture and discourse of students from that of teachers, quite irrespective of whether the teachers are conservative, radical, or middle of the road. On the one hand, students recognize the personal and cultural power that comes with mastery of the conceptual and communicative competencies the academy has to offer. They also recognize that these competencies may be a prerequisite for vocational success in the emerging global "information society." On the other hand, students still feel deep reservations about assuming the role of self-conscious intellectualizer and contentious argument-maker that is demanded by academic courses,

This essay appeared previously in *Notes in the Margins* (Spring 1995). Reprinted by permission.

including basic composition. Academic-intellectual literacy promises power, but at the cost of a personal makeover that may not look attractive, especially when there are no guarantees.

What is it about the role of intellectualizer and public argument-maker that looks compromising to students? First, such a role rests on a conception of citizenship that has become increasingly unreal since the late nineteenth century, with the erosion of small-town culture and the displacement of the urban citizen by the consumer. The diminished political role of the citizen makes it hard to imagine ourselves influencing public policy by exercising our rhetorical and argumentative skills. The standard expository composition assignment requiring students to develop a "position" on a public issue like homelessness or abortion rests on the increasingly hollow-seeming pretense that the arguments we make on such issues will actually make a difference.

Second, the discomfort students feel about affecting the persona of a public argument-maker is deepened by the traditional American suspicion of intellectualism, which is still often identified widely with aggression, aloofness, and snobbish elitism. Argumentation and intellectualism entail a distancing from one's experience in the "elaborated code" described by sociologist Basil Bernstein as characteristic of upper class speakers and writers. Americans both admire and distrust people with arguments—politicians, advertisers, eggheads, and others who seem manipulative or pretentious. The very word "argument" for many students (like the word "criticism") conjures up a vision not of discussions that go somewhere—how many arguments end, after all, with anybody's mind being changed?—but of negativism, sarcasm, and aggression, of contentious hair-splitting bouts in which competitors put each other down. In short, for many students, becoming the sort of contentious person that the academy rewards seems to mean turning oneself into a snob or a nerd, quite possibly alienating oneself from one's friends, relatives, and romantic partners. As the saying goes, nobody likes a smart-ass.

To put it another way, to assume the rhetorical posture of argument-maker you have to want other people to do something that they are not already doing, if only to think differently. Why should you as a student want to tell other people what to do? Students who have been socialized into the secular liberal pluralist outlook have acquired a philosophy of live and let live: I have my opinion, you have yours, so why not leave things at that? To set yourself up as the pushy kind of person that composition assignments ask for commits you to the seemingly arrogant proposition that other people should think like you, and that you have the right to speak for others.

Students from a more traditional religious upbringing, on the other hand, are no less likely to think their beliefs are self-sufficient and therefore not worth getting into a debate about. For such students, the secularized social types on campus may seem too far gone in their agnosticism to be persuadable. Whether secular or religious, then, the chances are that the American student has been trained to believe that adopting an argumentative rhetorical attitude is at best a waste of time and at worst asking for trouble.

A third factor that deepens student alienation from the culture of argumentation is the academic obsession with problems and problematizing, something that appears strange and counterintuitive not just to students but to most nonacademics. Standard expository theme assignments ask students not only to become aggressive know-it-alls, but to cultivate and cherish "problems" in a way that seems at best mysterious and at worst perverse.

My University of Chicago colleague Joseph M. Williams and his associate Gregory G. Colomb call this "the Problem Problem." In an unpublished manuscript, Williams and Colomb point out that a special stumbling block for inexperienced students is the act of "problem-formation" that launches most expository essays. These students have trouble accepting the fact that writers often have to work to "sell" readers on the reality and importance of their problems, to persuade them to see the writer's problem as theirs.

As students experience them, after all, problems often have a seemingly pre-given quality—being either out there in the world or in here in one's experience. The conventions of the academy, however, encourage us to invent new problems that nobody has heretofore been aware of—and to redescribe familiar problems in new ways. In fact, the less anyone has been aware of the problem you are announcing, the more credit the academy gives you for pointing it out. Such an assumption will appear perverse or silly if you believe there are already enough problems in the world without anyone inventing new ones. Here is why to students the problems that academics worry about often seem artificially fabricated, by contrast with real problems like getting a date or a job, paying tuition, and getting through the university.

The assumption that problematizing is always a good thing—that the more aware of problems we are, the better—is seen in the academy's habit of treating texts as problems of interpretation and meaning. Once we are socialized into academic culture, it seems so normal and natural to assume that texts have meanings that it is profitable to extract, analyze, and debate that we forget how profoundly counterintuitive this assumption is to most people (including ourselves before we became socialized). For many students the meaning of a text, say, by Plato on the nature of love is simply what Plato's text itself says. Anyone who wants to know what Plato has to say about love can simply go read the text, right? (It is such confusion about the rationale for hunting for "hidden meaning" that drives students to Cliffs Notes and Monarch Notes in order to complete a paper assignment.)

To make a problem out of Plato's meaning is seemingly to make a mountain out of a molehill. But then, making mountains out of molehills is precisely what humanities teachers notoriously appear to do in their self-serving trick of pulling elaborate "symbolism" out of texts that any sensible person can see is really not there. And if Plato's meaning seems a manufactured problem, then it will probably seem even more foolish to look for the deep social and philosophical meanings that academics find in trashy romance novels, or in events like the O. J. Simpson case.

A final reason why many students are ambivalent about intellectualizing roles is that this ambivalence is often reinforced by their teachers, who internalize their culture's negative view of such roles and feel uneasy about "imposing" their intellectualism on others. Writing students often receive contradictory signals from instructors: on the one hand, the instructor seems to say, "I certainly don't expect you to talk like me, and why on earth would you want to?" On the other hand, the same instructor ends up awarding A's to precisely those students whose talk and writing most approximate his or hers. In a contradiction that Pierre Bourdieu, Claude Passeron, and Monique de Saint Martin (1994) analyze in *Academic Discourse,* the academy systematically withholds its discourses from students and then punishes students for failing to speak those discourses competently.

For some progressive educators, this contradiction is an argument for getting rid of grades, which supposedly are at the root of the inequality between teachers and students. The inequality lies not in the existence of grades, however, but in the fact that teachers control the discourses of argument and intellectualization and students do not.

Some—though by no means all—current educational progressives go so far as to maintain that the primacy of argumentation in composition classes is a form of repression, from which students are to be liberated so they can discover their own authentic voices. This attack on argumentation—which does not hesitate to avail itself of aggressive argumentation to make its points—has led some "expressivist" composition theorists to try to shift the emphasis in writing instruction from exposition, analysis, and the thesis-driven essay to creative self-expression and personal narrative. (Some expressivists argue that working first in narrative genres will help students subsequently develop expository skills, but this has yet to be demonstrated.)

Though these views often present themselves as highly "transgressive," their effect ultimately reinforces the old genteel assumption that advanced literacy is for the few—as it can only continue to be if students are deprived of the argumentative skills needed to succeed. In some cases, however, the turn to personal expression derives not from any programmatic attack on argumentation or any assertion of the inherent virtue of students' voices, but from the frustration teachers often have in getting students to use the academic intellectual register. On those days when it is hard to get the students to talk at all, it is tempting to settle for an animated class discussion in a personal register and let academic discourse go by the board. Making a virtue of necessity in this way evades the problem, however, and in the long run does students no favor.

Another factor that occasions doubts about the primacy schooling accords to argumentation, intellectualism, and problematizing is the mounting recognition that these conventions are not universal but culturally specific, and that student resistances to those norms are inflected by cultural differences in class, ethnicity, and gender. Cultural differences influence cognitive styles, as for example when women or non-Europeans have trouble identifying with the aggressive rhetorical persona presupposed by the thesis-driven essay. Such works as Shirley Brice Heath's *Ways with Words* (1983) reveal that classroom difficulties that have traditionally been ascribed to incompetence or laziness are often rooted in different cultural learning styles, and that student performance can be improved once teachers understand and respect these different learning styles. From another direction, work by cognitive psychologists like Howard Gardner (1993) demonstrates that intelligence comes in different varieties and is not unitary but multiple.

Clearly, education has been advanced by these challenges to homogenized views of "the student" that ignore cultural and cognitive differences. Nevertheless (and I think Heath and Gardner might agree), there is a danger that this salutary emphasis on cultural and cognitive difference will blind us to student problems that transcend such differences, in however uneven a degree.

Though students' alienation from intellectualized, position-taking roles is indeed inflected in very different ways for non-whites and whites, females and males, and Westerners and non-Westerners (as well as for different cognitive types), and though it carries very different social consequences for these different groups, in my experience this alienation cuts across these cultural, gender, and ethnic differences. Though it is observably true that in certain classrooms some female students are less prone than some male students to speak up, it is also true that timidity in the face of intellectual discussion often crosses the male/female barrier. If anything unites white male and female students from the affluent suburbs with nonwhite male and female students from the inner city, it is their common disaffection from books, book culture, and the languages of intellectual discourse. Nor should this be surprising, given the fact that, as diverse as these student groups are, they are all subject to the anti-intellectual elements of American mass culture.

Because this disaffection is rooted in deep patterns of socialization, patterns that are reinforced rather than countered by much of the culture of campus life, it is not likely to be undone by a few hours a week in the interrupted and circumscribed environment of the classroom. If the best way to learn a foreign language is to live in the culture of native speakers, to socialize students more successfully into the foreign language of academic intellectual discourse educational institutions will need to create a more continuous and self-reinforcing intellectual environment. The academic curriculum has the potential to become that kind of intellectual environment, but not in its presently disconnected, disjunctive, and unfocused state. Writing centers, writing-across-the-curriculum programs, and student-run academic symposia (like those that have been developed in the first-year composition program at the University of Arizona) could eventually comprise a counterculture of intellectual discussion that would effectively compete with the surrounding culture, in part by making that culture an object of study. This argument cannot be pursued here but it is further developed in my *Beyond the Culture Wars* (1992, especially chapters 6 and 9).

In short, then, we educators will miss the point if our fixation on dueling over texts, canons, and political philosophies causes us to ignore the resistance students often have to the intellectualizing of experience that is presupposed by academic work. Nor will it help if we romanticize that resistance, though teachers do need to respect the reasons why students harbor it. The problem is not intellectualization or argumentative discourse but how to give our students access to it. Unless these issues are frankly discussed and thought through, we risk repeating the results of previous spasms of national enthusiasms for education reform, changing what is taught and how it is taught, perhaps, but not how it is received.

Exchange between Graff and the Editors on "The Academic Language Gap"

Y & L: We would like to pursue some of the points you make in your piece about the value of the kinds of academic "intellectualizing" that you describe as characteristic of academic discourse. First, at one point in your essay you write that "it seems so normal and natural to assume that texts have meanings it is profitable to extract, analyze, and debate that we forget how counterintuitive this assumption is to most people." This assertion seems to pinpoint one area where the academy is crucially out of touch with the mainstream culture that, by and large, is responsible for supporting or squelching academic inquiry of all kinds (particularly the discourses produced by the humanities which seem the most remote from moneymaking and the workaday world). For us, such a "perception gap" raises questions about the relationship of what we ask students to do in an academic setting and the kind of language practices they encounter in mainstream culture. So we're wondering about the place of academic "intellectualizing" in the broader culture.

GG: Yes, though before we get into those questions I should try to head off some confusions by clarifying the distinction between "academic" and "mainstream" language practices, a distinction that my essay misleadingly overstates. Even the term "academic discourse" is somewhat misleading, since there's a good deal of overlap and continuity between the writing in an academic book or article and the writing in a newspaper op-ed piece, a general interest magazine, or even in a government report. Maybe the term should be "public discourse" or "public argument" or something like that, rather than "academic" discourse, which implies something more specialized, rarefied, and opaque. In any case, it was this public discourse that I was talking about, part academic, part journalistic, from which many high school and college students are alienated.

But if academic discourse is understood in this way as continuous with journalistic and other public discourse, it would be misleading then to say that "academic" discourse is "out of touch" with "mainstream" discourse. Rather, it's those alienated students who feel out of touch with *both* academic *and* mainstream discourse insofar as they feel alienated from any form of public culture.

Y & L: One of your underlying assumptions in this essay seems to be that academic modes of inquiry—problem finding, position taking, argument building—are inherently valuable though widely misunderstood. What, precisely, *is* the value of problematizing, analyzing, and debating textual meanings for American society at the beginning of the third millennium? If, as you point out, "the role of intellectualizer and public argument-maker . . . . has become increasingly unreal since the late nineteenth century, with the erosion of small town culture and the displacement of the urban citizen by the consumer," why do we persist in teaching these modes of inquiry and expression?

GG: Again, I need to correct a misleading impression given by my essay. If role of "public argument-maker" had really gone out with the horse and buggy and the small town meeting, as my formulation implies, then it would indeed be a contradiction to argue for increased emphasis on that role in teaching. What I was trying to say, I think, is that, for various complex reasons, not just students but Americans generally have trouble imagining their views and arguments actually making a difference in the wider public culture. I was referring to the familiar sense of helplessness that most of us often experience in advanced technological societies, where decision making is felt to be in the hands of a "they" who does not consult the citizenry and whom it feels one has no way to reach. I didn't mean to say, however, that this pessimistic view is necessarily correct, for to leave it at that would be a kind of self-fulfilling prophecy that would surrender to fatalism. In fact, I think since the sixties there's been a good deal of discussion of the renewal of public culture and the role of the citizen, and the emergence of the Internet has given further impetus to this discussion. Even if the discussion turns out to be largely wishful thinking it's a promising development. In other words, I didn't mean to imply that I thought democratic public discourse is completely dead in the USA or a lost cause.

Y & L: Aren't students and the public right when they argue, in effect, that such discursive practices don't have anything to do with their (current) "real" world?

GG: No, they aren't right. They're making a miscalculation, in fact, that can be disastrous for their own career opportunities. In the global information-oriented society that's in formation today, those discursive practices are crucial forms of cultural capital (in Bourdieu's sense). More and more, you can't leave home without them if you hope to get a decent job, which doesn't mean the job is all, that education doesn't also produce social critics and public intellectuals, in and out of their day jobs.

Michael Bérubé has made this last point very effectively in his recent book *The Employment of English* (1998). Contrary to John Guillory's (1993) argument that English studies have lost the cultural capital they once had (and when was that, I wonder), Bérubé argues that our work now has *greater* potential as cultural capital than it ever had, but we haven't noticed this yet. We're so used to assuming that nobody cares about us that we don't see the public intellectual influence our kind of work is already having in the culture.

Y & L: On the other hand, if the majority are wrong about the relevance of our basic approach to texts—and to knowledge and discourse generally—what is it that they have missed?

GG: Check your daily paper, where it's the strong argument-makers (if not necessarily the makers of good arguments) who write the most influential pieces and who are written about in other pieces. What they've missed, again, is a form of cultural capital that's increasingly important as "spin control" and "buzz," and the power of communications technology, become ever more important.

Y & L: How might we correct the misperception that what we do is largely irrelevant?

GG: This is the key question, I think. In my view, our academic-intellectual discourse is not at all irrelevant to our students' needs, but we've done a good job of making it *look* as if it's irrelevant. For example, we obscure the overlap and continuity to which I referred above between the scholarly article and the op-ed piece or governmental report. Academics today are often concerned with the same public policy issues as are journalists and public officials, but our discourse tends to obscure that commonality. This is not just because we use too much jargon and technical

terminology, thought that's part of it. It's also because we frag-
ment our discourse into disconnected courses and groups that
don't communicate with each other, so that what *might* come
across to outsiders as a coherent academic conversation tends to
come across as an incoherent babble of voices. I've written about
the way the academic curriculum obscures the academic conversation in several chapters of my *Beyond the Culture Wars* (1992),
especially one on "The Course Fetish."

Y & L: Twice in your chapter you mention the anti-intellectual
elements of American mass culture and how those pressures also
serve to reinforce our students' perceptions that there is a real
world of discourse distinct from academic discourse. If "the traditional American suspicion of intellectualism, . . . [which is] identified widely with aggression, aloofness, and snobbish elitism,"
as you put it, works against the possibility of our students perceiving themselves as genuine participants and stakeholders in
academic discourse, doesn't the practice of indoctrinating students into the jargon and critical modes of our discipline reinforce those suspicions?

GG: It might, especially insofar as doing a more effective job of
socializing students into academic discourse (I prefer that verb to
"indoctrinating") might deepen the gulf between the discursive
haves and have-nots and the attendant resentments. I don't see
any choice for educators, however, except to give students as much
access as we can to those discourses of power that, as I noted,
constitute indispensable cultural capital. Lisa Delpit argues along
these lines with respect to minority education in her recent book
Other People's Children (1995), which maintains that progressive teachers who refuse to be prescriptive and try to get out of
the way of the students are helping to condemn minority students (I'd extend the argument to other students as well) to continued failure. To withhold those discourses or to content ourselves
with teaching them ineffectively, or teaching them to the select
few and not the many, seems to me a betrayal of our students.

Y & L: Can anything be done to counter anti-intellectualism,
either in the classroom or more publicly?

GG: Getting the issue out in the open for discussion with students and among teachers would be a start. Whenever I raise a question like "does analyzing everything spoil the fun?" I flush out very interesting ambivalences from students. I also find deep divisions among teachers as to whether it's a good thing or a possible goal to try to turn students into "intellectuals." Our culture clearly has a love-hate relationship with intellectuality, but the subject is so fraught with anxieties about snobbery and condescension that we rarely talk about it or debate the question. That evasiveness carries over into courses, leaving students often uncertain about what it is they are supposed to do. I think composition teaching would be more effective, for example, if we called it "Argumentation," or "How to Make and Exchange Arguments," rather than "Composition" or "Expository Writing," terms which are innocuous and uncontroversial and therefore nebulous, failing to indicate to students what the task is that they are expected to master.

Y & L: Near the end of your chapter you briefly offer a vision of an academic curriculum that can create "a more continuous and self-reinforcing intellectual environment," a vision you lay out more fully in *Beyond the Culture Wars*. We wonder about the role of English studies in such a curriculum. Would the field have a central role in such a curriculum? Or would it reconstitute itself somehow by focusing its attention on "culture" along the lines you describe in your book? How should English teachers understand their role in such a curriculum?

GG: It shouldn't be a question of choosing between "English" or "culture"; rather it's a question of connecting English with other disciplines, so that while the different fields still retain some integrity or definition—there has to be *some* division of labor—they connect with each other in such a way that students become able to see their different courses as part of a common study of culture, as well as able to use intellectual words like "culture." Insofar as argumentation is the common language across the disciplines (or as near to one as we are likely to find), however, persuasive rhetoric should be recognized as the central discipline of the university, the opposite of the low-status, low-pay job it is now.

Works Cited

Bérubé, Michael. 1998. *The Employment of English: Theory, Jobs, and the Future of Literary Studies.* New York: New York University Press.

Bourdieu, Pierre, Jean-Claude Passeron, and Monique de Saint Martin. 1994. *Academic Discourse: Linguistic Misunderstanding and Professorial Power.* Stanford, Calif.: Stanford University Press

Delpit, Lisa. 1995. *Other People's Children: Cultural Conflict in the Classroom.* New York: The Free Press.

Gardner, Howard. 1993. *Frames of Mind: The Theory of Multiple Intelligences.* New York: Basic Books.

Graff, Gerald. 1992. *Beyond the Culture Wars: How Teaching the Conflicts Can Revitalize American Education.* New York: W. W. Norton.

Guillory, John. 1993. *Cultural Capital: The Problem of Literary Canon Formation.* Chicago, Ill.: University of Chicago Press.

Heath, Shirley Brice. 1983. *Ways with Words: Language, Life, and Work in Communities and Classrooms.* New York: Cambridge University Press.

CHAPTER TWO

When the Multicultural Leaves the Race: Some Common Terms Reconsidered

VICTOR VILLANUEVA
Washington State University

I

A scene. A number of graduate students of color in English write an article for the school newspaper which gains a full-page spread. Its title is a paraphrase of a famous book on colonialism and race by Frantz Fanon. The banner reads "Black Masks, White Masks." The grad students write that they no longer wish to be reduced to wearing white masks if they are to succeed in the university, that the denial of their being of color affords them nothing but their silencing. Among their examples, they write of a Halloween party in which one of their fellows appears in blackface.

A meeting of grad students and department faculty. Tempers run hot. Blackface says he never meant to offend. He was paying homage to the great jazz and blues musicians of the past, playing Muddy Waters tunes. He would have been born in the 1970s, maybe unaware of a dark history of such homages.

> *Holiday Inn, Bing Crosby in blackface, singing, "Who was it set the darkies free? Abraham. Abraham." Mr. Crosby surely didn't mean to offend. But that was then, you say.*

Stunned silence. A student of color leaves.

A large-seeming fellow, red hair, small blue eyes, always earnest, always speaking with broad gestures from large, thick hands, all befreckled, a Boston-like mannah to his speech, always the one to find contradictions in meetings, in classes. He stands. Says that as he sees it, this thing about silencing doesn't wash, that those complaining about it are the very ones always speaking up in classes, and that (without a breath) he can't think of a one from among the faculty present who doesn't speak of multiculturalism, that the damned text used in the first-year composition program is really an ethnic studies book, for gosh sake (or words to that effect). The book is Ronald Takaki's *A Different Mirror* (1993), "a history of multicultural America," says the subtitle, its author a "professor in the Ethnic Studies Department" at his university, says the back cover. And all are effectively silenced for a dramatically long moment.

The South Asian who self-identifies as a person of color, surely the colonized from another's empire, British accent to her speech, dark chocolate brown skin, large black eyes, now seeming to well with tears, thick black mane framing her small face, clearly agitated, breaks the silence. She speaks about the difference between speaking and being heard, that if one is constantly speaking but never heard, never truly heard, there is, in effect, silence, a silencing. She says that speaking of ethnic studies or multiculturalism is less the issue than how race seems always to be an appendage to a classroom curriculum, something loosely attached to a course but not quite integral, even when race is the issue.

Suddenly, another voice. Spanish surname, Latina features, given to self-deprecating humor about her lack of Spanish ("*Hola, señor. Yo quiero Taco Bell*"). She is not among those who wrote the article of protest in the school paper. She says, "I don't get this at all. I don't see this racism. Could someone define "racism" for me?

II

The question posed by that student grew out of her training in English studies, an understanding that to get at an issue requires that we define. And that she could raise the issue at all, that English graduate students would be so confused by race and racism, makes it clear that there is something in the job of English that lends itself to the process of understanding race and racism as discursive practices, so that English studies becomes an integral part of the process of assimilation that goes on endlessly in the culture at large. On the one hand, English studies is complicit in assimilationist practices that allow racism to continue unabated; on the other, we can only understand all political action discursively. The ill and the cure are tied to language and the study of language.

I've said it too: "multiculturalism." I've said "race or ethnicity" as if they were somehow the same. But I'm thinking differently about it all right now. I'm beginning to say that ethnicity is not "race" for us in America. There's overlap, but not synonymity, even when physiognomy isn't an issue. "Multiculturalism" just confuses matters, jumbles the whole culture, ethnic, race thing up, the multicultural mixing with gender, sexuality, class as well. Bigotry isn't limited to racism. Yet it is racism that is the fulcrum of the race, class, and gender triad. Racism continues to be among the most compelling problems we face. Part of the reason why this is so is that we're still unclear about what we're dealing with, and must thereby be unclear about how to deal with it.

Antonio Gramsci (1957, 1971) helps to open a critical way of assessing the terms we use interchangeably and the ways in which that process might not be helping our approaches to racial issues in our classrooms. In his theory of hegemony, Gramsci explains the ways in which a society can contain a thick, dense, complexity and still end up serving the needs of a relative few. Hegemony, argues Gramsci, relies on our consenting to a system of rule because we either accept the idea that the goods of the system override the bads—that is, we accept the moral grounds for the systems we take part in—or we accept that the system serves our needs well enough, a prudential and rational choice, despite whatever faults clearly exist. We go along with the program, in effect consenting to hegemonic controls because we see what we believe to be the common good, despite our varied, contradictory, even oppositional challenges. Those whose interests are best served by the hegemony foreground the points of commonality among various, sometimes oppositional cultures by way of the moral good which becomes ideologically realized as "the common sense."

This is not altogether a conspiracy. Hegemony is a process, a process of incorporating ideologies. These ideologies are passed on through the institutions of civil society, institutions like the family, the church, the media, and the schools. We step into the system that precedes us, and it seems normal, the way of the world, so much the way of the world that we reproduce the basics of what came before, re-forming in various ways the things that came before in the search for making matters better. We tend to miss how things remain essentially the same because we are content with the foundations. Yet those foundations have more than the moral fiber of their society built on them. Those foundations carry compelling historical sequences that give rise to our current hegemonic configurations—the conditions that give rise to the current hegemony and its common sense.

And it is there that I see a problem with "multiculturalism" and with "ethnicity" as used interchangeably with "racism." The end of racism in America (or the world) will require a radical change in the current hegemony. Multiculturalism and ethnic sensitivity in America will not. Consider, for example, Mary Louise Pratt's "Arts of the Contact Zone" (1991) and the concept's application in first-year composition readers. How the concept plays out is that instances of conjuncture between the dominant culture and other cultures are presented, the speech of Young Chief Joseph, for example, "I Will Cry No More Forever." What we see are points of contact, including discomforting points of contact, where ideologies seem to clash. What remain are the appeals to a common sense of decency and morality that do not jar our common sensibilities. This is the story of this country, a place where cultures come in contact. Points of contact are part of the hegemonic process, points for some sense of conciliation. In other words, though it is good to recognize the rhetorical prowess of members of other cultural groups, and it's crucial to recognize points of identification among ourselves and others, no matter how seemingly different from our own cultures, these acknowledgments do not make for a radical change in the tendency toward racism.

Acknowledging a cultural plurality doesn't make for radical change in racist attitudes, because ethnicity is not the same as race—physiognomy notwithstanding. What I mean is that, at least when I use the words "race and ethnicity" as a single term, I am trying to acknowledge the ways in which a racial-like bigotry operates even when race is not apparent. I think of the word "spic," for example, a slur arising from Latinos in the U.S. who responded to queries with "no espic English"—no espic, espic, a spic. Here race is less an issue than a linguistic link to a particular ethnicity. But the problem with relegating this to ethnicity rather than racism is that with ethnicity comes the myth of assimilation. America has tolerated and in one sense or another has absorbed its various ethnicities. But America was not designed to do likewise with race. America is founded on racial terms, with the Naturalization Act of 1790—1790!—that denied rights of full citizenship to non-Whites (Takaki, 1987).

> A scene from The Godfather. Robert Duvall's character visits the movie mogul who's denying Johnny Fontaine his star-making movie role. Mr. Walsh, the mogul, says something about "dago, guinea, wop, gumba greaseballs." To which Tom Hagen says he's German-Irish. And Mr. Walsh says, "Well, let me tell you something, my kraut-mick friend." Always an ethnic slur at hand when needed. But that was then, you say.

Eventually, different ethnicities become part of the whole, unless, the common sense goes, a particular ethnicity willfully excludes itself from the whole. It's that sense that America's history is made up of different ethnicities who eventually melt into the pot that makes for the credible argument or perception that those who don't melt have chosen not to or are too lazy to do so. And that perception makes for counter–affirmative action laws and English-only laws, makes for a belief that lazy, recalcitrant ethnics are getting a free ride at the expense of the majority, a reverse discrimination which is countered by the long-standing forward discrimination. Although every ethnic group has had its hardships in becoming part of this country, "only blacks were enslaved, only Native Americans were removed to reservations, only Chinese were singled out for exclusion, and only Japanese Americans (not Italian Americans or German Americans) were placed in concentration camps," says Takaki (1987, 7), and, I'll add, only Mexican Americans were expatriated during the Great

Depression (Estrada et al. 1981), and only Puerto Ricans can be concerned about a citizenship conferred over three generations ago. It's history that dictates so much of what is constituted as a race. Omi and Winant write that an

> effort must be made to understand race as an unstable and "decentered" complex of social meanings constantly being transformed by political struggle . . . : race is a concept which signifies and symbolizes social conflicts and interests by referring to different types of human bodies. Although the concept of race invokes biologically based human characteristics (so-called "phenotypes"), selection of these particular human features for purposes of racial signification is always and necessarily a social and historical process. . . . A racial project can be defined as racist if and only if it creates or reproduces structures of domination based on essentialist categories of race [with Essentialism . . . understood as belief in real, true human essences, existing outside or impervious to social and historical context]. (1994, 55, 71, 187 n.57)

And part of what makes for those who would be categorized has to do with how a particular group entered into a society. America's people of color are those who meet Omi and Winant's notions of race and were the victims of colonialism.

> A news item from Universal Press syndicate:
> *"Seinfeld"—"the show about nothing"—ended up with a black eye as a result of the penultimate episode in which Kramer accidentally burned a Puerto Rican flag and then stomped on it. The episode generally portrayed Puerto Ricans as melodramatic, car thieves, and criminal mobs during the annual Puerto Rican Day Parade. . . . As a group, Puerto Ricans in particular have been historically misrepresented in popular culture as a government-dependent community of hot-tempered Latins, loose Marias and unemployed criminals. "It's not a coincidence that the 'Seinfeld' episode took place four weeks prior to the actual parade, which this year marks 100 years since the United States took possession of Puerto Rico," said Blanca Vazquez, the editor of the CENTRO Journal at New York City's Hunter College. . . .*
> *There's a common anecdote about immigration officials who detain Puerto Ricans: "But I'm Puerto Rican," says the detained citizen. "I don't care what kind of Mexican you are," says the official.*
> *Because of miseducation, many people barely seem to know that Puerto Rico is already part of the United States and that*

> *Puerto Ricans have distinguished themselves in every war since their US citizenship was conferred upon them in 1917.*
>
> *All this is taking place at a time when residents of Puerto Rico will determine, as a result of the recently passed Young bill (Rep. Don Young, R-Alaska), whether the island will stay a commonwealth, become a state, or an independent nation. While the measure is stalled in the Senate, the issue is not going away anytime soon.*
>
> *This radical piece of legislation has the potential to strip Puerto Ricans of their US citizenship, unless they vote for the statehood option. Some analysts believe that it could legislatively set precedent for taking away or denying the citizenship of other groups, possibly Mexican-Americans, Cubans, or Central Americans—depending on the focus of the nation's anti-immigrant hysteria. . . . "Seinfeld's" "yada, yada" is about "nada." The fate of Puerto Rico, however, is something. It has the capacity to determine the future and character of the United States. Perhaps NBC will see fit to educate people about this debate and the historic contributions of Puerto Ricans. (Gonzales and Rodriguez)*

So even though *race* isn't always the issue (so many Latinos and Latinas being racially White, for example), *racism* is the issue.

What makes for a need to see some ethnicities as racial is historically determined. Racism is the experience of those who came to this country under subjugation or became part of the country through colonialism, the subjugation of slavery itself being a kind of colonialism. Racism amounts to a kind colonial sensibility. Says John Rex: "Racial discrimination and racial prejudice are phenomena of colonialism" (1973, 75). Consider the victims of racism—those whose bodies were colonized (African Americans, American Indians, Asians); those whose lands were taken (American Indians, Alaska Natives, Spanish West Indians, Mexicans, other Latin Americans [like Panamanians], Pacific Islanders, especially Hawaiians and Filipinos). The United States continues to have colonial holdings in the Caribbean and the Pacific. To be colonized is to be conferred with a color.

People of color can sense the colonialism. It is a certain brand of alienation, shared to some extent by women, particularly in terms of the division of labor (Mies et al. 1988). It is a part of our social make up. Consider some of the litany of the 1980s with which E. San Juan Jr. opens his book *Racial Formations/Critical Transformations:*

Vigilante gunman Bernard Goetz catapulted into a folk hero for shooting down four black youths in a New York subway. Fear of Willy Horton, a black inmate helped elect a president. . . . Antibusing attacks in the early eighties in most big cities. The 1982 murder of Chinese American Vincent Chin mistaken by unemployed Detroit autoworkers for a Japanese. . . . The election to the Louisiana legislature of Republican David Duke, former head of the Ku Klux Klan. (1992, 1)

I can easily add the 1990s police beating of African American Rodney King, the police beating of Mexican immigrants suspected of being undocumented migrants in California, anti-affirmative action statutes in Texas and California, the passing of English-only or Official-English statutes throughout the country. The colonial status of people of color and the racism it engenders isn't the result of overactive imaginations. And these effects, both psychosocial and political-economic, are what Frantz Fanon called "internal colonialism." It's a term that has caught the political imagination from time to time even before Fanon. It was used by Lenin, Gramsci, Harold Cruse, Stokely Carmichael, Eugene McCarthy. It's a term still used to describe the Amerindians of South America and the American Indian nations of the United States, a term used in interdisciplinary world-systems theory (Blauner 1972).

For all that, the term "internal colonialism" has contemporary critical theorists concerned that the complexities of race in the United States are too great to be relegated to a simple binary between colonizer and colonized; in a word, the term's use is essentializing. Contemporary theory prefers the more complexly suggestive term for what happens to people of color—"hybridity," popularized by Homi Bhabha, who, in the foreword to the revised translation of *Black Skin, White Masks,* writes that Fanon came up with the term (cited in Sekyi-Otu 1996, 89). The problem with "hybridity," as many have pointed out, is that the term is at least too passive, at worst suggestive of something positive rather than painful and exclusionary (Bahri 1998). It is a positive term insofar as it has essentially the same resonances of the melting pot—a painful process in which something different and vital emerges. "Internal colonialism," however, maintains the separateness that prevails. In reviewing Bob Blauner's *Black Lives,*

White Lives: Three Decades of Race Relations in America, Samuel Farber (1990) cites Blauner's evidence that as of 1990 the same old bigotry prevails: racial intermarriages are still disfavored, and any form of affirmative corrective action concerning racial imbalances is seen as reverse discrimination, with the only change (if it can be considered a change) being that the middle class of color becomes good (recalling the credit-to-your-people/race sensibility) while the working class remains bad. I do believe the binary exists (as do others who, unlike Homi Bhabha, do not try to remove the charge of essentialism levied at Fanon but applaud it; see Sekyi-Otu 1996, 89, 244–45).

> I like citing the Puerto Rican poet Tato Laviera, since he speaks so clearly to me, who is of his same generation, of the more typical manifestation of hybridity. He writes, .
>
> > *i want to go back to puerto rico*
> > *but i wonder if my kink could live*
> > *in ponce, mayaguez and carolina*
> >
> > *tengo las venas aculturadas*
> > *escribo in spanglish*
> > *abraham in español*
> > *abraham in english*
> > *tato in spanish*
> > *"taro" in english*
> > *tonto in both languages* (qtd. in Flores et al. 1981, 214)
>
> Acculturated veins, yet not American in some sense and no longer quite Puerto Rican, linguistically a fool in both English and Spanish ("tonto in both languages"): the hybrid of internal colonialism.

III

Linda Chavez, on the Web site for the Center for Equal Opportunity, an organization for which she is co-president, argues the case that the fear about the browning of America is wrongheaded. She points to the many restrictions against immigration in the past, and how those who had been persecuted, the southern and eastern Europeans of the 1924 Immigration Act, have melted into the pot through the assimilation process. She concludes, then, that "assimilation, not race, is the issue" ("Immigration"). The irony is that she is from a Hispano background, New Mexican, not an immigrant herself nor from immigrant stock, claiming (like so many Hispanos) a direct link to seventeenth-century Spain. So she argues the case for assimilation—a figurehead (former president of U.S. English as well, the organization seeking English-only constitutional change), yet after four hundred years in this land she cannot be assimilated, not really, since so much of her position comes from being the Spanish surnamed arguing the ethnic case and denying the racist.

Still and all, she reflects the dominant sensibility, a sensibility that still informs school curricula. We are still colonial schools, trying to inculcate cultural assimilation. But consider a near analogy when assimilation gets coupled with cultural pluralism (or when the soup of the melting pot is poured into the salad bowl). Gail Kelly (1984) tells of French education in Vietnam. The French, confusing racism and cultural pluralism in much the same way we do, taught Vietnamese culture to the Vietnamese, though through French eyes and through the French language. Since, to use Frantz Fanon's words, "to speak a language is to take on a world, a culture" (1967, 38), the Vietnamese children found themselves ostensibly without a world or a culture: somehow distanced from their original cultural ways and somehow kept at a distance from the colonizers' in the manner of a Tato Laviera. Closer to home were the Bureau of Indian Affairs schools that would prevent American Indian school children from speaking their native languages though living in reservations; or worse, that would forcibly separate the children from their homes in order to accelerate the assimilation process. But that was then? Every argument against any form of bilingual education, every argument for a unified cultural literacy (Hirsch 1987) says this is now.

In *The Rage of a Privileged Class*, Ellis Cose tells of an interview with Hofstra's Dean Haynes, surely one assimilated, and successfully:

> Ulric Haynes, dean of the Hofstra University School of Business and a former corporate executive who served as President Carter's ambassador to Algeria, is one of many blacks who have given up

hope that racial parity will arrive [in] this—or even [in the] next—
millennium: "During our lifetimes, my grandchildren's lifetimes,
I expect that race will . . . matter. And perhaps race will always
matter, given the historical circumstances under which we came
to this country." [And he's angry, he says.] . . . "Not for myself.
I'm over the hill. I've reached the zenith. . . . I'm angry for the
deception that this has perpetrated on my children and grandchildren." Though his children have traveled the world and received an elite education, they "in a very real sense are not the
children of privilege. They are dysfunctional, because I didn't
prepare them, in all the years we lived overseas, to deal with the
climate of racism they are encountering right now." (1993, 8)

Assimilation is in itself insufficient. And the numbers of people
who have been a part of this country for a century (like Puerto
Ricans) and so much longer, hybrids insofar as they are no longer
parts of any nation but this one but who nevertheless feel outside
the mainstream even when carrying all the artifacts of the mainstream, make it clear that assimilation is insufficient.

From Ana Castillo:[1]

> We would like to give
> a thousand excuses
> as to why we all find
> ourselves in a predicament—
> residents of a controversial
> power. . . .
> We would like you to know
> guilt or apologetic gestures
> won't revive the dead
> redistribute the land
> or natural resources.
> We are left
> with one final resolution
> in our predestined way,
> we are going forward.
> There is no going back.

IV

A simple celebration of cultural multiplicity while maintaining
the literacy practices that have maintained the subjugation of too

many of America's people of color is insufficient. If we can't change the economic system that gives rise to the current hegemony, we should at least begin to consider how to make a radical change that will alter racism. And how we can go about that would have to be through our teaching. The trick, then, becomes providing a means for those who are of color to gain credentials of credibility—diplomas and degrees, positions of power—while maintaining a critical consciousness of the racism that pervades. The trick is to have White students appreciate the pervasiveness of racism without defending their privilege as White. The trick becomes increasing an awareness of the racism which pervades without turning into propagandists, since propaganda will surely fall on deaf ears.

In the composition program where I now work, writing process pedagogy is balanced by the use of nonfiction readings that extend beyond the short stretches of discourse provided by readers. The text currently in use is Ronald Takaki's *A Different Mirror* (1993). This text was chosen because it is written in a very conventional academic discourse, demonstrating the ways an argument can be sustained at length, demonstrating the conventions of academic discourse, while also demonstrating a critical viewpoint. Takaki relates an alternative view of history, beginning with the British colonization of Ireland and demonstrating how the attitudes engendered against the Irish are translated to attitudes toward American Indians and eventually toward others who are colonized or subjugated, taking us from colonial times to the 1992 riots in south central Los Angeles. With this richness of material, assignments concerning the book range from simple summaries (which aren't simple at all, since White students in particular are anxious to take Takaki on) to extended critiques.

It is during the process of formulating critiques that the work of providing a critical consciousness proves most difficult. Since to be critical, for most students, means to find fault, Takaki gets charged with displaying an unfair bias in his rendering of history because he's Japanese American (though students fail to note that he's fourth-generation, which he mentions, with U.S. ancestry dating back to 1880, longer than many of the melted students of the pot, suggesting that some folks don't melt; but then, that just increases the weight of the supposed bias in his historical rendering). Ad hominem arguments lead us to issues of Aristotelian logic, the preferred logic of the academic discourse community (see Villanueva 1993, 65–90, esp. 88). Ad hominem takes us to the differences between bias or world view and dishonest research, the myth of objective discourse versus the voice of reasonableness, objectivity versus an ethos of thoroughness and reasonableness. And questions of honesty in research take us to the library, to work out the contentions of common sense that arise in the classroom: Is there a reverse discrimination, for example? Whatever commonplace grows out of the reading is subjected to a dialectical process, is to be tested in library research and in interviews, subjected to the peer collaborative process, subjected to the writing process, eventually to be formulated within the conventions of academic discourse.

But to do this we must begin with where the students begin—guilt/defense, anger/blame. Students tend to place themselves on one pole or the other, poles usually predicated on racial identity. We begin with a focused freewrite. On the board: "We are reading a racial history of America because . . ." Students are to write without stopping: five minutes. Read-alouds. I ask for one-word reactions to the read-alouds. Overwhelmingly (and consistently), the single-word responses boil down to the four terms with variants: guilt or shame, defense or defensiveness, anger or hate, blame. What good is blame, becomes the salient question. How constructive guilt? Eventually, sometimes more quickly than others, we realize that guilt or blame is not the issue. Correcting the past or someone's sins of the past is not the issue. At issue is a fuller understanding of that past in order to rethink the ways bigotry creeps into all our lives, to rethink the things taken for granted or accepted as true—and to display that thinking in the way academics relate their thinking, since that will be the task put before them in any writing assignment: critical reassessment presented along sets of conventions.

Some students go down resisting. But most at least learn the conventions (like the first-year student who wrote an excellent paper on the contradiction of a Marxian world view and the claim of a strong religious foundation, claiming they cannot co-exist; religious faith must stand alone—something of a corrective of his instructor but not an attack, a reasoned argument, having long jettisoned the rhetoric of religious pamphleteering which affected his writings earlier in the semester). A dialectic between the common sense and the bigotry it can contain presented in the conventions of academic discourse, discovered through research and the discovery process which is writing, can help to create a critical consciousness, making within some people a utopian hope, the possibility for radical change in America's racialized—as well as multicultural and multiethnic—condition.

Note

1. Excerpt from "We Would Like You to Know" by Ana Castillo reprinted from *My Father Was a Toltec and Selected Poems*. Copyright 1995 by Ana Castillo. Published by W. W. Norton & Co., Inc., and originally published by West End Press. Reprinted by permission of Susan Bergholz Literary Services, New York. All rights reserved.

Works Cited

Bahri, Deepika. 1998. "Terms of Engagement: Postcolonialism, Transnationalism, and Composition Studies." *JAC: A Journal of Composition Theory* 18.1: 29–44.

Blauner, Bob. 1972. *Racial Oppression in America*. New York: Harper & Row.

———, ed. 1989. *Black Lives, White Lives: Three Decades of Race Relations in America*. Berkeley: University of California Press.

Carmichael, Stokely, and Charles V. Hamilton. 1967. *Black Power: The Politics of Liberation in America*. New York: Random House.

Castillo, Ana. 1995. "We Would Like You to Know." In *My Father Was a Toltec and Selected Poems, 1973–1988*. New York: Norton.

Chavez, Linda. "Immigration Is Not about Race." Center for Equal Opportunity. Available at http://www.ceousa.org/html/immigr.html ("Immigration" section of Web site).

Cose, Ellis. 1993. *The Rage of a Privileged Class*. New York: HarperCollins.

Cruse, Harold. 1968. *Rebellion or Revolution?* New York: Morrow.

Estrada, Leonardo F., F. Chris Garcia, Reynaldo Flores Macias, and Lionel Maldonado. 1981. "Chicanos in the United States: A History of Exploitation and Resistance." *Daedalus* 110.2 (Spring): 103–31.

Fanon, Frantz. 1967. *Black Skin, White Masks*. Trans. Charles Lam Markmann. New York: Grove Press.

Farber, Samuel. 1990. "Racism over Three Decades." *Against the Current* 26.1: 31.

Flores, Juan, John Attinasi, and Pedro Pedraza Jr.1981. "La Carreta Made a U-Turn: Puerto Rican Language and Culture in the United States." *Daedalus* 110.2 (Spring): 193–217.

Gonzales, Patrisia, and Roberto Rodriguez. 1998. "Puerto Ricans Complain about 'Yada, Yada.'" Column of the Americas, Universal Press Syndicate (May 15).

Gramsci, Antonio. 1957. "The Southern Question." In *The Modern Prince and Other Writings*. Trans. Louis Marks. New York: International.

———. 1971. *Selections from the Prison Notebooks*. Ed. and trans. Quiten Hoare and Geoffrey Nowell Smith. New York: International.

Hirsch, E. D., Jr. 1987. *Cultural Literacy: What Every American Needs to Know*. Boston: Houghton Mifflin.

Kelly, Gail P. 1984. "Colonialism, Indigenous Society, and School Practices: French West Africa and Indochina, 1918–1938." Pp. 9–32 in *Education and the Colonial Experience,* ed. Philip G. Altbach and Gail P. Kelly. New Brunswick, N.J.: Transaction.

Mies, Maria, Veronika Bennholdt-Thomsen, and Claudia Von Werlhof. 1988. *Women: The Last Colony.* 2d rev. ed. Atlantic Highlands, N.J.: Zed.

Omi, Michael, and Howard Winant. 1994. *Racial Formation in the United States: From the 1960s to the 1990s*. New York: Routledge.

Pratt, Mary Louise. 1991. "Arts of the Contact Zone." Pp. 33–40 in *Profession 91*. New York: MLA. (Originally presented as the keynote address at MLA's Responsibilities for Literacy conference in September 1990 in Pittsburgh.)

Rex, John. 1973. *Race, Colonialism and the City*. London: Routledge and Kegan Paul.

San Juan, E., Jr. 1992. *Racial Formations/Critical Transformations: Articulations of Power in Ethnic and Racial Studies in the United States.* Atlantic Highlands, N.J.: Humanities.

Sekyi-Otu, Ato. 1996. *Fanon's Dialectic of Experience.* Cambridge, Mass.: Harvard University Press.

Takaki, Ronald. 1987. "Reflections on Racial Patterns in America." Pp. 26–37 in *From Different Shores,* ed. Ronald Takaki. New York: Oxford University Press.

———. 1993. *A Different Mirror: A History of Multicultural America.* Boston: Little, Brown.

Villanueva, Victor Jr. 1993. *Bootstraps: From an American Academic of Color.* Urbana, Ill.: National Council of Teachers of English.

CHAPTER THREE

It's Not *an Economy, Stupid! The Education-as-Product Metaphor as Viewed from the English Classroom*

SCOTT A. LEONARD
Youngstown State University

A s I write, the twenty-first century has begun, and what was once a wet spot on the dam of public discourse about higher education is becoming a raging torrent of words: to wit, that public education, particularly at the pre-college levels, is broken and can't be fixed (cf. Hodges and Mechlenburg; Center for Education Reform). Increasingly, words like *productivity, producer, consumer, inputs,* and *outputs* are used to describe what education is and why its quality is worse today than it was in the early '60s. When these dire-sounding reports contemplate the humanities at all, they mention only English (apparently this term refers primarily to composition) and high school graduates' increasingly deplorable preparation in this area. Led by such politically influential figures as Jeanne Allen, Lesley Arsht, William J. Bennett, and Lynne V. Cheney, this growing congregation of dissenters from the High Church of Public Education fervently affirms the need for assessment and accountability for teachers, students, and administrators, as well as the efficacy of pluralism,[1] competition, and choice in "deliver[ing] and manag[ing]" public education (Allen et al. 1998, 4). That is, they insist on applying free-market economic principles to the schools by rewarding merit and productivity, punishing indolence and incompetence, and encouraging informed parents to shop around for the best education that they can afford in a diverse and highly competitive academic marketplace. Perhaps as a result of political agitation by such groups as the Center for Education Reform,

Standards Work, and Empower America, or perhaps simply as a response to strained budgets, many state governments are, increasingly, characterizing education as a manufacturing enterprise in which taxpayers invest a portion of their income in hopes of a future return. In these conversations, the value of the humanities—including most of what we now call English studies—is being implicitly and explicitly questioned in terms of what they contribute to state economies. In essence, everything boils down to resources (i.e., money) and how best to expend them. Thus, American cultural affairs have returned to—if, indeed, they ever left—a condition deplored by Ralph Waldo Emerson, who looked forward to the day when "the sluggard intellect of this continent [would] look from under its iron lids and fulfill the postponed expectation of the world with something better than the exertions of mechanical skill" (383). Indeed, the nineteenth-century's concern that America was only too adept at creating material wealth to the exclusion of an artistic and cultural life of its own was among the most powerful motives for institutionalizing academic English studies in the first place.[2] Thus, the modern perception that the nation's spending on the humanities—indeed on all public higher education—is an *investment* can be seen as the return swing of a pendulum set in motion over one hundred years ago. Today, America feels little guilt about its materialism and, thanks in part to the academy's own theorizing, the university itself no longer confidently asserts the numinous power of "culture" (defined as deep familiarity with "English letters") as a counterbalance to the crassness of getting and spending wealth.

As a result, the academy is being reimagined by legislators and university administrators not as a zone where art for its own sake is to be appreciated, nor where ideas, however insurgent against prevailing opinion or time-honored tradition, are to be articulated and debated, but rather as a vocational and technical training facility for the postindustrial future. An education, according to the metaphors most often employed by legislative and university decision makers, is a commodity for sale and *for use*. Concomitant with this view is the growing perception that universities are corporations or factories that *produce* an education which must be advertised and sold in an increasingly competitive marketplace. This metaphor might seem strained to those placed in so-called research institutions where endowments are large and enrollments competitive; however, most academics who, like me, work for small- to medium-sized "teaching" universities already know what it is to see their institutions open classrooms in the local shopping malls and open "extension campuses" in the suburbs. Our universities' public relations offices already aggressively sell the "convenience" of obtaining an advanced degree in these locations.[3] Similarly, we already know what it is like to open a newspaper or to turn on the radio or television and find our four-year schools slugging it out with vocational and technical facilities for student-customers. Billboards and the local paper feature photographs of our department chairs and deans in posed open-book encounters with student-models who feign rapt attention.

It is in this mercantile milieu that policy makers have begun to measure the relevance of English studies in dollars and in post-graduation employment figures rather than in terms of what individual human beings might learn and how they might grow intellectually. Moreover, as the dissonance between the nineteenth-century liberal arts model and the twenty-first-century commodity model of education intensifies, the academy is increasingly depicted as a remote ivory tower and the "knowledge workers" who inhabit it as symbols of all that is quaint, elitist, and simply wrong-headed in higher education.[4] This chapter will attempt to put a human face on these rhetorical constructs by considering the important human interactions that take place in the classroom and by comparing these exchanges both implicitly and explicitly with the cartoonish depictions so common on the floors of various legislatures and in the media. I will argue for the "relevance" of English studies from the vantage of a classroom practitioner—and one who sees tremendous disconnection between his professional practice and its current representation in the salons of power, in the media, and on the street. Moreover, I will argue that the relevance of English studies—indeed of all study—can and should be measured in other than monetary terms. Rather, the social value—the relevance—of any academic enterprise must be measured in terms of how individual human beings involved in focused collegiate study benefit personally and intellectually from their labors.

Despite the foregoing, the prospect of a reconfigured university that is, as a recent communiqué at my university put it, more "responsive to our student-customers," and likewise the dire rumblings from Ohio's state house about cutting wasteful programs and putting an end to the "underutilization of human resources," have, for me, tended so far to be a distant thunder. The whirlwind of blind, furious "right-sizing" might yet bring down the house, but in the meantime my usual contact with the needs and expectations of the taxpayer and student-customer mostly feels like a teacher/student rather than a vendor/customer interaction. It usually goes like this. In the morning, my first-year composition course meets. The students are deep into *inventio,* and today I will acquaint them with search strategies on the World Wide Web and show them how to make use of our virtual library's catalog and databases. They will download useful information from the Internet and walk to the library to raid the stacks. Eventually, they'll produce research reports on subjects of their own choosing. I'm hoping—expecting—that the researching and writing experiences I've designed will teach my students how to read critically and organize information logically, will teach them to incorporate the words and ideas of others seamlessly into texts of their own creation, and that they will learn how to give credit where credit is due in the form of a "Works Cited" page. In short, I will do what thousands of my colleagues across the country do every day: teach my students a set of literacy *skills* and give them opportunities to practice the *art* of expository prose.

In the afternoon, my upper-division British Romantics course will convene, and we will begin discussing William Blake. As usual, I will begin with a bit of contextualizing by providing biographical and historical information, then organize my students into small groups and provide them with a collaborative learning and writing prompt that will require them to think critically about and discuss the assigned reading before composing brief, team-written responses. During the second hour, my students will read their responses aloud and general discussion will ensue. I'm hoping that my students will learn how to enjoy intellectually challenging and historically remote poetry and prose both for what it meant in its time and for what it still could mean to them personally.

Eventually, they'll produce research papers that draw on research and writing skills which, presumably, they acquired in their first-year composition courses and through other academic writing experiences. Also presumably, this research will take them deep into the historical moment we're examining even as it leads them to a deeper appreciation of how literary art flows from and influences the currents of history. Here, too, I do what thousands of my colleagues in North America do every day: I present my students with historically informed aesthetic experiences that we hope will better orient them to their own world even as it fires their imaginations and quickens them to the pleasures unique to reading the carefully winnowed word.

In both of these classes, and in the mythology course that meets in the evening, my students quite naturally expect to learn something that they didn't know already. Quite naturally, they expect that what they read, discuss, think, and write about will provide them with portable knowledge and skills that they can use in their future careers. To use the cost-accounting language of the decision makers who craft educational policy in my state and across the nation, my students quite naturally expect a return on the investment of their money and time. Just as naturally, I'm doing all I can to give them their money's worth—but not because I recognize their right as customers to the product they're paying for. I simply don't see them this way. And it's not because I have an ethical obligation to my students (which I certainly do) that I design assignments that will give them practice at reading, writing, and thinking. Rather—and this sentiment seems very widespread among my colleagues—I believe right to my bones that the happiest future for democracy and for America lies in an informed, critical, and literate population. To summarize the consensus at the watercooler and coffee urn, we believe that by teaching students that words matter and in helping them learn how to carefully consider the nuances of meaning in a poem, in an essay, or in a novel, we're teaching them to evaluate all discourse intelligently. We believe that the kinds of reading that prove productive in teasing out obvious as well as subtle meanings in literature will prove equally effective when applied to the metaphors and cultural references embedded in advertisements and political speeches. We believe that by teaching students how to craft sound arguments and by directing them to pay close attention to word choice we enable them to participate more effectively in the political life of the nation, even as we enable them to make a significant contribution on the job. Thus, at bottom, we're working for the same thing that those who decry the undeserved privilege of us academics say they're working for: a literate public able to participate in a healthy democracy.[5]

The critical difference in perception between how "we" academics and "those" legislators, administrators, and pundits who would characterize a great deal of the intellectual labor that academics perform as valueless—or even invidious—to the Union comes down to this question: What is the university for? If the answer is advanced vocational training and the necessary "production" of a merely *functional* literacy, then most academics *are* working against the grain. The university is, for most of us who teach and conduct research there, not primarily a place where job training happens. Most of us still assume that our primary purpose is to teach students how to learn, how to question appearances, and how to test fairly the strengths and limits of all sorts of ideas and practices. Most of us further assume that our research—the Thesean pursuit of various lines of thought as far into the maze as we can go—enhances and enriches the content of our courses and exemplifies the strategies and modes of inquiry that we hope to teach to our students. In short, most of us hope that the facts, methods, and hands-on experiences that we make available to our students will stimulate them to a self-conscious engagement with their worlds. An admittedly abstract goal, but no more so than the goal of manufacturing "job-ready" workers—as if job readiness were just one, static thing. This is not to say that academics are unconcerned with the ultimate employability of their students. We would be cold-hearted indeed if we scorned as vulgar our students' desires to be self-sufficient and to have meaningful employment. Of course we know that our students must eat, must find an occupation that pays the bills and gives the person a sense of place and worth. Nevertheless, by predisposition and training, academics are unlikely to endorse blithely *any* one-dimensional world view; and, describing a college education as primarily a conduit to job security and financial independence certainly is one such view. Indeed, one of the chief distinctions between the academic and nonacademic worlds is that in the former sphere we actively seek out and attempt to give proportional weight to nuance, complexity, and exceptions to the rules. We don't believe in simple answers and easy solutions. Our detractors, by contrast, quite frequently discuss the goals of education as if all people were the same, all needs were one. We are told that if we only did "X" or "Y," *the* problem could be solved. Even so, we cannot say that academics as a class haven't been myopic and even blindly resistant to institutional change. The ivory tower caricature has some basis in reality. Generally speaking, academics have behaved as though the university were a space somehow above the darkling economic plain and not fully part of the struggle in which the armies of supply and demand, profit and loss clash by night (and day). Clearly we must take seriously the fact that resources are not infinite and that we have a compelling duty to the public weal both financially and pedagogically. Moreover, also generally speaking, the charge that the academy is insular and prone to dismiss rather arrogantly the ideas and wishes of the nonacademic world is not entirely baseless. In academic discourse communities, the standards of proof are exceptionally rigorous; reputations are made on one's ability to consider and account for the full complexity of every problem. Thus, we academics *do* tend reflexively to dismiss ideas and assertions that do not hew to such exacting standards. But such arrogance, if the insistence on careful thought and substantiated claims can fairly be called that, does not proceed from apathy about the cares of the world. College professors, just like everybody else, leave their offices after work and find themselves very much part of the so-called *real world*. We shop and cook meals. We participate in community associations and vote. We get the kids to lessons and games. We watch movies and pay for light and heat. It matters profoundly to most of us who's in the White House and what legislation is on the floor for debate; it matters to us whether our taxes go up and whether our interests are well looked after by other public employees. The image of the pipe-smoking, tweedy, *man* who obliviously reads esoterica while Rome (or America) burns—an image we find so often pilloried in the press and lampooned by legislators—grossly distorts the reality that students encounter in the modern public university. What they find are living, breathing human beings who have strengths and weaknesses, passions and antipathies just like everybody else they know.

But let's move away from generalizations and focus instead on what occurs when flesh-and-blood students meet with their flesh-and-blood teachers. Recently, one of my students—I'll call him Robert—followed me back to my office from composition class. Robert had spent the last seven years in the Army, expecting for most of that time to make a career of it. But eventually he got tired of how little one's military experience or personal interests are considered when it comes to job assignments: "All these new guys would get the job I was applying for while I was stuck— again—in diesel maintenance. Some of those guys didn't even want the job that I wanted, but they'd get it and I wouldn't. Finally," he says, "I just figured I could do more of what I wanted if I was a civilian. So, here I am" (Robert 1998). When asked, "What do you want to do now?" he gets a troubled look on his face and says, "Well, I sort of thought I could get into the medical-technical field; but, now, I don't know. That stuff we were doing today—the research and all—I really like that, too." How long have you been in school, I ask, thinking that he must be fairly well along. "Oh," with a shy smile, "this is my first quarter in college. This is my first English class."

Robert, like more than a quarter of Youngstown State University's students, is "nontraditional": 27 years old, married, with a new child (a daughter) born during the second week of class. Like nearly all of my students, Robert works to support himself[6] and takes a full academic load. Again, like many of my students, neither of his parents ever attended college. Robert's father worked in an extrusion plant that capsized in the wake of "Black Monday"—that infamous day in 1972 when the steel mills in Northeast Ohio locked workers out and then, one by one, went out of business or moved overseas. Neither his father nor mother read for pleasure when he was growing up, he says—a report that echoes dozens of others I've heard in the ten years since I came to YSU. In any case, Robert joined the military because, after his father's painful experience, the job security appealed to him and because he didn't need more than his high school diploma to "qualify." Why, exactly, is he in college? Robert believes what Youngstown State advertises in newspapers and on billboards: a college degree is the key to financial opportunity and self-determination. He's certain that college generally and, as he says, "that stuff" that he learns in his composition class will equip him for a good job. But he's also fascinated by the discovery that he likes "that stuff." It's a revelation to him that learning itself is, if not exactly fun, at least rewarding and engrossing. Naturally, Robert and I don't resolve his uncertainty about what he'd like to do for a living. Yet he's had a chance to think aloud about his future and to feel that he's not "funny" for not knowing exactly what he wants this early in his college career.

Robert leaves, and I check my e-mail. Posts to the North American Society for the Study of Romanticism (NASSR) listserv flood my mailbox. Picking up a thread in medias res, I find this post from a professor who specializes in Romanticism:

> Not to spoil a joke, but the article titled "The New U.: A Tough Market is Reshaping Colleges" in the Dec. 22, 1997, issue of *BusinessWeek* (pp. 96–102) makes for scary reading alongside the Trudeau cartoon for today. The lead-off example in the article is U. Florida at Gainesville, whose president is quoted as saying, "Let's pretend we're a corporation." The article then notes: "Defying traditional academic notions, departments now vie openly for resources. English professors must demonstrate, in essence, that Chaucer pays the bills using funds as effectively as engineering or business classes."

The Doonesbury cartoon referred to in this post depicts the plight of "gypsy scholars"; in one panel, a man with a megaphone says, "Okay, we need two romantic lit instructors today," as specialists on the market floor cry out, "Here!" "Over here!" "Ici!" This lengthy post to the NASSR listserv urges those of us in the humanities to consider the restructuring of the academy both as inevitable and as an opportunity to reconceptualize what we do in more culturally relevant terms. This professor sees our immediate future as technologically driven and multidisciplinary. He is not afraid of the changes this future will bring—at least not afraid for the technologically literate and the professionally flexible—and offers members of the NASSR listserv a "close reading" of the aforementioned Trudeau strip that invites us to observe that the strip in question is structured on the basis of a contrast between two understandings of knowledge work. In the first plate, the Kingman Brewster lookalike and his consultant (a provost?) are staring at a computer monitor whose spreadsheet is showing them glowing figures about the profitability of their college now that tenure has been eliminated and tuition hiked. In the last plate, where the cattle-call scene I earlier referred to illustrates that the quality of faculty hires can be kept up due to the desperation of the "buyer's market," the most advanced technology visible is a megaphone. In this view, the managers of the new knowledge economy are the networked; the victims are the non-networked and technologically illiterate whose paradigm of individual research has been assimilated against their will to a paradigm of individual competition ("Here!" "Over here!" "Ici!") that is inherently uncompetitive against advanced networked modes of competition.

The suggestion that what professors of English do is "knowledge work" and therefore a marketable commodity for dissemination through an increasingly corporate university elicits numerous responses on the listserv—most of which decry the ways in which the McUniversity of the near future is indifferent to traditional modes of academic thought and classroom practice.[7] Two of the most interesting responses came from outside academic English studies. I foreground them here because they articulate what, if the buzz at professional conferences and on the Internet is a reliable indicator, is a growing irritation with our discipline's perceived "elitism." In this context, elitism refers to how out of touch academics apparently are with what the general public endures. We have tenure where others do not have job security. We make better money and benefits than most. We have one of the greatest benefits of all, time flexibility. Moreover, the argument runs, what academics in the humanities do has no "practical" use and therefore no *real* value. So why should we professors be exempt from the supply and demand economics that govern the rest of society? English is particularly suspect, the argument continues, inasmuch as the antihumanist tendencies of much of the literary theory that passes for *serious* scholarship in our discipline demonstrate that we are ideologically bankrupt—even we don't believe in the ultimately beneficent effects of intimate acquaintance with the presumed content of our curricula. We're only about resistance and revolution, subversion and alterity. One respondent to the Romanticist, a professor of philosophy, takes a great deal of delight in dismissing our discipline's "theory stars" (he names Stanley Fish and Eva Cushner as examples) as purveyors of piffle.

> The current paedagogical mélange of theory, feminism, historicism and genderism are, in their sharp antihumanism, hardly designed to win university-wide, public, or business support. If the public actually knew the full scope of current academic thinking about the nonexistence of truth, the relativity of all values, the absence of author and authorial intention, the impenetrable and occluding power of belief, the hatred of western culture, the despite for democratic processes, the leveling of all distinctions of literary value, the critique of the family and the elevation of Foucauldian power to a Theory of Everything, they would never support us. And quite rightly never. . . . Departments of literature have only corrosive refreshment to offer the world. If you think not, look at the MLA conference catalogue, and then imagine trying to explain let alone justify the vast majority of the topics to ordinary taxpayers and businessmen.

He continues by asserting that

> most [English] academics seem to think all is essentially right with the profession if only the politicians and the public would just shut up, fund them as they wish and not interfere in the important business of writing more essays no one will read, constructing more jargon a few dozen only will use, undercutting the good burghers' social illusions about their country, resuscitating Marxism and in general reversing a few thousand years of cultural development.

Despite the generalization that a handful of "stars" whose "influence in shaping MLA policy on the nature of professional writing has been baleful" and has made English studies generally irrelevant and odious, most interlocutors in this virtual conversation generally agree with this critic. Another discussant, whose dissertation in the social history of the early industrial revolution did not earn her an academic post, sees the introduction of market-driven economic principles into the academy as long overdue. Demographics, she asserts, are at the root of the public's growing willingness to cut the humanities deadwood out of the groves of academe because

> my generation simply contains more workers in almost every field than the people ahead of us or following us do or will need. For middle and late "boomers" there were no academic positions to occupy, the tenured chairs all contained the well-planted bottoms of people, mostly male, only a little older than we, who were not about to move over to make room for their younger brothers and sisters.

To this notion that a dearth of jobs and an oversupply of job seekers lies at the root of academe's comparatively recent attempts to streamline, she adds this parting shot:

> For . . . every safely tenured humanist in America, I would venture that there are three or four equally capable, equally qualified people whose experience is . . . enough . . . to create a climate of deep lack of sympathy for the problems of the professors. . . . The rest of us have to spend a lot of time doing things for which we are marginally qualified, are not terribly interested in, and would rather not do, so that once in a while we can do the thing for which we were trained. If the most unfortunate turn your professional lives take is that you have to spend time teaching, and learning to appreciate, the literature of periods adjacent to your periods of specialization, then you are privileged indeed. As a taxpayer, a worker, and now the parent of a college-aged child, I am very, very skeptical of the complaints of supposed intellectuals who cannot find in themselves the creativity to make ordinary adjustments to the demands of the society that they live in.

This discussant, like the professor of philosophy, inveighs against the research agendas of those in the humanities—and particularly the academic Romanticists who subscribe to the NASSR listserv—characterizing them as mostly frivolous and certainly not essential:

> You really don't know how fortunate you are. Most of you have had the privilege of spending your days standing lost in wonderfully uffish thought about things that matter mostly to yourselves, without really having to worry about where your next paycheck is coming from. . . . What I see from this side of the glass is a privileged class worried that the feast is coming to an end. It

must have been lovely [but] research for its own sake is a very rare privilege, you must know. Even the remote Scholastics were not merely exercising their interests and following the aesthetic of their logic. Rather, they were actively searching for the answer to a problem which their society considered paramount and utterly practical—how to get souls into heaven.

Without doubt, these words sting. For those of us "knowledge workers" who have never enjoyed "release time" for research (for me, that includes the co-editing of this book), who find time to mow their lawns on weekday mornings only by making those hours up long after their neighbors have retired for the evening,[8] and whose constant concern is to provide their students with the best possible learning environment, this sort of drive-by criticism of the academic "feast" goes well beyond galling and has the distinct flavor of sour grapes.

But however unfairly this discussant might paint the vast majority of academics with the wool-gatherer's brush, she is right about one thing: she is not alone in her opinion. According to William H. Honan (1998) in an article in the *New York Times*'s "Education Life" supplement, the volume of complaints about perceived abuses in academe has grown louder even as the tone has become more bitter. The complaints that Honan cites are, by now, familiar: Faculties have usurped control of educational institutions and run them chiefly for their own benefit, not the students', they are accountable to no one, and colleges not only have failed to increase productivity but also cost too much (33). The litany continues as our

critics . . . contend that all too often, students are unable to graduate in four years because faculty members are off pursuing hobbies masquerading as scholarship or research, and not teaching enough sections of required courses. And, they say, as a final slap to the taxpayers who finance public institutions, professors have created an inflexible tenure system that guarantees them lifelong employment at a time when almost no one but Federal judges and Supreme Court Justices enjoys that privilege. (Honan 1998, 33)

Honan situates criticisms like those above in the context of statehouse scrutinies of education budgets and the Congressional debate concerning the "reauthorization of the Higher Education Act, a $40 billion package of loans, tuition tax deductions, financial aid and institutional grants that is the single most significant piece of Federal assistance to students, colleges, and universities" (33). Much of the Congressional debate has been informed, reports Honan, by the National Commission on the Cost of Higher Education, a "bipartisan group of college and university presidents and others knowledgeable about higher education" (44). The Commission, whose $650,000 budget was authorized by fiscal conservatives Bill Goodling of Pennsylvania and Howard P. McKeon of California, was conceived in response to perceived public anxiety over the rising cost of higher education. During the fall of 1997, says Honan, "some members were bent on exploring the suspicion that low faculty workloads and undeservedly high faculty salaries had been responsible for driving up college costs . . . [traveling] throughout the country asking openly hostile questions [like] 'Are faculties paid too much?' and 'Do professors work hard enough?'" (44). Despite receiving answers that did *not* support the assumptions provoking these questions, many in Congress—and many of their constituents—remain convinced that higher education is "overpriced" due to exorbitant payroll costs. One Congressional proposal proceeding from this assumption "is a carrot-and-stick approach, in which colleges that reduce tuition or increase faculty workloads would get Federal grants for their students, and those that did not would see their aid cut" (Honan 1998, 46). Congress is unlikely to pass this kind of proposal into law because even its own National Commission cannot agree that university costs are high because faculty are overpaid and underutilized. Nevertheless, during the 1990s Congress came to see its political bread as being buttered on the side of *appearing* fiscally conservative—and to see that political points can be made by bashing a professional group that the public perceives as not having "gone through the stress of downsizing or increasing productivity like everybody else" (Honan 1998, 33). Despite the fact that stereotypes of this kind—and, worse, making law based on such stereotypes—have the power to damage severely the quality of public education, Congress will likely continue building and burning selfish "intellectual elites" of straw because, as they say in some circles, it preaches well.

Further complicating this picture is what now appears to be a long-term trend of angry voter resistance to higher taxes in any form. This resistance is ironic given that, according to an August 1997 CBS News poll, "public pressure on budgets comes even as more Americans see college as a necessity and a right" (Arenson 1997, 1). When asked whether college was necessary to get ahead in life, 75 percent of the 1,307 people responding to the CBS survey said yes, a sharp jump from the 49 percent answering in the affirmative to a similar survey twenty years ago. Indeed, 86 percent of the more recent poll's respondents said that "every capable person has a right to receive a college education, even if he or she cannot afford it" (Arenson 1997, 1). Respondents in the same poll were, however, evenly divided about how we should pay for this "right." About 48 percent said that, yes, the federal government "was responsible for insuring that every qualified person gets a college education" (1). Into the vacuum created by this general ambivalence toward the costs of public higher education have leapt fiscally conservative legislators and governors who have been able to position themselves as leading the charge against ivory tower trough-feeders living the good life at public expense (cf. Honan).

But have legislative calls for greater accountability to the taxpayers' investment in higher education actually affected the humanities? It seems that they are beginning to. At the City University of New York (CUNY), for example, the liberal arts and programs duplicated within its fifteen-college system were designated a "luxury" that the hardworking public could no longer unquestionably afford. As a result, entire departments were shut down. David Yaffe (1996), writing for the *Village Voice*, reports that "City College took the worst hits in the [CUNY] system . . . losing [the] departments of nursing, classical languages and Hebrew, physical education, theater, and dance in [1996's] budget alone" (16). Invoking a decision-making power akin to martial law, CUNY's Regents hiked tuition by $750, raised lower-division class sizes by a third, and "retrenched" nearly twenty tenured faculty. In addition, budget cuts in the name of a remediation reformation have also had a chilling effect on hiring and, according to Steven Urkowitz, English department chair at

City College, are "diminishing the overall capacity of the colleges for everybody" (quoted in Yaffe 1996, 14). It bears mentioning here that one of the greatest sources of public anger at American universities is, bizarrely, that they "waste" so much money on remediation. The question is, once again, framed only in terms of tax dollars: Why should we—in effect—pay twice to teach students the fundamentals (first in high school, then in college)? Thus, universities, in an attempt to respond to Dr. Jekyll's stated belief that college is a basic American right by preparing the unready to take on college-level work find themselves outraging Mr. Hyde's hatred of taxes and weakness.

In my own state, during the early 1990s, Ohio's Board of Regents (OBOR), responded to what its former chancellor Elaine Hairston called our "era of constrained resources" by conducting a statewide graduate program review aimed at weeding out "unnecessarily duplicative" programs (Overview 1994, 2). OBOR appointed a blue ribbon panel (Committee on State Investment in Graduate and Professional Education, or CSI), that asked the following questions:

> How does investment in a given discipline connect to the state's economy and quality of life? How much should Ohio invest in a given discipline? What are the relative benefits to the state of investment in doctoral study in a particular discipline in comparison to other priorities—undergraduate education, for example? In light of overall priorities, how much should the state invest in graduate and professional education? (Committee 1994, 3).

One of the results of the panel's work was the recommendation that Ohio "disinvest" in four of its seven doctoral programs in English.[9] "Ohio," the report states, produces "more than its share of the national pool of graduates." As a result, the CSI recommended that the state scale back its "investment [in English doctoral programs] by 35–50%" because there is "no indication that the overproduction is justified by needs in Ohio" (Committee 1994, 35). Ultimately, the University of Toledo and Bowling Green University were largely "defunded," while Ohio University and Kent State University were ordered to completely overhaul their programs or lose them.

The above examples highlight several important features of the current sociopolitical landscape. First, some of the nation's most populous and influential states have begun to micromanage academic affairs as a means of controlling expenditures. While the actions in New York and Ohio may not be taken as definitive proof of a national trend, the fact that Minnesota, Illinois, Oregon, and Florida have also debated and drafted legislation to divest the public of supposedly unwanted programs, abolish or significantly alter tenure, and increase workloads at least suggests a trend in the making. After all, the conditions that impelled the actions in the above states exist throughout the nation. According to Kenneth Ashworth (1994), former commissioner of the Texas Higher Education Coordinating Board, lawmakers in all states face

> runaway health costs; an aging population; the deteriorating distribution, transportation, and utility infrastructures of our cities and states; increasing social service costs; escalating prison costs; costly court orders; expensive school reform movements and equalization of funding; and frequent mandates from Washington to extend state coverage into areas the federal government is unwilling or cannot afford to support. (8)

Secondly, we should pay attention to the language used in statehouses, university administrative offices, and the occasional opinion pieces in the media. The production-consumption metaphor has a powerful and persuasive logic: the academic industry produces commodities of value, to wit, college degrees. Different models of these commodities sell unequally on the market. Computer science degrees, for example, sell so well that the nation can't keep enough in stock. Witness the February 1998 Congressional hearings featuring Bill Gates and Silicon Valley technocrats lobbying for an expansion of the H-1B program which grants temporary work visas to highly skilled foreign technicians.[10] English degrees, on the other hand, sell so poorly that hundreds a year spoil while sitting on the "job market" shelf. Thus, the logic continues, if we expend academic resources on slow-moving models like fine arts or English, we reduce our ability to produce hot sellers like medicine or computer science. According to this line of thinking, the obvious solution to this manufacturing inefficiency is reallocation.

While the demand for computer scientists has proven as uncertain as the technological sector of the economy has proven volatile, an oversupply of English Ph.D.'s must be acknowledged. In that annual horror that even left-leaning academics call the job market, the '90s have been uniformly dismal. According to Bettina Huber's 1995 *ADE Bulletin* summary of the matter, the trend for more than a decade has been to graduate approximately one thousand Ph.D.'s in the field—fewer than half of whom found full-time, tenure track appointments. In the 1993–94 market, for example, America's various doctoral programs in English *manufactured* 983 Ph.D.'s.[11] The full-time, tenure-track *demand* that these Ph.D. *mills* were working to *supply* amounted to only approximately 41 percent of that number (or 403). The other 580 "units" had the choice of either sitting on the shelf for another year before competing with last year's and next year's 500-and-some "extras" or to take non-full-time, non-tenure-track appointments. According to Huber (1995), only about two-thirds of those receiving degrees ever report finding work in the field (51). Thus, the nation's English graduate programs *do* supply the market with more than it demands. Whether that market has been artificially depressed by the routine exploitation of the less-expensive labor of graduate students and adjunct faculty is another matter. But whatever the reasons for the depressed job market, the fact remains that there are substantially fewer jobs than qualified job seekers.

But important realities are elided when we view the university only through an economic lens. If the university-as-a-factory metaphor were truly descriptive of the world in which we live and work, the bosses would quite rightly reduce the number of shifts and transfer or lay off workers producing slow-moving humanities degrees and increase profits by increasing production (but, to keep prices up, never quite enough to match demand) of the quicker-selling science degrees. The company would remain profitable and, if some "knowledge workers" in the humanities sector were lost to market forces, at least the company would remain viable and the inevitable job losses in one sector would be made up for through increased employment in another.

But American universities are *not* stamping out automobiles, and "knowledge workers" are not low- to medium-skill workers who can be quickly retrained to operate new machines in a different part of the factory. Moreover, our "customers" are not buying tangible products with a variety of option packages to choose from. Whether they would acknowledge it or not, our student-customers are "buying" a series of thought- and behavior-transforming experiences that add up, yes, in part to job-training, but also to a particular kind of subject formation. That is, students pay to support and perpetuate an intellectual environment that will, to some significant degree, form them as people. Upon graduation, our students will not be driving off the lot as shiny, fully loaded sports cars. Instead, they will, ideally, "commence" from their universities with a range of skills and habits of mind that in large measure will determine how they think, define who they are, and shape who they might become. Indeed, the perceived value in a college degree is exactly this: it certifies that a unique and desirable kind of personhood has been achieved. Seen as an industry, higher education is in the bizarre situation of devouring its customers as raw material and reissuing them as units suited to producing and consuming other products. But universities are not mills. Rather, they are the most formally organized expression of a complex endeavor whereby human beings collect, sort, and disseminate forms of their knowledge and experience as a means of species survival. Despite the astonishing amounts of money involved in operating the nation's universities, we must not forget that universities are, at bottom, highly evolved expressions of the same impulse that makes lore-masters necessary to archaic cultures. Tried-and-true knowledge must be accumulated, preserved, and disseminated, or a tribe—the species—is doomed, quite literally, to reinventing the wheel, or antibiotics, or the Bible. Moreover, tried-and-true knowledge must be questioned, tested, experimented upon, and revised, or the human species is doomed, again quite literally, to the flat Earth, flightlessness, or the slide rule. The university is more warehouse than factory, more laboratory than warehouse. But why do we need such metaphors at all? The university is a unique sociocultural entity; it is like nothing else and should be treated and described as such.

Returning again to the classroom, we find that nowhere is the inappropriateness of the higher education industry metaphor more obvious than when we consider the needs and expectations of actual students. Consider, for example, "JoAnn," a single mother of two children. An African American woman who, as she proudly puts it, grew up in the "'hood" and witnessed at age twelve the fatal shooting of her mother, she has some very specific ideas about why she has come to college—indeed, why she somehow finds the money and inner strength to stay in college.[12] A near stranger to her father, and raised by her maternal grandmother, JoAnn managed to finish high school and complete a two-year nursing program with few of the advantages that most of my White, working-class students enjoyed. When she was laid off from her nursing job at a local hospital, she determined to get a four-year degree and earn the credentials necessary to work in hospital management. Living now on scholarships and student loans, JoAnn doggedly pursues her goal despite chronic depression and the isolation of being considered "too White" by her "street friends" and "too street" by her mostly White, working- and middle-class college peers. Like most of my students, JoAnn wants to be autonomous and self-sustaining, working in a position that cannot easily be made obsolete. She wants to be able to live in a place where her children can play safely outdoors and attend schools where there is little peer pressure to reject the middle-class values of education and the pursuit of a stable career considered "too White" by the exacting standards of "the 'hood."

When she talks about her education, JoAnn can sound like the poster child for the view of universities as retail outlets for job skills and practical knowledge. She complains, bitterly at times, about having to shell out hundreds of dollars per class for general education requirements that have no direct application to her chosen career. Most of the time, JoAnn doesn't see her education as a rite of passage or a chance to find herself: it's a way out of soul-killing poverty and mortal danger. During any number of conversations we've had in the past two years, JoAnn has made it clear that she *does* perceive education as a commodity—a thing to be purchased at significant financial cost and personal difficulty.

But despite her frequent complaints that the university seems indifferent to its hard-working student-customers, JoAnn has remarked to me several times that these past few college years have been the only time in her life when she has been able to imagine and exercise options for her life's direction. On campus, JoAnn once remarked, her opinions about race, class, and gender matter, and she can be respected for the quality of her thought as well as receive encouragement for efforts to take charge of her life. At one point she said, "I wish it could be like it is here on campus all the time. This is the only place where I feel like myself." Clearly, JoAnn is paying for a product and getting what she's paying for—a diploma "with all the rights and privileges pertaining thereunto." She's gaining valuable practical knowledge and experience that will be eminently useful in her postgraduate working life. But just as clearly, JoAnn is also slowly experiencing a personal transformation: she knows and thinks differently than do her family and friends in the "'hood." Her conversations about the literature, philosophy, and other general education courses that she's "forced" to take reveal that she finds these most interesting and thought-provoking of her college experiences. Reading Aristotle, reading the *Epic of Gilgamesh*, has provided her with important reference points and insights unavailable to her anyplace else. She's not, as she says, entirely "street" anymore, precisely because she has been formally and directly encouraged to read, think, and write about perspectives that were unavailable to her in her own community.

Can we say that JoAnn could make a living without having read a Shakespearean sonnet or a Socratic dialog? Of course. But—and this is the point I've been laboring to make all along— it is the extravocational knowledge provided by humanities courses that will enrich our students' "selfhood." They will think differently and, I would argue, better because they will have a broader view of human experience and thought. They will, at least ideally, be able to think more carefully and clearly because they have been trained to dig into texts and appreciate the nuances of language, to glean not only ostensible meaning but also its many subtler shades. This is what has always given a college education its cachet; it's one of the reasons that families are willing to incur significant debt to have their children *educated*. They want to ensure and signify, at least in part, that those children have more than job skills. They want to ensure and signify, at least in part, that their children have a specific and valuable kind of personhood. Whether the current, more pragmatic movement will succeed in redefining the social meaning of a college degree remains to be seen. Probably the image of college as a place of self-discovery and personal growth will continue to attach itself to the university experience no matter how much its growing vocational orientation erodes the humanities programs wherein our students' selves take definite shape as matters of taste, philosophy, and principle are investigated and debated. Now, far be it from me or anyone else to dismiss our students' pragmatic orientations as mere capitalist programming—honest work that gives us a sense of social identity and which others value is crucial to human happiness. But there truly is more to human happiness than meat and drink, work and a paycheck. There are relationships and ideas, intellectual interests and creative expressions which are enabled and ennobled by organized, disciplined contemplation in that unique environment called the university.

I know that most critics of the university and its faculty would not actually dispute that higher education is or at least could be the vital cultural center that I've claimed that it is. Rather, when such things are discussed at all, it's with a shrug and a sigh where it is ruefully admitted that we just can't afford such luxuries. Moreover, the university's critics point with a great deal of asperity and disappointment to the ways in which academics do not seem to be enriching the cultural life of the country. Whatever we academics think we're doing, the public reads our research activities as, at best, uninterested in American culture and, at worst, downright hostile to it. The NASSR listserv discussant's invitation to examine any MLA convention program and imagine explaining and justifying any of the hundreds of presentations to middle-class America should do more than make us feel defensive. How *do* we justify our "research?" How *do* we answer the charge that much of what gets exposure from conference podia and in professional publications would subvert (if only more than a few dozen converts cared about the message) the very society that employs us? Leaving aside such typical responses as "that's anti-intellectual" and "that's not fair," what's our *considered* answer to such questions about relevance? These criticisms are invitations to take our measure as a discipline and to formulate reasoned responses to our detractors. We don't have to demonstrate that *teaching* critical thinking, reading, and cogent writing are relevant. Everything we read and hear suggests that that's what the public considers vitally relevant. We do, however, have a serious public relations problem stemming from our well-publicized if ill-understood activities outside the classroom. Few outside the academy understand the pressures that force so many academics to publish quickly a great deal of not very revelatory work in order to keep a job that took at least ten years of education to land. Few outside the academy understand that it is more our administrators' needs for quantifiable data about faculty performance than indifference to students that accounts for the esoterica that finds its way into so many professional programs and journals. Few outside the academy understand or sympathize with the impulse to have and appreciate knowledge and arguments for their own sake that characterizes intellectual discourse. For that matter, few outside the academy understand that the jargon of any group—whether it's a gathering of English professors, carpenters, or rap musicians—appears esoteric and unnecessarily opaque to outsiders. The difference between now and a generation ago is that not only do few people outside academe understand the mandarin rules and medieval traditions governing collegiate tenure and promotion, the professional reputation game, but also it is now becoming almost a matter of public policy and tax savings to put a stop to all academic activity that cannot be readily understood by the layperson. We may be the victims of ignorance and cheap shots, but the world in which we now live is increasingly determined to have a say in what we do as part of our professional practice. And it's well past the time when huffing about the stupidity of the media, the salons, and the public makes any sense. The fact that almost nobody but English professors and their protégés even cares whether or not English departments continue to offer anything more than a few great books and composition courses should stir us to action. Indeed, we may have already squandered our best opportunities to direct the force of this cost-benefit thinking about education in ways that might truly benefit society and improve education.

The easy way to close this essay would be to urge us to get our message about the value of what we do out to the public. But even if we were to write op-ed pieces, convene committees, and issue reports, what difference are we really likely to make? Academics are too few, too isolated, and too internally contentious to figure very heavily in anybody's political calculus. We don't represent a large enough voting bloc; we don't have big money to spend; and we don't have sufficient public support. We do, however, have one venue through which we can make the case that what we do is valuable to society and well worth its "investment," and that is the classroom. We have the opportunity, every school day, to show and tell our students that what we do is vital to them and to society. I'm not just thinking about bringing our students in on the social, cultural, and political discussion outlined in this chapter. We certainly should be doing that, but we also need to make some practical and very difficult changes in how education is administered if we want to convince our students that we value them and we care whether or not they learn. For example, we can show that we truly value pedagogy and our students by refusing to cave in to administrative pressure to inflate classroom enrollments and to reduce course offerings. How can our students, who either are or soon will be voters, possibly give two figs for our concerns about the future of higher education when it appears to them that we've let them be herded by the hundreds into impersonal lecture classes? How else can those students feel anything upon graduating but anonymous and used for their tuition dollars when they have very little personal contact with their professors during most of their undergraduate years? When we let turf concerns and the political value of ameliorating our administrators' anxieties about budgets determine such pedagogical and curricular issues as class size, availability of information resources, staffing, and course offerings, we are communicating loud and clear to students that their desires for education and personal growth are not our first concern. I can well imagine someone asking "what do you mean *let* this happen? Enrollments are complicated matters over which individual faculty have very little control." True enough, but we have a great deal of control over how student-centered we are willing to be when asked by our administrators to ignore sound pedagogy in the name of cost savings.

Youngstown State, to draw an illustration from my own experience, is a "union shop." That is, it is a condition of employment here to belong to the Ohio Educators Association. While our union has not staged a walkout during my tenure, they have done so in the past, and the possibility that they will do so again arises every three years when a new contract is negotiated. Soon, negotiators from my union and my administration will face off over a bargaining table and such things as health benefits, salaries, and working conditions[13] will be haggled over and the results will make front page news here. Seen through a public relations lens, this faculty/administration wrangling is devastating. It shows my mostly working-class community that it's all about money and benefits—and I'm getting a better deal than they are. My job is more secure and my pay-and-benefits package is better. In short, they see just what they expect to see: the university is a big business that must keep its workers reasonably happy in order to continue pumping out its product. They do not get the impression that what happens in the classroom is even of the remotest concern in these negotiations. Sadly, our concerns about the quality of teaching never enter directly into these negotiations. Never has a headline read: "Teachers Threaten Walkout Over Tuition Increase!" "Teachers Strike for Better Conditions for Students!" But, why not?

Students care passionately about affordable campus day care and how much money they have to pay for books and tuition. They notice and care that while faculty all have new computers in their offices, the university can't seem to spring for toner, paper, and enough knowledgeable lab monitors to keep the computer labs open and running.[14] They notice and care that while the university continues to build multimillion-dollar buildings and to landscape lavishly, staffing shortages prevent the sufficiently frequent offering of required courses. If we really want to make the kind of news that would help us get our story out, then we ought to be ready to stage walkouts over the issues that concern our students most. We ought to be showing the public concretely that our professed interest in our students' intellectual and personal growth is more than talk. I'm convinced that if we show solidarity with our students and if we genuinely pour our considerable talents and energies into teaching and making our students' on-campus lives more humane, they will stand up for us when we ask for relief from the purblind pruning of the cost-cutters. Is teaching genuinely important to us or not? Are we genuinely interested in *communicating* the accumulated knowledge of our culture or not? If we are, then we need to show and tell our students so every term. If we are, then we need to strive tirelessly and effectively for real improvements in the classroom, in the lab, and in student services. But if we are not, then nothing in law or nature requires that English departments continue to exist. And, really, if making meaningful contact with students in the classroom and working for tangible improvements in their lives elsewhere on campus is not what we care most about, why *should* we occupy a publicly funded institutional space? Will there be English departments in any but private universities at the turn of the twenty-second century? Now, more than ever before, the answer depends on what we do in the classroom.

Notes

1. "Pluralism," in this context, means ideological plurality wherein views other than the relatively secular perspective of the public schools would be given voice. Thus, the Center for Education Reform suggests that parochial and charter schools receive public funding equal to that of public schools (cf. Allen et al.'s *A Nation Still at Risk*).

2. Compare, for example, Leverett W. Spring's "Literature and the Ministry" (1892), James Jay Greenough's "The English Question" (1895), and Thomas Whitefield Hunt's "The Place of English in the College Curriculum" (1886). The latter summarizes the concerns of the time when he says

> that the mission of America is not literary but industrial; that we are to expect an inferior order of literary art and a sluggish popular interest therein. It is stated, also, by way of palliation, that the country is too young as yet for any decided development along these higher lines of national endeavor. . . . The difficulty lies deeper. Most of it is found in the want of a more distinctive literary English culture in our colleges. Students are not kept long enough in contact with the inner life of English Letters to take on something of that spirit which is resident therein (120–21).

3. Just how commodified has higher education become at the beginning of the twenty-first century? My institution, Youngstown State University, has "outreach campuses" in two of the region's shopping malls. At both locations, gift shops selling university-related apparel and souvenirs are attached to the classrooms.

4. Consider, for example, Henry Hyde's remarks during Senate Impeachment Hearings where he deprecated the value of the testimony of academic experts in constitutional law by saying that "an academic is someone educated beyond his intelligence" (a sound bite included on NPR's "All Things Considered"). To cite another example of this sort of "drive-by criticism," we might consider Pat Buchanan's 1996 address to the Heritage Foundation in which he declared that the Supreme Court and an "intellectual elite . . . believ[e] the prevailing social order of middle class America is deeply flawed, unjust, corrupt, irrational, and calculated to restrain individual fulfillment" ("Remarks" 1996).

5. Compare Newt Gingrich's 1998 remarks during the enrolling ceremony for the Education Reform Bill: "This is about America. It's about our ability to compete in the world market by learning the skills of the Information Age. It's about our ability to be good citizens by having the knowledge to be able to make good decisions as voters and participate in our community" ("Remarks" 1998).

6. In fact my first conversation with Robert concerned his fear that he might sometimes be late to class. He worked the graveyard shift at the local auto plant and sometimes was required to stay past 8 A.M., which would not give him time enough to make the thirty-mile drive from work to campus, find parking, and take his seat. I asked him when he had time to study for his classes, to which he replied, "Well, I've got all morning classes. So I get home at 12:30, sleep until 7:00, eat dinner with my wife, and then study until I have to go to the plant about 10:30. Also, when it's slow, I'll study in the break room at work."

7. The basic resistance to this professor's remarks that emerged from this thread could be used to demonstrate what many critics have been saying: that academics have adopted an almost reactionary position against change, denouncing it as crass commodification and predatory profiteering. However, that would be only part of the story. After venting various pent-up frustrations, the more senior members of the list began proposing ways in which a reasoned, public dialogue could be created that would include businesspeople, students, policymakers, and academics. This changed the tenor of the conversation from fearful and angry to optimistic and thoughtful.

8. This is not the petty whining that it might seem, but an oblique answer to Claude Hendon, an education policy advisor to the Florida State legislature, who is quoted as saying: "It is Friday morning . . . the rest of us are headed for a day's toil at the shop or the office. But the professor is out there mowing his lawn. *His* [sic] weekend starts early" (Honan 1998, 33).

9. There were consequences for programs in other disciplines as well; here only those affecting English studies are reported.

10. The high-tech industry didn't wait for Congress to act, however. According to a *New York Times* report, universities began to feel marketplace pressures in unexpected ways. While the dot-com boom lasted, graduate and even undergraduate students followed the siren song of big, quick money, dropping out to take jobs in the rapidly expanding high-tech field (Bronner 1998, A1).

11. This figure comes from adding the reported number of males and females receiving Ph.D.'s for this year.

12. The violence that JoAnn takes for granted is staggering. On one occasion, in the fall of 1997, I drove her and her children to the emergency room after her domestic partner punched her into unconsciousness. Six months later, she dropped by my office with her arm in a sling because the unlicensed automobile mechanic working on her car ran her over during an altercation about the cost of repairs. Despite the pain, the fear, and the required court appearances to press charges against her attackers, JoAnn managed to stay in school—this despite the fact that she missed several days of class and even more study time. The most significant academic side effects of JoAnn's poverty and of the violence of the culture that she battles every term have been disappointing grades and the necessity to repeat a course in human physiology.

13. As a further indication of how little political clout even the state's educators association has, it should be noted that "workload" is no longer a negotiable issue in Ohio. It was removed as a "bargainable" issue anonymously and without public discussion in conference committee during the summer of 1994 and has not been restored. That same year, the Ohio Board of Regents mandated a 10 percent increase in the amount of time that professors taught. While, ultimately, most universities did not raise the number of classes its faculty were required to teach per year, it is instructive that there was absolutely no public outcry. Even the union said little and could do nothing. As academics, we expect ideas to be debated and we expect reasonable procedures to ex-

ist whereby change can be accomplished. There are, however, legislative means by which such things as workload, tenure, and programs can be changed to suit the university-as-business model that do not require a great deal of public exposure (i.e., debate) or political risk.

14. While it seems unlikely that my colleagues teaching at well-funded "research institutions" or at comparatively well-endowed private schools have ever suffered this embarrassment, I have several times had to ask my students to bring their own paper to class because the department's lab supplies budget had been exceeded.

Works Cited

Allen, Jeanne, et al. 1998. *A Nation Still at Risk: An Education Manifesto.* Washington, D.C.: The Center for Education Reform.

Arenson, Karen W. 1997. "Why College Isn't for Everyone." *New York Times,* 31 August, section 4: 1, 10.

Ashworth, Kenneth H. 1994. "Performance-Based Funding in Higher Education." *Change* 26.6: 8–15.

Bronner, Ethan. 1998. "Voracious Computers Are Siphoning Talent from Academia." *New York Times,* 25 June: A1.

Center for Education Reform. "The Education Forum: The Voice of the Nation's Stakeholders, Hosted by the Center for Education Reform." Available at http://edreform.com/forum/. Accessed on 2 March 2000.

Committee on State Investment in Graduate and Professional Education: Final Report. 1994. Committee on State Investment in Graduate and Professional Education. Columbus: State of Ohio.

Emerson, Ralph Waldo. 1985. *The American Scholar.* In *The American Tradition in Literature,* ed. George Perkins, Sculley Bradley, Richmond Croom Beatty, and E. Hudson Long. 6th ed.. New York: Random House.

Greenough, James Jay. 1893. "The English Question." *Atlantic Monthly* 71: 656–62.

Hodges, Michael W., and Bill Mechlenburg. "Grandfather Education Reform Report." Available at http://home.att.net/~mwhodges/education.htm. Accessed on 15 January 2000.

Honan, William H. 1998. "The Ivory Tower Under Siege: Everyone Else Downsized; Why Not the Academy?" *New York Times,* 4 January, section 4A: 33, 44, 46.

Huber, Bettina. 1995. "The MLA's 1993–94 Survey of Ph.D. Placement: The Latest English Findings and Trends through Time." *ADE Bulletin* 112: 40–51.

Hunt, Thomas Whitefield. 1886. "The Place of English in the College Curriculum." *New Englander* 45 (February): 108–24.

Overview of the Committee on State Investment's Recommendations for the Review of Doctoral Programs in Ohio. 1994. Ohio Board of Regents. Columbus: State of Ohio.

"Remarks by Patrick Buchanan, Republican Presidential Candidate, to the Heritage Foundation." 1996. Lexis-Nexis Academic Universe. 29 January 1996. Available at http://web.lexis-nexis.com/universe.5+3302e716ccfe943493d3df29038198fd.

"Remarks by Some U.S. Senate Members and U.S. House of Representatives Speaker Newt Gingrich (R-Ga) at Enrolling Ceremony for the Education Reform Bill." 1998. Lexis-Nexis Academic Universe. 25 June 1998. Available at http://web.lexis-nexis.com/universe.5+3302e716ccfe943493d3df29038198fd.

Robert [pseudonym]. Personal interview. Youngstown, Ohio. 8 January 1998.

Spring, Leverett W. 1892. "Literature and the Ministry." *Atlantic Monthly* 69: 546–54.

Yaffe, David. 1996. "CUNY in Crisis: Is This the Beginning of the End of Public Higher Ed in New York?" *Village Voice* 41.3: 13–17.

CHAPTER FOUR

Literacy, Gender, and Adolescence: School-Sponsored English as Identity Maintenance

MARGARET J. FINDERS
Washington University in St. Louis

L ike I care!" fifteen-year-old Angel, a European American mother of a two-year-old, yelled out on the first day I visited TLC Middle School. Expelled from a mainstream middle school and on probation, Angel vehemently denied literacy engagement and enacted a rigid set of rituals performed to preserve a sense of self. In a private interview about doing school work, another fifteen-year-old, Diego, told me, "It's like you gotta be bad. Like prove somethin'. Like in front of Tara, it's okay maybe, but now with Lopez around, no way."

The story I tell focuses on Angel, Diego, and the other students that I met at the Teen Learning Center (TLC). This middle school (sponsored by three school corporations and the local judicial system) is located in the rural Midwest and provides an alternative education program for middle school students in the county who have been expelled from school and who, as wards of the court, are ordered to attend. I served as the language arts teacher at TLC for the 1996–97 academic year.

I came to TLC as a thirteen-year-veteran middle school language arts teacher with an extensive research background on schooling for middle schoolers. Feeling confident yet challenged, I set out to provide a literacy education that would support the learning of Diego, Angel, and the rest of the TLC students. But

This project was supported by an NCTE Research Foundation grant and a Purdue Research Foundation grant.

this story will not be about what I taught Angel or Diego. In contrast, I'll attempt to share what the twelve- to fifteen-year-olds taught me about relevance and the teaching of English.

The teaching of English is always about power. And nowhere was that more evident than at TLC. But before I turn to the daily interactions there, let me situate literacy in terms of current understandings. Definitions of literacy have expanded beyond simply the ability to read and write, or, perhaps more precisely, such abilities are now understood as deeply enmeshed in wider circumstances. As James Gee (1990) explains, "Literacy as 'the ability to write and read' situates literacy in the individual person, rather than in the society of which that person is a member. As such it obscures the multiple ways in which reading, writing, and language interrelate with the workings of power and desire in social life" (27). Because language is now understood as situated within specific social, cultural, and historical settings, a reconception of literacy as necessarily plural emerges in current literature (e.g., Dyson and Freedman 1990; Gee 1990). Dyson (1992) explains that when people speak or write, they are engaging in a dialogue socially situated within multiple relations of power. She writes, "and they do so with a sense of the social and power relationships implicit in those dialogues" (4). Understanding the link between language and power makes visible the sociopolitical tensions that create and constrain social positions. However, drawing from poststructuralist theory, I would argue that neither teachers nor students are simply socialized into the profession. Davies (1993) argues that "people are not socialised into the social world, but that they go through a process of subjectification. . . . In poststructuralist theory the focus is on the way each person actively takes up discourses through which they and others speak/ write their world into existence as if they were their own" (13). She writes further that "through those discourses they are made speaking subjects at the same time as they are subjected to the constitutive forces of those discourses" (13). The constitutive forces of the discourses at work in schools create great challenges for those of us engaged in literacy programs.

Discourses shape how people come to understand the world in which they live, how they judge the worth and actions of self and others. But people are not simply defined by ideological constructs of what they should be. As Weiler explains, people "negotiate expectations, both external and internalized in their own consciousness, in the context of material need and desire through competing discourses" (Weiler 1998, 353). Before turning attention to literacy learning specifically, let me describe for you how the students at TLC negotiate their expectations and interactions in a broader sense.

"Just the way we are": Docility and Identity at TLC

TLC students came to school with a keen sense of identity, a well-articulated construction of desire, and a set of rituals performed to present a particular sense of self. Social relationships, attitudes, and perceptions of schooling shaped their sense of self. TLC students brought to the school context certain expectations for how individuals must act, and they judged the value of individuals in relation to these expectations.

It quickly became evident that C. J., Angel, and Diego were peer leaders at TLC. All fifteen years old, these students set the tone for social and academic competence in my English classroom.

C. J. lived with his mother, younger brother, and stepfather just outside of a tiny rural community thirty miles from the school. C. J.'s mother took a job in town because she was obligated to drive C. J. to and from TLC each day. C. J. was ordered by the court to attend TLC for the entire year because of state laws demanding that anyone arrested for carrying a gun to school must be expelled for one full academic year. "I made a bad choice," C. J. explained, "a real bad one. And I got in trouble and I thought I was some big tough man. Pretty dumb, huh?" At six feet tall, around 180 pounds, blond-headed C. J. commanded the respect of the other students at TLC.

At age fifteen, Angel was the senior student at TLC, having been enrolled at TLC since she was thirteen. Only the TLC head teacher, Jennie Carter, had been there longer, and Angel was not afraid to let anyone know that she considered herself in charge of much of the daily routines at school. Angel lived with her mother and her two-year-old son, Tyler. Angel claimed that it was her pregnancy at the age of thirteen that landed her at TLC; records attributed her enrollment there to frequent absenteeism and Angel's volatile nature in the mainstream middle school classroom.

Diego's arrival at TLC created a great deal of tension. When Diego entered TLC for the first time, Angel announced that she was proud to be a racist and began a long series of racial slurs to unite the other TLC students (all European American) against Diego, a Mexican American. C. J. stood up for the new student, and Diego quickly found a place at TLC.

Diego lived with his mother, twin sister, and younger sister. He worked over thirty hours a week at a fast-food restaurant to help support his family. When I wrote that his admittance to TLC was based on his refusal to comply with teachers' directives at his mainstream middle school, Diego corrected me: "No, I got kicked out for truancy. My probation officer tells me to 'choose to change.' I'm not choosing to change and all this other crap. He goes, 'Come with me,' and I said, 'F— you, man.'"

A sense of belonging permeated the TLC environment. Long histories of academic failures and court records united the TLC students. Robert Brooke (1991) writes that "we understand who we are in our society by identifying the group of people we belong to and by working out the degree of belonging we feel to these groups" (22). To instill a sense of belonging, Jennie Carter, the head teacher, started each morning by talking about TLC as a community. In what she named Family Meeting Time, Ms. Carter focused discussions on the importance of shared vision, goal setting, and positive attitudes. She initiated a reward system to recognize positive behaviors and academic successes at school. During Family Meeting Time, she might ask particular students to come forward to be recognized for earning 100 percent on an exam or perfect attendance for a two-week period. Angel characterized the sense of belonging that she felt at TLC differently: "You know we did a lot of things to prove we were the way we were. We were juvenile delinquents, and so we gotta be worse."

Davies (1993) created the term "category maintenance," which she describes as actions "whereby children ensure that the categories of person, as they are coming to understand them, are maintained as meaningful categories in their own actions and the actions of those around them" (18). I document how the category of "adolescent" creates a meaningful category that dictates particular behaviors. (See Finders 1997 and 1998 for a more thorough discussion of the normalizing discourse that serves to regulate adolescent behavior through the sociocultural invention of adolescence as a life stage.) Adolescence as a life stage emerged from a particular set of sociopolitical conditions. Yet adolescence is generally regarded as a part of the "natural" life cycle that is biologically determined. The discourse of adolescence holds that (1) adolescents sever ties with adults, (2) peer groups become increasingly influential social networks, (3) resistance is a sign of normalcy for the adolescent, and (4) romance and sexual drive govern interests and relationships. Driven by uncontrollable hormonal surging, the discourse holds, adolescents display meanness and conflict as signs of "normal" adolescent development: "It's like you gotta be bad," Diego told me. "Like prove somethin'." Taking up the discourse of adolescence that dictates that "normal" adolescents display conflict, TLC students, who were all early adolescents, enacted particular "adolescent" behaviors. Being tagged as juvenile delinquent furthered the need to display resistance. Recall Angel's comment: "We were juvenile delinquents, and so we gotta be worse." The tag "juvenile delinquent" created a readily available category that furthered the need to display resistant behaviors.

All students at TLC were there because of social and academic failure in mainstream schools. The TLC school context was set up for precisely these students. Robert Brooke writes:

> In identity negotiations theory, it is a context's ability to delimit a range of roles for the individual that is crucial. Each context holds certain expectations for how individuals will act and evaluates the worth of individuals in relation to these expectations. (1991, 19)

"And so we gotta be worse" as a defining mantra permeated daily life at TLC. Students and teachers at TLC both came with a set of assumptions and expectations that direct individuals on how to go about their daily rituals. Through official expectations, particular "resistant" students were subjected to what Foucault (1977) would call "normalizing judgments," judgments that placed them at TLC and judgments that dictated who they must be at TLC.

Theories of resistance point out that students who are either unwilling or unable to meet a school's compliance standards are labeled as deficient or deviant and destined by those labels for school failure (D'Amato 1987; McDermott 1987). Available roles for low-SES (socioeconomic status) students are often presented in dichotomies: victim and rebel. Note how Diego's probation officer's "choose to change" message was met with Diego's strong sense of identity: "I'm not choosing to change and all this other crap." Erickson (1987) argues that for low-SES students high school diplomas serve primarily as "docility certificates" (208). TLC School students (all low-SES) have earned reputations for not being docile. Angel explained it this way:

> We're not afraid. We don't care if we get expelled. We don't care at all. We're careless. And that's the big bad thing. We can do what we want. I don't care. It's just the way we are.

For TLC students, "just the way we are" demanded rigid adherence to particular performances. Walkerdine (1990) writes that "in a recent study an overwhelming number of girls of all ages gave descriptions of their ideal girls which included the terms 'nice, kind and helpful'" (51). This notion of the ideal, Walkerdine argues, connects good performance with docility and positions girls in roles that privilege helpfulness as the highest level of attainment. For Angel, terms like "nice, kind, and helpful" were contrary to her construction of self. Angel embraced a subject position as a highly sexualized being and she acknowledged explicitly how this was received by adults. She described herself through the eyes of adults in the following manner:

> The biggest thing is slut 'cause I had a baby. No teacher called it to my face. But they looked upon me like that. They looked at me like I was nothin' at all 'cause I had a baby when I was 13.

Central to the construction of identity for Angel was a home and family identity. But "domestic" and "docile" were by no means synonymous for Angel. Good performance for Angel was not perceived as being "nice, kind and helpful." In contrast, she called herself "She-Ra Mom" and perceived that her status as "mother" gave her power over and responsibility for her peers. She-Ra Mom physically and verbally whipped the younger boys into shape. Angel said of her peers at TLC,

> I'm the mom. They were my kids. She-Ra Mom is what they called me. I kept everybody in line. There wasn't a moment that anything happened there that I wasn't there, that I wasn't in the middle of. You know, everybody came to me with problems. It's like I was there. You know. I was their mom. I kept every body in place and it worked.

One can sense tensions in Angel's conflicting perceptions of her position as "mother." While she felt competent as parent ("You know, everybody came to me with problems. It's like I was there. You know. I was their mom."), she also felt her two pregnancies had cast her as incompetent as a student ("You're no good. You'll never amount to anything."). Proud of her position as a competent and fully functioning woman member of the community, Angel felt pressures from a set of expectations that cast her sexuality as deviant.

As noted earlier, students came to TLC with a keen sense of identity. Both males and females enacted their identities through displays of "being worse," but "badness" at TLC was distinctly gendered. Males at TLC displayed their prowess through their criminal offenses. Girls, on the other hand, displayed their prowess through their sexuality. Note in the following transcript how presentations of self are clearly gendered and distinctly delinquent. When a guest arrived at TLC, Ms. Carter asked each student to introduce him- or herself.

RICKY: I'm Ricky. I've been here since the beginning of the year. I got arrested for paraphernalia (possessing drug paraphernalia) and driving without a license.

WAYNE: Wayne. I'm in 8th grade. I threw a punch at Ferguson (middle school principal).

ANGEL: Uh. (Appearing to wake up.) Oh, I'm tired. I was out all night with my boyfriend if you know what I mean. I didn't get any sleep. Ha. You know what I mean.

Boys identified themselves through their criminal acts. Girls identified themselves through their bodies. Drawing from popular culture images of "gangstas," TLC students both male and female enacted a presentation of self as "you gotta be bad." Goffman (1959) describes such group negotiations as performance teams that are defined as "any set of individuals who co-operate in staging a single routine" (79). Therefore, membership in a particular "performance team" may demand the staging of particular routines. As a member of a performance team of juvenile offenders, each TLC student's actions were orchestrated for the purpose of category maintenance. The students felt constrained to operate within that role and were explicitly schooled by peers in behaviors to maintain the category of "juvenile offender." Surveillance and safety demanded a very narrow band of appropriate behaviors within the school context.

Family Meeting Time: The Making of Meanings through Multiple Expectations

In order to understand the social and cultural interplay in the construction of meaning, I turn now to the morning ritual of TLC to demonstrate how multiple expectations were enacted at the school. Multiple sets of rules—those defined by school authorities and those controlled by the peer dynamic operating within the classroom—demanded adherence to competing expectations. The Family Meeting Time was used to discuss issues and problems that emerged at TLC or at the national level. Students were asked to discuss such things as racial tensions and age-specific smoking laws at a national and local level. Often, school policies and regulations were discussed.

Family Meeting Time was set up by Jennie Carter to create a space for democratic interactions. Students were invited to freely share their views on issues. Most often, Jennie Carter or the teaching assistant, Jerry Brown, proposed a conversation about legal and moral behaviors and consequences for particular choices and actions. As you might guess, these conversations never became lively debates or heartfelt sharing times. Only when an issue hit too close too home, such as Jerry's insistence on imposing a dress code, did conversations take off, and in such cases they most often resulted in yelling, fighting, or even calling the police. At the end of the year, these meetings still never engendered lively debates. Jerry and Jennie struggled to create this sharing time, which never played out as they had hoped. Conversations did not evolve into lively engaged interactions. The exchanges were always forced and slow. While Jerry and Jennie constructed the family meeting as a sharing of the authority within the classroom context, TLC students did not recognize this talk time as any real opportunity for power. Diego told me privately, "If you talk about it, they'll use it against you." In a similarity with Foucault's notion of a normalizing gaze in which, through discourse, surveillance becomes an internal overseer, TLC students monitored their own interactions. While they all reported a strong affection, trust, and deep respect for Ms. Carter, their history as students constructed Family Meeting Time as school time, and that carried with it certain expectations of how one must act. And it could carry certain consequences: "If you talk about it, they'll use it against you."

TLC Middle School was designed as a transitional school. Students came and went as the judge and probation officers deemed appropriate. School officials expected that students would benefit from the attention provided in a small-group atmosphere and viewed the goal of TLC as modifying delinquent behaviors. The court system and school officials envisioned this happening through a system of punishments; Ms. Carter's vision was a reward system. Neither worked.

The temporary community at TLC had its norms called into question every time a new student arrived. And there were many new students (sixteen during the time I was there). On days when a new student arrived, Ms. Carter set in motion a ritualized performance by asking students to discuss their academic success with the newcomer. She worried to me privately each time a new student was to arrive that there would likely be a fight. And so in order to reduce the threat of violence, she would set the tone for the day by making public the standards of acceptable performance and showcasing particular students who were doing very well at TLC. Ironically, the new student came with much symbolic power gained by recently being arrested and, in a sense, challenged the more successful students in recreating their community as a community of juvenile offenders. What was valued by these teens was the opportunity to display status and position—not by how far one had come but by how bad one had been. Conflict is one of the means these students had available to them to get norms on the table. During morning break right after the community-building exercise, the students would go beyond the eyes and ears of the teachers in order to reestablish their positions as powerful. This norm checking most often resulted in physical fighting.

Clearly the system of rewards and punishments did little to modify behaviors of juvenile offenders. On the contrary, it became a means to confirm them. Here's the bind: each of these students had a much more powerful community outside of school, a community that constructed them as competent members, so every time a new student came and Ms. Carter led them in another discussion on the philosophy and vision of TLC, the older students who were becoming quite successful at TLC were quite literally positioned in dual memberships.

As noted earlier, Erickson (1987) argues that for low-SES students a high school diploma is nothing more than a docility certificate. TLC students would agree. Being positioned as competent members of one community of youthful offenders and deemed incompetent in their schooling makes the performative choice an easy one. And their identity as resistant students must be preserved. In private interviews, I asked students why there was a fight each time a new student arrived. "Just gotta happen that way," said Brett, and Diego explained:

> That's because you know, we don't know them so we try to start something. Like at break, Tom had his first day and Sherry was gettin' in his face and later on somebody asked, "Tom, hey, what's you think of Sherry?" and he goes, "I think she's a slut."

C. J. explained it this way:

> Everybody gets adjusted to the way it was before they came, and they have to readjust when they come. Like Wayne when Ricky came, he had to show he was the big tough guy, and Ricky didn't take it. So, see, when Jade came Chenelle had to do the same

thing. And before when Angel was there and before Jade came, Angel said she had to take care of Jade. LeeAnne said that about Tara and then Tara said that about Sherry. So it's sort of like girls have to prove themselves to girls and guys have to prove themselves to guys.

At TLC physical conflict and verbal abuse were ways of getting norms on the table, of establishing and maintaining hierarchical rankings. Physical prowess for both boys and girls was called into question every time a new student arrived. Ms. Carter set out her version of the school norms explicitly on the first day. This arrival ritual created a crisis of identities, a confrontation of rival demands. Situated within competing demands, TLC students had to reestablish themselves as competent and powerful.

The juxtaposition of demands was evident as each new student arrives with symbolic power as a youthful offender. Successful TLC students carried symbolic power, recently earned through the court systems. Yet those students who were succeeding within the school structure could not school the new TLC student into their established norms because that would diminish their established identities as competent juvenile offenders. The new students actually carried the most currency in "being bad." They held the most recent arrest records, granting them the most power.

Students who were becoming successful at TLC were trapped in conflicting values. Since their identities were constructed through their deviant behaviors, the reward system and the emphasis on a community of successful students worked against positive change. Students did not want to be singled out as doing well in school. Jennie's overt requests to reform could not compete with covert demands to be bad.

The School Game: Gender Enforcement and Literacy Learning

What West and Zimmerman (1987) call the "doing of gender" was played out in school performances at TLC, and it specifically governed literacy learning in distinct ways. As a juvenile offender, each TLC student's actions were orchestrated for the purpose of category maintenance. Students felt constrained to operate within that position and were explicitly schooled by peers in behaviors to maintain the category of "juvenile offender." These students established firm boundaries for their actions.

For male TLC students, "literate learner" and "juvenile offender" were constructed as mutually exclusive categories, and these students have had far too much success with the latter to risk recategorizing themselves. Recall Diego's statement: "It's like you gotta be bad. Like prove somethin. Like in front of Tara, it's okay maybe, but now with Lopez around, no way." I can provide very few examples of literate engagement for students like Diego. Whether cajoled or threatened, Diego sat firm, producing very little. When asked to write about "what mattered most," he wrote such things as "I'm writing about this stupid school. The students here are narks." Or, "Listen, this is not an admission but an ass kickin' to you, you fakes." When asked to participate in a reading workshop, Diego slept or pretended to sleep.

"Category maintenance" thus constrains literate engagement in this court-ordered transitional school for youthful offenders. Yet the dominant discourse of adolescence, which constructs resistance as "normal" adolescent behavior, made these boys' performances somewhat acceptable and made these boys seem reachable to TLC teachers, including me. We operated from a "boys will be boys" perspective, if you will. For females, "you gotta be bad" came with a very different set of expectations and consequences. The discourse of female sexuality underscores many traditional elements of a woman's place, particularly that she must be controlled. Determined to establish themselves as powerful, females at TLC enacted identities as highly sexualized beings, as out of control. One girl, for example, began writing an advice column. She wrote letters and responses in two different voices and inks:

> Dear Dying, I need your help because next year I am going back to (mainstream middle school) and I am afraid I'll get kicked out again because I don't like to get up in the morning and leave my man. I won't get up in the morning and I'm usually late to school. I usually stay up late with men. And man, I am tired in the mornings. Please help.
>
> —Too much in bed.

Dear too much in bed,
I know what you mean. Are you supposed to pick school over
men. No WAY! I say who needs school? School should be late so
you could sleep in HA! sleep in with your man and still go to
school. But you better go to school so you can get a good job like
that. I hope you can party and go to school.

Girls at TLC engaged freely in literate activities. For them,
"literate learner" and "youthful offender" were not mutually
exclusive categories. They read and wrote regularly. They were,
in fact, competent readers and writers. They used reading and
writing to prove they were bad, and they proved it through their
bodies. They spoke, read, and wrote about their sexuality. The
distinctly gendered patterns that Angel and the other girls brought
to my classroom created obstacles for me and for the other adults
at TLC.

Classroom teachers too bring to the school context certain
expectations for how individuals must act, and they judge the
value of individuals in relation to these expectations. The construction of the female self as a highly sexualized being created
great boundaries for their middle-class teachers, especially me,
who preferred girls to be nice, kind, and helpful but found these
girls to be mean, obscene, and disgusting. For us, "literate learner"
and "sexualized adolescent" female may have been exclusive categories. Category maintenance was in operation for the adults as
well as for the adolescents at TLC. This, of course, denied the
girls' positions as competent communicative members of the classroom. Adults, denying these girls positions as competent members, left them no possibilities for moving beyond a defensive
stance.

As noted earlier, the connection between good performance
and docility places girls with their nurturing teachers in positions
that privilege helpfulness as the highest level of attainment. This
notion of "good performance" is based on middle-class, white
cultural views. Fordham's (1993) research documents the diversity of gender constructions. She writes, "Because womanhood
or femaleness is norm referenced to one group—white middle-
class Americans—women from social groups who do not share
this racial, ethnic, or cultural legacy are compelled to silence or
gender "passing" (8). Clearly, the denial of diversity of gender

roles in the school context serves to marginalize girls like Angel, working-class and lower-class girls, whose actions do not match their middle-class teachers' view of "good performance" and private sexuality. The institution has a responsibility to respond to the needs of students like Angel rather than to continue to construct them as incompetent members.

"You don't have a clue": Relevance to TLC Students' Lives

For adults at TLC, "just the way we are" demands rigid adherence to particular performances, too. Just like the TLC students, I came to TLC with a keen sense of identity. Bringing experience as a middle school teacher and what I perceived as a vast body of knowledge about effective literacy pedagogy, I cast myself as a competent middle school teacher, although, as I was to discover, the category of middle schooler that I had come to understand clearly did not match my students. For me, a self-monitoring system was in operation which regularly and systematically reestablished a traditional view of literacy, and a middle-class view of female sexuality, both of which denied TLC students, especially female students, positions as competent members of the classroom.

"You don't have a clue," fourteen-year-old Brett told me early in the year when I asked him about his homework. Brett was right. And if I forgot it throughout the year, others reminded me. Angel told me, "You don't have a clue, do you, Peg? You don't understand anything about me. You think that reading some book is going to make some big difference."

"Reading some book" was central to my identity as English teacher and as English education professor. "Reading some book" did make some big difference to me. "Reading some book" was the centerpiece of my view of what counts as literacy instruction. Relevance to my students' lives was the cornerstone to my pedagogical approach, but I must admit that my view of relevance was naive at best.

So what might all of this mean to the literacy educator? After teaching language arts at TLC for one year, I would argue that our first move is to change our views on what counts as literacy, to give the students power and powerful texts. I came to TLC with what I thought was a broad definition of literature. I also believed that students should have more authentic purposes for engaging in literacy tasks. But my field notes chronicled a constant struggle to push the TLC students closer to a traditional definition of literature. For example, while I was willing to work with popular magazines, I viewed them as a bridge into "more appropriate reading materials." I was so constructed as an English educator that I had to constantly monitor my own assumptions of what it means to teach literature. In 1985, Scholes argued that we must stop teaching literature and start studying texts (16). Yet the solution is more complex than simply taking this advice. "Category maintenance" was for me a self-monitoring system in which I regularly reestablished a traditional view of literature. Applebee's historical studies of the teaching of writing and of literature reveal that while there is no nationally mandated curriculum for high school English, there is a homogeneity in the English curriculum across the nation (1974, 1981, 1990). While innovative practices are abundant in professional literature, "category maintenance" is certainly at work in public school English departments across the nation. It was clearly at work in adults and students at TLC, including and especially in me. Students had not lost interest in literacy in general but in the kinds of literacy experiences most often available to them in middle schools. Thus I would argue that our first move is to disrupt the dominant discourses that position some students as noncompetent members of the classroom. Angel, for example, was a highly competent reader and writer. Yet the combination of her sexuality and my views on sexuality prevented me from viewing her as competent.

We must not only begin to articulate a pedagogy that makes visible the discourses that situate us, but we must also begin to move beyond the more reductive of these discourses. It may seem particularly naive that I entered TLC with such an optimistic view of my abilities to work with unsuccessful middle schoolers. But for me the most important learning that I can share here is my destructive reading of Angel. Because Angel did not fit my category of middle schooler, I must admit I found it very difficult to work with her. Yet her behaviors and comments made my sexist and classist views visible. In the end, we came to appreciate each other. The very strength of Angel was her ability to articulate her views directly, something I admire in women. Yet I struggled to assert my authority over her. Docility can no longer be the means by which we teach our students (young women or men) to succeed in school.

Rather than work to recategorize juvenile offenders, I suggest that we work explicitly to recategorize literacy. The newspaper, the Internet, and magazines have much to offer, not simply as bridges to school-sanctioned literature but as worthy texts in and of themselves. Once I was able to work to recategorize myself, I came to see the potential power in such works. In terms of economics and rhetoric, these texts are extremely powerful. Examining how culture works to construct our desires presents a powerful pedagogical alternative. The local newspaper, which reported the criminal offenses of TLC students, offered texts that were powerful and extremely relevant to students' lives at a very immediate level.

Students came to TLC with a narrow and negative view of texts. Texts had been used against them to prove them incompetent in the classroom and in the courtroom. Awareness of political and social consequences had limited TLC students' literate choices. Most often, classroom conflicts were based upon substantive social and political issues. Wrestling and wrangling with political complexities and intellectual uncertainties should be modeled and practiced, rather than denied. While it has become sound pedagogy and is common practice to select literature that relates to students' experiences and to make "authentic assignments" based on real-world situations, emphasis in schools has remained on the aesthetic rather than the political. TLC students were particularly accomplished at examining political issues in court documents and at constructing texts to persuade legal and school officials.

Also, as we work to encourage engagement, we must abandon the notion that to capitalize on free choice is enough. We must monitor and examine the constrained choices available to our students and draw from them how our own choices and desires are shaped by outside forces. We must also be attuned to ways in which we can influence outside forces through our rhetorical choices. Examining the category maintenance at work in texts is a beginning to opening up categories that students *and* teachers may inhabit. I advocate an emphasis on cultural production and on ethnography in order to reveal how texts serve to define and constrain available social roles. Such a focus allows a teacher to mobilize the readings, to construct a pedagogy that situates reading not simply as an aesthetic experience but as a political act as well. It is this shift in emphasis that proved relevant to the TLC students. Our focus shifted to the politics of textual worlds. We began to explore the politics at work in textual representations of the students and of adolescents like them. As literacy educators, we must provide opportunities and models for examining what counts as competence in our language arts programs. We must monitor and expand our category of "competence." Literacy educators must take up a critical stance that deepens understandings of the influence of both language and culture upon lives and classrooms.

During language arts time, TLC students and I brought in texts and began reading as ethnographers, looking at how the characters were constructed in particular texts and contexts, looking for "official voices" embedded in the newspapers and court documents. We focused on uncovering the implicit values and assumptions that governed the actions and judgments of particular characters. In other words, we examined the discursive positioning at work within the texts. We read for assumptions, attitudes, and values implicit in texts (e.g., the local newspaper, *Lowrider Magazine,* court documents, and *The Outsiders*). During our literacy class, I began asking students to look at how a given text constructed individuals and events. Together we began examining the social, historical, and cultural constructions of particular positions available—in texts, classrooms, and the larger culture.

As we struggled together that year to make literacy learning relevant, two means of access became evident. First, relevance depended on real and immediate purposes for literacy with real and immediate audiences. Second, performance offered a means of entry into a literate experience without disrupting one's identity maintenance.

At first reading, the suggestion for real purposes and audiences may appear as nothing new in terms of appropriate pedagogy. Scholars and practitioners have long recognized a focus on the "authentic" as a key to success in teaching. But it was the degree of need for real and immediate purposes that I began to understand as I worked with the TLC students. While we were exploring how young people were represented in magazines and music videos, a series of articles about the possibilities of relocating TLC was published in the local newspaper. Community members wrote letters expressing their concerns with placing a school for juvenile offenders in their neighborhoods. Drawing on her critical skills, Angel reflected on the local newspaper's construction of herself and her peers: "So they've constructed us as juvenile delinquents. They make it look like we are all in trouble or on welfare or something like that. They try to make it look like we are all wards of the court. That's BS." Her work as an ethnographic reader led her to organize classmates to write the following letter, which was published in the newspaper:

> We the students of TLC would like to speak out on our own behalf and rights. We are not all troubled kids or wards of the welfare system and most of us asked to return to TLC. It is true that we have had trouble in the past, but we are taking positive actions to change our behaviors so we can be respected, trusted and looked upon as young adults rather than juvenile delinquents. We have a 95% attendance rate at TLC. We earn A's and B's. If we earn lower than a B, we redo our work until we are successful. The atmosphere at TLC supports our learning. We feel respected as people. We take responsibilities for each other and ourselves. No one here laughs at others. We respect our differences and learning needs. TLC is a school for second chances. Everyone deserves a second chance. We are proud to be TLC students.

Like Angel, C. J. came to understand the social and rhetorical moves that helped TLC students in the classroom, the courtroom, and beyond. C. J. reported that he was extremely proud of his own work in the newspaper, stating, "And we wrote that response to the newspaper. I just think it's kind of neat we responded to it and it actually got in the newspaper. I still got that clipping. Got my name in the paper for something good."

Proving something to probation officers, social service providers, and the juvenile court judge proved to be a key to success at TLC. Each month we produced a school newspaper. Our goal was to demonstrate our success in school. Relevance was immediate and the consequences prompt. At first, students viewed this as a somewhat fraudulent practice, designed to "fool" the officials. C. J., for example, explained about another student's article in our school newspaper: "He just said that to impress his probation officers and make it sound good with everybody, but he didn't mean a word of it." This comment helped us continue conversations about the politics of literacy.

The second key to relevance was performance. Performance offered a way into literacy learning. Performance proved successful because students do not need to give up their presentation of self. They simply could take on the persona of another. We invited key officials to TLC to a drama performance created by the students. The audience was real and present. Again, this had real and immediate consequences.

Performance and Promise: School-Sponsored English and Identity Maintenance

I asked C. J. what was the best thing he had done this year. Without hesitation, he replied, "I'm really proud of the Outsiders Trial." I had designed a trial after reading S. E. Hinton's young adult novel *The Outsiders*. Students served as lawyers, defendants, and witnesses to determine if the main character Pony Boy should continue living with his older brothers or go to a foster-care home. TLC students acting as trial attorneys presented their case to the real judge whom they had met in more adverse settings. Their parents served as the jury.

C. J.: It was cool. I liked that real well. 'Cause we actually got the chance to be the prosecutin' people [laugh] instead of being prosecuted. That was pretty neat.

FINDERS: Did your view of Judge Jackson change at all because of that trial?

C. J.:	He seems pretty cool. He was a pretty good guy that day, I thought. But I know you don't want to make him mad. You know what his nickname is?
FINDERS:	No.
C. J.:	Father Time.
FINDERS:	Why?
C. J.:	'Cause he'll put you away for a long time.
FINDERS:	That's interesting 'cause the only time I met him was when we had our trial. And he seemed like such a good nice guy. So maybe if you run into him again, he'll remember what a good prosecuting attorney you were.
C. J.:	Hire me on? [Laughs]
FINDERS:	Right. Hire you on. Remember what he said to you? Remember when he said you were really good at that? That you should consider becoming a lawyer.
C. J.:	Yeah, and I said to him, "Is that a good thing?" [Laughs] It was a good thing. I guess we kinda proved ourselves to him that day.

C. J. was "really proud of the Outsiders Trial" because he perceived himself to be competent and powerful in front of another powerful person, "Father Time," the juvenile court judge. And that's all I think these students were looking for.

The teaching of English is always about power. Texts had been used against C. J., Angel, and Diego to prove them incompetent and powerless in the classroom and in the courtroom. Keen awareness of the power of texts had limited TLC students' literate experiences. Explicit attention to that power could serve them.

"Prove ourselves": Literate Consequences and Identity Maintenance

Because students were so tied to their performances as youthful offenders, taking on the role of someone else in a dramatic performance freed them to redefine their positions as competent students. As C. J. said, they "actually got the chance to be the prosecutin' people instead of being prosecuted." Likewise, when students perceived that engaging in literacy experiences could have positive social consequences, as in the writing of newspaper articles, they embraced the activities. And the consequences of such a performance did not disrupt their identity maintenance. The consequences served their needs at a real and immediate level. In fact, in performing for the juvenile court judge, as C. J. said, TLC students "kinda proved [themselves] to him that day." Literacy educators should not demand that students recatogorize their identities within their peer group. Such a demand, I would argue, cannot be met. Rather, we must recategorize our approach to literacy instruction.

Not without adversity and controversy did we undertake this new approach to literacy. The TLC students' defining mantra, "You gotta be bad," created obstacles in this approach to literacy. Internet access to pornography and to the strong lyrics of well-liked groups such as Wu Tang Clan created roadblocks. Although I banned these particular materials after discussing the constructions of "academically appropriate materials" as viewed by school and judicial justice authorities, other adolescent content was used. Yet by appropriating exclusively owned adolescent content such as gangsta rap music into a curriculum, by changing the perceived boundaries, any critique will lose some of its power by the very fact that placement within the context of the classroom has lessened the appeal and has stolen ownership. If "you gotta be bad" can be enacted through one's choice in music that advocates sexual and physical violence, for example, then what happens when that avenue becomes sanctioned by authorities within the school context? The key is to tap into these resources without co-opting them. Often, I overstepped the boundaries. It is not so much attending to text selection alone but attending to how that text gets read (how a text might be mobilized) that can serve us as we strive to work with resistant learners like Diego and Angel.

Regardless of a text's content, the dynamics of literacy experiences as enacted at TLC or any school demand particular performances, and classroom-based examinations will, of course, create a social space in which students stand to gain or lose status among their peer groups. There are no easy answers. At TLC, surveillance was external and internal. TLC students monitored their own actions and monitored the actions of others. Their history as incompetent students and competent juvenile offenders constructed school time in a particular way that carried with it certain expectations of how one must act. And it carried certain consequences.

I'll allow Diego, Angel, and C. J. the final words on the matter:

DIEGO: It's like you gotta be bad. Like prove somethin.

ANGEL: You know we did a lot of things to prove we were the way we were. We were juvenile delinquents, and so we gotta be worse.

C. J.: Everybody gets adjusted to the way it was before they [new students] came, and they have to readjust when they come. Like Wayne when Ricky came, he had to show he was the big tough guy and Ricky didn't take it. So, see, when Jade came Chenelle had to do the same thing. And before when Angel was there and before Jade came, Angel said she had to take care of Jade. LeeAnne said that about Tara, and then Tara said that about Sherry. So it's sort of like girls have to prove themselves to girls and guys have to prove themselves to guys.

Works Cited

Applebee, Arthur. 1974. *Tradition and Reform in the Teaching of English: A History.* Urbana, Ill.: National Council of Teachers of English.

———. 1981. *Writing in the Secondary School.* Urbana, Ill.: National Council of Teachers of English.

———. 1990. *Literature Instruction in American Schools.* Report Series 1.4. Albany, N.Y.: Center for the Study and Teaching of Literature.

Brooke, Robert. 1991. *Writing and Sense of Self: Identity Negotiation in Writing Workshops.* Urbana, Ill.: NCTE.

D'Amato, John. 1987. "The Belly of the Beast: On Cultural Differences, Castelike Status, and the Politics Of Schools." *Anthropology and Education Quarterly* 18.4: 357–360.

Davies, Bronwyn. 1993. *Shards of Glass.* Cresskill, N.J.: Hampton Press.

Dyson, Anne Haas. 1992. "The Case of the Singing Scientist: A Performance Perspective on the 'Stages' of School Literacy." *Written Communication* 9.1: 3–47.

Dyson, Anne Haas, and Sarah Warshauer Freedman. 1990. *On Teach-
ing Writing: A Review of the Literature.* Occasional Paper No. 20.
Berkeley, Calif.; Pittsburgh, Pa.: Center for the Study of Writing;
Carnegie Mellon.

Erickson, Frederick. 1988. "School Literacy, Reasoning, and Civility:
An Anthropologist's Perspective." Pp. 205–26 in *Perspectives on
Literacy,* ed. Eugene R. Kintgen, Barry M. Kroll, and Mike Rose.
Carbondale, Ill.: Southern Illinois University Press.

Finders, Margaret J. 1997. *Just Girls: Hidden Literacies and Life in
Junior High.* New York: Teachers College Press.

———. 1998. "Raging Hormones: Stories of Adolescence and Implications for Teacher Preparation." *Journal of Adolescent and Adult
Literacy* 42.4: 252–63.

Fordham, Signithia. 1993. "'Those Loud Black Girls': (Black) Women,
Silence and Gender 'Passing' in the Academy." *Anthropology and
Education Quarterly* 24.1: 3–32.

Foucault, Michel. 1977. *Discipline and Punish: The Birth of the Prison.*
Trans. by Alan Sheridan. New York: Pantheon.

Gee, James Paul. 1990. *Social Linguistics and Literacies: Ideology in
Discourses.* New York: Falmer Press.

Goffman, Erving. 1959. *The Presentation of Self in Everyday Life.* New
York: Doubleday.

McDermott, R. P. 1987. "The Explanation of Minority School Failure,
Again." *Anthropology and Education Quarterly* 18.4: 361–64.

Scholes, Robert. 1985. *Textual Power.* New Haven: Yale University Press.

Walkerdine, Valerie. 1990. *Schoolgirl Fictions.* New York: Verso.

Weiler, Kathleen. 1998. "Reflections on Writing a History of Women
Teachers." Pp. 347–69 in *Minding Women: Reshaping the Educa-
tional Realm,* ed. C. Woyshner and H. Gelfond. Cambridge, Mass.:
Harvard Educational Review.

West, Candace, and Don Zimmerman. 1987. "Doing Gender." *Gender
and Society* 1.2: 125–51.

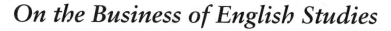

CHAPTER FIVE

On the Business of English Studies

STEPHEN M. NORTH

University at Albany, State University of New York

I want to begin this essay by making what should not be a particularly controversial assertion: that the enterprise characterized as "English"—or, of late, "English studies" or "English Studies"—has only the most meager tradition of dealing with the economic dimension of its own operations. Thus, the primary means of referring to the mélange of activities undertaken in the name of "English," especially in the context of postsecondary education, has been based on a somewhat fuzzy conception of a "discipline" (or, sometimes, "field") as a collective and for the most part research-based enterprise whose constituents are united by their fealty to some combination of method, subject matter, and telos—with no suggestion at all, in short, that this enterprise involves anyone earning a living. We might allow that everybody "really" knows—at least in a nod-nod, wink-wink sort of way— that to be "in" English has been and still nearly always is to be an English "teacher," an English "professor"; but that is nevertheless, and often quite pointedly, not a knowing that this understanding of discipline is designed to encompass. Indeed, it may be that the most appropriate emblem in this context is the Modern Language Association's dogged maintenance of the notion of the "independent scholar," a term which, while for all practical purposes a euphemism for "un- or underemployed academic," nevertheless hangs on as a way to assert—however hollowly— that one can still be fully "in" English, be practicing the discipline, whether one holds an academic post or not.

Secondarily, however—when, that is, it is necessary or convenient to acknowledge that this enterprise actually might have some such economic dimension (and the still powerfully pejorative sense of "careerist" in many circles, to take one obvious indicator, suggests just how hard such acknowledgment can be to come by)—the operative term has nearly always been "profession." This notion, too, has always had a certain fuzziness. So, to take what is perhaps a minor but symptomatic concern, the name of the enterprise has never been amenable to the same sort of agentification as the names of other, seemingly comparable enterprises: economics is carried on by economists, history by historians, biology by biologists . . . but what do we call the people who "do" English? What is it they are engaged in, and why can't they—or why don't they—find some verb in the very language under whose name they operate to describe it? Still, the invocation of profession does at least allow that the enterprise's members are understood to be individually qualified experts, licensed by the disciplinary collective (self-regulated, as it were) to carry on whatever this work turns out to be in some sort of economic context—are experts, in other words, in a way somehow comparable to lawyers, say, or doctors, or maybe ministers, so that whatever it is they do by virtue of their disciplinary training, it results in marketable goods or services—even if it doesn't do much to clarify exactly what such goods or services might be or, therefore, exactly how or why professionals might be remunerated for their efforts.

Founding the Franchise

Nor is it hard to see where the use of these terms to characterize what has long been an almost exclusively educational enterprise would have gotten its start. Like so many things in American higher education, that is, the origins of this somewhat fuzzy conflation of discipline and profession can be traced to the formative influence the nineteenth-century German university system exercised over its fledgling U.S. counterpart. And the key element of that influence here—the central figure in the development of this particular disciplinary/professional mythology, if you will—was the German professor, or at least the image of him imported to this country by German university enthusiasts. Here was an academic figure who seemed to hold enormous potential for a new and growing country with an already well-developed predilection for rugged individualists. James Morgan Hart's "the-German-professor-is-not-a-teacher-in-the-English-sense" rendering of this figure in his 1874 *German Universities,* brought to our contemporary attention by Gerald Graff's *Professing Literature,* has gone on to acquire something of a bumper-sticker ubiquity in this regard. To help dramatize the kind of appeal it might have held for Hart and his fellow enthusiasts, though, I would ask that you read it this time aloud, giving it as much of a John Wayne–style drawl as you can muster: "The German professor is not a teacher in the English sense of the term"—think Rooster Cogburn, now, and feel free to stand up and swagger around the room—"he is a specialist. He is not responsible for the success of his hearers. He is responsible only for the quality of his instruction. His duty begins and ends with himself" (qtd. in Graff 1987, 55).

Just so we're clear, let me stipulate that, so far as I know, this characterization was intended to be positive. That is, despite the many contexts in which such a formulation would be overtly objectionable—"his duty begins and ends with himself"?—this is supposed to be praise, admiration, adulation: represents, as it were, what Mr. Hart wanted to be when he grew up. And I suppose it really is possible to see the appeal such a figure might have held for Hart and the other eager young white male enthusiasts for whom he can be said to have spoken. By all accounts, the position occupied by the comparable U.S. college teacher of the time—the one such young men would have been tutored from or could have anticipated holding—would have seemed to them quite unattractive: that of a glorified schoolmaster who, far from functioning as any sort of autonomous knowledge maker, might have been most positively described as a moral and behavioral disciplinarian charged with shaping pupils nearly all of whom were already his social superiors. By contrast, then, the status these professors at Berlin and Heidelberg were imagined to enjoy would have seemed remarkable indeed—the academic equivalent, perhaps, of an industrial Carnegie or Gould or maybe, as with our swaggered reading, the hero of dime-store Westerns—but in any case a man whose hallmark, as Hart would put it later

in the same argument, was his single-minded devotion to reputation and to power: "The professor has but one aim in life: scholarly renown. To effect this, he must have the liberty of selecting
his studies and pushing them to their extreme limits" (qtd. in
Graff and Warner 1989, 21).

The catch in all this, however—the fly in this durable and
presumably soothing mythological ointment—is that, for economic purposes at least, English as discipline and/or profession
never developed in such a way as to produce or support such
creatures. In a broad sense, of course, this is true for all of the
disciplinary entities whose development has been connected with
the rise of the U.S. academy. That is, despite American higher
education's enduring love affair with what might be called the
spirit of the German university—and indeed despite some early
attempts to enact that spirit institutionally, most notably at Johns
Hopkins and Clark—members of the American professoriate have
found their livelihood to be linked much more directly with undergraduates and the undergraduate curriculum: have found themselves working in institutions designed not so much around
entrepreneurial research stars (and certainly not stars who negotiated their individual budgets directly with the state) as around
the department, a far more ensemble-oriented unit whose primary
institutional function has been to provide undergraduate teaching in exchange for tuition dollars or their subsidized equivalent.

Moreover, this U.S. arrangement provided the professoriate
with at least two significant economic advantages. First and most
obviously, it created a fairly stable and predictable revenue stream.
That is, while maintaining undergraduate enrollments has never
been absolutely automatic (so that postsecondary institutions and/
or individual departments have occasionally failed because of lost
enrollments), and while other sources of funding (e.g., endowments, grants) have certainly had a role to play in making the
system work, tuition dollars—and, again, their subsidized equivalents—have nevertheless proven over the long term to be a very
reliable income base. Second, this revenue stream also turned out
to be usefully and quite consistently expandable, with the result
that the full-time professoriate has not only seen its standard of
living gradually improve over most of the course of this century,
but seen its ranks increased—again, gradually but substantially—

as well. Obviously, the processes by which these two changes have come about involved a whole range of other factors: the growing influence of accrediting agencies, the establishment of tenure, the extension of collective bargaining to the academy, and so on. But the basic dynamic has been simple enough. For a very long time, both new institutions trying to get started, and existing ones looking to expand, were generally able to find the students they needed, and therefore to either hire more faculty or compensate those already in place at a higher rate.

These advantages notwithstanding, however, what this department-centered model has clearly *not* done is make research or the researcher the professorial economic *raison d'etre* in the American system that it was in the German. This is obviously not to say that research has ever disappeared entirely from the mix. While its status has varied considerably over time and across both disciplines and institutions, and while it has been the subject of exhaustingly chronic debate, it has nevertheless held firm as an integral feature of all academy-based disciplinary identities. Strictly speaking, however, the American professor—*as* professor—has never stood any real structural chance of becoming the full-fledged, autonomous, knowledge-making specialist of Hart's imaginings. Rather, every department's first obligation, and therefore at least indirectly every professor's first obligation, has always been to supply the requisite number of filled undergraduate seats. Support for research, then—and, in particular, *time* for research—has had to be generated in ways convertible to that currency. In other words, either funds from sources other than tuition have had to be somehow transformed into teaching labor, thereby freeing up the professor for research activities, or else the amount of teaching labor generated per tuition dollar invested has had to exceed the threshold established for a given campus economy, so that the surplus—again in the form of no-longer-needed professorial classroom time—could then be distributed to the faculty for research purposes.

For a disciplinary enterprise like English, therefore—one which, by contrast to chemistry and geology, say, or even psychology and sociology, has turned out to have no significant access to any such nontuition funding sources—this pattern of development has put nearly the entire burden of sustaining any sort of research agenda entirely on the latter option. To be sure, there is a certain chicken-and-egg quality about its having evolved in this way: that is, it is hard to say whether English has developed its rather insular academic existence because its research agenda has had no remunerative currency elsewhere in the culture, or whether its research agenda has had no remunerative currency elsewhere in the culture because English has developed this rather insular academic existence. Either way—or both ways or neither way, for that matter—the net economic result has been the same: from fairly early on, the only reliably remunerative practice carried out under the banner of English as a disciplinary enterprise—the only real *business* of English, in this sense—has been teaching.

Boom

And on the whole, it is a business at which English has done quite well. During its first seventy-five years as a more or less distinct entity—from, say, 1875 to 1950—both the number and the size of English departments grew right along with the country's system of higher education in general. To be sure, English did not always keep pace with the leading edge of such growth; it was not, as I have already suggested, either directly responsible for or directly connected to the college- and university-sponsored activities that generated most of the nontuition dollars. What English *did* have to offer, though, was a research agenda made viable by the nationalist/racialist appeal that gave its philological forebears their start, extended in various permutations to the study of the British and subsequently the American literary tradition, and, more directly to the point here, a means of supporting that agenda (and its propagation among majors and graduate students) by assuming a good-sized chunk of the classical curriculum's disciplining function at the lower division, most notably in the form of mandatory first-year writing and required general education courses. And in order to effect the necessary exchange— the key mechanism, that is, by which tuition generated through such lower-division teaching was transformed into faculty research time—was a practice I call *discounting*: farming out as much of such instruction as was practicable to workers paid at less than the going professorial rate, with the savings thus generated allowing tenured-faculty teaching loads to be reduced in terms of preparation and class size (i.e., allowing such faculty to teach small upper-division seminars in their specialities), or in terms of course load, or both. It is not clear whether English departments invented this mechanism, and they were certainly not the only units to employ it, but—especially in the case of first-year writing—they seem to have done an especially good job of institutionalizing it as an accepted part of their operations. Long before the end of World War II, then, English departments had established themselves as sturdy, if not exactly imposing, fixtures on the college and university scene.

English really hits its full economic stride, however—the business of English becomes really *big* business, as it were—during the post–World War II period that saw such dramatic transformation in both the scope and the mission of American higher education. The general sequence of events should be reasonably familiar: the various incarnations of the GI Bill, the post-Sputnik scramble that produced initiatives like the National Defense Education Act, the coming-of-college-age of the Baby Boom generation, and—that bottom line of bottom-line causes—the sustained expansion of the post–war/Cold War economy. To be sure, this was an economic and demographic tide that lifted all departmental/disciplinary boats, but English seems to have done particularly well. Its flagship Ph.D.-granting departments, for example, doubled in number between 1950 and 1972, going from about 60 to about 120; attained some rather impressive sizes, with units featuring 60 or 70 or even more full-time, tenure-track faculty members; and, not surprisingly, vastly increased their collective output of Ph.D.'s, jumping from around 200 in 1950 to around 1,400 in 1974.

And this tremendous growth at what might be called the "top" of the enterprise—this dramatic increase in the number of graduate faculty (read "research") positions *and* the vast numbers of new Ph.D.'s, nearly all of whom would have been led to aspire to comparable positions themselves—was fueled by a concomitant expansion in its discounting operations. After all, it is not as though English had suddenly found some other way to fund its operations. The effects of this expansion are most dramatically obvious, no doubt, in the Ph.D.-granting departments (especially, but not exclusively, at public institutions), where the long-standing practice of using teaching assistants (TAs) as part of the instructional labor pool grew enormously: legions of TAs, assigned course loads comparable to (and sometimes greater than) the courseloads of faculty, freeing the latter to concentrate on upper-division and graduate instruction—and, of course, research.

But it had related effects in other sorts of units, as well. When these newly credentialed Ph.D.'s found themselves employed in M.A.- and B.A.- and A.A.-only institutions—where, given the brute arithmetic of the system, the vast majority inevitably landed—they understandably sought to fashion positions suitable to their training and aspirations. In some institutions, this involved developing still more M.A. programs, and then using the students thus enrolled as TAs in roles similar to those played by Ph.D. students, even—depending on state and campus regulations—as instructors of record. In others, it meant differential workload policies of various kinds, with tenure-track faculty teaching 2-2 or 3-3, say, and other employees (labeled as instructors, lecturers, adjuncts, and so on) teaching 4-4 or more. And whether differential course loads were possible or not, at four-year institutions the Ph.D.-holding, tenure-track faculty tended to reserve for themselves whatever research-oriented advantages they could—teaching in their areas of specialization, smaller class sizes, sabbatical leaves, and the like—an option always made possible, whatever the limits of scale, by some form of the same discountable labor that greased the research skids elsewhere in the system.

Bust

As I assume most readers know all too well, however, this period of expansion—what might be called, albeit not without a good-sized dose of irony, the Golden Age of English—came to what was by institutional standards a screeching halt beginning in the mid-1970s. In retrospect, it is possible to identify warning signals even earlier, but as this passage from Don Cameron Allen's

1968 MLA-commissioned *The Ph.D. in English and American Literature* suggests, the giddily prosperous leadership of this enterprise—an enterprise I confess to thinking of as College English Teaching, Inc.—was definitely not seeing them:

> The shortage of fully trained teachers of English [i.e., Ph.D. holders] has unfortunately been increasing in an order that is not consonant with the increase in undergraduate enrollment. In 1953–54 only 29 percent of all new teachers of English had a doctorate; ten years later, this surprising percentage had fallen to little more than 12 percent. . . . The decline in trained personnel revealed by these percentages for English is true of all other disciplines but not to the same degree. While the number of beginning English teachers with Ph.D.'s was being halved, the average for all fields was falling from 31 percent to 25 percent. It seems almost a natural law that the more trained English teachers are required, the fewer are available. Can this shortage be solved or should we regard it as chronic? (Allen 1968, 17–18)

The answer to Allen's closing question, of course, was that this shortage not only could but indeed would be "solved," and in very short order; supply would not so much catch up with demand as get whiplash watching it pass by, heading lickety-split in the other direction. Thus, by the time Cameron Allen's book was in print, nearly all of the doctoral students who would make up the enterprise's two largest Ph.D. classes—more than 1,300 in both 1971–72 and 1973–74—were already on track to graduate into an academic job market of such rapidly diminishing prospects that it would, along with other factors, lead to a halving of the Ph.D. graduation rate in just over a decade: between 1973–74 and 1986–87, the rate would fall from over 1,350 to under 700.

The economic factors that applied the brakes so effectively are, at base, pretty straightforward. As the 1970s wound down, the country's higher educational system as a whole hit a kind of enrollment ceiling—discovered, in essence, that it had created enough spaces to accommodate all of the undergraduates who could afford to pay enough, either on their own or with various subsidies, to support what by then had become fairly well established ratios of full-time, tenure-track faculty and steadily expanding administrative overheads (the role of which often seems ignored in this equation). It wasn't, in other words, that postsecondary education had somehow become universal; although it was far more widely available than before World War II, say, there were still plenty of prospective students who did not yet attend. Nor was it a question of academic credentials, a shortage of ostensibly "qualified" students; subsequent developments—most notably at the community college level, perhaps, but in plenty of other venues as well (e.g., college sports)—make it clear that such qualifications were and are, for all practical purposes, entirely negotiable. It was, rather, about money. With the middle-class portion of the baby-boom bulge waning, with federal support for higher education gradually diminishing, with interest rates in the teens, with the overall U.S. economy no longer expanding at its early 1950s pace, the market for college instruction, at least as that instruction had come to be delivered by full-time, tenure-track faculty, reached its limit.

To make matters worse, this was a limit that was pretty much guaranteed to recede, a ceiling that would get lower for quite some time. That is, between continuing appointment and a tight job market, tenured college and university faculty—the vast majority of them still decades from retirement age—were not going anywhere: could neither be made nor expected to vacate their positions. Yet with every passing year, at least if minimal employee morale was to be maintained, the overall cost of their salaries and benefits would increase, while the number of students they taught would either stay the same or—given the effects of age, infirmity, seniority privilege, and the like—decline. In short, from a tuition-generating perspective, at any rate, the faculty would constitute a fairly serious long-term liability.

Institutions responded to this problem in a number of ways, all of which are familiar by now: increasing faculty course loads or course sizes; constraining the growth of faculty salaries or benefits; offering early retirement incentives; combining or retrenching the more vulnerable units; raising tuition; and so on. (It may be that some institutions also cut administrative overhead, but I have no concrete information on that score.) As far as I can tell, however, their most durable and effective long-term strategy has been to refine and expand the system's version of what elsewhere in the economy has come to be called "outsourcing" or "contracting out": in essence, circumventing the tuition-generation problems an aging tenured faculty creates by assigning various portions of that faculty's instructional work to either non-tenure-track and/or nonfaculty employees at a lower cost.

And while it seems safe to assert that one or another form of this practice has eventually been deployed in nearly every sort of academic unit, it is hard to imagine that any of them have been more amenable to it—provided a more fertile ground for this scheme—than English departments. As I indicated earlier, after all, these departments had been engaged in a comparable practice—what I called discounting—for a very long time, and their rationale, albeit usually implicit for obvious marketing reasons, has always been plenty clear: certain courses English departments offered were considered less than fully disciplinary, and could therefore be taught either by the less than fully qualified (e.g., TAs, ABDs) or by the underemployed (i.e., Ph.D.'s hired as adjuncts, lecturers, or the like) for less than full compensation. When colleges and universities began to target such courses as a site for contracting out, then, English departments were hardly in a position to protest. Having spent the better part of a century of making it increasingly clear that they absolutely did not need tenured professors to teach first-year writing, say, or creative writing, or advanced composition, or even such general education fodder as introduction to literature, they had no plausible grounds for (nor, it has often seemed, any genuine interest in) arguing otherwise now.

What has ensued over the past twenty years or so might be characterized as a slowly widening spiral of discounting. It has played out in various ways on various campuses, of course, and it has not been—symptomatically—the sort of phenomenon where anyone has kept a neat, comprehensive body of centralized or self-evident data, but there is no mistaking the general trend. Consider, to begin with, that even after the higher educational system hit what I called a ceiling with regard to a certain range of paying customers in the mid- to late 1970s, undergraduate enrollments have managed to climb at a slow but gradual rate—so that, to take one obvious indicator, the number of B.A. degrees awarded inched its way up from about 887,000 in 1971–72 to about 1,173,000 in 1996–97 ("Facts" 1995; "Digest" 2000).

Next, consider how well English departments have done in holding onto their share of this slowly expanding clientele. According to two longitudinal studies conducted by the U.S. Department of Education over roughly the same time span, for instance, English not only offered what was by far *the most frequently* taken and completed college course in the country—English composition, which consistently accounted for more than 3 percent of all college credits earned, an astonishing 1.5 percentage points more than its nearest competitors; it also placed three other courses in the top thirty-five (introduction to literature, English literature, and American literature), which together accounted for another 2.5 percent of all credits earned, meaning that English departments accounted for more than 5 percent of all college credits earned over this time span ("Facts" 1996). In addition, while its English-major customer base did suffer a rather serious decline between 1972 and 1985—after a decade spent over the 7 percent mark (1963–64 to 1971–72), it sagged to a 1980s average closer to 3.5 percent—even that number enjoyed something of a resurgence well into the mid-1990s, going from a low of about 3.4 percent back to a peak of nearly 5 percent before edging back toward the mid– to low 4 percent range as the century wound down. And it is worth noting, too, that since the number of B.A.'s granted was slowly climbing throughout this period, the raw *number* of English majors who were graduated increased pretty steadily from the mid-1980s until a 1993 peak of more than fifty-six thousand (the highest such number since 1972), so that even though this number began to tail off in the second half of the 1990s, it remained closer to the fifty-thousand mark than the more desperate figures in the low thirty thousands that were characteristic of the mid-1980s ("Bachelor's" 1).

In these various bottom-line ways, in other words, business for English departments has been quite good, with demand for their undergraduate services not merely holding steady, but in fact gradually increasing. Judging by the measures available to us, however, it also seems fair to say that this demand has not translated into prosperity for the enterprise of English as a whole. Thus, while we don't have comprehensive data on the hiring patterns of English departments (deaths, retirements, and so on), what information we do have indicates that the employment prospects for new Ph.D.'s—their chances, that is, of landing the full-time, tenure-track positions they have generally believed themselves to be training for—have been chronically poor throughout most of this same period. Indeed, according to MLA's periodic surveys of the employment status of such graduates—the organization conducted ten such surveys between 1976–77 and 1996–97—the worst year had for some time been 1983–84, when only 36 percent of all Ph.D.'s granted (i.e., not simply those with known employment status) were reported to have found tenure-track employment, while the best had been 1991–92, at 45 percent. But that long-standing low point was actually supplanted in the most recent survey (1996–97), when 372 of the 1,226 people reported as having earned Ph.D.'s were also reported to have found full-time, tenure-track positions—a very scant 30 percent, which, when averaged in with the other nine surveys, produces an average of just about 40 percent (Laurence 1998, 59–60; Huber 1995, 48).

In short, something on the order of four hundred new English Ph.D.'s per year have been finding tenure-track jobs over the past two decades—which translates, assuming that there are about 3,500 English departments in the United States, to an average entry-level (full-time, tenure-track) hiring rate of just over one position per department per decade. (This does not account for all hirings by any means, but it makes an obvious benchmark figure for the system's overall economy.) Even more to the point here, of course, is that an even greater number of these new Ph.D.'s have *not* immediately found such employment, with a substantial portion of them—more than 30 percent of those with known employment status in every survey—reported as having taken academic positions that are other than tenure-track, that is, positions that are non-tenure-track (renewable), one-year (nonrenewable), or part-time.

And this group—some 200 to 350 people per year—along with a cadre of TAs which has also been growing steadily since the mid-1980s, has been folded into an ever-growing pool of discounted laborers. A 1996–97 sampling by MLA indicates that in the B.A.-granting departments polled, an average of 50 percent of all first-year writing sections were taught by non-tenure-track faculty; in M.A.-granting departments, 64 percent; and in Ph.D.-granting departments, 96 percent (Gilbert et al. 1998, 29). At the two-year institutions, meanwhile, the Department of Education estimates that, as of 1993, 64 percent of *all* community college faculty held part-time appointments, so that it seems eminently safe to assume that the percentage of part-timers teaching first-year writing is at least that high, and likely higher. Combine these percentages with the results of MLA's 1991–92 survey of under-graduate English programs, which reported that composition accounted for 46 percent of all English sections mounted in this country (Huber 1996, 47), and factor in that we know a good many other courses are staffed in much the same way, and the scope of English's discounting operation begins to come clear. In fact, I am willing to contend—by virtue of a certain amount of extrapolation, to be sure, but with little fear of contradiction—that more than half of the undergraduate English courses mounted in the United States every year are now taught by someone being paid less than, and usually far less than, a full-time, tenure-track faculty wage.

(Let Us Call the Next) Chapter (In the Saga of College English Teaching, Inc.) 11: Bankruptcy and Reorganization

As the enterprise of English studies reaches the end of its first full century, then, the majority of its members would seem to be fur-ther than ever from having access to anything like the "disci-pline" or "profession" in the image of which the College English Teaching, Inc. franchise was—however ambiguously—founded. Indeed, if my extrapolation is correct, we can now say that teach-ing college English has officially become a non-tenure-track oc-cupation: that is, more courses are being taught by people who have no prospect of becoming tenured faculty than by people who already have been or might be tenured. And there is every reason to believe that this will become more and more the case: that the operation is likely to become even more extensively dis-counted. After all, in addition to the 46 percent of all sections that MLA's 1991–92 survey reported were composition courses (a number which I suspect has itself grown in the subsequent decade), writing courses in general—all of which, so far as I can tell, have traditionally been considered discountable—constituted 65 percent of all courses taught. Add to these at least one-third of the 28 percent of all sections that survey reported as featuring literature—to account, that is, for the courses in this category that are routinely discounted, often on a large scale, such as introduction to literature and lower-division electives—and you have the profile of an enterprise with plenty of discountable potential left to tap.

The gravity of this situation as a threat to corporate operations has not gone unnoticed. Indeed, MLA—the closest thing postsecondary English has to a central corporate intelligence—has taken remarkably visible positions with regard to it. Thus, as I noted above, it was one of the ten organizations to sign the 1997 "Statement from the Conference on the Growing Use of Part-Time and Adjunct Faculty." Even more pointedly, it formed the Committee on Professional Employment, whose own final report deals with employment practices in the departments of all of MLA's constituent language groups, but with English departments treated as a distinct category. Last but not least, MLA's Executive Director, Phyllis Franklin, took the occasion of her "Editor's Column" in the fall 1998 *MLA Newsletter* to write a piece called "Setting Standards: Acceptable Ratios of Full- to Part-time Faculty Members," her response to two essentially identical "calls" passed by the organization's 1997 Delegate Assembly. One, a motion offered by the Graduate Student Caucus, "requires the MLA to 'determine minimum standards of acceptable full-time/part-time ratios by various institutional circumstances' and to 'report those standards' by the time of the 1998 MLA convention" (Franklin, 5). The other, derived from the "action agenda" of the aforementioned "Statement from the Conference on the Growing Use of Part-Time and Adjunct Faculty" (1998), calls upon "concerned organizations to work together 'to define the appropriate ratio between full- and part-time faculty appointments that would ensure quality education with due consideration of the diversity among disciplines and among institutions of higher education and then to reconsider this ratio at stated intervals with respect to the rapidly changing conditions within higher education'" (Franklin, 5). Franklin's immediate aim in the column, then, is to prime the pump for discussion of such ratios at the 1998 convention. To this end, she outlines the general issues, reports on survey data, and offers the following "Possible Standards for Discussion":

1. Seventy percent of the courses and course sections in English and foreign language departments in B.A.-granting colleges should be taught by tenured or tenure-track faculty members.

2. Sixty percent of the undergraduate courses and course sections in English and foreign language departments in Ph.D.-granting institutions, excluding first-year writing and language courses, should be taught by tenured or tenure-track faculty members.

3. Fifty-five percent of the course sections in first-year writing and language courses in Ph.D.-granting institutions should be taught by tenured or tenure-track faculty members.

4. Establish a standard for first-year writing and language courses only. (6)

The most remarkable feature of these documents—the two statements and this column—is the fact of their existence: they represent an explicit level of, and overt concentration on, what I have been calling the business of English studies to a degree that is, so far as I can tell, unprecedented in the history of MLA. Thus, while the organization's constitution does define its purpose as being "to promote study, criticism, and research in the more or less commonly taught modern languages and their literatures and *to further the common interests of teachers of these subjects*" ("Constitution" 1996, 621, my emphasis), it has heretofore rarely—I am willing to say never—sought to define those "interests" in anything like the starkly economic terms on such prominent display in this excerpt from Franklin's column, and readily available in both statements as well. This is the stuff of beleaguered CEOs and companies trying to stop the bleeding, not the executive directors of scholarly societies: it is more about the business of doing business than about "study, criticism, and research," and—especially given the levels of discounting under serious consideration—far more a matter of which teachers' interests will be subordinated to others' than of which ones might be furthered in "common."

And in this sense, of course, the substance of these various proposals is much less noteworthy than their visibility: they aren't so much new as newly—and rawly—visible. In fact, this fin-de-siècle scramble might well be understood as a last-gasp effort to preserve whatever is left of the old franchise, to negotiate a ratio of discounting whereby some full-time, tenure-track faculty can earn six-figure salaries, thus keeping alive the myth of the (almost) autonomous disciplinary and professional specialist, without provoking one or more of the several other interested parties—employees, creditors, and customers, if you will—into taking the kind of action that might bring the whole system down.

Will it work? Frankly, it's hard to see how: there is too much pressure from too many directions for the situation to be stabilized by so facile a gesture. To begin with, even if MLA were to endorse guidelines such as those Phyllis Franklin proposes—and that is certainly conceivable, not least since a vote to support what in other contexts might well be construed as objectionable labor practices ("Hey, I know: let's discount the wages paid to our co-workers in 30 percent or 40 percent or 50 percent of our courses!") is here being framed as an effort to resist such practices, and hence as a *reform* measure—surely their most immediate impact would be to boost the relatively young but growing labor movements among TAs and adjuncts: the endorsement of these levels would constitute, that is, an important form of leverage for the purposes of negotiating lower teaching loads for the former and better employment opportunities for at least some of the latter. And it is hard to see why, once that leverage created any serious momentum, the reform process would stop. So, for example, the TA unions might eventually reach course loads (and/or the creation of fellowships) they found satisfactory; demand from that quarter is at least conceivably finite. But reform there would obviously manifest itself first as an even greater pressure to staff classes with non-tenure-track, and especially part-time, faculty. Would those workers, fresh from collective bargaining success as TAs, happily settle into responsibility for 45 percent of the first-year composition course, say, and not press for more? Even given the skill with which English departments have traditionally managed to keep these two groups from seeing their common interest, it seems unlikely.

Meanwhile, with or without such guidelines—and the burgeoning power of organized labor among the currently discounted notwithstanding—I expect that at least some college and university administrators will continue testing the lengths to which discounting can be taken. Why not? The labor pool is already there—Ph.D.-granting English departments have made and keep making sure of that—and the profit margin is awfully tempting. In fact, if the academic equivalent of full-fledged departmental bankruptcy hasn't already been visited upon an English department somewhere, it is bound to be fairly soon: some enterprising dean or provost or board of trustees will try running a fully discounted English operation, staffing all courses under the English rubric with no tenure-track, and maybe even no full-time, faculty whatever. Even now, it would be no problem to document instances where—in both two- and four-year institutions—60 percent or 70 percent of a department's undergraduate sections have been staffed by non-tenure-track people, and without any particularly vehement public outcry. If that's possible, why not at least *try* 80 percent, or 90 percent, or 100 percent? It is, as they say, easier to apologize than to ask permission. In this direction as well, then, the chances of anyone playing the autonomous scholar diminish: if we are all discounted, there need be no such stars.

Lastly, if there is a wild card in all this—a constituency whose tendencies are more unpredictable, and perhaps also more pivotal, than the others—it is the students and their financial supporters (including parents, of course, but there are obviously lots of arrangements these days, with a lot of parents also being students), and then also, at least to some degree, the legislators, trustees, regents and the like who might be said to represent them. As the members of this group become more savvy consumers of higher education, they have already begun to regard discounting operations with some skepticism—almost as a kind of bait-and-switch scam—and to respond accordingly: If I pay full-fledged tuition (or, at the public schools, full-fledged taxes and tuition), I want full-fledged instruction delivered by full-fledged instructors in return.

Up to a certain point, then, English may well want to harness this constituency in its campaign to slow or stop any further discounting: "See that," the field's members can say to administrators. "We need full-time, tenure-track lines because the students and their financial supporters demand to be taught by the real thing!" The catch, of course, is that English departments as traditionally constituted would only want to make such claims up *to* that certain point—the one where discounting provides the right amounts of research time—and no farther, and that would likely prove to be a far more difficult trick. After all, the value English-as-discipline places on its research and publication agenda is not, so far as I know, shared very fully by many members of the larger public; nor is it my sense that the enterprise would be anxious to have its productivity along these lines subjected to careful scrutiny—and especially not with comparisons made to fields better able to attract external funding. Thus, while there might be some short-term advantage for English in collaborating with its customer base, as it were, in a campaign against discounting, such a campaign might very well lead to places English doesn't necessarily want to go: to the floors of legislatures and the boardrooms of trustees, say, where votes to give those customers more access to those full-time, tenure-track professors they believe they are paying to study with would translate into higher teaching loads for the full-time and tenure-track. If it is possible at all to sell these consumers on any version of the marquee scholar—and I have my doubts about that—it won't in any case be a version of that scholar whose "duty begins and ends with himself." If as an undergraduate I can't take Professor Marquee's courses—and take them often—what exactly am I paying all that tuition *for?*

It is tempting, and even something of a custom, to close out such analyses of labor practices by waxing moralistic, arguing that some "we" must stand in solidarity with our graduate students and colleagues and take action to end their "exploitation." I am not going to take that route. For one thing, if moral suasion were sufficient to turn this tide, it would have done so long before

now; it's not that this is a new issue, or that wonderfully elo-
quent writers—James Sledd has long been my favorite—haven't
made the moral case many times over. For another, while there
are clearly all sorts of disparities between the parties involved—
disparities that obviously might be and often are characterized as
inequities—I am sufficiently procapitalist to believe that exploitation is not a term that has a very secure place in these particular debates. Nobody I know has ever been *forced* to enroll for
graduate study in English, to study through the years required to
earn a terminal degree, to join the ranks of the underemployed,
and so on; that would be a long time to have what would surely
be a curious-looking gun held to your head . . . and who, exactly,
would hold it? At most, I might be willing to characterize the
system as involving something like elective exploitation, a course
of study and a mode of employment people choose to pursue in
part because they like the work (and what they often characterize as the lifestyle), but also in part because they imagine that it
might win them a version of that full-time, tenured research position enshrined in the field's mythology—the closest thing to
which, in the United States, has traditionally been made possible
by precisely the kind of discounted labor they are willing to provide in order to stay in the game. The odds of climbing to the top
of this corporate ladder have always been lousy, but they have
never been secret. People with this much education have real
choices in U.S. society. If they stay in this business, it's because
they elect to.

That perhaps rather hard-nosed position notwithstanding,
though, I will in fact close out my analysis by arguing—predict-
ably, I should think—that the business of English really does need
to reform, to reorganize, and to do so in particular with regard
to this practice I have called discounting. And the basis for my
appeal, even to those who hold the very best positions the enterprise currently has to offer, is crass self-interest. I don't claim to
know exactly what will happen to English studies or English departments as the next century unfolds; the analysis I have offered
here can most charitably be characterized as quasi-economic, and
therefore—given the vagaries of even genuine economic analyses—is hardly the basis for grandiose predictions. But given the

trajectory the enterprise has been following, and given the kinds of indicators I have reviewed, moving into that future armed with an unworkable mythology and its concomitantly muddled indifference to institutional economics strikes me as a formula for disaster: a great way to ensure that working conditions for everyone—even those traditionally best insulated—will get a good deal worse before, and maybe even if, they ever get better.

Works Cited

Allen, Don Cameron. 1968. *The Ph.D. in English and American Literature*. New York: Holt, Rinehart and Winston.

"Bachelor's Degrees Granted in English, 1950–1997." 2000. Associated Departments of English. Accessed 19 January 2000. Available at http://www.ade.org/images/BAtrends.gif.

"Constitution of the Modern Language Association." 1996. *PMLA* 111.4 (September): 621–27.

"Digest of Education Statistics, 1999: Chapter 3—Postsecondary Education." 2000. National Center for Educational Statistics. Accessed May 2000: Table 249. Available at http://nces.ed.gov/pubs2000/digest99/d99t249.html.

"Facts and Figures." 1995. *ADE Bulletin* 110 (Spring): 52.

"Facts and Figures." 1996. *ADE Bulletin* 113 (Spring): 59.

Franklin, Phyllis. 1998. Editor's column. *MLA Newsletter* (Fall): 5–6.

Gilbert, Sandra M., et al. 1998. "Final Report of the MLA Committee on Professional Employment." *ADE Bulletin* 119 (Spring): 27–45.

Graff, Gerald. 1987. *Professing Literature*. Chicago: University of Chicago Press.

Graff, Gerald, and Michael Warner, eds. 1989. *The Origins of Literary Studies in America: A Documentary Anthology*. New York: Routledge.

Huber, Bettina. 1995. "The MLA's 1993–94 Survey Of PhD Placement: The Latest English Findings and Trends through Time." *ADE Bulletin* 112 (Winter): 40–51.

————. 1996. "Undergraduate English Programs: Findings from an MLA Survey of the 1991–92 Academic Year." *ADE Bulletin* 115 (Winter): 34–73.

Laurence, David. 1998. "Employment of 1996–97 English PhDs: A Report on the MLA's Census of PhD Placement." *ADE Bulletin* 121 (Winter): 58–69.

Sledd, James. 1991. "How We Apples Swim." Pp. 145–49 in *Composition and Resistance,* ed. C. Mark Hurlbert and Michael Blitz. Portsmouth, N.H.: Boynton/Cook.

"Statement from the Conference on the Growing Use of Part-Time Faculty and Adjunct Faculty." 1998. *ADE Bulletin* 119 (Spring): 19–26.

Economies, Politics, and English Studies

MARGARET J. FINDERS

STEPHEN M. NORTH

SCOTT A. LEONARD

VICTOR VILLANUEVA

Margaret J. Finders

Gerald Graff and my teenage daughters agree on schooling in at least two ways. First, that the stuff of their literacy curriculum is the "same old deadly 'school stuff.'" And second that there is an enormous chasm that separates the culture and discourse of their teachers from that of their peers. My daughters might articulate it a bit differently. But their views of schooling match Graff's in these discouraging ways, evident in their apathy at waking to another day of what they would call "mind-numbing boredom." A book on relevance and English studies would be very short indeed in their minds. "Relevance? To what? To me?" When I posed the question to them, they, in fact, evoked Leonard's economy metaphor—with more than a bit of sarcasm, I might add: "Yeah, mom, we need to get good grades so we can get into a good college and with a degree from college, we can get a good job." When I asked specifically about their English classes, they went on, "Oh, yeah, like reading *Billy Budd* is gonna help me get a job." They are keenly aware of the need for a college education. Since ninth grade, their class ranking has appeared on grade reports with the implicit subtext that unless they are in the top half they won't get into a "good" school. So they understand the need to play this deadly school game by the rules set by the adults.

And they play it with finesse and grace, subverting the dominant culture whenever they can with the savvy of pros, borrowing from adolescent culture to co-opt a teacher's authority. The school game for my daughters is about walking the tightrope between these two distinct discourse communities, each with the potential for great profits and greater consequences.

The discourse borrowed from teachers and guidance counselors ("a good high school education equates with a high grade point average, which is a ticket into a good college") collides with the discourse of their peers that dictates the need to display resistant behaviors. Subverting the teacher's authority is about seizing power and forming strong bonds within their peer network. Both of these discourses of schooling ignore what individual human beings might learn and how they might grow intellectually. One says, "Oh yeah, if you get into a good school, then you can get ahead and get a good job." The other, "This has nothing to do with real life. It's all just a bunch of BS." Borrowed discourse of the teachers ("if *you* get into a good school, then *you* can get ahead and *you* get a good job") emphasizes the individual and the need to take care of oneself first and foremost. While my daughters both mock such ideas, they accept the rules of this venture. So they see their English studies as a game that must be played, although they see no real relevance to their present or future lives. The texts they read and the essays they write are simply required drills to get them to the next level with grades piling up like pennies in a piggy bank.

Unlike the students that I write about in my chapter in this volume, my daughters are for the most part successful high school students, coming from a middle-class culture that matches school expectations. Yet youth culture makes them more like Angel and C. J. than their teachers might anticipate. While both would agree that the literacy curriculum could be described as "the same old deadly 'school stuff,'" they would disagree on the benefits of it. My daughters buy (excuse the pun) Leonard's metaphor of education as economy. They have grown up with the educational mantra, "Work hard in school, get good grades, and you'll get a good job." Students like Angel (more like the students in Willis's [1977] and MacLeod's [1987] studies) also articulate the need of an education to get a good job, but they know they are denied access. And actually they are savvy enough to know that other avenues of work may be more profitable for them.

So how might we begin to make English studies relevant to all students? We must change such defining and constraining discourses. While Graff notes that students are alienated from intellectualized, position-taking roles, I fear that teachers are often alienated too. As I argued in my chapter, category maintenance may prevent some teachers from engaging in the kinds of literacy education that might actually begin to change the discourse of schooling. Discussions of the profits of a good education attend too closely to what the individual might get and pay little if any attention to what human beings might learn. Teacher education programs must begin to help beginning teachers ask critical questions and then act on them in a responsible way. To reap the economic benefits, to reap the social and political benefits, the discourse of schooling must be intellectualized. The profits of the game must be expanded to attend to what individual human beings and entire sociocultural groups might learn and how they might grow intellectually.

Stephen M. North

For me, the most powerful collective message of the chapters assembled in this section of the book—one influenced, to be sure, by my own preoccupations—has to do with graduate training, and especially doctoral training, in English studies. That is, while the concerns raised by these five essays are quite varied, and while the academic politics of their authors—were we to be assembled, say, in a single department—might well prove to be more various still, all five nevertheless invoke an English studies professoriate populated by people whose backgrounds (in the broadest sense), interests, and training are quite different from the ones embodied by those who have defined this discipline-cum-profession for most of its American history. And one key set of sites for mounting the kind of campaign any such population shift would require—if not indeed *the* key set—is comprised of the 150 or so programs that offer the Ph.D. Both curricular logic and institutional history suggest that changes not certified at these sites, no matter how right-minded, are almost certain to be marginalized or short-lived. In short, if English studies is to be "relevant" in the ways these chapters suggest, some serious changes will need to be made in the way the professoriate goes about replenishing its ranks.

So, for example, one such change—suggested by both Gerald Graff's and Margaret Finders's chapters—would lead doctoral candidates to place considerably more formal emphasis on the study of their current and/or prospective students than has heretofore been the case. Neither Graff nor Finders says as much directly; the graduate curriculum per se is not their immediate concern. Still, Graff makes it eminently clear that the general trajectory of disciplinary development in English—a trajectory which, on the whole, moves the professoriate further and further out of touch with the discursive universe(s) of the students who enroll in their classes—poses a serious educational problem. And the implication, at least, is that this problem ought to be addressed, this trajectory altered, as early as possible—that is, when the future members of the professoriate begin their training.

Finders's report on the Teen Learning Center presents an even more radical challenge. Her study seems to me important, interesting, well-written and—most directly to the point here—quite unlikely to emerge from, or even appear on reading lists for, most extant English Ph.D. programs. I won't say it couldn't emerge from *any* such program. There are some—especially those with a strong rhetoric and composition emphasis—where work like this might appear as a dissertation. And there are a few more where such a study, or inquiries understood to be "like it" in some way (with Shirley Brice Heath's *Ways with Words* enjoying a canonically token status in this respect), might appear on the reading list of one or another course. Still, I would hardly be going out on a limb to claim that the vast majority of English doctoral students will earn their degrees without *ever* formally studying the writing or speaking of any students at all, let alone the writing or speaking of troubled high (or middle or elementary) school students, and that fewer still will do any serious or extended writing about such matters. This sort of inquiry might be sponsored in schools of education or the odd sociology or anthropology program . . . but not in English. If we are to take Finders seriously, though—and I certainly believe we should—this state of affairs would have to change, and the impact on advanced work in English would be dramatic indeed.

Victor Villaneuva's chapter, meanwhile, presents comparable sorts of challenges. Thus, to begin to work with undergraduates on issues of race, he says, "we must begin with where the students begin," an imperative that presupposes much the same kind of understanding as that advocated by Graff and Finders, and—accordingly—a mode of doctoral training that would feature one or more disciplined approaches to gaining it.

But his essay also calls attention to another dimension of prospective reform in English doctoral education: that is, he raises questions not only about *what* and *how*, but also about *who*. In this sense, I was struck by what might be called the demographics of his opening scene: "A number of graduate students of color in English write an article for the school newspaper." It is true, of course, that the "face" of English doctoral education in this demographic sense has probably changed more than that of any of the traditional disciplines in the post–World War II era, if only because of a remarkable shift in gender balance: that is, more English Ph.D.'s have been awarded to women than men each year for more than a decade now. The scene he describes here, though, could not plausibly take place in most English doctoral programs—or could not, at least, without rather fudging on what "a number of" means in a proportional sense. Moreover, if we extended his concern with race to include such factors as class and career goals, so that English Ph.D. programs were genuinely hospitable, in ways they have rarely been, to students whose first degrees are from community colleges, say, and whose career ambitions are along the line of directing the sort of Teen Learning Center Finders studies—and here again, I believe such changes would indeed be salutary—then those programs would have some serious revising to do.

Lastly, even Scott Leonard's chapter—one which seems to suggest that the major problem facing English studies lies in its inability to effectively "get its message out"—seems to me to imply, if perhaps unwittingly, the need for reforms in doctoral education. Near the end of the essay, where Leonard suggests actions that English faculty might take to help students and the larger

public appreciate their value, he wonders why, "if making meaningful contact with students in the classroom and working for
tangible improvements in their lives elsewhere on campus is not
what we care most about, . . . should we occupy a publicly funded
institutional space?" On the whole, I don't agree with the way he
defines this mission elsewhere in the essay—his notion that the
faculty somehow confers on students "a specific and valuable
kind of personhood," for instance, makes me most uneasy. Still,
assuming we could agree that some version of making these meaningful contacts and tangible improvements is indeed paramount,
and that doctoral education, as our ultimate formal certification
process, should reflect these *as* priorities—in the place, that is, of
the generating of long lists of publications, which is what we
actually value in assembling our graduate faculties—then Leonard
and I might actually end up agreeing, too: that if English studies
is going to be "relevant" in the next century, its regimen of doctoral education needs some serious reworking indeed.

Scott A. Leonard

To the degree that each of us writing in Section I has addressed
the relevance question(s) motivating this book, we have, not surprisingly, discussed the ultimate beneficiaries of much of our work
—our students. Yet, reading the essays in this section has reawak-
ened in me a familiar ambivalence that irritates like virgin wool
on damp skin. And I itch most intensely when I put my anecdote
about JoAnn alongside Victor Villanueva's sampling of ideas related to Frantz Fanon's *Black Skin, White Masks*. Villanueva
claims that the discursive practices of the mainstream are responsible for the continued subjugation and estrangement of those
positioned as other within the dominant discourse. "We are," he
says, "still colonial schools, trying to inculcate cultural assimilation." He makes it clear that this is "painful and exclusionary" to
students not positioned in the mainstream by the dominant discourse. I agree with most of what Villanueva says; cultures are,
almost by definition, assimilation engines, and that which is
unassimilable is pushed to the margins, and those so positioned

receive less of what the mainstream has to offer, including justice and opportunity. Who could deny this? Yet the implication that we can't help but reinforce the historical inequities of the dominant culture when we teach—no matter how enlightened or well-intentioned we might be—is the crux of my concern. I admire the aesthetic of this theory; it's self-consistent, it explains at the abstract level all there is to know about "the way it is." Yet how could anyone but a stone-cold cynic teach if he or she truly believed this to be true?

When I first entered graduate school in 1986, nearly all the composition research we read and imagined ourselves conducting centered on classroom practice, the observable writing process, and related issues in developmental psychology and their relationship to basic rhetorical concerns. This research seemed to have as its goal the creation of knowledge that could ultimately facilitate student efforts to master the discursive codes necessary to their academic and postbaccalaureate success. In the intervening years, composition studies has more or less abandoned the formal, sustained study of writing practices and the practical applications that such knowledge would have. One needn't have read every issue of the profession's major journals nor to have read every CCCC program in the last ten years to know that identity and technology issues now get most of the ink and presentation space. Have you conducted a six-year study of students collaboratively producing texts, and do you want to write up your findings about what does and does not facilitate successful group work? Don't stake your professional fortune on its seeing print. Not only is collaborative writing passé as a publication area—after all, it enjoyed a three- or four-year vogue about ten years ago—but so-called empirical research just isn't "hot" anymore. Indeed, despite the hundreds of presentation slots available at the 1999 CCCC meeting in Atlanta, only sixteen were given to empirical research methodologies and reports of research. Compare this to the seventy slots granted to presentations falling under the Writing and Difference rubric, a number that doesn't take into consideration sessions devoted to such cognate areas as Colonial Theory, Disabilities, Social/Democratic Action, and Social Issues, nor the forty-four presentations devoted to Computers and Writing.

This drift away from the classroom and away from observation-based research has had important consequences. So far, no thread of inquiry has been developed to its fullest potential. All those questions raised fifteen years ago about the writing process, about the viability of empirical research for investigating literacy behaviors, about whether or to what degree skills and knowledge developed in the first-year writing classroom are portable to other writing situations, about group dynamics, about cognition, about brain function—all those questions remain questions and the subjects not of disciplinary knowledge but of practitioner lore. As a discipline, we take up a thing for a few years, drop it and take up another. Ours is not a scientific culture but a culture of essayists. We, unlike our colleagues in the social sciences and sciences, are looking for something new and original to say and not to establish knowledge from which descriptive rules and fact-informed practices can be derived. This is the value of theory to our discipline—it gives us novel ways of discussing the same old problems and of pointing out new ones. Thus, unless we can change our organizational culture, we will not produce the discursive equivalents of the First and Second Laws of Thermodynamics, because we reward the raising of questions, the display of forensic skill, and the rhetorical revolt against the percepts and precepts of our antecedents rather than the creation of knowledge. But while English studies, in its neverending search for something new and clever and surprising to say, appropriates partially digestible methodology, philosophy, and terminology from other disciplines and drifts from hot topic to hot topic, we further advance the perception that we aren't about any specific thing.

English studies may well pursue this desultory path into perpetuity, but we have to ask ourselves why we'd bother. What do we do for our students and for the oppressed by persisting in scholarship that takes little or no responsibility for the social and pedagogical consequences of its theorizing? Mere novelty and theories that problematize without proposing and testing solutions are, at best, empty exercises. Speaking now of identity theorists generally and not of Villanueva specifically, let me ask what difference it makes to observe that discursive practices shape subjectivity and that the consequences of such shaping can be painful? Don't we already know that oppression is painful and that language is its tool? What can we or should we do with this knowledge when we teach Monday morning? English studies needs an open and honest discussion of what, if anything, it collectively can or should do about social evil. That discussion, I strenuously assert, should be closely tied to observation-based research of the most rigorous kind—of the kind Margaret Finders, for example, engages in. We need as a discipline to commit ourselves to establishing working principles, to deriving methods appropriate to the phenomena we study, and to investigating in sustained fashion all discursive practices—mainstream and otherwise.

If such institutional change is to occur, however, it will have to be led in a conscious, organized way by the discipline's de facto decision makers. Editorial boards for our journals and publishing houses will have to make long-term commitments to encouraging sustained observation-based research and to publishing work that bridges the theory/praxis gap. Ph.D. programs will have to orient their curricula toward the classroom careers upon which most of their graduates will be embarking. Indeed, the profession needs to take a collective step back and ask itself what the goals of its collective activities should be and discuss and implement ways of achieving those ends. The annual meetings of MLA, NCTE, and CCCC should make this disciplinary soul-searching a long-term focus. This would mean fewer sessions, fewer speakers, and very likely more genuine and productive dialog among the membership. If these possibilities are but partially realized, we may find that English studies not only survives the next century but thrives.

Victor Villanueva

I am never not amazed at the place I find myself at (improper dangling preposition and all). And it's never that I don't feel as though I belong, because after all this time I realize I do fit, even if awkwardly at times. Fit. Place. And race. My baggage. And the baggage always has me thinking in decidedly political terms, so that I sometimes get surprised when the political is assumed, not made explicit, when there seems to be more of a handshake with politics than an embracing of the political. Or maybe that's unfair. Maybe what I mean is that I can read these essays and see something of my life through them—as the high school dropout from the slums, as the graduate assistant, as the faculty member making demands. And if it isn't Freire I'm reading, then I'm reading Gramsci; and if it isn't Gramsci, then it's something like a materialist political economy. That's what I read, but only in the spaces. So let me write in between those lines, a brand of politics within which to reread the section, maybe.

I'm compelled to do a quick glossary—terms and concepts all over these essays. I want them to be explicit. Forgive me if I tell what is already known. And to the initiated, forgive my over-simplifications (though obscurity is the great sin of the cultural/political discourse of the time).

The language of the left begins with two antithetical terms that describe two ancient philosophical camps: idealism and materialism. Idealism operates on a kind of faith, believes that the answers to metaphysical questions (metaphysical questions being those that ask how nature and reality come to be and how they change), are spiritual, nonmaterial. The word for studying this spiritual cause of change is teleology. Hegel believed in the spiritual. Materialism looks to physical causes. The earliest philosopher normally seen as a materialist is Democritus, who lived during the fifth and fourth centuries B.C.E., a particularly fertile era in Western thought. Democritus created atomic theory. A slightly older contemporary was Protagoras, the sophist who said that "man is the measure of all things," that there is no natural, gods-given social order. And there was Socrates, who believed that religion is not the same as morality, and in a way very much like a Paulo Freire, said that doubt is the way to truth.

The traditional notion of materialism is mechanistic. It is eternal, unchanging, in a sense, in that the mechanisms set in motion in the beginning, that first beginning, the big bang, say, are the same mechanisms in operation today, in motion but never changing, not really. Take on this position for social or human behavior and what results is an ideology—the way of the world, unchanging. The idealists had a concept that was more dynamic than mechanistic materialism: the dialectic.

Actually, the dialectic in the way we tend to discuss it in rhetorical circles is Aristotle's. Aristotle, a pragmatist, in some sense anticipated Marx by seeing social conflicts in terms of who holds power. But in terms of dialectic, for Aristotle the dialectic was a logic system. In the eighteenth century, the dialectic gets another use through Immanuel Kant. Kant says that we can't prove reality, because for every thesis the mind produces, the mind can produce an equally valid antithesis. To prove his point—yes, to prove that nothing is provable—he set up four contradictions of pure reason as four sets of theses and antitheses. Comes Fichte and then Schelling and they create the synthesis, the solution to the contradictions that neither accepts nor rejects the thesis or the antithesis. Hegel comes along, about a generation after Kant, to posit a dialectic which is a threefold process in which reason is revealed through reality, and reality is reason and spirit. Marx says, "good idea, but forget spirit," or something like that. Marx creates dialectical materialism, in which the conflicting reality isn't mind and spirit; it's physical reality and society: capitol and labor.

Dialectic, in the language of the left, is the struggles and the contradictory interests between capitol and labor. And the classes that represent them are the bourgeoisie and the proletariat. The bourgeoisie own the money, the tools, the workplaces for a product; they are the owners of the means of production. Most of the rich we might know are not likely the bourgeoisie; most, even CEOs, work for someone. And the proletariat are those who must earn wages in order to survive. Collar colors, blue or white, make no difference. As long as there is a chain to that collar, that paycheck, we are the proletariat.

And as the proletariat we are subject to exploitation (which is very different from coercion; guns to heads is coercion). Exploited, we become alienated. We are exploited because we don't earn what we are worth. If we did, the capitalists couldn't realize a profit. The professoriate, then, is exploited, even when well paid, if we think in terms of real use value. TAs and non-tenure-track faculty, then, are decidedly more exploited, since they do much of the same work as tenured faculty—often more class-room work—and get paid decidedly less. So we work for some-one else, with relatively little control over when and how we'll work, or where or for whom, little control, even, of what we'll do. Most teachers know something of administratively imposed curricula, of the higher administration using "higher" as their excuse, who in turn say "the school board" or "the regents" or "the legislature." And most teachers have felt, at some time or another, powerlessness—or worse, too much under the influence of other powers. This is alienation. The solution, according to Marx, is to form unions.

In America, at least, there grew the great alliance of capital and labor by way of the unions. In other words, unions took on a mediating role between capital and labor, serving themselves and the interests of capital in the name of the workers. Unions became another decision maker for labor. Alienation remained.

And alienation—an estrangement of the individual from the self, the natural environment, social life—sounds awful. It sounds like what we all endure and sometimes try to do something about through counseling or backpacking or weekends at the lake. But why do we endure rather than seek to overthrow? The answer: ideology and hegemony.

The simple definition of ideology is "world view": our individual conceptions of the self, the relation of the self to the collectivity (which could be as small as the family, as large as humanity), the self to the physical environment, the way of conceiving society, its nature, and the way of thinking about history. When ideology is decidedly political (as the word tends to be used), then it contains the program for political action, with "program," then, marking the difference between ideology and culture: ideology is systematic, a set of principles, even if consciously unrecognized and thereby unquestioned, whereas culture can contain random, disassociated beliefs. For Marx and most marxisms, the set of principles are imposed. We haven't a clue.

But this is a problem, addressed by Antonio Gramsci, who developed the concept of hegemony. Hegemony argues that though we know that we are being exploited, we either accept the idea that the goods of the system override the bads, that is, we accept the moral grounds for the systems we take part in, or we accept that the system serves our needs well enough, despite its faults, or despite the greater profits realized by those we work for. We go along with the program, in effect, consenting to hegemonic controls.

So hegemony, which can contain any number of ideologies, gets passed on through rhetoric, through the conscious use of language aimed at persuading others to accept particular world views. But the party line, so to speak, would be that ideology is passed on through a process of reproduction (which Louis Althusser called "interpellation"). Essentially, ideology is passed on through the institutions of civil society, civil society being the complement of the State. Those institutions would be things like the family, the church, the media—and the schools.

And so we step into the system that precedes us, and it seems normal, the way of the world, so much the way of the world that we become subject to reification, reification being the contemplation of the way of the world—maybe even its study—without questioning, without looking at the big picture, without seeing the totality (another bit of jargon, but not a tricky word).

Education, then, takes on a pivotal role, especially an education which is concerned with the rhetorical—composition, literacy, English studies. Education as an institution is an institution of civil society that tends to prefer idealism over materialism, promoting particular ideologies—in America, the combination of liberalism and laissez-faire capitalism, which boils down to "every man for himself and let the best *man* win." And in this alienating ideology the schools promote critical thinking (problem *solving,* the problems already preexisting) rather than critical consciousness (problem *posing,* trying to get at the potential problems within or underlying the preexisting).

These terms—*critical consciousness, problem posing*—come from the work of Paulo Freire. Paulo Freire is kind of a stew of modern trends in marxism. There's a dash of Lukacs, a couple of cups of Althusser, some chunks of Sartre's and Lefebvre's existentialism (which smells a lot like liberalism), and a healthy portion of Gramsci. At the heart of Freire is *conscientização.* *Conscientização* has been translated to "critical consciousness."

Critical consciousness is being able to see the dialectical relation between the self and society, the causes of alienation, the recognition that society contains social, political, and economic conditions which are at odds with the individual will to freedom—the very heart of the essays in this section.

For Freire, personal lives must contend with social, political, and economic situations. For Freire, the more students are aware of the dialectic, the more they can affect changes in their selves and in their environments. In short, the more the dialectic is recognized as such the greater the chance for lessening alienation. Freire says that in changing the word we can change the world.

So we recognize the political. We have students engage in social dialectical processes. And in what they produce in the classroom, perhaps, they come to know more about an inequitable system, come to know—consciously and explicitly—that there is a dominant language and there is a dominant set of ways with that language that reflect power relations. And in that knowing, the students might consider change. And it is in this same kind of knowing that curricula change, and economics can move to political economy, including how best to do what we do best in the classroom and thereby assure a changing and thereby ever relevant English studies.

Works Cited

Fanon, Frantz. 1967. *Black Skin, White Masks.* Translated by Charles Lam Markmann. New York: Grove Press.

Heath, Shirley Brice. 1983. *Ways with Words: Language, Life, and Work in Communities and Classrooms.* New York: Cambridge University Press.

MacLeod, Jay. 1987. *Ain't No Makin' It: Leveled Aspirations in a Low-Income Neighborhood.* Boulder, Colo.: Westview Press.

Willis, Paul. 1977. *Learning to Labor: How Working Class Kids Get Working Class Jobs.* New York: Columbia University Press.

PART II

CHANGES: ENGLISH CLASSROOMS IN AN EVOLVING WORLD

CHAPTER SIX

The High School English Teacher: A Relevant Member in a Good Tribe

DONALD L. TINNEY
Middlebury Union High School, Middlebury, Vermont

In Chris Crutcher's *Ironman* (1995), a difficult father, Lucas Brewster, tries to convince a childless high school teacher to stop meddling in his life and to stop imposing his agenda on his son, Bo Brewster. The teacher, Mr. Nakatani, is relentless in his commitment to all of his students.

"I won't involve myself in your life, like you asked. But let me tell you somethin'. I'm an adult, an' your son's a child. In a good tribe every adult is a parent to every child, so don't ask me to take myself out of Bo's life as well" (201).

The belief that teachers are parents to all children who enter their classrooms allows me to see that the work I do—teaching high school English—is important work. I am part of my students' lives. Acknowledging my own relevance in the tribe allows me to not only define the mission of my work, but to declare the meaning of my life. If I am to believe that I am relevant, that my life has real value, then I must believe that my work has real meaning and value, as well. In other words, I am important. What I do matters.

My belief that I am an important person in the lives of my students might strike one as pure arrogance, but I see this belief as being crucial for my effectiveness in the classroom and for maintaining the highest level of responsibility for the teaching of literacy. High school students want the genuine article before them and can sniff out a phony, and his or her academic jargon, before they open their notebooks. If I am going to matter to them, they must also matter to me, as all children matter to their parents.

As a teacher of students who will be entering the workplace, getting married, raising children, running for office, and so on in the twenty-first century, I have been wondering what I should be doing now to prepare these young ones for successful lives in an exciting and uncertain future. Until recently, I was close to being overwhelmed by trying to keep up with the latest computer technology, trying to decide what assignments to drop to make room for Internet projects. Then I had a delightful conversation with the mother of one of my students from the class of 1989. She was telling me about her son's highly successful career, how he has been working for one of the "Big Three" automakers, living in New York, traveling to Germany. He designs Web sites. In 1989, when I was struggling to get this young fellow to read Dickens and to revise an essay or two, we would have thought that a Web site was where a spider made its home. How could I have prepared him for an exciting career grounded in this new technology? Any teacher with more than ten years of experience could tell a similar anecdote. I know this is not a unique story, but it does speak to the futility of attempting to prepare our students for tomorrow by teaching them what we think tomorrow will bring, usually at the expense of the more human aspects of the humanities. We need constantly to remind ourselves of what is truly important about our subject matter and not get sidetracked or seduced by the sizzle of new technology.

The high school English teacher keeps and shares the stories of our culture, the stories which lead youth to the wisdom of their elders. As Toni Morrison said in her Nobel lecture in 1993, "Narrative has never been merely entertainment for me. It is, I believe, one of the principal ways in which we absorb knowledge" (7). The English classroom, filled with narrative, filled with stories, is a real place for our students to absorb and use the knowledge that will allow them to be prepared for the new millennium.

The stories of our world live in the English classroom. I often wish we could change the name of our academic division from "English Department" to "Story Department". Stories are what allows us to think about our lives, to give our lives definition, to find a structure, to make meaning. Stories allow us to see how unique each one of us is, but they also allow us to see how much alike we all are, how much we have in common, how every life has a beginning, a middle, and an end. Each story has a hero. Each story has a conflict. Each story has a lesson. Where do students learn or hear stories? Where do students learn stories other than those of their immediate families or of their church?

While the story is an effective vehicle in which to transfer the cultural heritage from one generation to the other, the story also allows the reader the opportunity to experiment with emotions, ideas and, albeit vicariously, decisions and subsequent actions. As young adult novelist Katherine Paterson (1997) has pointed out, books are practice for life and children need practice before they experience certain realities. On the occasions when people tell her that they have given *Bridge to Terabithia* to a child who has lost a friend, Paterson says she can't help thinking, "too late, too late. The child needs to read it before experiencing the loss" (1997).

Story has been used for generations as a teaching tool, and many elementary and secondary teachers would argue that it remains one of the best teaching strategies. A teacher needs only to observe students learning from narrative text in the primary grades, then observe them struggling with expository text in the middle grades, to see how naturally effective the story is as a learning device. Native American storyteller Joseph Bruchac (1997) reminds us that Native Americans never disciplined their children in the way we do today. All discipline was managed by the elder telling the youth a story about someone in similar circumstances. The child was never made to feel bad or wrong, but was allowed to learn about where particular choices and behavior might lead. Storytelling is teaching.

Katherine Paterson (1989, 139) sees the story as a critical component of our curriculum. There is no need for me to seek to convince you who are teachers that reading and writing are vital to education. You know that. But I do want to encourage you to feel that stories are at the center, not at the edge, of that process. They are at the center not only because stories help us shape our lives and our society but also because they have the power to lure us into learning.

High school students are faced with innumerable decisions about how they will live their lives. These choices are real; they are not let's-play-house kinds of decisions of childhood. Teenagers are faced with difficult choices about drugs, alcohol, friendships, careers, money, love, sexuality, and family, to name just a few. Far too often, adults discount the decisions the adolescent needs to make, because the adult has had to make similar decisions hundreds of times and forgets that the adolescent is faced with this myriad of choices for the first time. Adults can base their decisions upon their beliefs and upon their experience, but what can adolescents base their decisions on? Stories can provide an opportunity for teens to explore the issues facing them, before they make life-defining decisions. For years, high school students have explored the decisions Holden Caulfield faces, without facing his consequences in their own lives. A narrative can also enable healing for the reader, as Katherine Paterson points out.

> The word heal means "to make whole." This is more than patching up, it is more than simply catharsis, the purging of the emotions. We are concerned here with growing, with becoming. We don't come into this world fully human. We become human, we become whole. And contrary to what our president (Reagan) might imply, stories are not frills in the curriculum of life. They are vital nourishment in this process of becoming fully human, of becoming whole. (1989, 144)

Without the lessons of stories, adolescents would be wandering through foreign, threatening territory. They cannot afford to try everything once, to walk down every path, nor would they survive the experimentation they would need to do in order to collect enough data upon which to make an informed decision. Without stories, would they have names for the emotions they feel? Would they know the universal nature of their isolation and loneliness with which they are coming to grips? Holden, Hamlet, and Hester can speak to teens in a way that Seinfeld and Beavis would never be able to do.

As Judith Langer (1995) points out, readers build "envisionments" while reading a story, allowing themselves to empathize with many of the characters and to imagine themselves as part of the story. They can see the consequences of their decisions, how their actions affect their relationships, and discover alternatives to their own particular circumstances, allowing them to continue to grow:

> Literature plays a critical role in our lives, often without our notice. It sets the scene for us to explore ourselves and others, to define and redefine who we are, who we might become, and how the world might be. . . . As we read and tell stories through the eyes of our imagined selves, our old selves gradually disappear from our recollections, our remembrances of yesterday become firmly rewritten, and our new selves take on a strength and permanence that we believe was and is who we are. All literature—the stories we read as well as those we tell—provides us with a way to imagine human potential. In its best sense, literature is intellectually provocative as well as humanizing, allowing us to use various angles of vision to examine thoughts, beliefs, and actions. (7)

Our children need stories and they need a variety of stories. They need stories about people falling in love. They need stories about what it means to be a woman, what it means to be a man, a parent, a leader, a follower, a citizen, a neighbor, a friend, a worker. They need stories to help them find the strength and courage necessary to live in this ever-changing world. They need stories to understand a human being's unlimited capacity for love and compassion, as well as the capacity for hate and violence. They need stories to learn how human beings are meant to be connected to each other, to be in partnership, not to be alone. They need stories to allow them to accept their differences from the majority; gay, lesbian, and bisexual teens desperately need stories with healthy gay, lesbian, and bisexual characters, just as Latino and Latina teens need stories with Latino and Latina characters.

We cannot afford to underestimate the power of story in our personal lives, nor can we afford to fail to teach our students about this power in our culture. We need to teach students why stories are as powerful as they are and to demonstrate the impact our stories have on our lives, even when students might not know the actual story. For example, we need to teach students about the power that Bible stories have had in our culture, whether or not we choose to delve into the religious issues. Our students need to see that many of our beliefs about the world have histori-cally been based upon and/or explained by Biblical stories. In recent years, scientists have challenged many of these beliefs with new stories: scientific ones.

Our traditional stories also allow our students to discover how our society functions, to see how the culture has an impact on the individual. For example, *Romeo and Juliet* provides an opportunity for students to learn how the context of the environ-ment—in this case, the hatred, anger, and violence of Verona—affects the content of our lives, such as the experience of falling in love and getting married. Popular songs on the radio might convince teenage lovers that their love will be strong enough to endure everything and anything, but Shakespeare gives us a story we can use to teach our students that love affairs do not happen in isolation from the rest of the world.

Given the value of stories in our lives and given the fact that stories are learned in English classes, how could anyone question the relevance of English? In fact, formal literary analysis or tradi-tional literary criticism might easily lead one to doubt the rel-evance of English. What is the value of breaking a novel into bits and pieces to analyze the structure and technique of writing? Far too many adults today do not read, simply because literature was ruined for them in the high school or university English class.

As a critical thinking skill or advanced intellectual pursuit, literary analysis might have its place in certain academic settings, but I would never defend the attempt to turn high school stu-dents into serious literary critics. Our students need to read works of literature, talk about them, write about them, argue about them, construct personal meaning from them. They need to find role models within them, draw connections to their own lives, and think a little more deeply about those lives and the relation-ships within those lives. After all this important work is done, how could anyone in high school have time to play literary critic?

I sometimes think that we adults are not patient enough with our young people. We forget how difficult it can be to construct meaning. We forget that we are always struggling with meaning-of-life questions. We forget that our students need time to ex-periment with ideas and philosophies. In English class, the real answers are not in the back of the book, not even in the teacher's edition. More than anything else, the English teacher needs to be patient, as all good elders in a good tribe are.

While our children need to hear the stories of their tribes, their cultures, their worlds, they also need to learn how to tell their own stories, how to become storytellers. They need to find their own voices and they need to be heard. Their stories will enable them to define their own lives. They need to be able to say, "This is who I am." Where can a teenager do that? Where is a teenager allowed to say—and encouraged to say—"This is who I am"? Teenagers can find plenty of places in their world where they are told, "This is who you are" and "This is who you should be" and "This is what you should look like" and "This is what you should act like." Church, family, the mass media, the back of the school bus, and the shopping mall are all places where our young people receive external lessons about how they should act, feel, and look, about what they should believe, about what they should say.

Some would say that the teacher treads upon dangerous ground when creating the English class as a place where students can explore their own beliefs and begin to define themselves. It can be a place of inquiry, a place of intellectual, emotional, and spiritual experimentation. It can be a challenging place. Why would it be anything less? If we do not allow our students to define themselves, what are the alternatives? They will be defined by external forces, such as social institutions, trends, peers, politics, and the media. How will these externally defined young people make their decisions? What kinds of citizens will they become? What kind of democracy will we have? What kind of community will we have when all of its members have been defined by external forces? Who will have the power in our society?

The power in our society rests with the source of the definition. If we allow the church to define us, the church has the power. If we allow the mass media to define us, the mass media have the power. If we define ourselves, we have the power to live the lives we choose to live. I know that I am not the only person who believes strongly in the power of self-definition, but I might just be left to stand alone if attacked at a local school board meeting. Our communities are sometimes filled with people who simply do not want our children and adolescents defining themselves. It is a rocky climb. Who has the patience to listen to a fifteen-year-old espouse a sophomoric philosophy of life? Can we afford to let all these teenagers become self-actualized human beings when there's so much work to be done? With the overwhelming prevalence of the mass media—soon, we'll all be wired, networked, and somehow tied to a yet-to-be-imagined media construct—the notion of being completely defined by external sources is close to becoming a frightful reality in the next millennium. It is imperative that we allow our students to take a critical look at what corporations can do via the mass media to define human beings in our culture.

If English teachers are to remain relevant members of the tribe, they must accept their own importance as the keepers of stories and continue to fight the good fight against the dangerous influence of the mass media with their most powerful message: your value is determined by your consumption. Our stories send another message: your value is determined by your contributions.

How do we go about this important task—I see it as my mission—of allowing our students to define themselves? They can tell their stories. They can write about their lives—their personal histories, their hopes, their dreams, their plans, their beliefs. When we allow them to tell their own stories in a variety of forms, they will find their own voices and take their own stands. We are responsible for giving them a place where they can articulate their own needs, wants, and desires, as well as their fears, and where they are able to communicate with at least one other person in the world—an authentic audience—who will listen.

Recently, when a student of mine wrote about growing up in a series of foster homes, her peers and I were able to acknowledge the inner strength she has drawn upon to survive a painful decade. She is able to see that her will to survive and her commitment to her own life have kept her going. If she didn't have a place to tell this story, I wonder if she would see that she has an extraordinary source of personal power. Similarly, when a student read an original poem about how her father never hugs her, she articulated both her genuine emotion of sadness and her human need for affection, coming a bit closer to receiving what she needs and allowing others to appreciate what they have.

This is risky territory. Our students will be vulnerable. We will be vulnerable. We risk getting our hearts crushed. We risk losing our composure. We risk being fully human. But how else do we create powerful writing, writing which allows us to say, "This is what I want you to know. I am desperate for you to know this"? The effective English classroom is a place of vulnerability, a place of intimacy, a place of open communication. The effective English teacher is an active participant in that classroom, being the adult against whom many adolescents will bounce, as they struggle to become themselves. If we want our students to find their true voices, we need to allow them to write about what truly matters to them.

We crave intimacy. We crave communication. We crave affection. We crave acceptance. Very few people wake up in the morning saying, "Gee, I really hope I get rejected today!" We want to be loved. We want to be held and hugged. Many of us take our intimate relationships for granted and few of us talk about them publicly, but we all have fundamental human needs that can be met in loving relationships. The adolescent is no exception, yet I wonder when and how often adolescents are truly embraced. When do they allow themselves to be intimate with other human beings? When are they genuinely close to other people? They're often rejecting their parents' love and affection as they progress through the process of individuation, but they rarely find or create new sources of love, affection, and commitment simultaneously with that rejection of parents. We should never be surprised when teens bend to peer pressure, attach themselves to unlikely sex partners, or run with the wrong crowds. The adolescent's need for love, affection, and acceptance is no less serious than the toddler's or the adult's.

The adolescent will struggle to meet those needs and will find some of them met in our classrooms. If not, can we expect our students to declare who they are? We need to learn how to articulate our needs and desires, as well as how to control them. We cannot express all that we feel through physical means, so we need to express our thoughts and emotions through writing, speaking, and other forms. The English class needs to be a community where that can happen, where the poem can be written or discovered, where the raging heart can be released in prose, where the journal can be filled. It needs to be a place where students can see themselves as learners, as readers, as writers, as storytellers, as citizens, as lovers, as children, as parents—as human beings. When we work to meet the adolescent's need for acceptance, the need to be listened to, and the need for honest communication, we come closer to creating a community where students will grow.

With the start of each school year, I ask my students a basic question: "What do you expect from me?" This first question usually sets them aback, because they expect me to say, "This is what I expect from you." By acknowledging the fact that they have expectations of their teacher and by giving them the opportunity to explain how their teacher can effectively meet their needs as learners, I begin to create a context for dialogue and partnership. I also believe that when teachers ask their students to articulate what they need from a mentor, they are also demonstrating that students are responsible for both their own learning and their relationship with the teacher. If students do not see this responsibility early, they will most likely play the victim's role, and education will be something that is done to them.

Following the exercise in which they define an effective teacher, I ask students to define this entity we call English. They write about it, talk about it, think about it, and write about it again. The conversations are more than interesting to me, but students are usually frustrated in answering the question "What is English?" I use this opportunity to discuss how difficult it is to define something as varied and as abstract as English. We compare defining the teacher, a real person with whom they're in a relationship, with defining the subject area.

The next exercise is less abstract. Students collectively write a class declaration, which could also be described as a mission statement (see the chapter appendix for examples). Students declare what their class will be and define their commitments. In other words, they state what they will create in the school year ahead. Every year, my students are amazed at how long this process takes, but they are also always proud of the statement they all sign. We take time to talk about why the process takes time and energy, constantly reflecting upon the decisions students make along the way. Students articulate what they need from the class in order to be successful learners; they almost always say they need acceptance, trust, and respect. This lesson is twofold: it gives all students a chance to see that they are in a position to meet the needs of others while also creating an effective context for their own learning.

This class declaration becomes the students' first real standard in their class. It is clear to them, because they wrote it. They know what their commitments are and what the classroom environment will look like when they fulfill their commitments. We've all talked about the concepts of student ownership and building a community of learners for years, but this is one exercise which brings these concepts to life.

The writing of the class declaration is the first activity upon which I ask students to formally reflect. All students write weekly commentaries in which they evaluate their work for the week. They comment on things like their level of participation, their contributions, questions, problems, solutions, and plans. Right away, I ask them to read their class declaration and reflect upon whether or not they did what they said they would do. We can return to these declarations as often as we need to, just as executives can refer to their mission statements to see if they're on course.

Within a few days of the completion of the class declaration, I begin asking students to write about what they will create, either in class or in another aspect of their lives. I never insist that they read these personal declarations aloud, but I do insist that they see themselves as people who are always creating something. We define that which we create. We own that which we make. We can give only that which is our own. We talk about commitment and contribution very early in the academic year, so that we can discuss the commitments and contributions of the literary characters we will meet in the coming months, but we also need to look at our own commitments and contributions we make to the world around us. Whom and what we care about are reflected in everything we do.

In this class owned by students, I cannot be the traditional English teacher giving traditional assignments to be graded and returned promptly. It would be too easy to say, "OK, you've declared who you are as a class, so now I'll tell you what you're going to do and learn." I need to simply be a good elder, a guide, a mentor, a fellow learner. This is, as is almost everything in life, easier said than done. I am an authority figure in the community, but I need not impose that authority where it is not needed. For example, I can assign a four-page argumentative essay (mandated by the curriculum, perhaps), but I have no need to assign a specific argument, and this is in fact a choice which must belong to the student. Students need to struggle—and they will—to make their writing their own, to give themselves assignments. Many students will resist owning their work, but most will eventually relish the opportunity to say what matters to them. With this freedom of choice, I think students find their own voices, because they are telling their own stories and making their own arguments. This authenticity allows them to be accepted and respected as human beings, not simply approved and graded as students. We English teachers talk frequently about voice, because it is voice that allows a piece of writing to "sound like the writer." It is also the voice that needs to be heard amidst the din of our busy world.

I am encouraged by the alternative forms of assessment I have seen in recent years: writing portfolios, demonstrations, authentic assessment. I believe that many students have refused to take full responsibility for what they create out of their fear of being judged with the red pen and a letter grade—an inhuman process in which anything less than an "A" is some sort of failure. As we move into this new century, we need to continue adjusting our assessment practices to reflect the fact that our students are human beings with souls. We need to continue our conversations about standards, but we must always be listening for the standards our students bring with them to the schoolhouse door. Our students need to accept our assessment of their work as feedback, not judgment, and allow it to contribute to their growth as learners.

We prepare our children for adulthood by effectively meeting their needs in childhood; the adolescent is no exception. The adolescent needs to feel loved and accepted, needs to establish an identity, needs to be listened to, needs to ask questions and search for answers, needs to hear the stories of adults who have found their own way. Our students need to acquire literacy—skills and strategies that will allow them to negotiate their world—and they need to establish their own personal identities. They cannot do this on their own. They need the support and assistance of their parents—all of their parents in the tribe, including the high school English teacher.

Works Cited

Bruchac, Joseph. 1997. *Tell Me a Tale.* San Francisco: Harcourt Brace.

Crutcher, Chris. 1995. *Ironman.* New York: Bantam.

Langer, Judith A. 1995. *Envisioning Literature: Literary Understanding and Literature Instruction.* New York: Teachers College Press.

Morrison, Toni. 1997. *Nobel Lecture in Literature, 1993.* New York: A. A. Knopf.

Paterson, Katherine. 1989. *The Spying Heart.* New York: Lodestar.

———. 1997. "What Is Literature for, Anyway?" Keynote address, Vermont Center for the Book conferences, Mt. Ascutney, Vermont, November 7.

Appendix: Examples of Class Declarations

We, the people of English 9, declare that we will respect each other and create a safe learning environment. We will be free to express our opinions and ideas and have fun while learning. We will generate and accept feedback while supporting and listening to each other. As a class we will fully participate in activities and discussions. We will challenge each other to be successful learners.

We, as a class, will work to improve our reading and writing strategies. We will listen to one another, participate with a positive attitude and maintain equal rights for all. As we learn and understand our lives and our world, we will be responsible for our own education.

We are dedicated to the experience of life and to the acceptance, appreciation and trust of each and every individual.

We thrive on our desire to learn, our quest to reach our dreams, and our struggle to become individuals with responsibility, maturity and integrity. We challenge each other with questions and we share our independent thoughts. Understanding, acceptance, and respect result from our giving to and receiving from each other. We are committed to our dreams and, above all, to the future of a world that is ours to create.

We create an opportunity to experience reality in a way that allows us to discover, express and understand ourselves through knowing each other.

CHAPTER SEVEN

Promoting a Relevant Classroom Literacy: Personal Growth and Communal Action in a Middle Grades Curricular Development Project

SARAH ROBBINS
Kennesaw State University

with

MARY MIESIASZEK
Simpson Elementary School, Norcross, Georgia

BETH DAVIS
Simpson Middle School, Marietta, Georgia

W hy are we doing this?" Teachers of English language arts hear this question frequently, framed sometimes as the direct query of a hesitant learner who is asking about a particular instructional activity she or he may be experiencing for the first time (e.g., finding information on the Internet about a specific topic, or editing a peer's essay). Other times the question may challenge progressive educators less directly:

- ◆ in the gently probing comments of those "involved" parents who, during a PTA classroom visitation night, subtly question the relevance of homework they've seen a child doing—homework that may not look much like the sentences they had to diagram or the spelling lists they memorized when they were in school;

- ◆ in the puzzled look of a "traditionalist" principal "observing" a teacher who, instead of lecturing, is facilitating an interactive lesson such as a student reading workshop with multiple texts being studied about a common theme, but without an instructor-directed, whole-class discussion;

♦ in those moments when we're asked to turn in lesson plans or reports that show a match between the student-centered, generative activities we want to carry out in our classrooms, on the one hand, and the more skills-oriented curriculum guidelines provided by a school system or state department of education, on the other.

We believe that educators who fail to engage such questions fully and respectfully do so at great risk—to their students and to their teaching practice. In fact, we are still learning so much from our own shared efforts to address this type of probing query—in regard to specific instructional moments and in regard to an extended curricular program that we initially tried out in 1995–96—that we'd like to urge others to come along on a narrative revisiting of that year's collaboration. The collaboration involved the three of us as co-teachers and co-researchers along with about 140 eighth-grade students at East Cobb Middle School in Marietta, Georgia.[1] As teachers, we were piloting a local version of a national curricular-development and teacher-enrichment project aimed at helping students use their own literacy to explore health-related topics they identified and to problem-solve around those issues most important to themselves and their community.[2] As researchers, we were addressing the kinds of questions that lie at the center of this book: What is the relevance of English studies in the schools today? How do we create and refine curricula so that they are clearly responsive to the needs of particular students, yet also responsive to community-made standards and expectations?

Anticipating and Answering Critics, Challenging Our Own Assumptions: The Relevance of Understanding Historical Conceptions of Literacy

The question posed at the beginning of this essay actually drove much of our planning as we taught together at East Cobb in 1995–96. Before we began the project, we had many discussions about our goals for student literacy development. These talks helped us identify the core beliefs we shared about how an "ideal" English class would be relevant to students' own self-identified needs, with such a course also able to play a meaningful, constructive role in the larger community. Many of these conversations moved back and forth between specific plans for a particular instructional activity—for example, how we could sensitively invite students to share their responses to a story or poem on a troubling topic—and broader, more theoretically oriented (though always very informal) talk. As we've revisited our 1995–96 collaboration, one striking theme that has emerged is our struggle to establish a workable balance between, on the one hand, our wish to nurture the excitement our students were showing at inquiry-based learning, and, on the other hand, our understanding of our responsibility to prepare them to respond to others' less generative conceptions of literacy (e.g., state-level standardized tests measuring literacy "skills"). In analyzing our collaboration with the extra benefit of a time-distanced perspective, we can portray this difficult balancing act more clearly if we situate it in a larger history of competing conceptions of literacy held by educational leaders in the United States from the very beginning of the Republic to contemporary times.

Several now-familiar, late-twentieth-century polemical texts have called for a standardizing approach to teaching "English" and related school subjects—one that seeks to create a strong sense of national unity, at least among the educated elite, based on students' sharing of common knowledge. Thus in such texts as E. D. Hirsch's *Cultural Literacy* (1988), and in related instructional programs, "literacy" is cast mainly as the ability to display a collection of discrete bits of information acquired in classrooms operating with a kind of "banking" concept of the term. English teachers, in a pure version of this scenario, would need to "deposit" culture-making knowledge in student brains that would otherwise be empty vessels. Frequently, advocates for this conception of literacy (see, for example, Allan Bloom's *The Closing of the American Mind* [1987]) invoke a rhetoric of deficiency, contrasting today's sorry pupils with supposedly superior past generations, who are depicted as more fully literate by virtue of their knowing information such as the titles of Shakespearean plays, phrases from the Declaration of Independence, or details about the lives of Benedict Arnold and Abraham Lincoln (Hirsch 1988, 24–26).[3]

What's often missing from such views—which cast literacy making in the schools as a passing-on of universally agreed-upon bodies of knowledge—is a detailed sense of the history of education in the United States and, more specifically, a thoughtful engagement with ways in which "literacy" itself has had differing meanings with accompanying variations in schooling goals at different times in our national history. Just as literary critics have shown that "canonical" writers such as Herman Melville and works such as the poetry of John Donne have not always been at the center of university English curricula, so too some historians of American education are now highlighting ways in which being "literate" has meant different things at different time periods.[4] Along those lines, works like Carl F. Kaestle's *Literacy in the United States* (1991) and Miles Myers's *Changing Our Minds: Negotiating English and Literacy* (1996) emphasize that our ways of conceptualizing "literacy," along with our approaches to "measuring" it, have shifted over time within the context of specific national needs at different historical moments. For example, Myers relates the development of an "assembly line" model of industrialized corporate culture to a whole array of shifts in thinking about literacy in American schools. He explains how such texts as Frederick Taylor's *Principles of Scientific Management* helped promote parallel visions of school literacy as a decoding/analytic activity, best measured with "objective testing using multiple-choice items and machine scoring" (Myers 1996, 97). Overall, Myers emphasizes, our ideas about what makes effective teaching and learning today need to be shaped by an awareness of how "changes in standards of literacy are explained by (and associated with) occupational shifts, ideological shifts, national debate, and changes in the nation's form of schooling, models of mind, and literacy assessment" (16). We should realize, in addition, that any "new" campaign and associated school reforms are bound to encounter resistance from advocates of other models, because an awareness of the shifting conceptions of literacy that have dominated public discourse and educational decision making also teaches us that no single vision (whether it be "Signature Literacy," "Recitation and Report Literacy" or "Translation/Critical Literacy") can be expected to govern teaching everywhere at any one time (16).

Using approaches similar to that of Myers, Carl Kaestle and his colleagues have sought to debunk some of the myths (e.g., about declining test scores) that have often dominated decision making about school literacy programs in the United States. In doing so, Kaestle's influential anthology, like Myers' book, has emphasized how our changing understandings of and goals for national literacy are linked to "tensions between modern capitalism and political democracy" (Kaestle et al. 1991, 51). As an example of another scholar shaping this developing tradition of literacy studies, Lawrence Levine's (1996) insightful treatment of trends such as the development of Western Civilization courses in colleges and of "Americanization" classes for immigrant factory workers situates them within the larger context of dynamic national political goals.[5] What all these texts share is a view of literacy as ideologically charged, with particular educational practices necessarily implicated in the issues of particular historical moments. In place of the seemingly transcendent views of literacy imbedded in such works as *Cultural Literacy* and *The Closing of the American Mind,* then, studies like Levine's, Kaestle's, and Myers's all insist that we historicize our views of literacy and thus recognize that the instructional decisions we make every day are grounded in social values and customs which are subject to change, and therefore naturally open to challenge.

Along those lines, if in an even broader international, theoretical, and sociolinguistic context, Brian V. Street's *Social Literacies* (1995) reminds us of the ways in which geographic and psychic *place* as well as time can shape different conceptions of literacy. While explaining that his book's title is designed to stress "the *social* nature of literacy and . . . the multiple character of literacy practices" (2), Street calls for a "New Literacy Studies" attuned to cross-cultural differences in literacy practices (an approach that is aware, for example, of the varying beliefs and practices governing the role of orality in different cultures). Most important for this essay, perhaps, Street insists that we need to give greater attention to "the cultural nature" of literacy (6), and in particular to the ways in which social "power structures" shape "literacy practices" (161).

With historians, education theorists, and sociolinguists pushing us to consider literacy in increasingly complex and shifting terms, it may be refreshing to see apologists like Hirsch expanding his canon of texts to include more nontraditional materials. Yet what are we to make of an educational reformer like Theodore R. Sizer ruminating in the MLA-sponsored anthology *The Right to Literacy* (1990) on the "public literacy" that virtually all Americans share, the "set of widely accepted symbols and ideas that give meaning to being American" (10)? True, Sizer identifies public literacy as more dependent on popular media (through oversimplified logos like McDonald's arches and watered-down publications like *People*) than on traditional academic fare, but he acknowledges that E. D. Hirsch has played an important role in reminding us of the importance of unity-building "content" in our schools—even as he tweaks Hirsch for needing to be more mindful of how that content is situated in a "context—gregarious, changeable, reflected and used in a rich variety of media" (12). In other words, as much at odds as scholars studying literacy have sometimes been, there does seem to be an emerging meeting of the formerly opposed minds, a recognition that the emphasis on individuality and process in progressive theorists' work might be at least partly reconcilable with traditionalists' valuing of literacy's potential to build unity through shared acquisition of more content-based literacies. As Carl Kaestle has observed, "At any given time, literacy can serve both cultural diversity and cultural consolidation, but the mix between those functions shifts over time" (1991, 272). Perhaps we are in or are approaching a moment when literacy—especially as it is enacted in classes labeled "English" or "English studies"—can be seen as affirming both impulses simultaneously, with the special challenge to the teacher being to seek a proper balance between individualization and community building. Certainly, such an aim was one of ours, especially since we perceived it as one way to make our curriculum more "relevant," to use this volume's key term. Thus, we would not argue that such a balance-seeking goal represents a full-scale *retreat* from the critical pedagogy espoused by thinkers like Peter McLaren (1994) and Henry Giroux (1988). But we would advocate a reconception of the role of "resistance" in classrooms as potentially being more pragmatically and constructively aimed at social reform.[6] And certainly, within the context of this anthology, ongoing examination of the various conceptions of literacy that do/should guide our teaching seems in order.

Our work together with our students, in fact, addressed just such a broadening and deepening of our own and our students' concepts of school literacy. We sought to affirm each student's unique needs for learning, but in ways that would promote community building as well. We tried to enact a view of literacy which, in both epistemological and political terms, would ally itself with curricular models like those seen in Patricia Stock's *The Dialogic Curriculum* (1995) and Shockley, Michalove, and Allen's *Engaging Families: Connecting Home and School Literacy Communities* (1995), as well as university-school collaborations such as Dave Schaafsma's with Antonio Tendero and Jennifer Tendero (1999) and Colleen Fairbanks's with Audrey Appelsies (1997). In particular, we sought to make our English class *relevant* by celebrating the diversity of our students' interests, needs, and abilities, but also by encouraging them to pool their unique, diverse literacies for shared social action. Literacy in our classroom involved multifaceted learning in which students were encouraged to

- explore topics of interest to them,

- extend their knowledge intertextually and through interaction with their peers and the larger community,

- reflect upon and critique their own learning processes,

- use language self-consciously to create and nurture a sense of community, and

- use their literacy proactively for individual and communal change.

With this focus guiding us, we tried to ask, "Why are we doing this?" about each instructional activity, and if our own answer couldn't identify a link between a proposed learning plan and our basic goals for literacy development in the classroom, we pushed ourselves to reformulate the plan. Using this general outline, we invite our readers to review our 1995–96 classroom experiences with us, noting both those times when our practice seemed clearly aligned with our beliefs about making literacy development individually and communally relevant to our students, and those times when we fell short of our goals.

Background on Our Collaboration: From Getting Started Together to Writing about Our Work

Although some elements of our literacy philosophy have become clearer to us as we've shared our work with other teachers in staff development workshops and with educators in English education courses, the central principles that guided our work were in place from the beginning, in large part due to sensitive guidance by the Cobb County Schools middle grades language arts coordinator, Meribeth Cooper. Meribeth met with Sarah during the preliminary planning stages of the project and helped sketch out the framework of core literacy principles that would direct our work. She then facilitated a meeting with administrators of East Cobb, the county's middle grades lab school, where the project would be housed.[7] Having to articulate our principles from the outset turned out to be invaluable throughout the year, since that process later supported specific project-related tasks such as writing an introductory letter and periodic updates to parents about our plans, as well as outlining our goals to students. Perhaps more important, maintaining a focus on our beliefs about personal and community literacy gave us a way of evaluating our work formatively—a process that seemed especially crucial since we were heading out on a journey without a detailed road map. We trusted that, if we created and tried out instructional plans grounded in our shared philosophy about proactive school literacy, the students themselves would also see the specific reading, writing, speaking, and listening tasks we were asking them to do as meaningful and productive. Therefore, as we planned together, we quizzed ourselves constantly, asking, "What do we hope the students will gain, in terms of the project's overarching goals for inquiry-based learning?" If we couldn't answer that question in light of our ideas about the relevance of the curriculum and its links to our view of literacy development, we knew we needed to revise our plans.

Interestingly, when other educators at East Cobb and around the school district would ask "exactly" what we were doing during that initial project year, we found it hard at first to describe our work. Part of the problem in these conversations was that many teachers seemed to want us to give them a recipe book or a detailed set of steps which, followed in order, would help kids in their classrooms generate the same kind of energy ours were showing. Meanwhile, partly because we had broader questions driving our work, we resisted seeing anything we were doing as lockstep. We were trying to respond to signals from our students to revise as we went along, while keeping our principles foregrounded. Once the school year was over and we reflected on our learning by doing several informal workshops (e.g., at the 1997 NCTE Spring Conference), we *could* identify the broad outlines of "phases" that we believed our own inquiry project had gone through and that we hoped other teachers would be able to adapt for their specific classroom cultures.[8] Then, with Mary taking the lead, we prepared a resource booklet for other teachers interested in our work—one that did *not* offer a set program of study but that instead invited students and teachers to generate their own approaches by setting their practice within the broad context of our literacy concepts. Our review below of the writing process we used to draft that resource material is intended in part to show how teachers' revisitings of their past classroom practice can lead them toward more abstract levels of analysis of the (often unspoken) literacy principles operating in their classrooms than they usually have time for during a typical school year as it's unfolding.

One of the most revealing steps in that shared writing process was our discussions about the right title for the booklet, since we wanted the cover to provide a capsule statement about our work but to do so in a way that would underscore the belief system about English language arts learning that we felt had shaped our teaching. We chose "Student Literacy for Community Action" because we thought it signaled the balance between individual learners' personal literacies, which we had tried to emphasize during the first period of the project, and the kind of broad, social action which we hoped students would be encouraged to use their literacies to achieve.

The introductory rationale we wrote for the resource booklet builds on our title to outline our school literacy philosophy in more detail:

> Student Literacy for Community Action is an inquiry-centered language arts curricular program based on the premise that students learn to read and write more effectively if they read and write about issues that are of serious concern to them. Student Literacy for Community Action promotes social action and community building—students learn that the competencies of literacy include not only the ability to read with understanding, to write movingly and persuasively, but also to promote change and solve not only their own problems, but the problems of others as well. Students read an array of different texts, and work collaboratively with others to make important connections to what they read and how this information relates to their own lives.

This opening section of the rationale, with its emphasis on students developing "competencies of literacy," including problem solving, underscores our belief that school learning can be proactive, but this passage does so in a way that would probably be acceptable, if not downright appealing, to most educators and parents. In the next section of our rationale, though, we offer more specific references to our 1995–96 classroom work and more details about our principles that, we suspect, might make some teachers less enthusiastic about trying to adapt our approaches to their own settings:

> The project [at East Cobb in 1995–96] promoted a strong sense of community among our students and provided opportunities to connect with other students, parents, preservice teachers, professional experts and others. Students began to see how their own problems and concerns were shared by others and how connections to these issues were literally everywhere they looked: on television, in books they read, in the newspaper, in magazines, on the Internet, in relationships around them, etc. The project literally opened their eyes and made them AWARE—aware that they could empower themselves through literacy. Eighth graders

deal with a multitude of problems and emotional turmoil, and many feel they have no control over their problems and concerns and are, in fact, powerless to change their lives or to effect changes around them. Student Literacy for Community Action gives students the opportunity to use their own lived lives as a source of inquiry. While researching their issues and concerns, they are able to gain access to information that enables them to find solutions and answers, and enhances their ability to make informed, responsible decisions.

Rereading this rationale statement now, we can see that for some teachers, trying to implement an English program like ours might prove exciting, whereas for others it would be unappealing or perhaps even untenable. For one thing, some might feel that promoting "a strong sense of community" in the classroom is not an appropriate goal, especially when it encourages students "to see how their own problems and concerns [are] shared by others." Implied by this statement, after all, is the idea that students can productively share "problems and concerns" in the classroom—a view of literacy-for-problem-solving which may lead to teachers' having to address very sensitive issues (e.g., abusive home situations). Another element in this rationale passage that we expect some teachers might resist is its valuing of popular culture texts as worthy objects for classroom study. Specifically, when we comment that the issues which matter to young adolescents are "literally everywhere . . . : on television, in books they read, in the newspaper, in magazines, on the Internet," we affirm our belief that such materials have an important role to play in school literacy development—a commitment some teachers may not share. Foregrounding such statements early in the resource booklet was purposeful, because we suspected it would allow casual "visitors" to that text to stop reading early on if they found themselves unable to affiliate with our guiding literacy principles. However, we imagine that such an emphasis on an undergirding philosophy for English language arts learning would not discourage readers of *this* volume from proceeding further. Rather, we hope that, through critique of our practice as an attempt to act on our beliefs, our readers can examine their own views about making English studies relevant by linking curriculum development to a proactive brand of personal and communal literacy.

As an attempted enactment of our ideas about individual, school, and community literacy, our project-related instructional program in 1995–96 moved through five phases: (1) reading and writing to begin community building, (2) selecting inquiry topics based on community interests and needs, (3) developing owner-ship of the inquiry topics, (4) researching, responding, and re-flecting, and (5) initiating community action projects. While each of these phases, in retrospect, appears to have been distinctive, and while the students did seem to progress through them in a loose sequential order, it's also important to note the recursive nature of the so-called "phases." That is, phase one, "reading and writing to begin community building," represented conscious steps we took early in the year to invite the students to identify common interests and to see themselves as a group. But this "phase" was more accurately a recurring activity that did not stop on a particular day when we suddenly determined, "There's a sense of community now." Keeping the recursive nature of the project activities in mind, we invite readers of this volume to revisit with us the "phases" of our inquiry learning from 1995–96 and, at the same time, to consider them in light of our views about literacy outlined earlier.

1. Reading and Writing to Begin Community Building

In this phase, students responded to various writing prompts and read a wide variety of texts about individuals' relationships with their various communities (e.g., family, neighborhood, school). Whole-class and small-group oral discussions played an impor-tant part in this aspect of our work, as we tried to make visible key elements in our students' individual literacies (both the con-tent of their interests and the methods of literacy action they tended to use well). Often, we noted that every student perceived prompts differently, whether the prompt was a poem to read or a suggestion for something to write about. While the differences in responses never disappeared, we did note more common threads emerging as the weeks progressed and the class had a larger and larger bank of shared experiences to draw upon. One way that we encouraged a buildup in that shared "bank account" was by highlighting intertextuality. For instance, when our students read a poem with a first-person narrator who was considering suicide because of pressure to excel academically, we asked them to write a "letter" to the speaker in the voice of a parent or another caring adult. Later in the year, when the students wrote similar responses to literature, we alluded to details from their earlier letters or from the poem itself to help give directions or explain related themes in other texts.

Meanwhile, the three of us were very busy reading as well—reading students' written responses and "reading" their voices and behaviors in class to see what topics seemed most important to them. These topics, in fact, were beginning to be generated by the students themselves as they signaled specific questions and issues that they found engaging in what they read and discussed. On the couple of occasions that students pushed us toward subjects we weren't (yet) comfortable having the whole group pursue, we connected with those students individually to try to meet their personal needs. (For example, for one child who wrote about not being able to cope with his parents' impending divorce, we sought help from the guidance counselor. Interestingly, as outlined below, "divorce" did eventually become one of the formal inquiry topics for the class's research.)

At the same time, we were trying to ensure that parents understood our instructional goals and our rationale for addressing them. We sent a letter home, asking students to return it with a parent's signature. In addition, we did a brief, informal presentation at a PTA-sponsored event. We felt it was very important that parents be aware of the complexity of the project from the very beginning, not only to prevent possible misunderstandings, but also because parents might turn out to be resources when students did topic investigations later. In other words, we were striving from the start to establish the kind of "partnership" relationship with our students' homes that Shockley, Michalove, and Allen have advocated (1995, 7).

In general, throughout our first phase, we found class discussion to be more productive when we asked students to write before responding aloud. Their thoughts were more organized and coherent, and they were more comfortable with sharing. Below are summaries of some of the instructional activities that helped our students develop a sense of community.

◆ Students wrote about their own communities, neighborhoods, homes, families. In this case, our suggestions for writing included these: "Where I Live," "My Home," "What I See Every Day," "What I Like about Where I Live," "What I Would Change about Where I Live," and "What I Worry About."

◆ Students read and responded to excerpts from *The House on Mango Street* by Sandra Cisneros. Students illustrated a vignette/story they particularly liked. After we had discussed several of Cisneros's vignettes, we juxtaposed one with a Robert Frost poem ("Tree at My Window") and asked students to choose one to respond to and illustrate.

◆ Students compared and contrasted their lives/communities with the communities described in the Cisneros narratives.

◆ Students responded to numerous issue-oriented poems. (In this case, we chose poems with topics which, based on discussion and writing already completed, we anticipated at least some kids would find very compelling, such as pressure to succeed in school.) Students wrote in a wide variety of genres (e.g., jot-lists, "counter" stories rewriting their readings) for a range of purposes, but in each case their writing encouraged them to problem-solve around the topic they were exploring.

◆ Students traded narratives about their neighborhoods with preservice teachers, who wrote back global responses. In expanding the students' audiences beyond the classroom, we were trying to prepare them to think about the various "communities" where they could use their literacy in proactive ways.

◆ Students created pictorial illustrations for one of the texts we had read, "toured" each others' illustrations in a class museum, then wrote a reflection about their own or another's work. In this case, we were especially pleased to see students situating their literacy practices in relation to other texts, as they made many comparisons and contrasts during the tour and, later, in oral and written references back to this exercise.

In all these introductory activities, as we assessed the students' work formatively for both content and process, we were also trying to look for topics and questions that interested significant numbers of our students. At the same time, we urged them to note such commonalities themselves and to begin to value each other as readers and writers—thus recognizing each other as potential resources when we began the more formal inquiry work later in the year.

While we were using reading, writing, and discussion activities to bring our students' interests and needs to the surface of our classroom culture, a deeper goal of this phase of our project was to encourage our students to develop a voice, a sense of ownership, and a curriculum-forming power in the community of learners. Along those lines, when we repeatedly referred to specific texts students had created for themselves as sources of information and models for more text making, we were gradually beginning to define the intellectual content and the genres we would all be exploring through the rest of the year on the students' own terms. Thus, as Charles Schuster has advocated, we were trying to initiate a sustained shift in authority, as we (the teachers) authorized our students to become "speaking subjects" who could help "establish the accepted forms" that would shape future uses of literacy in the classroom and the larger culture (1990, 231).[9]

2. Selecting Inquiry Topics

Based on student writing/responses during the initial phase, we tentatively began to identify themes and issues of interest to pursue. In general, topics that were showing up in the writing and/or oral comments of a notable number of students became candidates for our list, which initially ranged from specific health concerns like "smoking" and "taking drugs" to broader subjects such as "peer pressure." To narrow the expanding list to a manageable number for ourselves and our students, we used a number of strategies that would simultaneously involve the students in the process and make others' interests clearer to each student in the class:

◆ We composed a survey based on issues and themes gleaned from student writing and oral comments in class. We invited all our students to select a few themes (four, for example) that they would be interested in researching and to explain their choices. While this surveying was helping us choose subjects for extended research, it was also giving us a chance to teach about techniques for conducting a survey, one of the primary research approaches we hoped students could use later themselves.

◆ We repeated the survey process with a shorter list of choices.

◆ As students began to make their tentative choices for inquiry topics, we asked each to keep a television log of things he or she saw about any of the issues emerging as class members' tentative research choices. Contributing to individual and group identification of inquiry topics, this activity also provided an opportunity to discuss another research technique.

Overall, one of our key aims during this phase of the project was to help our students begin to reconceptualize research as a *social* more than an individual activity. In conceiving of research as "we-search," we hoped our students would recognize the following about literacy as inquiry:

◆ Topics of interest to an individual are actually socially constructed: they're "out there" being debated in the larger culture in a variety of ways.

◆ Popular culture texts like television news stories and radio interviews can be viewed as a "literate" form of we-search, involving multiple collaborators, but following different discourse protocols than traditional academic research.

By linking our students' initial efforts to identify *what* they wanted to research with an exploration of the multiple ways others in the larger culture were already examining those issues, we hoped to help class members begin to see that literacy acquisition involves more than learning facts, that it also requires learning socially constructed methods for using language to communicate and to foster change. Thus, our teaching certainly focused at times on highlighting the specific traits of various "genres" we wanted our students to be able to use themselves, and on giving them opportunities to try out those very genres through reading, writing, and presenting. But we were also aware of the limits identified by Street (1995) in such "dominant literacy" (135) instructional programs. That is, we wanted to combine what Street calls learning about how specific "genres of literacy" operate to dispense power in the larger culture (e.g., "in the higher reaches of commerce and government" [139–40]) with learning about how to critique those genres and, when appropriate, re-form them.[10]

3. Developing Individual and Group Ownership of Inquiry Topics

The main purpose of this phase was to allow students to make personal connections with their topics. Since we believe individual instructional activities in the English classroom are more relevant for students if they see links between their own needs and the particular literacy-based tasks they are assigned to do, we tried to help our students ask themselves whether or not the topic they *thought* they wanted to explore could really sustain their interest for an extended period of time. With that in mind, we provided a series of reading and writing prompts to help kids do some tentative exploration of their issues:

- ◆ Using magazines as a resource, students created collages to *represent* the issue they had chosen.

- ◆ Students wrote a poem, story, letter, script, dialogue, play, or other creative text about their issue.

During this phase, as in our earlier ones, we frequently provided opportunities for class members to share their work with their peers. (For example, we held a poetry performing day.) We felt this kind of public sharing process not only supported our continued community-building efforts but also exposed students to each others' inquiry topics in ways that might steer individuals away from a subject that seemed appealing at first (often due to its dramatic nature—e.g., gang fights) toward some that were less obvious but at least as complex. At the same time, these activities helped students refine their inquiry topics to narrower, more manageable forms (e.g., gang dress and its connection to peer identification versus "gangs"). Most important, this phase aimed to make the inquiry process itself more dialogic. Specifically, we were asking students to use text-making exercises to situate themselves in relation to their topic *and* others' (classmates' and professionals') interactions with that topic. In other words, we were encouraging the students to see themselves as entering an ongoing public conversation about the topic that would link them to others doing similar work.

Overall, we hoped that the creation of pictorial and performance texts during this phase of our project would reinforce for our students a conception of their literacy as multifaceted along the lines described by Margaret Voss (1996). Like Voss, we understand that most school-based opportunities to exercise literacy are tied to "the print literacies of reading and writing." But we also affirm her sense that "the term *literacies* [can be extended] to mean personal competencies and literacies, which may be *expressed not only in words* but [also] in performance, always recognizing them as aspects of an individual's particular culture(s) as well as his or her specialized talents" (14). So, especially during this phase of our project, we encouraged our students to express their multiple, culturally constructed personal literacies through such means as picture making, oral performance, and the designing of meaning through manipulation of symbols and signs.

4. Researching, Responding, and Reflecting

In preparation for their more extended writing about their chosen subject, students learned about Ken Macrorie's (1988) I-search inquiry model. After exploring differences between I-searches and traditional school research approaches, students drafted a reflective plan. They then researched by using a variety of techniques, including interviewing, doing library study, making field visits, and hearing from expert presenters. Part of the student research was done on their own (for example, accessing the Internet, reading newspapers and magazines, and watching relevant television programs at home), and part was done in small-group clusters and whole-class exercises.

Our students focused on four issues: divorce, domestic violence, gang violence, and peer pressure. For certain class-time activities, we formed two umbrella groups to combine issues: peer relationships, and family relationships. Students selecting divorce or domestic violence were grouped together under "family relationships" and students selecting gang violence or peer pressure were grouped together under "peer relationships." For purposes of class discussion and response to the various readings, we felt the larger grouping was more productive, because we wanted to encourage class members to work together on problem solving associated with their issues.

Students drafted the first sections of their I-search paper before beginning their research. These sections, titled "What I Know" and "What I Want to Know," allowed students to identify knowledge they already had and helped them form specific questions they would like to have answered through their research. Throughout the formal search process, we tried to encourage the use of a wide array of sources of information, both traditional and nontraditional. One reason for this approach was to try to allow students to develop inquiry skills they could use later, both in and outside of academic settings, to address issues of personal concern. Some examples of approaches we used are given below:

- ◆ Students brought in their own topic-related artifacts from popular culture (e.g., a magazine article, newspaper article, or a summary of a television program, commercial, or event they had witnessed).

- ◆ Students read *and responded to* short narratives, poetry, and other texts relating to the specific issues chosen. (Some of these texts were created or discovered by individual students who, before long, began to bring in "found" resources, such as videotapes of news segments, for the whole class to share. See "artifacts" above.)

- ◆ Students read adolescent novels relating to specific issues and maintained a reader-response journal. Specifically, we read *What Daddy Did* by Neal Shusterman for the issues of domestic violence and divorce and *I Know What You Did Last Summer* by Lois Duncan for the issues relating to peer pressure. During discussions of these novels' portrayals of our inquiry topics, we emphasized to our students that reading literature is often an effective way to learn more about an issue, but that we needed to develop a critical eye for distinguishing among the various "blurred" genres providing narrative accounts of a "lived" issue—ranging, for example, from a short story or novel to a fictionalized memoir to researched "nonfiction" stories such as journalistic feature articles. We compared and contrasted newspaper and television "stories" about issues with "purer" fiction treatments to help our students draw distinctions between various kind of texts crafted for different audiences and purposes.

◆ Students took a field trip planned to provide access to important research information about issues/topics, but to do so in ways promoting use of a range of research techniques. Specifically, our classes visited Kennesaw State University for the day, where they heard formal presentations by experts, conducted informal interviews with faculty members, and used the Internet in a computer classroom.

Throughout this phase, we encouraged class members to share resources they found on their own and through collaboration. In addition, as each student began to draft an I-search paper, we planned a number of class activities to promote peer reading and response to drafts and, later still, peer editing. By sharing information and reading each others' work, the class members made their I-search papers into "our-search" papers, which was consistent with our beliefs about links between individual and community literacies. Along these lines, we also involved preservice teachers in the research and writing processes, as a group of KSU students who were enrolled in a reading methods course became "research buddies" to our eighth graders, visiting the class to assist with writing and revising. (Earlier, that same group had sent representatives to facilitate small-group discussion of the young adult novels students were reading in relation to their topics.) As with our written exchanges with another group of Kennesaw State students earlier in the year, these oral and written dialogues promoted an extension of our inquiry community and thus situated our students' developing literacy in a broader social context than some school learners are encouraged to experience. Overall, we hoped our students' extended composing and publishing processes for their I-search papers, constantly nurtured by their multiple collaborative encounters with a variety of kinds of texts exploring the same issues, would help them develop an understanding of their own literacy along the lines that Robert Gundlach has advocated, whereby they would recognize "that becoming literate is a matter of learning the social roles, knowledge, skills, attitudes, and values needed to participate in specific communities of readers and writers" (1992, 365–66).

5. Making a Difference through Community Action Projects

In this last phase, students carried out a program that would help them see themselves as having a positive impact on their schools and their communities. Specifically, our students visited seventh-grade classrooms and presented their I-search papers, thereby providing information on timely topics to a near-peer audience, while also exposing those younger students to some of the literacy learning techniques that had been used in the eighth-grade program. By inviting our students to serve as role models, we hoped to help them see that their literacy could have a direct impact on others' learning and daily lives outside of school.

In terms of the theory/practice link we were striving to maintain in our yearlong program, this is the point in our work where we felt we had been least successful in meeting our goals. With the calendar running out, we did not have adequate time to do the kind of sustained community action projects we had originally envisioned. For example, students focusing on divorce as an issue could have worked together to produce help sessions for other students experiencing this painful process. Students focusing on issues like gang conflict/violence could have developed plans for a peer mediation program at the school. If we had followed through more fully on our own conceptions of literacy as proactive, in other words, we would have more closely approached the purposeful vision Deborah Brandt has called for, wherein learners move beyond print-based knowledge transmission as the prime means of exercising their literacy to a multifaceted, craftlike enterprise "embodied in a doing" (1990, 193).

Looking back at the entire year, it was easy to see that we had devoted so much energy to community building and issue identification that we did not have much time left in the late spring to do the kinds of complex, extended reading and writing necessary to carry out problem-solving (or problem-addressing) group projects. In other words, we came to recognize that the shared community action projects we had planned for the end of the year were as much a form of community-building literacy as the exploratory activities we had done at the beginning, but with the added benefit of underscoring for our students the possibility of associating literacy with communal agency. In other years, with other groups, we became better managers of the school calendar so as to allow more time for *group* action projects growing out of our inquiry. Although we clearly could have done better in 1995–96, we've been pleased with the opportunities we've had to build upon that learning in a number of settings. Besides being able to call upon many of the principles and specific instructional strategies outlined here in our own teaching since then, we've also learned from collaborating with other teachers interested in community literacy connections. Thus, even though the initial collaboration at East Cobb ended several years ago, that shared inquiry still guides much of our teaching and continuing research today.

Notes

1. During that school year, Mary and Beth were on the same five-person teaching team. Both had several classes of "reading" in addition to the six sections of language arts (three apiece) that they taught. About 140 language arts students (roughly 70 per teacher) took part in this project. Over the course of the year, on days when we were focusing on learning activities for this project, Mary's and Beth's students sometimes met together and sometimes worked in separate classrooms. Sarah, who was teaching in the English department at Kennesaw State University, regularly visited East Cobb, often facilitating lessons and sometimes taking home student writing to read and evaluate.

2. In the fall of 1995, the three of us had been invited to join a network of teachers sharing ideas about student-centered instruction under the auspices of a program funded by the Bingham Trust and Michigan State University. Dubbed "Write for Your Life," the project appealed to us both because of the opportunity it offered to learn from other educators around the country and because of the clear indications we received from project coordinators Janet Swenson and Dave Schaafsma that each participating classroom should develop its *own* instructional approaches for promoting proactive student literacy, consistent with local needs and expectations. Thus, we joined a lively and challenging national-level collaboration that encouraged us to try out context-specific strategies for helping young adolescents acquire and nurture personal

literacies supporting their own health and well-being in a changing American culture. Throughout the year, in fact, we were able to link our own and our students' inquiry-based learning to other classrooms trying out similar approaches by way of such methods as a listserv for participating educators, professional literature about literacy provided to teachers by project coordinators, and occasional in-person meetings. We want to express our great appreciation to the Write for Your Life project teachers and to the Bingham Trust and Michigan State University for their support of our research.

3. Here is a passage from Bloom's *The Closing of the American Mind* (1987) which uses the kind of rhetoric of deficiency we describe: "Young Americans have less and less knowledge of or an interest in foreign places. In the past there were many students who actually knew something about and loved England, France, Germany, or Italy, for they dreamed of living there or thought their lives would be made more interesting by assimilating their languages and literatures. Such students have almost disappeared, replaced at most by students who are interested in the political problems of Third World countries and in helping them to modernize, with due respect to their old cultures, of course. This is not learning from others but condescension and a disguised form of a new imperialism" (34). And here is another from Hirsch's *Cultural Literacy* (1988): "Once we become aware of the inherent connection between literacy and cultural literacy, we have a duty to those who lack cultural literacy to determine and disclose its contents. To someone who is unaware of the things a literate person is expected to know, a writer's assumption that readers possess cultural literacy could appear to be a conspiracy of the literate against the illiterate, for the purpose of keeping them out of the club. But there is no conspiracy. Writers must make assumptions about the body of information their readers know. Unfortunately for the disadvantaged, no one ever spells out what that information is" (26).

4. See, for example, an excellent collection of essays edited by Cathy Davidson, *Reading in America* (1989). Several essays in this anthology underscore how class, race, gender, and regional differences have also had an impact on our understandings and exercises of literacy in the United States. In particular, see E. Jennifer Monaghan's essay "Literacy Instruction and Gender in Colonial New England" (53–80) and Barbara Sicherman's portrait of the class-based reading habits of a well-to-do Progressive Era Midwestern family ("Sense and Sensibility: A Case Study of Women's Reading in Late-Victorian America," 201–25).

5. Levine might be surprised to see his work positioned within a cluster of texts that more overtly theorize public school literacy, but I would

argue that we should read his effort to counter Bloom and others in the title of this history *(The Opening of the American Mind)* and in his careful marshalling of historical detail as underscoring both a growing possibility for alliances between progressive educators and American studies scholars and the potential benefits that K–12 English teachers may find for their pedagogy in a methodological turn to history.

6. Our position, then, could be seen as affiliated with calls like Swearingen's for a move beyond deconstructive critique and postmodern theorizing "to an examination of their potentials as agents of change." Invoking Jonathan Culler, Swearingen asks for a reconceptualizing of "oppositional criticism" that will allow for more self-conscious efforts to produce social change (1990, 222–23).

7. As a collaborative laboratory setting, the school maintains a partnership with Kennesaw State University's teacher education unit. East Cobb, which opened in 1963 as a junior high school, is now one of a dozen middle schools in the Cobb County system. The student body now includes about 1,300 enrolled students and is rapidly approaching a point at which students of color will be in the majority. Especially in terms of trying to serve the multiple overlapping literacy communities involved in our project, the importance of the continued support of Cobb County School District administrators like Meribeth Cooper and Ellen Cohan cannot be overestimated.

8. We wish to thank Kennesaw State University faculty members Pam Cole and Carol Harrell, who participated in our spring conference presentation, for their help in developing the framework for analyzing the "phases" of our project year.

9. Schuster draws quite effectively on Mikhail Bakhtin's concepts of "utterance and addressivity" to advocate a pedagogy of empowerment that is similar to other calls for student-centeredness in its tone, but with a greater emphasis on the need to promote "active responsiveness" in "those branded as illiterate" through moves that are self-consciously crafted to help them acquire power. More specifically, Schuster suggests that since "illiterate people find themselves on the margins of the dominant-culture speech genres," it is the responsibility of the "dominant classes within society" to help "create speaking subjects out of individuals currently considered illiterate" (1990, 229, 231). While we don't mean to suggest that our students were "illiterate" in the everyday sense of the word, we see a potential benefit for classroom teaching in Schuster's descriptions of how learners can acquire a more socially powerful brand of literacy if they are assisted in their efforts to enter "into the territory of the utterance—shaping it, giving it evaluative accents, . . . forming it

from within" so that shared culture is created through "mutual responsiveness" in language use (1990, 228–29).

10. Street's insightful critique of a range of pedagogies centered in varying conceptions of literacy aims ultimately to promote an "approach that sees literacy as critical social practice" (1995, 141). A particularly interesting element in Street's discussion is his effort to show that both the Hirschian model of "cultural literacy" acquisition, on the one hand, and more purportedly student-empowering approaches such as the Freirean model and the teaching of dominant genres, on the other hand, may all prove inadequate if they are not sufficiently grounded in and productive of an understanding of the role that particular cultures and their ideologies play in literacy development or in constraints on its use. (See especially pages 135–41.)

Works Cited

Appelsies, Audrey, and Colleen M. Fairbanks. 1997. "Write for Your Life." *Educational Leadership* 54.8: 70–72.

Bloom, Allan. 1987. *The Closing of the American Mind*. New York: Simon & Schuster.

Brandt, Deborah. 1990. "Literacy and Knowledge." Pp. 189–96 in *The Right to Literacy*, ed. Andrea A. Lunsford, Helene Moglen, and James Slevin. New York: Modern Language Association.

Davidson, Cathy N., ed. 1989. *Reading in America: Literature and Social History*. Baltimore: Johns Hopkins Press.

Giroux, Henry A. 1988. *Schooling and the Struggle for Public Life: Critical Pedagogy in the Modern Age*. Minneapolis: University of Minnesota Press.

Gundlach, Robert. 1992. "What It Means to Be Literate." Pp. 365–72 in *Multidisciplinary Perspectives on Literacy Research*, ed. Richard Beach et al. Urbana, Ill.: National Council of Teachers of English.

Hirsch, E. D., Jr. 1988. *Cultural Literacy: What Every American Needs to Know*. New York: Vintage.

Kaestle, Carl F., et al. 1991. *Literacy in the United States: Readers and Reading since 1880*. New Haven: Yale University Press.

Levine, Lawrence W. 1996. *The Opening of the American Mind: Canons, Culture, and History.* Boston: Beacon Press.

Macrorie, Ken. 1988. *The I-search Paper: Revised edition of Searching Writing.* Portsmouth: Heinemann.

McLaren, Peter. 1994. *Life in Schools: An Introduction to Critical Pedagogy in the Foundations of Education.* New York: Longman.

Myers, Miles. 1996. *Changing Our Minds: Negotiating English and Literacy.* Urbana, Ill.: National Council of Teachers of English.

Schaafsma, David, Antonio Tendero, and Jennifer Tendero. 1999. "Making It Real: Girls' Stories, Social Change, and Moral Struggle." *English Journal* 88.5 (May): 28–37.

Schuster, Charles. 1990. "The Ideology of Literacy: A Bakhtinian Perspective." Pp. 225–34 in *The Right to Literacy,* ed. Andrea A. Lunsford, Helene Moglen, and James Slevin. New York: Modern Language Association.

Shockley, Betty, Barbara Michalove, and JoBeth Allen. 1995. *Engaging Families: Connecting Home and School Literacy Communities.* Portsmouth: Heinemann.

Sizer, Theodore R. 1990. "Public Literacy: Puzzlements of a High School Watcher." Pp. 9–12 in *The Right to Literacy,* ed. Andrea A. Lunsford, Helene Moglen, and James Slevin. New York: Modern Language Association.

Stock, Patricia Lambert. 1995. *The Dialogic Curriculum: Teaching and Learning in a Multicultural Society.* Portsmouth: Boynton/Cook.

Street, Brian V. 1995. *Social Literacies: Critical Approaches to Literacy in Development, Ethnography and Education.* New York: Longman.

Swearingen, C. Jan. 1990. "Bloomsday: Doomsday Book for Literacy?" Pp. 215–24 in *The Right to Literacy,* ed. Andrea A. Lunsford, Helene Moglen, and James Slevin. New York: Modern Language Association.

Voss, Margaret M. 1996. *Hidden Literacies: Children Learning at Home and at School.* Portsmouth: Heinemann.

CHAPTER EIGHT

Women in Mind:
The Culture of First-Year English and the Nontraditional Returning Woman Student

PATRICIA SHELLEY FOX
Armstrong Atlantic State University

Re-vision—the act of looking back, of seeing with fresh eyes, of entering an old text from a new critical direction—is for women more than a chapter in cultural history: it is an act of survival.

ADRIENNE RICH, *"When We Dead Awaken: Writing as Re-Vision"*

Thinking of writing as academic writing makes us think of the page as crowded with others. . . . Students write in a space defined by all the writing that has preceded them. . . . [T]his is the busy, noisy, intertextual space—one usually hidden in our representations of the classroom.

DAVID BARTHOLOMAE, *"Writing with Teachers: A Conversation with Peter Elbow"*

Among the store of cultural and historical misinformation that my eighteen-year-old students bring to my first-year composition and literature classes is this: that there was, at some unspecified time in the past, a historical movement known as the Women's Movement, which produced something called Equal Rights. And now that that's taken care of, they seem to imply, we can all get on with the rest of our lives. Meanwhile, the handful of twenty-eight-, thirty-five-, or forty-two-year-old first-year students, their classmates—mostly women who have been away from formal education a decade or more—are far less certain. Their life experiences, since they were last in school, have given them reason to doubt this particular version of reality. The world as these returning women students have experienced it is more complex, and the education in life that they have received outside of school often makes them question—though seldom out loud—the cultural narratives that their younger classmates so readily accept as truth.

Increasingly, women who choose to enter college some years after they last attended high school come to schools like the one at which I teach, a four-year state university with an enrollment of just over five thousand, in which women, overall, make up more than 70 percent, minorities over 30 percent, and students over the age of twenty-five more than 50 percent of the undergraduate population. As a teacher of composition and literature, I continue to be struck by the energy and commitment of these returning women students, by the complicated circumstances of their lives, and by the value and significance they place on this stage of their education. My work with them has prompted me to reflect upon this growing population of a particular group of women whom no one, least of all themselves, ever expected to see in a college classroom, and to wonder if and to what extent coeducational institutions such as mine have these women's particular talents and needs in mind as they shape their programs. To what extent, that is, are their educational experiences relevant to who they are as they enter or reenter school (an important factor in whether or not they continue and succeed) and, beyond that, relevant to developing the kinds of literacies—both personal and professional—that will best prepare them and sustain them for the rest of their lives.

Speaking at the Modern Language Association convention in 1971 on a panel organized by the Commission on the Status of Women in the Profession, Adrienne Rich noted those who were absent:

> Like Virginia Woolf, I am aware of the women who are not with us here because they are washing the dishes and looking after the children. . . . And I am thinking also of . . . women who are

washing other people's dishes and caring for other people's children. (Rich 1995, 38)

When I left my seventh-grade classroom six years ago, after twelve
years as a middle school teacher, and moved to the local university to teach first-year composition, I felt well prepared, ready
for the challenge in many ways. After all, I had taught first-year
composition as an adjunct some dozen years earlier, had earned
a second M.A. in writing in the interim, and had worked with
teachers in graduate courses during the summer with our writing
project. Yet I found something in that first year in my classes that
I had not expected to find. In the intervening years between the
late 1960s when I had gone to college—like the average first-
year student at that time, fresh out of high school—and the mid
1990s, the demographics had changed. In 1970 women represented 41 percent of the college population, while women over
age 25 made up just 10 percent, this by comparison to males
aged 18 to 21, who represented 28 percent of the total college
population. By 1995, however, while the percentage of women
in college had risen by one-third to 56 percent, the college population of women over age 25 had increased by more than two
and a half times, from 10 percent to 26 percent—to one of every
four undergraduates; by contrast, the college population of males
from age 18 to age 21 had shrunk from 28 percent to 18 percent
during the same period (*Digest of Education Statistics,* 1996).
    Not only are the numbers themselves remarkable, but what
is even more important in terms of women's lives in our culture is
that the increase has come from a nontraditional population,
precisely the population whose absence Adrienne Rich had noted
in her comments to the Commission on the Status of Women in
the Profession—that is, not only those women who had, in 1971,
been "washing the dishes and looking after the children" but
also those who had been "washing other people's dishes and caring for other people's children." Between 1970 and 1995, while
the female undergraduate population increased by 137 percent,
the undergraduate population of middle-class White women students leveled off. During that same period, however, the population of undergraduate working-class and minority women more
than doubled, increasing by 216 percent. That is, a significant

number of mature women who have entered colleges and universities in the last twenty-five years have come from families and communities that had never before imagined the possibility or purpose of higher education for women.

What I had not expected to find in my first-year classes that year were these mature women, women who, because of personal, family, economic, or cultural circumstances had ended their formal education ten or more years earlier and were just now returning to pursue college degrees and, even more important, to pursue power and purpose in their own lives. I want to look here, then, at the phenomenon of the nontraditional returning woman student, from the perspective of a teacher of first-year English, as it is represented in excerpts from the work of four students, and, in light of current literacy debates, to explore the implications of their growing presence in institutions of higher education.

The last thirty years have, indeed, been a time of significant social changes which have had an impact on the lives of women in several spheres, although not in the neat and precise ways that my younger, traditional students have imagined. In particular, we have seen a dramatic rise in the number of mature women enrolling, many for the first time, in colleges and universities. In addition, the last thirty years have been a time of significant changes in the economic and cultural demographics of higher education—changes that have prompted a rethinking of traditional approaches and curricula. Most notably, open admissions policies in the early 1970s saw an influx of immigrant and minority populations whose work challenged traditional ways of teaching. The field of composition as we know it grew directly out of the work of Mina Shaughnessy, Janet Emig, and others who began to look more closely and systematically at the work of these nontraditional students and, in the process, to extend and enrich our understanding of what it means to write. Likewise, in an effort to make college English and the study of literature relevant to the lives and histories of an increasingly diverse population, teachers sought out and included new texts, and, in the intervening years, they have continued to add to a growing multicultural canon. And while women's studies programs began to appear on the nation's campuses, in response to the growing feminist movement in the 1960s and 1970s, their impact has most often been seen in the development of special programs and upper-level courses. So while composition studies and multicultural studies grew in response to the increasing ethnic and cultural diversity of undergraduates, and women's studies programs grew in response to an increasing interest in feminist issues, there is little evidence that anything in particular changed—either in the way we teach or in the way we think about our practice in first-year English—as a result of the dramatic increase in the population of nontraditional returning women students, in spite of the fact that those of us who teach first-year courses and have worked with these mature women know how different they are as readers and writers from traditional first-year students, and know, too, how that difference enriches, even as it complicates, the conversations in our classrooms.

In 1988, in what has become a landmark essay exploring the intersections between theories of women's development and composition studies, Elizabeth Flynn wrote that "the emerging field of composition studies could be described as a feminization of our previous conceptions of how writers write and how writing should be taught" (1997, 549–50). Analyzing the "narrative descriptions of learning experiences" of four traditional first-year students, two females and two males, in view of theories of moral and intellectual development that see women's patterns of valuing interpersonal relationships in contrast to men's patterns of valuing individual achievement (Chodorow 1978, Gilligan 1982, and Belenky et al. 1986), Flynn finds that while "the narratives of the female students are stories of interaction, of connection, or of frustrated connection . . . the narratives of the male students are narratives of achievement, of separation or of frustrated achievement" (1997, 554). And while the student stories that she shares are certainly contrastive in the ways that Flynn notes, they are nonetheless, in important ways, more similar than different. That is, the stories of Kathy and Kim, of Joe and Jim, are all similarly uncomplicated familiar tales written by eighteen-year-olds, stock pieces that follow standard, predictable narrative formats: They are lost and they are found; they overlook the obvious and then find it, right in their own backyards, so to speak. Kathy is "the real hero" of her story, according to Flynn, while Jim is the "hero of his adventure" who "achieve[s] his goal in the face of adversity" (1997, 556). And while they are also marked by the gendered relational patterns that Flynn notes, if there's a larger pattern here that unites all four, it is one of a faith in traditional narratives, a certainty that the world is an ordered and predictable place; and it is this same kind of certainty that I recognize as that which marks the work of my traditional first-year students. They are all—male and female alike—similarly writing from the perspective of received knowers, still reading and writing the world, that is, from within the frame of the available cultural narratives.

David Bartholomae sees this pattern of students falling back on standard narratives and received forms, of writing from a perspective of certainty and a unified world view, as one of the dangers of an expressivist orientation. Delineating the differences between his sense of the kind of work we should be encouraging students to do in first-year English and Peter Elbow's, Bartholomae writes,

> As Peter phrases the issue, the question he faces as a teacher is "whether I should invite my first year students to be self-absorbed and see themselves at the center of the discourse—in a sense credulous; or whether I should invite them to be personally modest and intellectually scrupulous and to see themselves as at the periphery—in a sense, skeptical and distrustful." . . . Peter comes down on the side of credulity as the governing idea in the undergraduate writing course; I come down on the side of skepticism. ("Interchanges," 1997, 501–502)

What Bartholomae and others (e.g., James Berlin 1992) writing from a similar postmodern perspective are skeptical about is the kind of unified voice and faith in traditional narratives that mark the work of students like my traditional eighteen-year-olds and those of whom Flynn writes. French philosopher Jean François Lyotard has defined postmodernism as "incredulity towards metanarratives" (1984, xxiv), and Bartholomae and others like James Berlin have continued to frame our work as that of necessarily complicating the world for our students and encouraging their incredulity. As Berlin notes, "Each of us is heterogeneously made up of various competing discourses, conflicted and contradictory scripts, that make our consciousness anything but unified, coherent, and autonomous" (1992, 18). Both reject the romantic notion of the writer as unified subject and offer instead a sense of an "I" as contested, struggling through writing to read and write a self within and against these competing discourses. Bartholomae, again, writes, "Thinking of writing as academic writing makes us think of the page as crowded with others—or it says that this is what we learn in school, that our writing is not our own nor are the stories we tell when we tell the stories of our lives—they belong to TV, to Books, to Culture, to History" ("Writing," 1997, 481). While this conception may account for the work of a certain kind of student population, it does not fully account for the work of nontraditional returning women students; and this failure to account for their work is, I think, a consequence of what Joseph McDonald calls "our habitual association of the intellectual with the academic" (1996, 10).

By comparison to their younger classmates, who are, both male and female similarly, "received knowers" (Belenky et al. 1986), returning women students are not the naive readers assumed in so many of our discussions of first-year composition. The traditional first-year students we often imagine are those, untested yet by life, for whom the reading and writing they do in our first-year English courses will serve to push them out of their comfortable nests for the first time. Returning women students, on the other hand, are no longer received knowers in Belenky et al.'s sense of "listening to the voices of others"; no longer, that is, women who see the world simply or who compose the simple, heroic—David Bartholomae (1997) calls them "sentimental" ("Writing" 484)—narratives that Flynn's eighteen-year-olds write. Their very presence in our classrooms is evidence of their resistance to the metanarratives of domesticity and womanhood which have dominated the thinking of their home communities, and evidence, too, that their lack of "academic" experience does not equate to a lack of "intellectual" work in their lives.

While I will focus, in some detail, on the work of four women, I actually have in mind, as I write this, ten women—women who are, as a group, representative of the population of mature returning women students with whom I have worked over the past several years. These are women whose work I have held onto and continue to wonder about and study because I believe it has much to teach us—not just for women but for all our students— about the impact of a certain kind of "incredulity" and "skepticism," of a certain kind of attention to "busy, noisy, intertextual spaces," and of a certain kind of response to the "various competing discourses, [the] conflicted and contradictory scripts" that together make up the texts of all our lives. Their work, it seems to me, brings to our classrooms a kind of richness and complexity in the literacy practices of reading and writing to which we have not yet fully attended in our own narratives of first-year English. On average, these women are thirty-seven years old. The oldest, Billie, a retired jazz singer and twice-divorced mother of seven, is sixty-five; the youngest, Carole, a secretary and single mother of one, is twenty-seven. Of the group, two are single, three married, and five divorced. The eight who are mothers have twenty-four children among them. Two are African Americans, eight are White; and eight of the ten were born and have lived their whole lives in rural communities within sixty miles of the university. Six of the ten receive need-based financial aid. Five are majoring in health sciences, three in education, one in criminal justice, and one in English.

What I discovered that first year in working with my nontraditional women students was how rich and complex their histories were in comparison to those of their younger, traditional classmates, and how the atmosphere of a composition classroom allowed them valuable opportunities—most for the first time— to do the kind of serious and sustained "re-vision," that is, "looking back . . . seeing with fresh eyes . . . entering [old texts] from new critical direction[s]," that Adrienne Rich sees not only as "an act of survival," (1995, 35) but also as essential to becoming "a self conscious, self-defining human being" (45).

The theme of my first-quarter English course is education, and while we read a number of pieces throughout the quarter as we research the idea of education, I generally begin by asking students to write their own literacy narratives. I ask them, that is, to think back and recall the experiences they have had as readers and writers through the years, to recall moments in school and out of school that tell their stories as people who live with and through language. Later, they use their own stories, along with the reading, as data for use in doing research on school literacies and home literacies and in beginning to formulate some of their own theories about learning. What struck me so powerfully that first quarter were the literacy narratives of two returning women students, Willa and Margaret.

Hyperkinetic Willa blew like a whirlwind through my classes and, from all visible evidence, through the rest of her life too. At age forty-five, a single mother of two challenging teenagers, she worked in a florist's shop and was known to hitchhike the thirty-five miles to school on the regular occasions when her car broke down. An omnivorous reader, she coveted books and was equally voracious about her education in general. She was in school this time, she said, "on a mission: to become educated and to make something of my life." But school had not always been so inviting to Willa, as she recalled in an early draft of her literacy narrative:

> School was a foreign place for me. Like Richard Rodriguez, I "felt the intense pleasure of intimacy with my family at home," but at school I felt off balance and alone. Forced to stay still all day, I tried to grasp what was expected of me, besides the impossible. As long as I obeyed the rules—no running or loud voices inside, no interrupting the teacher, no self-initiated activities—I was treated pleasantly, which didn't happen often. I've never been able to sit still and being forced to, in itself, kept me from being creative. I needed to spread out, to talk, to move around. I would say that I was a very mediocre student in school. My mind was on five things at once, which were more interesting to me than what the teacher was narrating. I'd have to stop and pull my mind back into the classroom. Easily embarrassed over mispronounced words and mistakes, I sat in class daydreaming and brooding, hating school, definitely set on not learning at times.
>   Even then, without knowing it, I agreed with Paulo Freire that "only through communication can human life hold meaning." But how do you communicate when someone else is doing all the talking and the only acceptable way to talk is her way? I was an object, "a receptacle to be filled." Freire also said that "the more meekly the receptacles permit themselves to be filled, the better students they are." I was neither meek nor a fitting receptacle, yet the school world required me to sit still and "mechanically" memorize (whether it made sense to me or not) what

the teacher narrated. By violating most of these classroom norms, I became a problem that threatened the well-regulated world of the classroom. Success in school, I've since learned, depends largely on the student's ability to meet middle class standards of discipline and self control. Students from homes like mine, that allow free emotional expression and provide few controls on behavior, are therefore at a disadvantage. Teachers who were so well mannered, so icily, academically correct, could chill me with a mere glance and leave me feeling cold and scared inside.

Willa's narrative of education is "crowded with [the voices of] others" as she interweaves her reading of class texts with her reading of the larger narratives of school and culture and the texts of her own experience. And it is only in "entering an old text from a new critical direction," in looking back at her younger self struggling to conform to the expectations of the school world, that Willa realizes that in order to be successful she had to leave part of herself aside, that school had required a kind of dis-integration of self in order to survive. What she asserts here is her incredulity towards the cultural narrative of school, which bell hooks names this way: "From grade school on, we are all encouraged to cross the threshold of the classroom believing we are entering a democratic space—a free zone where the desire to study and learn makes us all equal" (1989, 235).

Margaret's literacy narrative followed a pattern, similar to Willa's, of synthesizing personal narrative and cultural critique. It reflects an emerging understanding of the ways in which women like her have been written into the dominant narrative of domesticity, and it illustrates many of the themes of women's experience articulated by feminist scholars—from patterns of "dominance and subordination" (Miller 1986) to the "conflict between the concept of rights and the ethic of care" (Gilligan 1982) to "metaphors of voice and silence" (Belenky et al. 1986). Paulo Freire wrote that "illiteracy" is a "typical manifestation of the 'culture of silence'" (1982, 160), and while Margaret was not, strictly speaking, illiterate, her opportunities to engage in acts of literacy had been denied her as a member of a culture that silenced women.

Thirty-two years old and the mother of three children, she was raised in the deep South as the sixth of sixteen children born to a Pentecostal minister and his wife. Her father, she says, was strict and held his family to rigid codes of behavior, speech, and dress that were particular to his faith and view of the world. As Margaret now looks back on her growing up, she says, "We were like those Amish people." In spite of being marginalized and embarrassed at school by the constraints of her father's strict dress code for women and the family rules against socializing, she loved school, admired her teachers, and, most of all, loved reading and writing. But Margaret lived in dread of the time she knew she would have to quit and come home, because it was her father's rule that the girls in the family would go to school only through the eighth grade. His reasons were both religious and practical: Because they were girls, they would help their mother with housework, meals, laundry, and the younger children; and, as girls, they would be safe from the temptations of a godless world during their high school years. Neither Margaret nor her mother nor her sisters had any voice in the matter. With a yearning to return to school always inside her, she earned her GED in her twenties, and when, at thirty-two, she entered college for the first time and was placed in developmental courses in reading and writing, she found herself angry as she realized the extent to which she had been deprived of her voice in the process of having been deprived of the literacy opportunities enjoyed by her peers who had been allowed to continue their schooling. Having been separated from school and denied access to the kinds of opportunities that school literacy offers, but having grown and matured in her interests and in her thinking in the twenty years she had been out of school, she now returned to school a married working mother, and the question arises: To what extent did the curriculum presented to her offer her an "authentic dimension as thought-language in dynamic interplay with [the] reality" (Freire 1982, 161) of her own life?

Having successfully completed her developmental courses, Margaret then found herself in the next quarter in English 101 where, in addition to writing her literacy narrative, she read one piece —Margaret Atwood's "This Is a Photograph of Me"—which in particular made a powerful impression on her and gave her an opportunity to reflect not only upon her own life as a woman but also on her mother's life and the lives of the women in her community. Margaret's younger traditional classmates struggled to read Atwood's poem, which describes a photograph—"smeared" and "blurred"—of what seems to be a rural, domestic scene. What apparently threw these younger readers off balance was the idea of a narrator who claims that "the photograph was taken the day after I drowned." Literal-minded and bringing a son's or daughter's limited perspective on domesticity to their reading, many of Margaret's classmates saw this as the puzzling and rather ridiculous monologue of a dead person. Margaret, on the other hand, whose sense of the world had grown more complex and sophisticated over the years as she took on the roles of wife and mother herself and had occasion to reflect upon her mother's life, immediately saw the drowning as a metaphor and the narrator as a woman.

Judith Fetterley has argued that, in traditional educational practice, "regardless of how many actual readers may be women, within the academy the presumed reader is male" (1986, 150)—or, I would add, a reader trained to read from a male perspective. She has also noted that this traditional "equation of textuality with masculine subject and masculine point of view" has hindered readers like Margaret in reading certain texts. Fetterley would have us note that Margaret can read Atwood's text in ways that her classmates cannot because of who she is and because of the perspective, from life experience, that she brings to her reading. Her education in life, not her education in school, has made her a better reader, for, as Fetterley notes, "Women can read women's texts because they live women's lives" (150).

Sensitive to the domestic responsibilities in which a woman might find herself "drowning," Margaret's response to the poem drew upon her memories of her mother's life as well as her own, and, like the readers Fetterley describes, she tells her own story to get at the truth of another's:

> I just saw that woman's eyes looking back from under the water, pleading for someone to notice her . . . "if you look long enough, eventually you will be able to see me" . . . and I thought of my mother. Sixteen children. Can you imagine? And she never had anything . . . no nice things, no clothes, no help or any real attention from my father or any of the boys. He was in charge. He wanted his clothes just so for preaching, wanted his dinner on

the table at night. There were times when I could see it in her eyes, now that I look back, but I had no way of knowing then what it must really have been like. She was drowning all the time, crying out from behind those eyes for somebody to notice, but nobody was there to save her.

What made it even worse was that our family was looked up to. Because we were the preacher's family, everyone thought our lives were so perfect, which must have made it even harder for my mother. That's what I thought of when I read the line, "and, to the right, halfway up what ought to be a gentle slope, a small frame house." There's so much tension in that "ought to be," so many "ought to be's" out there, for women like my mother, especially.

Such moments in her journal were a revelation to Margaret throughout the quarter, insights derived from similar acts of revision, looking back on incidents in her own life "with fresh eyes" seeing old texts "from a new critical direction." And while she struggled, at times, with feelings approaching guilt over what she sometimes saw as impulses that were disloyal to her father and uncharitable—feelings that Gilligan says "raise the specter of selfishness, the fear that freedom for women will lead to an abandonment of responsibility in relationships" (1982, 129)—she grew more assertive as her vision became clearer and her emerging sense of rights came to balance her ongoing sense of responsibility.

Three years ago, when Karly first walked into my 8 A.M. section of Comp II as a first-year student, she was eight and a half months pregnant with her fourth child. She had married at eighteen and had left her husband just after the birth of their third child. Now—three years later, pregnant again and, at age twenty-nine, back in school for the first time in twelve years—she was living with her partner, Ernie, having decided from her own traumatic experience that a marriage license was no guarantee of safety, much less love. Although we were on a quarter system and the class met daily for just ten weeks, I was curious to know how she planned to handle both her courses and childbirth, which appeared to be imminent. "Oh, that's not a problem," she assured me. "I was up and around the next day last time. I'll miss a day or two maybe, but that's all."

As part of the reading for the course, we looked at a variety of pieces—from essays, to short stories, to poems and plays, as well as print advertising and electronic media—to see the ways in which social roles appear to be already written for us by culture. What, we asked, are the messages that we receive from these cultural texts about what it means to be male or female, young or old, rich or poor, white or black or yellow or brown? I invited students to read their own lives, too, as texts alongside the others they were reading to see what they might find in them that would affirm or complicate the ideas that were emerging. Karly used the occasion of her first paper to write a piece she called "Yes, We Have No Mini-Vans," the story of her own quest to live up to the domestic ideals she had embraced while growing up:

> As a kid I can remember thinking that I wanted everything in my world to be "perfect." I wanted to barbecue with the neighbors, to take my family to Disneyworld, and to leave the mailman a Christmas card each year. My friend Wendy and I used to cut school and sit in my living room and pretend that we were waiting for our husbands to come home from work. We would sit, smoke cigarettes, drink coffee and talk about our imaginary kids who were all honor students. We had perfect little families and perfect little lives. When we were done, in anticipation of our husbands' arrival home from work, we'd dispose of the butts and pray that the Country Fresh Lysol would eliminate any trace of forbidden smoke. Then we'd put on lipstick and fix our hair.
>
> I'm not sure how we ever thought that having a husband and kids was all there was to happiness, but I blame our delusions on "Happy Days" and Good Housekeeping magazine. We expected to have a happy home and to play our roles perfectly. Just find a fertile wife who knows how to cook and clean, or a handsome husband with a good job who will give you children. Easy as pie. As I soon discovered, however, neither pie nor the task is easy.

After marriage at eighteen and the birth of two children before Karly's twentieth birthday, her husband lost his job, grew morose and eventually abusive.

> He ended up choking me one night when he discovered that there was no more Captain Crunch in the cupboard. He busted up the kitchen while he spewed forth his anger. Our daughter woke up

and I let her cling to me and paid no mind to the pressure she was putting on my full womb. The next morning I packed the kids into Wendy's car and left as he sat crying in the window of our third floor apartment. Wendy and I went to her house, smoked cigarettes, drank coffee, and talked about how far-fetched our fantasies had been.

Karly is at work here, constructing, in response to the intersections of the television and print texts of the larger culture and the text of her own experience, what bell hooks (1989) calls "an oppositional world view." And in the process, by an act of revision, she recognizes, as Bartholomae suggests, "that our writing is not our own, nor are the stories we tell when we tell the stories of our lives—they belong to TV, to Books, to Culture, to History" ("Writing," 1997, 481).

Fran was another student in my first-year composition class during the second quarter. Wiry and edgy, a two-pack-a-day smoker, Fran was a thirty-year-old divorced mother of three juggling the competing responsibilities of parenting, two jobs, and a full load of classes. But despite what seemed like impossible demands on her time and energy, she was a passionate student: "You don't understand," she would say to me when I asked how she was managing to keep her busy life together. "This class is what saves me. What I'm learning in here, about myself and about how the world works, is what is keeping me sane."

An avid reader and journal writer, Fran would wear out her dialogue journal partner with her elaborate responses and with her promptness in turning her own journal over and her partner's journal back to her. For the final paper of the quarter, she chose to write about images of motherhood in Henrik Ibsen's *A Doll's House* and Tillie Olsen's "I Stand Here Ironing," and in conference one day she explained how she had considered her own story as a text alongside the others when she wrote her paper. Ibsen's play tells the story of Nora Helmer, a doll-like wife of the ultimate patriarchal husband, who eventually realizes that, rather than living the ideal life she had always imagined, she is living no life at all and decides to set off in search of herself, leaving her husband and children behind. Olsen's story tells of a woman who, abandoned by her young husband at age nineteen during the

Depression, is left to raise her daughter on her own and, years later, suffers guilt for having been a less-than-perfect mother. Fran asserted that, at that point in the quarter, having had occasion to look closely—not only at the texts we had read as a class but also back at her own life as a woman, daughter, wife, and mother— she had as much authority as any man (in this case Ibsen) to shed light on women's experience; and, as a single mother, she felt she had much to add to Olsen's story. She worked feverishly over a period of two weeks and conferenced with both her writing group and me over drafts as she sought to get clear what she wanted to say. The final draft of the paper she wrote was an amazing synthesis of research, literary critique, autobiography, and cultural criticism called, ironically, "Choices." It begins,

> "Mother throws two children off bridge," reads the headline of the Savannah Evening Press, February 22, 1995. Why would a woman make such a tragic choice? What could possibly push her to feel such hopelessness? The story in the evening paper goes on to say that this single mother, a victim of domestic violence, had just lost her job. In Henrik Ibsen's A Dolls' House, Nora Helmer makes the difficult choice to abandon her children and husband to search for her own identity. Why would a mother choose to leave her children behind? Are these women insane, or have society and circumstances perhaps left them little actual choice?
>
> After reading Ibsen's play and Tillie Olsen's "I Stand Here Ironing," I have come to understand, in ways that my own experience had surprisingly not yet made clear, how social forces and economic conditions can push a mother to acts of desperation. . . .

Fran goes on to read Ibsen's and Olsen's texts as stories that call into question classical liberal notions of individual freedom and choice. Then she turns her analysis to the contemporary texts she has gathered from research:

> Our society today has an estimated 7.7 million single mothers. Three out of five of these women live at or below poverty level. According to a study released recently by Washington D.C.-based Women Work, ten percent of all single mothers are unemployed. The $4.25 an hour minimum wage is $2.75 an hour less than the $7.00 an hour needed to keep a family of four out of poverty. In

the United States today, single mothers who work are likely not only to receive low wages but also to qualify for much lower public assistance benefits than in the past. Fifty percent of single mothers don't even have child support orders or are unaware of their legal rights to child support, and of the fifty percent that do, only half are receiving what their children are entitled to. . . . "The perception is that there has been a dramatic change for women," says Women Work Executive Director Jill Miller. "The troubling thing about the surveys is that they show it's not that way."

In the following section of her paper, Fran tells her own story as "a member of the rapidly growing group of single mothers" whose own experiences with unemployment and welfare since her divorce have forced her to rethink the world as she knew it as a middle-class housewife. Fran goes on to tell of the idyllic early days of her marriage, then of her husband's alcoholism, her decision to take her three young children and leave him, and finally her struggles to support her family and continue her education. She juxtaposes her experience and her "choices" against those of Nora Helmer in Ibsen's play and the mother in Olsen's story and wonders what real "choices" women in similar circumstances have. And in her conclusion she writes:

How can we cast judgments on mothers who have, in many cases, given up their lives to support their children? I'm here to say that while I love my children without question, I understand Nora Helmer's choice. My life since the divorce would have been a thousand times easier without them. I could have gotten a smaller or cheaper apartment and a job with any hours, not to mention the difficulties that children present to romance. Try finding a date and keeping him when he finds out it's a package deal. Yet as a single parent, worse even a single mother in these hard economic times, I have grown from my experiences since the divorce. That's why I am now attending college, because I feel that education is not only a key to our financial security but also the key to finding myself.

As a postscript, I just heard that our government is trying to cut $20 billion in student aid. I guess I'll choose to leave school if they do. Does it ever stop? How is a single mother struggling to better herself and support her children supposed to make it? I feel if I am willing to try to pick myself up from the gutters of poverty, then I should be allowed the chance to do so. If I study hard and have the desire to make myself financially independent, then why not at least give me, and thousands more just like me, the chance? I don't want charity or pity. I only want to be strong and independent, to feel proud of myself and my accomplishments, and to hold my head up in the eyes of my children.

Fran's seeing her own story as a feminist text—worth studying alongside those of the published authors whose works she read and alongside the research data she gathered—was a bold move, and bolder still is her assertion that in the end she has found no easy answers. It is a measure of her having gone beyond silence, beyond received knowledge from appointed experts, to become an expert in her own right, a connected knower (Belenky et al. 1986) able to affirm her own voice among many as one who has light to shed on a complex situation, but finally, no easy answers. In this sense, she is like the women in Gilligan's study: "Searching for a way to resolve the tension they feel between responsibilities to others and self-development, they all describe dilemmas that center on the conflict between personal integrity and loyalty in family relationships" (1982, 138). And her questioning of the classical liberal notion of individual freedom, the clarity with which she asserts that the freedom of choice is differently available in our society, depending upon a complex intersection of factors including gender and economics, shows her raising questions and working to conceptualize and articulate (to return to hooks's term) "an oppositional world view." But then again, so is Willa when she questions the traditions of classroom decorum that put her at risk, and Margaret when she wonders about the privileges of patriarchy and its consequences in women's oppression, and Karly when she critiques her inherited cultural ideals of domesticity.

I spoke to Fran last fall. It had been four years since she was in my class, and she told me that she had been one of 18 students accepted from a pool of 120 applicants to a program in radiological science. While it has taken her four years to complete two years of course work, and she figures she has another "two to three years to go," she carries a 3.75 GPA and feels that she is finally "over the hump." She continues to struggle financially, though. Her ex-husband regularly misses his support payments, and when that happened again last August, just as she entered the radiology program, Fran and her children were thrown into a state of crisis:

> When I started the program it blew me away the money it cost just to get started. I needed three hepatitis shots which were $150, a physical, uniforms, and $450 worth of books. Keeping up with the school loans has completely drained me. When I get the money from the school loans that's how I pay the rent. I was working at Jim Walsh's RV World doing title work, but I had to quit. I couldn't keep up with my school work. But then here come all the bills, and I felt like I was drowning. It was Maslow's hierarchy. I mean, I need to meet the basic needs. My kids are taking cold showers. I can't pay the rent.
>
> I considered quitting. But they follow us pretty closely in the program, and the head of the department asked, "What's wrong with you?" When I told her, she said, "You were chosen for this program because we value you and your work," and then she said that the department had funds to cover me. But I don't go crying to professors. I was so proud to be in this group, but when all this started to happen I just pulled away.

Having overcome this last obstacle, however, and seeing the end in sight, Fran spoke about the personal satisfactions she has gained from being a student again and how she dreams of the luxury of being a student forever:

> I still keep a daily journal. I don't hold anything back. It helps me think and put things in perspective. And I've kept all my English books because I think someday I can go back and read them for pleasure. Even in my papers for my science courses, I always want to put poetry in. I went back to our old anthology to look for poetry last week when I had to write a paper on Elizabeth Kubler Ross's *On Death and Dying*. I just can't write scientific and dry. I think the semester system will be wonderful [commenting on the university system's conversion from quarters to the semesters], and I feel cheated that I didn't have it with my core courses. English, sociology, and philosophy . . . those professors you never forget, those you take with you. Maybe I just get far too emotional about things. My friends think I'm crazy, but there are some things you want to hold on to. When I'm rich and famous and successful in a career, and my kids are successfully launched into the world, I want to come back and be a student again. Isn't there a program where you can come back

for free when you get old enough? I love that I see myself as a little old lady, a career student, like Socrates: I know how much I don't know.

So much of how we have conceived of the work of first-year English, it seems to me, has been predicated upon the assumption that we have in mind an audience of traditional eighteen-year-old students, fresh out of high school. We imagine them to be callow, untested, anticipating a life as yet unlived. In this light we see our jobs as teachers, and the roles that reading and writing will play for students, in terms of pushing them from credulity to incredulity. As a consequence, we offer them texts that we believe will complicate a world view that, until now, has rested upon received truths and inherited cultural narratives. But the work of nontraditional returning women students brings a new kind of text and a new kind of reader into our classrooms, one who comes poised—in ways that traditional students are not— to do the real intellectual work of the academy, and who in many cases has already begun to do so. By challenging our inherited cultural narratives—of schooling, of domesticity, of womanhood, of individual freedom—they work within and among the competing discourses in their lives to offer us an oppositional world view. It is students like Fran and Margaret, Willa and Karly, students I never expected to find, who, because of their rich, complex, and often contradictory life experiences, enrich our work and the conversations in our classrooms. Their voices, both written and oral, tell the stories of their encounters with ideas and texts that, often for the first time, offer them (and those of us who work with them) ways of seeing and naming women's lives that allow them to make sense, to lay claim, and to move forward.

Works Cited

Bartholomae, David. 1997. "Interchanges: Responses to Bartholomae and Elbow." In *Cross-Talk in Comp Theory*, ed. Victor Villanueva, 501–4. Urbana, Ill.: National Council of Teachers of English. Originally published in *College Composition and Communication* 41.6 (1995): 84–92.

———. 1997. "Writing with Teachers: A Conversation with Peter Elbow."

Pp. 479–88 in *Cross-Talk in Comp Theory: A Reader,* ed. Victor Villanueva, Jr. Urbana, Ill.: National Council of Teachers of English. Originally published in *College Composition and Communication* 41.6 (1995): 62–71.

Belenky, Mary Field, Blythe Clinchy, Nancy Goldberger, and Jill Tarule. 1986. *Women's Ways of Knowing: The Development of Self, Voice, and Mind.* New York: Basic Books.

Berlin, James A. 1992. "Poststructuralism, Cultural Studies, and the Composition Classroom: Postmodern Theory in Practice." *Rhetoric Review* 11 (Fall): 16–33.

Chodorow, Nancy. 1978. *The Reproduction of Mothering: Psychoanalysis and the Sociology of Gender.* Berkeley, Calif.: University of California Press.

Digest of Education Statistics, 1996. 1996. Washington, D.C.: U.S. Department of Education.

Fetterley, Judith. 1986. "Reading about Reading: 'A Jury of Her Peers,' 'The Murders in the Rue Morgue,' and 'The Yellow Wallpaper.' Pp. 147–64 in *Gender and Reading,* ed. Elizabeth A. Flynn and Patrocinio P. Schweickart. Baltimore: Johns Hopkins University Press.

Flynn, Elizabeth. 1997. "Composing as a Woman." Pp. 549–63 in *Cross-Talk in Comp Theory: A Reader,* ed. Victor Villanueva, Jr. Urbana, Ill.: National Council of Teachers of English. Originally published in *College Composition and Communication* 39.4 (1988): 423–35.

Freire, Paulo. 1982. *Pedagogy of the Oppressed.* New York: Continuum.

Gilligan, Carol. 1982. *In a Different Voice: Psychological Theory and Women's Development.* Cambridge, Mass.: Harvard University Press.

hooks, bell. 1989. *Talking Back: Thinking Feminist, Thinking Black.* Boston: South End Press.

Lyotard, Jean François. 1984. *The Postmodern Condition: A Report on Knowledge.* Minneapolis: University of Minnesota Press.

McDonald, Joseph P. 1996. *Redesigning School: Lessons for the 21st Century.* San Francisco: Jossey-Bass.

Miller, Jean Baker. 1986. *Toward a New Psychology of Women.* Boston: Beacon Press.

Rich, Adrienne. 1995. When We Dead Awaken: Writing as Re-Vision. *On Lies, Secrets, and Silence: Selected Prose, 1966–78.* New York: W. W. Norton.

CHAPTER NINE

Community College English:
Diverse Backgrounds, Diverse Needs

KATHLEEN R. CHENEY
Adirondack Community College

A s the summer began and I attempted to bring some closure to the previous semester, clearing my desk and sorting and recycling the paper collection strewn across the worktable in my office, Nancy, a former student, appeared in the doorway. On her way to deliver a paper to another professor, she had noticed my open door and stopped to say hello. It didn't take long to recognize a weariness in her after an initial bright-smile greeting. Nancy had enrolled in college for the spring semester one year ago and was now taking summer classes, just as she had the previous summer, to complete all the coursework required to become a registered nurse. Having lost her job as a result of NAFTA, she had returned to school to be retrained and was expected to complete her degree in two years to have NAFTA cover her tuition expenses. That timeline necessitated taking classes even in the summer. She had accepted the challenge of a two-year schedule despite a daunting number of prerequisites needed even to be accepted into the nursing program, but the strain of it all showed. We visited briefly, then she hurried off to deliver her assignment. Since that visit, I've thought about Nancy's courage and how it is representative of what I often see in my students.

Many are in the classroom by choice, believing that a college degree, whether two-year or four-year, will open doors otherwise closed to them. But almost as many in a community college classroom have returned to school out of desperation. Lost jobs, inadequate incomes, job-related health issues, or changes in lifestyle, like a divorce, necessitate that they reassess the choices they've made. A college education, once inconceivable or uninteresting, is now perceived as the antidote for the ills in their lives. And so they arrive in the classroom, like Nancy, with clear goals—to be an RN, a lawyer, or a CPA; but just as many come to nurture their hope of a better life, somehow, in some yet unknown field of work. And the community college, with its open-door policy, is the path to an eventual four-year degree or a career that will take them back into the community with some measure of increased financial opportunity. Some graduates commute to the nearby capital area for a job; others gain employment locally.

Situated in northeastern New York, near the high peaks of the Adirondack Mountains, the service area for our community college covers two counties of predominantly rural countryside. Farming, manufacturing, and industry related to paper provide a livelihood that is supplemented by a seasonal tourism industry: vacationers to nearby ski slopes in winter and the trails and lakes for summer activities. The summer tourism in the nearby lake town generates a significant increase in employment needs, but these seasonal demands create job insecurity. Many high school graduates and GED recipients, young and old, although initially willing to tolerate the inevitable employment situation determined partially by the lack of a postsecondary education, eventually become frustrated and reexamine their decisions about attending college.

Who are the students who walk through our classroom doors? Each year there seem to be more nontraditional-age students. They range from as young as seventeen to as old as their sixties. More juniors and seniors in the area high schools are taking advantage of college course offerings and early admission programs. They are highly motivated students who see the community college as a way to complete the basic course work that they then can transfer to their chosen four-year institution. On the other end of the age spectrum, more students between the ages of forty and sixty are entering. They, too, are highly motivated, but, despite a wealth of life experiences, they are often intimidated by the academic world. In between these age groups are the traditional-age college students, motivated or not, who are following a sequence of events—high school then college—presumed to provide the means to participate in the good life, the American dream. When I think of these diverse groups, several students come to mind.

Ed, like Nancy, has returned to school to be retrained. A Vietnam veteran, Ed is in his mid-forties. Since leaving the service, his work had always involved heavy lifting, but he suffered an incapacitating back injury on the job. Because of this injury, he can no longer lift and he has difficulty standing or sitting for extended periods of time. Ed came to college in hopes of earning a degree in a field that could accommodate his disability and allow him to support his family. His high school years of heavy drinking and rebellion interfered with his early education, and lack of motivation and poor attendance created significant deficits in his skills. Over the years he developed a very negative outlook on school, a place where he felt harassed, and he brought this history to his experience of college. He knew how to read well enough to get through the occasional *Sports Illustrated* that he might pick up; he never wrote anything. To him, taking English was a waste of his tuition money. Nonetheless, a degree required English courses. He spent his first semester of college in a program called College Survival. Along with fourteen other students identified as weak in skills necessary to succeed in college, he spent the semester working to improve academic survival skills like time management and test taking and developing math, reading, and writing abilities in a seminar class with a math teacher, an English teacher, and a counselor. As the English instructor in that program, I worked hard to invite, push, cajole, and challenge Ed to give writing a chance. His initial animosity toward me gradually began to diminish. Later in that first semester, when he was faced with a research paper in a history course, he turned to me with his sense of panic. We worked together and he got through it—and well! It was that confidence builder that allowed Ed to see that he could improve his writing. Finally, he decided to really work on it. Although still filled with writing anxiety, he was willing to give English a chance. Progress was slow and influenced by a complex dynamic created by experiences in and out of the classroom.

Ed feared others' reactions to his writing. He knew his essays were weak, although he identified that weakness as merely his inability to write without error. Peer reviews meant exposing that.

But finally, and more importantly, it exposed his inability to clearly express his ideas in a way that others could understand. Reluctantly, Ed also came to recognize that college demanded writing that conceptualized and analyzed. This was even more daunting for him, and he began seeking assistance from me and the college writing tutors. Writing conferences that resulted in his increased understanding of ideas and that improved his strategies for meeting academic expectations kept him motivated. His fear diminished, and his self-confidence grew. After two semesters of intensive basic writing instruction and many visits to the Center for Reading and Writing, Ed was sitting in the same first-year composition classroom as Miriam.

Miriam was one of the younger members of the student body and one of an increasing number of high-school-age students who are choosing to attend college courses while finishing secondary school requirements. Some split their days, spending class time in both locations—the community college campus and the high school. Others have doubled secondary courses in their sophomore and junior years so as to spend their entire senior year at the college completing work that satisfies high school degree requirements and that transfer to a four-year institution. Unlike Ed, Miriam's educational background consisted of college preparatory course work completed in a fashion that placed her in the top 10 percent of her class. She had eagerly engaged in all the academic writing that Ed had avoided. She was not intimidated by a college research paper, having already successfully completed a research project in high school. With parents who were educators, Miriam had grown up surrounded by reading material and exposed to a world of ideas written about and discussed in her daily home life. While Ed had years of life experiences, he lacked the writing skills needed to work with those experiences. Miriam, on the other hand, had already developed strong reading and writing skills and was seeking the life experiences. Despite their different backgrounds and levels of academic ease, they were in the same English classroom.

Although the numbers of nontraditional-age students, both younger and older, are increasing at the community college level, there are still a significant number of traditional-age students, that is, eighteen- to twenty-year-olds. Kyle was one. He commuted daily from a rural hamlet where he worked in a local store to support himself and contribute to home expenses managed by a single parent, his mom. For Kyle, college was a way to escape being trapped in the small, isolated town where he grew up. He wasn't particularly inspired by school but had an essentially sound educational background and a curious mind. His artistic talent and the courses taken to nurture his interest in art kept him in college long enough for him to begin to see writing as another avenue for creative expression. For him, English became more than just a hoop to jump through to get a two-year degree.

These students—Nancy, Ed, Miriam, and Kyle—are representative of many more like them at my college. Most are white, working-class, first-generation collegians struggling for fifteen to thirty hours a week in low-paying jobs, while carrying at least twelve credits to maintain full-time status and qualify for financial aid. For the most part they are traditional in their views of family and conservative in their politics. Their opinions about the world are more heavily influenced by parochial experiences and the comments of family members and friends than by reading or the news media. And exposure to computer technology is limited to games and chat lines rather than the vast resources of information available on the Internet. Despite complicated histories and very real financial limitations, the students I see are survivors to whom a "middle-class life is an apparently attainable dream that represents to them social respect, self-esteem, material comfort, and job security" (Shor 1996, 9).

Whether a given student's goal is to "just take some courses" or to earn an associate or four-year degree (or beyond), each will ultimately enter the workforce and be a member of various discourse communities on the job, within the family, and within the public sphere. What are the literacy skills they need from their experience in an English studies classroom like mine? My students need to learn how to learn; they need skills that allow them to access ways to be informed, to support their development as participatory citizens empowered to act through their ability to use language as a connection to community. James Berlin explains that the goal of an English course "is to encourage citizens who are actively literate, that is, critical agents of change who are socially and politically engaged—in this way realizing some of the highest democratic ideals" (1996, 104).

My students have varied degrees of involvement within the community. Most of them have jobs, some still live with their parents, and many are parents themselves. The majority do not have life experience that one would describe as being "socially and politically engaged." They do not feel in control of their lives. Rather, they see themselves as hard workers, struggling to enact behaviors that will reap the rewards of a better life. Those who rejected postsecondary education and resisted the message that college buys success have been beaten up by demeaning jobs and low salaries and have returned to the educational institution. They now believe that a college degree will liberate them from the dehumanizing conditions of their lives. Although a degree may position them better, what is also important is that they develop increased awareness of those conditions. These students need to give voice to their circumstances and recognize the difference between being an active participant and being a passive observer. They need to see language not only as a tool for communicating but also as a means for identifying the world, a way to reflect on their existence in that world, and a way to problematize decisions or actions within their communities.

The English studies classroom offers students the opportunity not only to practice literacy skills but also to examine critically the cultural codes that determine what we think, what we say, and how and to whom we say it. An English course becomes a place where "students begin to understand that language is never innocent, that it instead constitutes a terrain for ideological battle" (Berlin 1996, 131). I see student writers and myself taking action and being acted upon. We are continually moving through experiences that arrange and rearrange our perceptions of the world and our actions in the world. It is this experience that a writer brings to writing. As members of a variety of discourse communities, we possess literacy skills that influence and are influenced by our participation in those communities. The writing and reading done in an English course can be an invitation to understand the intersections of our individual and internal multiple voices.

To illustrate this, let me introduce Nino, a member of a basic writing course I am currently teaching. After progressing through a noncredit program that focused on skill development in English and math, Nino is continuing in a two-semester composition course sequence as one of my students. From the beginning, Nino has demonstrated a questionable commitment to academics. Although his comments in class discussions were often insightful and delivered with a sensitive honesty, his attendance was unpredictable. If it hadn't been for a romantic relationship with another student in the class, Nino might have disappeared from class altogether. With the support of several people—his girlfriend, classmates, and teachers including me—Nino is still in school, although English is likely to be the only course he'll finish this semester. I wonder why English? I can't answer with certainty, but I do know that the reading he has done, the discussions to which he has contributed, and the writing he has submitted in the course all engage him in sorting through a myriad of gender, race, and class influences that create the context for his life. Fundamentally, Nino refuses to be passive even though I have observed, at times, a conflicted acceptance of the invitation to learn. The conditions of his life have been oppressive, but Nino refuses to acquiesce and instead is searching for a path to his dream. His quest began in the projects of New York City, from which he fled, but not before he had become a parentless teen involved in drugs and crime. This is what he wrote in one of his compositions: "I was at the bottom of the poor ladder. . . . [It's] all about how [to] survive the struggle. That's what being poor is, a struggle. So what I did was went against all odds. I moved [to] upstate New York . . . to at least finish high school." From there he enrolled at the community college and, eventually, in my English course. The theme in Nino's current course with me is that of social class. The previous excerpt is from an essay written for that course. Nino powerfully describes how he sees himself with regard to class position. His writing is a mix of standard English and vernacular that captures in vivid terms the poverty and marginalization he knows so well. His voice was heard by me, his teacher, but also by his fellow students. We talked not only about what he said but also about how he said it. He, and hopefully the other students, understood the power of his opening lines in the essay: "It's all about the Benjamin's. That is how America tells what class you belong in. How many Benjamin's do you receive in your paycheck? That separates the poor, the middle, and the rich class in our country. Who ever makes more money is the better person and who ever lives in the projects are scumbags and are no use to America." As we discussed and acknowledged the impact of his language, I wanted Nino and all the students to recognize the value of not abandoning their cultural history. As we talked, Nino clearly stated that he understood the usefulness of his language choices, but he also indicated that he did not want to be patronized. He went on to explain his awareness that success in the world depended on an ability to meet standards set by the majority.

In "Confronting Class in the Classroom," bell hooks captures Nino's concern: "Those of us from diverse ethnic/racial backgrounds learned that no aspect of our vernacular culture could be voiced in elite settings. This was especially the case with vernacular language. . . . To insist on speaking in any manner that did not conform to privileged class ideals and mannerisms placed one always in the position of interloper" (1996, 238). I wanted Nino and his classmates to see that it is possible to negotiate both worlds as they move in and out of various discourse communities. My English course can assist them as they work to "creatively invent ways to cross borders" (hooks 1996, 239).

But border crossing is not likely to happen among people who feel powerless, as most of my students do. Although many want to be in my classroom, they have internalized years of messages sent by the educational system that reinforce a position of powerlessness. They have heard, most often implicitly but occasionally in explicit form, that their task as students is to receive. Paulo Freire (1990) calls this the "banking concept" of education, and it is practiced extensively in our schools, my own included. As much as students are to be the receivers, I am to be the sender. Having the credentials of teacher signifies to the students that I have the knowledge and therefore the power. This arrangement of power fosters not engagement but passivity, not a dialogical classroom experience but one that is monological. In my view, in contrast, it is my job throughout the semester to find ways to connect with students and to help them effectively interact with each other. If they are to function as "reflective agents" capable of influencing "their own consciousness as well as the democratic society of which they are an integral part," they must learn to speak, to listen, and to negotiate (Berlin 1996, 124). And it all begins on day one of the semester.

This first meeting is critical. It initiates the participatory nature of the course; it invites the students to be active. It also begins the process of deconstructing the *student* and *teacher* positions that traditionally construct the teacher as the unilateral power. Over the years I've wrestled with what should happen in the first meeting of the semester. There have been times when I've arrived armed with all the materials students have come to expect: a syllabus and either the required book or handouts of the first reading assignments. But in recent years, my instincts have told me to worry less about bombarding them with the seriousness of the course and the challenge to improve their writing and instead spend the first few classes establishing connections. Through this foundational work I hope to personalize the educational experience, to begin to develop an environment in which there is enough human connection and trust that students will be willing to speak up, challenge, and in general take risks that will allow their voices to be heard both in discussions and in their writing. By midsemester, after several weeks of small and large group discussions, students often comment that English is one of the few courses in which they know other students and talk with them. That always amazes me, but it indicates the number of courses in which students are lulled into passivity and thus enter a kind of isolation from their educational community.

If people are to feel empowered to act and effectively influence the conditions of their lives, they need to develop literacy skills that they can use to challenge their existing economic, political, and social situations. The English classroom is a place where Nancy and Ed can share their common concerns about finding a job that both satisfies them and supports a comfortable lifestyle for their families; it is a place where students like Miriam and Nino can recognize the diversity in their backgrounds yet assert their common concerns for a positive self-image, a secure job, and a respected position in society. My intent is to encourage reading, analysis, discussion, and writing that transfers to the experience outside the classroom. The selected reading material is organized around a theme. This is my attempt both to unify our class experience and to present alternative ways of making sense of common experiences. Through these interactive processes—reading, discussing, and writing—students can engage with language to create a discourse community in which they can gain a sense of power as they present an observation, challenge another perspective, or write to produce different texts.

For the last few semesters I have focused my course on education in America. I want students to take what they practice and make it work for them as they attempt to enact the literacy skills they are learning. I hope, for example, that a discussion of Mike Rose's *Lives on the Boundary* (1989) helps students write in order to make sense of their own educational histories. By encouraging close examination of Rose's own struggle to attain literacy skills and his powerful description of his professional experience as a teacher of literacy, I want to give students an opportunity to use language to make sense of their world. It's a Freirean notion that Berlin describes like this: "To learn to read and write is to learn to name the world, and in this naming is a program for understanding the conditions of our experience and, most important, for acting in and on them" (Berlin 1996, 97). My efforts to help students become empowered have met with moderate success. Many begin to see their own complicated educational histories as a mix of a multitude of discourses giving rise to varied class, race, and gender positions. Several young women in my classes have spoken and written powerfully of their sense of being silenced in the classroom, marginalized by the experience of being unheard and frequently feeling disconnection rather than connection in the classroom environment. Their socialization, the cultural codes regarding their gender, have disadvantaged them.

Miriam is one such woman. Her sense of being marginalized motivated her not only to speak of it in our classroom discussions about education but also to investigate it in a research project. Her findings validated what she had experienced, and she shared that with the class as part of a presentation. In addition to creating a feeling of being marginalized, the banking model has too often reinforced the cultural message that males have greater powers of rationality. In *Women's Ways of Knowing*, the authors argue that women students benefit from observing both male and female professors who sometimes succeed and sometimes fail in their efforts to solve problems: "They need models of thinking as a human, imperfect, and attainable activity" (Belenky et al. 1986, 217). In a classroom immersed in dialogue rather than subjected to a teacher's monologue, the fits and starts of growing, learning, and thinking play themselves out in full view. Students can be active, participatory members of the educational community. Let me illustrate this kind of classroom involvement.

Several times throughout the semester in my English courses, our discussions center on giving feedback to students who are writing a response to an assignment. Everyone in the course gets a copy of a student's essay, and we give both written and oral feedback. This has many benefits. Not only is it useful to the writer, but it also has numerous benefits for all students, even though the process initially produces a great deal of anxiety for the writer. First of all, as we struggle to sort out an idea and the language that best represents it, the thinking process is revealed with all its messy characteristics. Students may challenge an observation I make or they may make a fine observation about something that I did not see. They also confront each other directly. In a recent discussion about a paper written on social class in America, one of my woman students confronted the writer of the paper about a generalization he had made. In effect, he commented that poor people get on welfare because it's an easy way to get money. The feedback he got from this young woman not only challenged that stereotype, but it also validated the young woman's personal experience, which she shared as a way of contradicting the myth. It is occasions like this that provide students with an opportunity not only to refine their literacy skills but also to use those very skills to acknowledge, understand, and redefine their roles in the educational community, as well as their roles in the many communities they encounter outside the classroom.

Our discussions of education and social class have uncovered a mix of attitudes. At times many students have been complacent, sometimes because they were satisfied in a hierarchical arrangement that placed them comfortably in the middle or up-per middle class. Or like many in America they "describe them-selves as middle class, whether they are . . . sanitation workers or lawyers" (Tokarczyk and Fay 1993, 4). But inevitably there are several students who are publicly angry, frustrated, or defensive about their class status. They feel victimized and disempowered, and while desperate to grab the brass ring in the educational merry-go-round, their reach is limited—by money, job obliga-tions, personal crises, health, and/or a general unfamiliarity with the academic world. One or another of these categories poses a real dilemma for some students; for others, *all* of these areas present problems. For the instructor, the challenge to teach to literacy needs is a complex one.

I'd like to focus on several problematic areas that appear each semester within our student population. Some issues can be placed in a context that pits "real" life against academic life. I don't mean to imply that the classroom is not a significant expe-rience with various obligations and rewards connected to it—in other words, not "real life." But it seems that more of my stu-dents than not see the classroom only as a passage that one must go through to get to what really counts: a career, or a job that provides a chance at a comfortable lifestyle, or at least enough to pay the bills. Earning that degree more often than not has an urgency about it, and in the interim the classroom experience is no more than the means to the end. Of course, there is some sense to that perspective—hopefully, attending college will, for example, result in Nancy working as an RN in a hospital. But when college is viewed primarily as a passageway, the demands of academic work often fall low on the priority ladder.

A recent conversation with a current student illustrates a common story. On the day that a major project was due, Janet did not attend class. I was surprised, since I knew she had been eager to do the research and was committed to presenting her results to the other students, results that she felt would enlarge what she described as their mostly narrow perspective about the welfare system. Shortly after I returned from the class, Janet called my office. Close to tears, she indicated that she was thinking of withdrawing from the course; her paper wasn't finished. Manag-ing other courses along with all the job hours that paid her living expenses strained her time management skills. She had completed her research, but her job and school obligations did not allow for the extra time she needed to get to a computer to write the paper. Since she had no money to buy a computer, she could only rely on friends or the computer center at the college, both of which required coordinating her time with their availability. Our conversation quickly moved from her paper to sorting out a dilemma—should she attend college full-time or part-time. The predicament of finding time, not to mention energy, to complete her English project highlighted for her the need to evaluate what she could successfully manage as a student. We agreed on an extension to the assignment; then I encouraged her to finish the course and to contact a counselor who could advise her about her status as a student. Janet needed support, understanding, and a willingness on my part to be flexible enough to accept a late assignment so she could finish my course despite all the complications.

As I indicated, Janet is not unusual. Typically, the community college student has many more obligations than just academics. There are job commitments. Most students of traditional age work full-time during the summer and then, especially in the first semester, continue to do that or cut their hours only slightly, perhaps to thirty hours, as the semester begins. With some help in the form of financial aid, the job pays tuition, buys books, pays for rent and food, and provides a dependable car and the money to insure and maintain it. After all that, there may be some remaining money for a social life. The students are trapped. Without the job, they can't meet their college expenses; but with a heavy load of hours on the job, they are unable to attain the desired academic success. As a teacher, I encourage these students to review their goals and reevaluate their priorities, something that often meets with great resistance. They are understandably reluctant to give up a car, or move back home with parents, to cut costs and reduce the need for the bigger paycheck provided by a thirty-hour work week rather than a fifteen-hour one. But they are also resistant to altering their intended timeline for a degree. They don't want to attend college part-time so they can work the numerous job hours. These unpleasant choices tarnish their hopes for reaching that American-dream lifestyle.

In my English course, I try to offer students an opportunity to begin to sort out the economic conditions that place them in the position to have to make such difficult choices. As their teacher I'm able to introduce reading materials, initiate discussions, and invite writings that encourage them to critically examine the various educational, social, economic, and family circumstances that determine their choices, because "only through articulating the disparate positions held by members of the class can different ways of understanding the world and acting in it be discovered" (Berlin 1996, 102).

Since the community college is also a place for adults to return to academic pursuits, their presence in the classroom introduces another problematic time management concern that affects academic progress: how to parent children and still succeed academically. These student-parents are unprepared for the rigors of college, not because of lack of motivation or discipline, nor because of skills that are any weaker than those of traditional-age students. Contrary to most jobs they've experienced, college study is not confined to daily starting and finishing times, like punching in and out on a clock. Their success is dependent on time spent on academics in the evenings and on weekends. And this is time that frequently conflicts with parenting demands, or at the least requires an adjustment to familiar patterns of family interaction. Many students, especially single parents, are overwhelmed by their obligations to school and their obligations to children. They have little support as they enter what is often a foreign world. Typically, the circumstances of their lives have not provided a solid educational foundation on which to build a college degree. The consequences of life choices have badly bruised their self-esteem and diminished their sense of being in control of their lives. Unlike their memory of school, college consists of large blocks of unscheduled time between classes and no teachers pursuing them for homework or makeup work. Managing time in order to manage academic studies requires self-discipline, since there is nothing built into the system as there is in high school. And that self-discipline comes from establishing clear priorities and making difficult choices. For example, it may require attending to a sick child instead of visiting the writing center for help with an assignment. In this sense, my work in the English department is not limited to teaching English, at least not in any way that I once imagined. Along with instruction in reading and writing, I participate in problem solving, counseling, evaluating, and supporting the students as they attempt to negotiate the complex experience of student life at the community college.

Each of the students I've introduced has encountered personal and academic situations that invited me to do more than just meet my classroom obligations. Nancy needed encouragement when the demands of her academic load conflicted with her teenage daughter's need for attention and supervision. When Ed was struggling to get through the reading assignments in a history course, we met to discuss strategies that might help him manage that reading. Midway through the current semester, Nino stopped by my office to get help with a writing assignment. Although we spent time discussing his writing, we spent even more time looking at his history, his current academic problems, and his doubts about continuing in school. If students are to succeed in college, if they are to attain the literacy skills necessary to be active citizens in our democracy, then I as an instructor of English studies need to situate my teaching so as to acknowledge the reality of students' lives.

A semester is about to end and the students are preparing for final exams, projects, presentations, and papers. All those I have mentioned are surviving, although with varying degrees of success. Ed has one final semester and then he will have completed a degree in corrections work. He worries about passing his science course and hopes that if he has to retake it, he will be able to manage the final-semester course load. We plan to talk during exam week and further evaluate his situation. Nancy will also be graduating, with a nursing degree. This should get her a position as an RN, but only if she's willing to commute. The budgetary needs of the local hospital, where she did her clinical practice, won't allow for significant hiring. Nancy knew about this situation, but not until she had entered the nursing program. Because of the guidelines for NAFTA, which paid for her tuition, she was unable to change her degree program once she began courses. As a single mother with two teenagers at home, she'll have some difficult job decisions ahead. Will she be able to commute? Will it be necessary for her to move her family? Kyle will be using the break between semesters to visit four-year schools in the South. He has decided to pursue a degree in English and he is eager to investigate a part of the country different from the hamlet where he grew up. Miriam has already moved on. Our community college was only a two-semester introduction to college study. She has now completed a full semester at her chosen four-year school. I look forward to a possible visit with her to hear about her experiences. Finally, there's Nino. School holds no enchantment for him, nor does he see it as the path to financial comfort or class mobility. He is weary of being poor and having to struggle to succeed in the academic world. He wants a weekly paycheck sooner than a college degree can provide. During the next semester he is thinking of going to a trade school, which seems to him a quicker, less painful means to his end.

I began this discussion by referring to the courage of students like Nancy, who, in the face of daunting needs, obligations, and complications, pursue their dreams. As I finalize my thoughts, those students are all around me on campus—the fresh new faces of first-semester folks and the less exuberant but persevering seasoned faces. For all of them, for all of us, courage is necessary—to meet our goals, to conquer our fears, to challenge the system that threatens to constrain us, to attain the dreams we so carefully cherish. As Mike Rose states, it is the stuff of "everyday heroics" (1989, 242) that plays itself out on campuses nationwide.

Works Cited

Belenky, Mary Field, Blythe Clinchy, Nancy Goldberger, and Jill Tarule. 1986. *Women's Ways of Knowing: The Development of Self, Voice, and Mind.* New York: Basic Books.

Berlin, James A. 1996. *Rhetorics, Poetics, and Cultures: Refiguring College English Studies.* Urbana, Ill.: National Council of Teachers of English.

Freire, Paulo. 1990. *Pedagogy of the Oppressed.* New York: Continuum.

hooks, bell. 1996. "Confronting Class in the Classroom." Pp. 235–45 in *Writing Lives: Exploring Literacy and Community,* ed. Sara Garnes, David Humphries, Vic Mortimer, Jennifer Phegley, and Kathleen R. Wallace. New York: St. Martin's.

Rose, Mike. 1989. *Lives on the Boundary.* New York: Penguin.

Shor, Ira. 1996. *When Students Have Power: Negotiating Authority in a Critical Pedagogy.* Chicago: University of Chicago Press.

Tokarczyk, Michelle M., and Elizabeth A. Fay, eds. 1993. *Working-Class Women in the Academy: Laborers in the Knowledge Factory.* Amherst: University of Massachusetts Press.

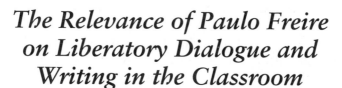

CHAPTER TEN

The Relevance of Paulo Freire on Liberatory Dialogue and Writing in the Classroom

CRISTINA KIRKLIGHTER
University of Tampa

When many think of Paulo Freire, they inevitably think of *Pedagogy of the Oppressed* (1993)—the book translated into countless languages with over half a million copies sold, the book of revolutionary pedagogy that so influenced international concerns of education and literacy, the book of inspiration for so many compositionists and educators in this country today. Yet when I, as a personal essay scholar and liberatory teacher, think of Paulo Freire, I envision him coming alive and speaking to me in two of his last books—*Pedagogy of Hope: Reliving Pedagogy of the Oppressed* (1994) and *Letters to Cristina: Reflections on My Life and Work* (1996). Admittedly, I could not verify that I was indeed practicing a revolutionary pedagogy similar to his until he disclosed to me the life behind the teaching.

I wonder if other liberatory teachers feel the need, as I do, to hear Freire tell them of the time when a Brazilian Northeast worker accused him of not visiting their houses and experiencing their hardships. Do they need for Freire to say he was at first angry with this man, but then years later understood the significance of this brave peasant's words? Is it important for him to tell them of the countless times peasants would say "Excuse us, sir. . . . Excuse us for talking. You're the one who should have been talking sir" (Freire 1994, 45)? Should he show them the arrogance of those in authority—the four East German educators who believed that "in bourgeois societies, . . . you have to talk about this, and fire the students up about it. Not here. We know what the students should know" (115)? Should they listen as he recounts the words of a janitor who chastised so-called liberatory professors for not practicing liberatory methods with their own staff: "I am happy with my day-to-day life. I am humble. But there are some things that I don't understand and should mention to all of you. For example, when I enter a director's office with the coffee tray and he is meeting with other professors, no one looks at me or answers when I say good morning to them. They only grab their coffee cups and never once say, even to be different, thank-you" (96). If certain liberatory teachers like myself come from the middle class, might they identify with Freire's middle-class fear as he agonized whether to ask a peasant where the bathroom was—a location that he feared might present shame to those who usually housed their bathrooms under the mango trees? On a personal level, as a teacher of mixed Honduran/Southern Angla origins, I acutely sensed Freire's frustration as he desperately tried to convince a group of Chicanos, African Americans, and Whites to unite in diversity at a conference—a plea to meet together instead of apart in separate rooms. I experienced his sadness as they ignored his words and dispersed to their isolated chambers. Freire was a man who pushed these others into dialogue, or tried to anyway.

Perhaps some in the distant theoretical arena of English studies would perceive these personal accounts by Freire as "personal fluff" or as secondary to the profound theoretical implications of his pedagogy. However, I would like to argue in this essay that the personal represents the heart of Freire's teachings and writings—the profound liberatory experience of encouraging all participants in the pedagogical dialogue to share their lives of study in relation to the world. It is here where we witness the profound liberatory experience of enacting Freire's secondary theories.

As I say this, I'm staring at last year's NCTE *Council Chronicle* photograph of Paulo Freire with his arm around Ira Shor. Many of us can probably recall this photograph memorializing Freire in our discipline. I often think about what it would be like to have a dialogue with Freire in person. For all the fire and energy in his writings, I see in this picture a warm, grandfatherly figure smiling at his friend Ira. I see someone who understands and values the company of "others." In my eyes, the picture reveals the truth behind his later, more personal writings. I continue to observe Freire in our dialogue of silence as I try to comprehend why he waited so late to complete his *Letters to Cristina* and share the stories that inform *Pedagogy of the Oppressed*. Perhaps what he says in the beginning pages of this book offers a clue to this delay:

> What is expected of those who write with responsibility is a permanent and continuing search for truth that rejects puritanical hypocrisy or veiled shamelessness. In the final analysis, what is expected of those who teach by speaking or writing, by being a testimony, is that they be rigorously coherent so as not to lose themselves in the enormous distance between what they do and say. (1996, 2)

Perhaps Freire waited so we would have more to go on for "the final analysis"—to run a thorough test on the man and his theories. After reading this quote, I, as an essay scholar, understand that this "testimony," this test in writing, is aligned with a form not commonly carried out in academic journals or classrooms—the essay that assays. Freire's notion about "being a testimony" through personal writing is not a new idea, but one that dates back to Michel de Montaigne's words in his *Essais:*

> In everything else there may be sham: the fine reasonings of philosophy may be a mere pose in us; or else our trials, by not testing us to the quick, give us a chance to keep our face always composed. But in the last scene, between death and ourselves, there is no more pretending; we must talk plain French, we must show what there is that is good and clean at the bottom of the pot. (Montaigne 1967, 55)

Freire's last books represented one way for readers to assess what was "good and clean" at the bottom of his pot. As Freire approached the new millennium, he brought us to a writing form that captured and complemented his liberatory theories and pedagogy— a writing form that bears witness to our ethical responsibilities in adhering through testimonies to our theories and practices. Perhaps, for the new millennium, Freire presented us with his letters (which are actually written in essay form) as a way to convey to us that as academics, as students, we need to develop a liberatory writing form spawned by liberatory dialogues where our personal experiences are never far from our research and teaching practices.

Yet sometimes I wonder where our oral and essay testimonials fit in with the U.S. political battlefield that is English studies. With all the distant battle cries about standards, literacy, and pedagogical reforms, where, in this turbulent stew of national politics, is there room to test what is "good and clean" at the bottom of our English studies pot? In our quest for a democratic educational mission, how might we undermine our democratic goals if we choose to neglect the personal test in our classrooms and academic writings? How can liberatory writing and a democratic community be more fully realized if we do not designate spaces for composition and literature classes that allow students to play out the relationships between concepts they confront in academia and the experiences that shape their lives?

Fortunately, in the spring semester of 1998, I was given an opportunity to apply this personal test by teaching a U.S. women of color literature class in the women's studies department at the University of South Florida. The participants (more commonly known as students) validated their needs for liberatory writing and dialogue through their letters to the Paulo Freire Institute. They, more than Freire or myself, are the ones who know the worth of these pedagogical practices. At the beginning of this semester, these twenty junior- and senior-level participants who come from places like Belize, Chicago, Puerto Rico, Haiti, Tampa, Jamaica, Michigan, Missouri, and Mexico, who are a mixed bunch of races, who are all female except for one, came to this class with no knowledge of Freire. On the first day of a three-hour class, I extracted many quotes from Freire's books and asked participants to discuss in groups the quotes they were drawn to. Many of the participants gravitated toward the following sentences from the excerpts:

> The oppressor is solidary with the oppressed only when he stops regarding the oppressed as an abstract category and sees them as persons who have been unjustly dealt with, deprived of their voice, cheated in the sale of labor—when he stops making pious, sentimental, and individualistic gestures and risks an act of love. (Freire 1993, 31–32)

Narration (with the teacher as narrator) leads students to memorize mechanically the narrated content. Worse yet, it turns them into 'containers,' into receptacles to be 'filled' by the teacher. . . . Education thus becomes the act of depositing, in which the students are the depositories and the teacher is the depositor. Instead of communicating, the teacher issues communiqués and makes deposits which the students patiently receive, memorize, and repeat. (Freire, 1993, 53)

Self-sufficiency is incompatible with dialogue. Men and women who lack humility (or have lost it) cannot come to the people, cannot be partners in naming the world. (Freire 1993, 71)

The role of the progressive educator, which neither can nor ought to be omitted, in offering her or his 'reading of the world,' is to bring out the fact that there are other 'readings of the world,' different from the one being offered as the educator's own, and at times antagonistic to it. (Freire 1994, 112)

As I watched their eyes light up and their voices speak with impassioned fervor, I suspected that the participants had not come across many Freires in academia. Their letters that they addressed to the Paulo Freire Institute seemed to confirm this. As a liberatory teacher, I am a strong advocate of having participants converse through writing with the authors of the texts they read instead of just with their teacher. It seems to give an added dimension to liberatory writing. Here are some of their words:

RENEE: Reflecting on my last three years in college and throughout my high school years, I can honestly remember only a handful of teachers who believe in the role of "progressive educator" and exemplify the quote beginning with "self-sufficiency is incompatible with dialogue."

TIFFANY: Many history books are from the 'white' societies point of view and leave many things that minorities have accomplished out. With the use of your theory with "problem posing" education, students would be allowed to share what their culture had to do with a certain issue in history. "Problem posing" education should be enforced in classrooms today so that our students won't be limited to only what authors or teachers think we should know about.

ANITA: The dedicated teacher opens communication between teacher and student and allows for interaction to take place. I want to be a teacher myself, and I believe that the only way for a student to actually learn and feel like a part of the learning process is to actually partake in the discussion.

NORMA: We should respect to hear each other out and learn to accept one another for our differences. I am passionate about this statement that you made because I can relate. Being a Haitian immigrant in this country, I had to endure a lot of derogatory comments and many stereotypical stigmas that are placed on us. The best way that I chose to fight against this ignorance was through education. I educated them about the culture, people and discrimination I experienced as a Haitian woman.

SHERELYN: With your suggestions, the society can be reassured that the graduates are well informed individuals. They will be people with whom education and the teachers who impart their knowledge have been assured of intellectual growth. Because of the teacher/pupil interaction, they will have learned a vast amount of knowledge that will have been cross-culturally different. They would have truly learned and would become citizens of the world.

IVIS: An act of love you say . . . 'to risk an act of love.' That would mean to risk one's own comfort.

Ivis's words about risking "one's own comfort" to impart our love to others seemed to be the answer to why participants couldn't locate Freire in many of their teachers. At one time, I was one of those teachers. It took me six years of practicing so-called liberatory teaching to finally understand the risk I had to take, to relinquish my comfort by sharing with others the kind of love advocated by this man. It took me six years to reveal what was "good and clean" at the bottom of his pot and to realize that this love, this risk, cannot be extracted from our textbook knowledge, our journals and conferences, or our many readings of Freire, but must come from a personal commitment within. When we make this commitment as teachers, we begin to hear the voices of brutal honesty—those in the academy who have been silent for too long. With this commitment come the words of liberatory participants who want to be loved. I hear it in their liberatory voices and see it in their liberatory words. What a relief it is to approach the new millennium in this way.

The beauty of sharing Freire from the beginning is that he continues to be with us as the class and I make a conscious effort to fulfill his words, as we attempt to resurrect what many perceived to be an idealist. I feel committed to not letting them down, to not letting them experience the "enormous distance between what they [we] do and say" (Freire 1996, 2). They're quick to point out when they think my "distance" tendencies creep up, and we feel comfortable enough to laugh about it and work together toward revising our roles in the classroom. When I look into the participants' eyes and listen to their voices, I feel Freire's presence in stark ways.

I am also less afraid, just as they have become, to share personal experiences in relation to the texts we read. If I had succumbed to the "distance," we would have missed Maria's response to a passage in Sandra Cisneros's "Only Daughter" that read, "Even now my father's hands are thick and yellow, stubbed by a history of hammer and nails and twine and coils and springs. 'Use this,' my father said, tapping his head, 'and not this, showing us those hands. He always looked tired when he said it" (Cisneros 1987, 159). As a Mexican who has lived in this country for seventeen years, Maria, who told us on the first day that she didn't like to talk in class, movingly recounted to us the callused hands of her parents who labored so hard to give their children a better life by sending them to college. "Cisneros is describing my parents," she quietly said. As she said this, the class fell silent in a moment of closing distance between these texts and lives. In that moment, Maria confirmed Cisneros's words through her testimony, forced the words to jump off the page and into the hearts of those around her. I could see it in their faces as I looked around the room. I could see some whose parents also worked with their hands nodding in silent and pained agreement. If I had decided not to pursue this risk of love and instead had chosen specific stories or passages in the Latina anthology that I liked, we might not have heard Maria's testimony. We might have also missed Maria's words about the infamous Benetton experience that Patricia Williams was subjected to, as recounted in her moving autobiography *The Alchemy of Race and Rights* (1991). Like Williams, who testified of her experiences with those who barred her from entering a Benetton store (home of the "United Colors of Benetton" brand), Maria testified about a bank who humiliated her mother by asking for her resident alien card instead of her driver's license as a form of identification. While Patricia Williams fought back by placing a poster describing this incident on Benneton's window, Maria fought back by helping her mother pull her money out of the bank and asking for a letter of apology. After Maria's testimony, the class clapped in approval, and I saw a proud smile come across her lips. As a Chicana, Maria understood an African American law professor's will to fight those who oppress others. Maria performed an act of love toward Patricia Williams, toward the class, and toward her mother by speaking out even though she had never before felt comfortable with doing so in a classroom setting. I wonder why she had previously felt so uncomfortable, and why she was so comfortable now. Did someone fail to risk that act of love with her? As teachers, the powers in the act of love come when we can relinquish a part of our agendas so others can be heard.

I'm sure some might say that I'm not much of a scholar if I use this act of love as the center of my pedagogical scholarship. Where are the theoretical implications in the act of love, some might say? It may seem simplistic, but it is a powerful source for retrieving the accumulated knowledge and experiences in the classroom. It is the driving force that a progressive educator needs to empower the disempowered in an ivory tower that too often still clings to the ivory. It is the motivator that sends us off to learn more through conferences, books, articles, films, and the like about the cultural, historical, and political literatures and lives of those we encounter in our classrooms. As we begin the new millennium, I hope the act of love that Freire imparted to us is not forgotten. It would be a tragic loss of English studies' relevance if this were to happen.

It is also important to emulate Maria and tell our own stories, as painful as they may be. I've noticed that there seems to be a growing movement in English studies for scholars to come "clean" with their personal forms of writing. Fortunately, this cleaning of the "pots" is no longer viewed by many as a domestic activity in academia. Just the other day I picked up a copy of H. Aram Veeser's *Confessions of the Critics* (1996) and found renowned critics that I knew only from distant scholarly articles telling me where they came from before they entered academia, why they chose a particular academic path, and how their backgrounds collide with their research and teaching interests. After reading these "confessions," I would not be intimidated to approach one of these scholars and discuss their works and their cleaning techniques. I've noticed that a more personal form of writing can lessen the distance from those we might label as "other." By revealing themselves in relationship to their scholarship, these established scholars open doors so "others" can meet Freire's definition of a radical—a person not afraid "to confront, to listen, to see the world unveiled. This person is not afraid to meet the people or to enter into dialogue with them" (1993, 21). When "others" provide us with personal and critical scholarship, we're enticed to draw them into dialogue. I've watched with growing curiosity over the years how an academic from working-class Nuyorican origins mesmerizes predominantly Anglo/Angla audiences with his personal/critical liberatory speeches and writings. When I'm around Victor Villanueva at conferences, I never fail to see an Anglo or Angla eagerly come up to him and tell him how much they enjoyed his speech or his autobiographical/critical book *Bootstraps* (1993).

We also need to include scholars unafraid to enter into dialogue with others among the texts we study in the classroom. Liberatory voices and writers in the classroom need liberatory role models. In the women of color literature class, I brought in testifying role models like Ana Castillo and Patricia Williams. Women—and especially women of color—need to hear Castillo's comments on why their voices in scholarship and the classroom are seldom heard:

> In our experience with dominant intellectual society, both within and outside academia, women—especially women of color—are often dismissed for our attempts to use personal experiences and perceptions as the basis of our theories. Because of the pretense of 'objectivity' in traditional scholarship, our deductions are

viewed as biased and therefore invalid when we base them on our experiences and perceptions. (Castillo 1994, 206)

They also need to hear Patricia Williams's words in response to a law professor who accused her of being too personal for an academic audience:

> I say: Writing for me is an act of sacrifice, not denial. (I think: I'm so glad I didn't try to write this down.) I deliberately sacrifice myself in writing. I leave no part of myself out, for that is how much I want the readers to connect with me. I want them to wonder about the things I wonder about, and to think about some of the things that trouble me.
>
> What is 'impersonal' writing but denial of self? If withholding is an ideology worth teaching, we should be clearer about that as the bottom line of the enterprise. We should also acknowledge the extent to which denial of one's authority in authorship is not the same as elimination of oneself; it is ruse, not reality. And the object of such ruse is to empower still further; to empower beyond the self, by appealing to neutral, shared, even universal understandings. In a vacuum, I suppose there's nothing wrong with that attempt to empower: it generates respect and distance and a certain obeisance to the sleekness of a product that has been skinned of its personalized complication. But in a world of real others, the cost of such exclusive forms of discourse is empowerment at the expense of one's relation to those others; empowerment without communion. (Williams 1991, 92–93)

Like Ana Castillo and Patricia Williams, I too feel a sense of loss when I cannot commune with others through my personal writings. From my own experiences with liberatory personal writing, I've discovered that I can bring "others" together in small ways. This coming together of "others" is empowering and ironically purifying for someone of "mixed" Honduran/Southern Angla origins like myself. I almost feel whole when I receive positive responses to my personal writing and teaching from both my Latina/Latino and my Angla/Anglo audiences.

Yet, for others I've spoken to, this personal writing shared with others is usually saved for journals, for conferences, for any place except the classroom. When I passed out a personal essay published in the *Americas Review* that intersected my Honduran/Southern Angla experiences of discrimination in relation to some of Patricia Williams's testimonies in *The Alchemy of Race and Rights,* I anguished all week about returning to the next classroom session. I feared letting these participants love me in return. This act of love is the hardest to let in; the one that leaves us so vulnerable, so human, to those we teach. However, it is necessary in a liberatory classroom not to deny participants a window into ourselves as they have not denied us. We have to tell ourselves that it's okay to let love go both ways if it's done right without any disempowering motivations. I discovered that it was okay when I returned to the classroom and an African American participant, Nikki, said she'd like to read a letter that she wrote to me. One part of her letter read, "Although I've had different discrimination, I can relate to those ghosts from your past that follow you around. I too have those family ghosts that will always be with me." Tears streamed down my face as she read that letter, yet I did not experience the shame that I thought I was supposed to as a teacher. Instead, in that moment, we seemed to gain respect for each other's cultural lives and experiences. Instead of a loss of respect, what followed was a powerful session in which participants of all colors extracted passages from Patricia Williams's words that made her a role model to these soon-to-be graduates.

What followed, after Nikki's reading of her letter, were testimonial dialogue tapestries of discriminatory practices that the lives in the classroom endured—testimonies which enlightened our reading of Williams's autobiography in stark ways that I could never have done alone through my personal essay and teachings. At one point in the discussion, Patricia Williams's account of mistreatment at Benetton was validated over and over through testimonies from the class. Keetha (an African American who left Jamaica as a young child) testified of the countless times she was ignored by salespersons. "I wait five minutes, I wait ten minutes, and no one at the jewelry counter even tells me that they'll be with me in a minute. They think I'm black and can't afford it," she says in the strong tone that we in the class have come to recognize as Keetha. Sherelyn (an African Belizean) recalled the time when she was shopping with her mother in a nice dress shop in California and a well-dressed African American salesperson told them, in a snooty tone, to go to the sales rack. "It happens in our own race," she said. Tiffany (an African American originally from St. Louis) told us that, as an employee of a better department store, she was trained to watch and follow African Americans. "I was recently written up by my supervisor because I failed to follow two African American women around. Well, they happened to be my Aunt Josie and cousin," she angrily exclaimed. Renee, an Angla student (originally from Tampa), chimed in with another story about how a salesperson called security on her Latina friend and herself when they complained to this salesperson about the ill-treatment they received. "The salesperson told us that we would pay for our comments and headed towards a phone to call security," she bitterly recounted. Shannon (an Angla from Michigan married to a Colombian) jumps up from her chair next to me and vividly acts out the physical confrontation that a salesperson had with her mother as she was followed around the store. "Don't treat my mother like that!" Shannon almost screams as she recreates this experience for us. Over and over again, these students, who together have more than four hundred years of accumulated, varied experiences compared to my measly thirty-eight, confirmed the mistreatment by others that Williams testified to in her autobiography. We, as teachers, are clearly outnumbered in the classroom, so to silence participant's voices, their written testimonies, would be a crime against accumulated age and wisdom. As teachers, we also have the responsibility to analyze with the class these testimonies, the why of these varying degrees of discrimination. When we risk an act of love, we prevent crimes against our society's and classroom's humanity.

When we risk an act of love as teachers, we must also remember those from our own school days who inspired us to love. It is important to remember the few teachers who paved the way for classroom humanity, who may never have read Freire, but who carried similar feelings of love. These are the inspirations that make us remember what it was like to love as a student. We must never forget those love moments.

I remember my first "true" love in a senior high school English classroom. His name was Mr. Patrick Welsh, an Irish-Catholic, middle-class high school teacher and law school graduate who wrote the best-seller *Tales Out of School* (1986) and who has written countless articles for the *Washington Post* concerning the plights of students in an urban public school system. I remember him just as Mr. Welsh—the teacher who gave us Supreme Court cases such as *Brown v. Board of Education* and *Regents of the University of California v. Bakke.* I remember myself as a seventeen-year-old student with a dictionary in hand, plowing through the rulings by Justice Brennan, Justice Marshall, Justice Burger, and many others. I remember how good it felt when he let us take sides and analyze these Supreme Court justices' words. What wonderful liberatory dialogues and writings came out of this class. How empowering for a student of seventeen. Years later, when I learned about Linda Brodky's problems with introducing Supreme Court cases in an English curriculum at the University of Texas at Austin, I was baffled by UT's actions. How could they possibly not understand the relevance of these cases to English studies? How closed-minded they must have been. Maybe they had forgotten to visit the classroom and witness the love within. What a sad moment in our English studies past.

I remember how Mr. Welsh shared our writings with the class, how he stated that some of us could write as well as he could in his *Washington Post* articles. I remember writing about the personal effects these Supreme Court cases had on me and how he listened. I remember that he, unlike some teachers at my high school, never treated me as lesser than because of my Latina heritage. I remember how proud I was when he read my writings to the class made up of White, middle-class males destined for the University of Virginia, Penn State, and other top schools throughout the country. If it were not for his love for us, I do not think I would have had the confidence to pursue an English major. I also remember that he never took advantage of this young, attractive, Latina's professional admiration for him. He knew where to draw the line with love in unselfish ways.

I see Freire's teachings in Mr. Welsh. I see Freire's teachings in the participants of the classroom. I see Freire's teachings in the authors of the readings I and other participants bring to the classroom. When I bring them all together, I am better equipped to see Freire's teachings in myself and impart this knowledge to others. All of this and probably more inspires the personal commitment to love. As this essay draws to a close, I wonder what personal commitment to liberatory dialogue and writing we in

English studies will make in this new century. Will it be one of risking an act of love, or will we go the easier way and dismiss it as sentimental idealism? How unselfish are we willing to be in designating spaces for those who want to practice this particular love of teaching? How will we make love relevant?

Works Cited

Castillo, Ana. 1994. *Massacre of the Dreamers: Essays on Xicanisma.* Albuquerque: University of New Mexico Press.

Cisneros, Sandra. 1997. "Only Daughter." Pp. 120–23 in *Máscaras,* ed. Lucha Corpi. Berkeley, Calif.: Third Woman.

Freire, Paulo. 1993. *Pedagogy of the Oppressed: New Revised 20th Century Edition.* Translated by Myra Bergman Ramos. New York: Continuum.

———. 1994. *Pedagogy of Hope: Reliving Pedagogy of the Oppressed.* Trans. Robert R. Barr. New York: Continuum.

———. 1996. *Letters to Cristina: Reflections on My Life and Work.* Trans. Donaldo Macedo with Quilda Macedo and Alexandre Oliveira. New York: Routledge, 1996.

Kirklighter, Cristina. "Traveling Academic Homes: An Autobiographical Visit to and from *The Alchemy of Race and Rights.*" *The Americas Review* 22.3–4 (1994): 37–43.

Montaigne, Michel de. 1967. *The Complete Works of Montaigne.* Trans. Donald M. Frame. Stanford: Stanford University Press.

Veeser, H. Aram, ed. 1996. *Confessions of the Critics.* New York: Routledge.

Villanueva, Victor, Jr. 1993. *Bootstraps: From an American Academic of Color.* Urbana, Ill.: National Council of Teachers of English.

Welsh, Patrick. 1986. *Tales Out of School: A Teacher's Candid Account from the Front Lines of the American High School Today.* New York: Viking Press.

Williams, Patricia J. 1991. *The Alchemy of Race and Rights.* Cambridge: Harvard University Press.

CHAPTER ELEVEN

Surviving Intact: African American Women Negotiating Scholarly Identities through Graduate School Writing

JUANITA RODGERS COMFORT
West Chester University

A moth is drawn to the light and is ultimately consumed by it. I do not want graduate school to be such an experience for me. The question hovers: how close to the light can I get and not be drawn into destruction? I must be cautious. I must resist impulse. I must survive, wings and spirit intact.

MAYA, a doctoral student

Karla Holloway asserts that "Black women have a specific need to keep their instincts and childhood memories pure, immediate, and healing . . . because we can grow into women who impart feminine spiritual wisdom" (Holloway and Demetrakopoulos 1986, 19). Even as African American women are increasingly attracted to doctoral studies in English, these future academics often engage in tremendous struggles to achieve credible, influential voices by the time they leave their graduate programs. One of the greatest challenges facing Black women in doctoral programs is how to effectively negotiate the various cultural trade-offs they feel they must make in order to survive in predominantly White discourse communities, which often distance them from the home communities where they will be respected more for the wisdom alluded to by Holloway than for the mere designation of "Ph.D." after their names.

Along with most other graduate students, African American women pursue doctoral degrees in English because they are attracted to the profession generally and because they have a strong scholarly interest in language, literature, rhetoric, composition, cultural studies, and/or pedagogy. Many of these women also aspire to contribute substantially to educational, professional, community, and faith-based programs outside the academy which cater to the needs of people whose interests have been ill-served by society's dominant institutions. They see their academic status, which signifies membership in one key institution, as a valuable credential which will enable them to more effectively influence a range of public issues. They anticipate that audiences for their discourses will range well beyond academic conference panels and the bookshelves of their colleagues.

This essay addresses my particular concerns about the relevance of English studies for a cohort of students whose voices and interests have been largely ignored. It is admirable when a program is able to announce that it attracts and even graduates a significant number of "minority" students. However, I am concerned that those students are too often led to believe that they must set aside the very subjectivities that distinguish them in their public and private lives in order to pledge allegiance to the dominant voices in their academic fields.

As a framework for and an assertion of rhetorical identity, the course papers, comprehensive examinations, and dissertations that doctoral students produce are media through which they are expected to demonstrate mastery of the modes of reasoning and the stylistic conventions that mark scholarly discourse. It has been argued by a number of literacy scholars that the typical discourse of the academy usually identifies a writer as a White European, middle- to upper-class, male voice. Such discourse does not fully accommodate the styles and modes that mark many other voices, nor does it adequately address the struggle of Black women to write without "replicating the 'White' and 'male' models of power that excluded and marginalized both Black women and their texts from the class and curriculum in the first place" (Henderson 1994, 435).

As I consider the relevance of English studies for African American women in graduate school in these terms, I must also ask a reciprocal question: *How relevant are these women to English studies?* How, if at all, does the "feminine spiritual wisdom" that Karla Holloway speaks about support and enhance the agenda and vested interests of the disciplinary communities these women seek to join? Certainly, it would seem reasonable to think that by their day-to-day participation in their programs—their intellectual exchanges with faculty, the conference papers and journal articles they author, the original research they ultimately publish as their dissertations—they help to transform both processes and products of academic knowledge making as they open up important discursive spaces for their distinctive voices. However, Alexis De Veaux, who was an assistant professor at SUNY–Buffalo the year I received my doctoral degree, advances a rather somber argument that I think is worthy of consideration by those who teach, mentor, and evaluate the work of graduate students. De Veaux charges that scholarship produced by Black women "is of little real interest to the academy, because the academy is interested in studying, not improving, Black people's lives." She continues,

> The further we advance, the closer we come to our degrees, the more the academy fears, rather than embraces, the ideas we bring to it. We know that the fear of our scholarship is directly linked to the potential of our ideas to alter the very structure of the academy. Our ideas will influence the intellectual growth of generations of students. Our ideas will become books that help to reshape social, political, and cultural images of Black people. (1995, 110)

Her reasoning suggests that unless the academy reins in the voices of Black women as they move through their programs, their work may pose a significant threat to the cultural stability of their disciplines.

One approach that has been used to rein in those voices involves ensuring that students have "mastered" the discourse conventions approved by the academy. Pat Belanoff critiques a position taken by proponents of conventional academic literacy. Participation in the academy's knowledge-making enterprise, these proponents insist, requires using the dominant language of the academy. The hidden premise: that such language carries the power and the respect of the academy's Eurocentric, masculinist, middle- and upper-class factions. If writers wish to wield disciplinary power, it is reasoned, they must use discourses invested with power. Those who choose not to comply faithfully run the risk that their voices simply will not be heard. Even now, at the turn of the millennium, cultural and political power is heavily invested in discourses that maintain the value systems and social hierarchies that have silenced many voices in the last century.

Even as the content of scholarship opens up, its discursive rules do not. As Belanoff articulates this viewpoint, "Although women, minorities, and Third World thinkers and writers are increasingly integrated into course content, *the language with which one writes about them should not be altered*" (1993, 264; my emphasis). For African American women trying to write not merely as students but also as "insurgent intellectuals," to use a term coined by bell hooks and Cornell West (1991), their negotiation of a critical consciousness may be further complicated by their awareness, as expressed by Patricia Hill Collins, that "oppressed groups are frequently placed in the situation of being listened to only if we frame our ideas in the language that is familiar to and comfortable for a dominant group. This requirement often changes the meaning of our ideas and works to elevate the ideas of dominant groups" (1991, xiii).

In the introduction to this volume, Robert Yagelski suggests that the relevance of English might be defined, to a degree, according to its capacity for teaching students to become "critically aware citizens who can read, write, speak, and think in ways that enable them to resist political domination or hegemony." If this is so, then it seems appropriate for students to expect their graduate training to help prepare them for the kinds of discursive battles they will have to fight in order to define a meaningful space for themselves in the profession.

To what extent, then, are graduate faculty proactively mentoring students to become critically aware academics who can resist the political domination and hegemony that certainly exist in English studies today, *including in their own classrooms?* I have seen firsthand that the mere presence of Black scholarship in English studies still irritates some people who see it as an invasion of privileged intellectual territory. Let me describe two incidents I can recall from my own graduate school days that made a significant difference in how I "composed" myself both in the classroom and in my writing.

Scene 1: I took a graduate seminar on intersections of literary and rhetorical theory, along with one other Black woman whom I'll call Julia and approximately fifteen White students. On the first night of class, a reading list was distributed which included about twenty critical pieces, two of which were authored by Black scholars, Houston Baker Jr. and Henry Louis Gates Jr. As we moved down the list (the Black-authored pieces were placed toward the end), we eventually heard two loudly whispered voices exchanging these comments, as one of the White students nodded in our direction:

"Why do we have to read *these* things?"

"Because *they're* in here."

Julia and I nervously quizzed each other after class about our first-day experience, with mistrust steadily growing in our minds: Had the professors who were team-teaching the course heard the students' racist comments, too? And if they had, did they share the students' attitude? What preconceptions about us as intellectuals would we have to contend with for the rest of the term? How were we supposed to raise our own voices confidently in discussions before classmates who, we felt, probably would not be inclined to value our contributions?

I was particularly nervous about writing a seminar paper within this classroom environment, even though the assignment represented a chance to speak from a vantage point that I had been holding back all term. Aside from reviewing the two Black-authored critical pieces, our classroom discussions had done little to engage issues of cultural diversity in rhetorical or literary studies. My initial enthusiasm for writing quickly faded as I obsessed over how I might develop a paper that attended to one of those issues, and whether my intellectual ability (and, indeed, presence in the program) would be questioned if I failed to do a good job with it. For weeks, I struggled with almost every aspect of composing—from topic selection, to appropriate support, to stylistic elements. With time running out, I decided that what I originally planned wasn't going to work, so I took the fall-back position of composing a standard comparison of two schools of thought. It was a simple replication of previously established points, conveyed without personal investment—a timid little piece that satisfied neither the professors nor myself. The most disappointing part of this experience was that I had not enriched myself as a writer. While the markings on my graded draft pointed out certain missteps in logic and form, the comments did little to help me address what I most wanted to know: how to approach future writings in ways that would not compromise my own standpoint.

Scene 2: I took a nineteenth-century American literature course with about twenty-five other students. There was only one other Black student, a man. The reading list contained no Black-authored works and only three authored by women. Shortly after the course started, a White female student sent a letter to the professor (and made copies for the class), asking why the authors were not more culturally diverse. The professor entered the classroom the day after he received the letter and began to chastise the student for questioning his selections, calling the letter a "hysterical" response (he even wrote that word on the board). A few days later, he handed out a faded (nearly unreadable) mimeographed bibliography of slave narratives, remarking only that "some of you might be interested in these."

This professor liked to read aloud passages from the works, in order to give us an appreciation for the language. But when he enlisted some poor student to stammer through a passage of Jim's dialect from *Adventures of Huckleberry Finn* (eliciting giggles from many classmates, unchecked by the professor), I was so insulted that I vowed never to speak a word in that class. Also, early in the term, I had started working on an essay project which would examine the rhetorical significance of Frances E. W. Harper's *Iola Leroy,* one of the first novels written by a Black woman. But I threw those notes away and deliberately dashed out a routine essay on Whitman and Dickinson as "love poets."

I silenced my voice in that class and reconstructed my project as well-considered acts of resistance: I did not respect or trust the professor enough to position myself as his teacher. I feared that he would merely fold my ideas into his lecture notes and take credit for updating his course. I don't know whether he even noticed that I never spoke. I only regret that by not writing the paper I had planned, I passed up an opportunity to do some important critical work (by the way, the paper that I did submit received an A).

A Rhetoric of Cultural Negotiation

For Isaiah Smithson, English studies, particularly in its movement toward cultural studies, concerns "relations among texts, writers, readers, and cultures" (1994, 1). In his view, texts are

> part of a complex network leading to and from diverse cultural phenomena in and out of the academy . . . [,] all texts are cultural texts [,] and . . . all writers and readers write and read differently according to the cultures that produce them. (12)

Within this context, self-portrayal in texts is often a difficult negotiation for those who locate themselves primarily in non-White, non-male, working-class or economically disadvantaged cultures. Their work develops out of a series of well-considered trade-offs made in an effort to achieve the goals that are important to them. As they receive and send messages about themselves, they are deeply concerned with what numerous facets of society (including the academy) expect them to be, as Black persons, as women of a particular age, as students, as teachers, as emerging scholars, as community leaders, and so forth. They are keenly aware of conflicting expectations held by Blacks and Whites, conflicting expectations within Black communities, conflicting expectations held in academic and nonacademic settings and in other societal institutions. In negotiating their roles and statuses with respect to these communities and institutions, these women must map out an effective vantage point from which to speak. As emerging professional women, they have much at stake in terms of their future rhetorical success, both materially, in securing the kind of publications necessary for tenure and promotion, and more intrinsically, in becoming voices that expand the parameters of their disciplines. But they face a number of specific pitfalls as they attempt to use academic prose for their own purposes. bell hooks has observed:

> For Black women scholars and/or intellectuals, writing style may evoke questions of political allegiance. Using a style that may gain one academic acceptance and recognition may further estrange one from a wider Black reading audience. . . . Choosing to write in a traditional academic style may lead to isolation. And even if one writes along the lines of accepted academic style, there is no guarantee that one's work will be accepted. (hooks and West 1991, 157)

The more strongly a Black woman's writing signals to readers that she holds a different social status from theirs, that she writes as a person who is noticeably different from her readers and who seeks different goals, the more readily in turn she may be identified as an outsider, with all the consequences that follow. Given the often competing constraints imposed by her academic rhetorical situations and her culturally grounded rhetorical resources, she must continually negotiate positions in her texts—sometimes comply, sometimes resist—on her way to establishing an effective scholarly voice that is also comfortable for her. Of course, if they are to reach any level of success in the academy, African American women must learn how to pull off this negotiation successfully, regardless of whether their graduate faculty have taught them how to do so.

It may be true that an identifiable Black voice is deemed acceptable—even expected—in writing assignments that raise obvious issues of race, gender, and/or class. But for other topics (unmarked by cultural "otherness"), where established authority is reserved for the sanctioned positions, viewpoints, authorities, or lines of arguments of the disciplinary establishment, it is infinitely more difficult for students to speak from a self-defined standpoint. Faculty readers have the power to shut down the voices of otherness as they see fit.

Bowser, Auletta, and Jones put forth several alternatives for addressing the general problem of "racial exclusion and putdowns made by even the most well-intentioned White colleagues" (1993, 17). They categorize these as "three no-win choices" which parallel certain writing strategies:

First, he or she can mention the offense in conversation, but this not only violates the middle-class, European-American's social rule of politeness but presents additional costs: Besides being considered rude and possibly maladjusted, the injured party usually will be ignored, excluded, or labeled a troublemaker from then on. Second, he or she can avoid speaking up. Say nothing long enough, however, and the victim is left to struggle with mounting internal anger, pain, doubt, and blame. Third, he or she can disassociate from other people of color and work toward being accepted as an individual apart from his or her race. This approach also has its price. The individual is never perceived simply as such. At best, this "honorary White" status lasts only as long as he or she is seen to be like a real White person *and supports White interests.* (17; emphasis added)

I have seen (and used) all three approaches at various points in my own education. My faculty evaluators, by virtue of their positions and status in the Eurocentric, masculinist, class-conscious, insistently secular academic culture, brought an unequal power relationship to the texts they assigned for class. But when students foreground their own cultural perspectives in their writings, they are, in a sense, asking their professors to *participate* in those cultures—inviting a closer meeting of minds where each side identifies itself with the other (*mutual* identification).

When these students complain about the negative ways in which faculty readers respond to their work, they indicate that they believe their *ethos* has been judged according to the same kinds of racist, sexist, class-conditioned values that the students have often encountered outside the academy. They are concerned about being placed in relationships with these faculty readers yet feeling stymied by rules of engagement those readers have established for the relationship. They are particularly frustrated in struggling to assess the implicit agenda behind readers' stated expectations. In such situations, they see themselves as "outsiders within"—being let through the door but not being shown the secret handshake. Such marginality, according to Collins, provides Black women with a unique angle of vision, one that enables them to take an important critical stance toward the mainstream of academic inquiry (1991, 12).

As these women assert that they write with audiences in mind that range beyond their faculty evaluators, they also acknowledge that their goals and agendas don't always coincide with those of the academic establishment. They profess that they wish to use their educations, even as graduate students, in ways that could level the playing field, empowering those who previously have been oppressed, and in ways that would bring them to the academy in increasing numbers, perhaps jeopardizing the intellectual and material positions of those already there.

As with the other areas of negotiation, what these writing subjects believe about their effect on readers is important. Where extensive help is not available and an attitude of "you're on your own . . . either you pass this test or you don't" prevails, it is usually left up to these writers to pick up whatever they can in the way of audience assessment, and hope that it works. When evaluations are inconsistent from one paper to the next and one course to the next, it is hard to develop a range of reliable feedback upon which to base a comfortable, relatively stable scholarly identity. If there are inconsistencies within the range of each woman's writing experiences, frequent misreadings of rhetorical context and audience expectations, and lack of confidence in who she is supposed to be to her readers, her negotiation of rhetorical identity can break down and the resulting confusion in the text can negatively influence readers' opinions of her and her abilities.

The task that these women face is not to leave one community in order to enter another, but to reposition themselves in relation to several overlapping and often conflicting communities. As they continue to press for changed attitudes within the disciplines they have joined, they also need to continue to assess ways in which their textual self-portrayals can move them further toward the center of their disciplines.

Cases in Point

A few years ago, I developed a series of case studies for my dissertation which chronicled the efforts of a group of Black women doctoral students from a range of disciplines at my institution to use their course papers as vehicles through which to develop their scholarly voices. My plan was to determine how these women used the compositions they produced to cope with and even influence their faculty readers' perceptions of them, and thereby establish themselves as credible scholars in their instructors' eyes. I also wanted to know the extent to which these women believed they had control over their own discursive practices. Many of their struggles were also my own.

Four of my seven study participants were also my peers in the English graduate program. (I will identify them here by the pseudonyms they selected for the project.) At the time of my study, Alice was pursuing studies in folklore, Bernice in American literature, Carol in rhetoric and composition, and Maya in English education. These women were responsive and responsible intellectuals who wished to "use their thinking and their feeling . . . their whole being," as Maya once remarked, in developing their academic writings. After interviewing them, I came to a greater understanding of their quest to exert agency as they learned to develop rhetorically useful identities that their academic audiences would find appropriate.

Three of these four women had returned to graduate school, as I did, at midlife, after—or while—raising children, working for years in government and the private sector, and/or serving in the military. Two were already accomplished poets and storytellers. Representing Baptist, Pentecostal, *Ifa* (a Nigerian religion), and African Methodist Episcopal faith traditions, they had vital spiritual lives that governed their everyday activities, and they participated extensively in religious and civic functions in the communities surrounding the campus. And perhaps most significant, they reported that they had been profoundly influenced by elders in their families, churches, and communities whose authority is derived not only from formal education but also from lifetimes of hard work, a special brand of common sense known as "mother wit," and the pressures unique to what some sources have called "the crucible of racism."

As they grew older, their families, churches, and communities conferred upon them the respect and authority that comes with the territory of being mature Black women. They had already undertaken the task of preserving and passing down the collective wisdom and knowledge of these communities, as writers and teachers in both formal and informal settings. They viewed their advanced education not merely as an employment credential, but also as valuable preparation for careers devoted to lifting others as they climb.

The epigraph by Maya that begins this essay eloquently expresses the desire of African American women in graduate school to avoid the kind of cultural assimilation that they believe would rob them of a hard-earned sense of self. Biases which exist both in the academy and in the larger society have affected many of them, both in their personal interactions with others and in the negative assumptions about them that they believe pervade their disciplines. As a rhetorician, and as a Black woman who has survived my doctoral program relatively intact (despite incidents like the two I described earlier), I understand that the dynamic of enfranchisement in academia is at least partially related to the graduate student's rhetorical effectiveness in her program, particularly in the impression of her scholarly identity that she suggests in the minds of her faculty readers. Her character, as perceived by those readers, plays a significant role in "composing" the student as a member of her academic community. Judgments about her, based on the "quality" of her written work—and, through those judgments, on the accordance of collegial respect and the distribution of material rewards—are made by readers who have the power to accept the student into, or exclude her from, their intellectual community. Evidence of this evaluative process can be seen at all levels of a graduate program, from the disposition of course papers and comprehensive examinations to reactions to the dissertation itself.

I remember how well my study participants and I understood that our academic writing had been crucially shaped by the course of our lives, *whatever that course entailed for each of us.* We wished to make our field acknowledge its growing diversity; thus, we saw that we must do more with our school writing than demonstrate our capability to produce texts for scholarly audiences. We sensed that our writing must also prepare us for the real-world writing we expected to use to accomplish our political and social goals, which might include coordinating fund-raising activities, developing community projects, revising teaching materials for special needs, and other public service endeavors. And we knew that if we were to be effective scholars within our disciplines as well, while retaining a sharp sense of ourselves as

African American women, our writing must certainly project a distinctive identity. We desired to learn in graduate school how to balance the expectations of our academic audiences with those of other audiences we wished to reach.

Maya and Carol in particular tended to tap into experiences and voices related to Black experiences, and they claimed that their work is recognized and appreciated by Black audiences. However, the extent to which these women and others can find a place for those kinds of voices in their academic writing varies considerably. Carol recalled a successful analytical paper she wrote on Jamaica Kincaid's "At the Bottom of the River," in which she was able to match the creativity of her nonacademic writing. "This seminar paper reflected a voice I had heard before," Carol said. "There is a distinct voice that comes through in [Kincaid's] work. I was able to adopt that voice in writing about it, and when people read my paper they can read into it that extra something." She also remembered another paper, on the success of African Americans in composition classrooms, that she constructed as a "double narrative." "I did the academic portion, and then I did my own personal commentary on what it feels like to be an African American woman and a graduate student going through this type of research," she said. "The double narrative came about with the frustration I felt in not finding [the success stories] I was looking for and in fact finding things much worse than I had expected."

Maya aspired to return to the place in California where she had been a classroom teacher for many years. She understood that much of her writing as an educator would be directed to members of communities that she already knew well—communities where concepts of faith and morality comprised an important backdrop for dealing with issues related to the education of children. She saw opportunities in some of her class assignments to practice the kind of writing she anticipated would meet needs and expectations of audiences in those communities. Her rhetorical strategies therefore included occasional references to biblical passages to serve as metaphors for her views, a narrative strategy that could be characterized as "secular parable," sentence patterns structured as litanies, and word choices that are often used in spiritual contexts. Taken together, these features engendered a tone of spirituality. Because of her extensive teaching experience, she expected that her professor would read her work carefully and perhaps engage in a dialogue with her on concepts that Maya hoped the professor would find provocative. But Maya revealed that she was disappointed to discover that the professor's comments on her work practically dismissed not only her voice but also her vantage point as an experienced teacher in predominantly Black schools. Few, if any, of the professor's comments actually engaged the ideas presented in the papers. Most directed Maya to express herself in more conventional disciplinary prose, arrange her points in a thesis-support rather than a narrative pattern, and use more authoritative sources.

Nevertheless, Maya found a way to maintain control of her own writing, even if she had to make significant concessions in order to succeed in the course. Assuming the burden of making twice the work for herself, she began to compose two papers for each of her assignments. In the first version, she said, she always wrote for the real-world audience that she envisioned would appreciate her words and be instructed by them. She then reworked the paper in the style that the professor wanted. Maya lamented that she was never satisfied with the versions submitted in class, that they did not contain the "fullness" of what she intended to say. For Maya, the conventions and constraints imposed by the professor's requirements diminished her ability to express certain nuances of a topic that she believed were essential to conveying her message.

I learned in the course of defining what my research project would be that a number of my peers share purposes and strategies, agonies and insights, as writers. Through their discursive choices, they attempted to control on numerous levels what they would say in particular composing situations and how it would be expressed. As they came to understand more about how their experiences as African American women related to their scholarship and teaching, they increasingly claimed the right to say to their academic audiences, "We know some things better than you do, our ways of knowing are vigorous and productive and, in many matters, you would do well to listen to us on our terms—precisely because of *who we are*."

And in saying these things to their faculty audiences, they claimed that they were paying a severe price. As students, regardless of their roles and responsibilities outside the academy, they faced challenges from faculty as they attempted to claim authority to speak from a position of Black womanhood. They were burdened with anxiety over course papers returned with their words crossed out and others' words inscribed, over graduate reports lamenting that they did not yet know how to construct arguments, over research topics rejected by professors who claimed that those topics did not merit scholarly treatment and would not generate "sufficient interest" in the field. While these experiences are not uncommon among graduate students of all colors and both genders, their effects are complexly intertwined with the race and gender issues I have been discussing. And so, these women wondered, where in these evaluative gestures could they find affirmation of their efforts to assert subjectivity as intellectual women of color? Aren't these gestures really designed to force them into less disruptive locations within the established academic landscape? Many times, my study participants indicated, they simply could not be sure which messages were encoded in these kinds of responses to their work. And upon receiving such messages, they were often unsure of the best response. Instructors' judgments regarding the writing ability of their students often hinge on the extent to which students are able to negotiate politically and ethically complicated linguistic terrain, often with little substantive guidance by those instructors.

Obliged as they were to follow the instructions given by their professors and other academic readers, these students of course perceived that their advancement within their programs depended on conforming to the expectations of those readers. Some of those readers had greater insight than others into the dynamic of writing for multiple, culturally diverse audiences, and thus could recognize and appreciate what the writers attempted to do. Other readers, however, at least *as they were perceived by the women in this study,* not only were ignorant of the nature of these women's attempts at self-portrayal, but sometimes seemed threatened by the presence of a "nonstandard" voice.

Alice's experience provides a case in point. Having been educated in all-Black schools, she earned a bachelor's degree in English at a historically Black university. After graduating magna cum laude, she joined the military reserves while working, first, as a state employee and, later, for a major automaker. She then advanced to active military duty, serving both stateside and overseas and eventually rising to the rank of major. She went on to earn a master's degree in English education, obtaining a teaching certificate in the process. She revealed to me that some of her experiences with faculty in the predominantly White graduate programs she has attended had led her to believe that they operated from the assumption that students like her, coming from Black colleges, are not adequately prepared to be effective thinkers and writers at the upper levels of graduate work at predominantly White institutions. In our interviews, Alice often stressed her obsession with overcoming this perception of her.

Alice came by to see me one day, her confidence badly shaken. She knew that I was in the composition program and was a writing center tutor. She wanted me to look over a graded paper that had been returned to her by a professor in one of her literature classes. What I saw, even without reading, saddened me deeply. Line after line, for page after page, was marked through in red ink. Copious notes were scrawled between those lines. Alice was not even allowed to keep her title—it too had been crossed through and reinscribed with the professor's words. As I read through the paper, trying to ignore the professor's markings, I saw much to celebrate about the way she approached her topic, making connections to her own mixed African and Native American heritage. I also saw some vibrant, innovative uses of language. Alice spoke to me at length about the choices she had made in composing that paper and the particular effects she had hoped to achieve at the very points the professor disapproved of. Looking at those points in her paper, I could see that while not all her strategies were successful, her intentions seemed fairly obvious from what she had written. Yet there were no words of encouragement anywhere on the draft. There was no attempt to explain why certain choices were not effective for the given writing situation. Instead, Alice was simply told what to say and how to say it.

Experiences such as Alice's were not uncommon among my study participants. They often wondered how they were supposed to find any affirmation in such gestures that would validate their subjectivities as intellectual women of color, or whether these gestures were designed to force them into less disruptive locations within the established academic landscape. The messages encoded in faculty comments on their work were sometimes confusing, even contradictory, and the women were often unsure of how they should respond.

Investing in the Discourses of English Studies

It is encouraging to note that graduate programs in English are now interrogating their own cultural groundings more specifically. As progressive as they are becoming, however, I believe that these programs can be made even more relevant to students who identify themselves with groups which traditionally have been marginalized by the academy. What I envision for English studies at the doctoral level is that faculty who teach, mentor, and examine doctoral students invest themselves more intensely in helping them negotiate professional roles which resonate more closely with the students' own goals and values.

I return to the reciprocal premises that inspired this essay: the relevance of English studies to African American women and the relevance of these women to English studies. After all that I have said earlier, I do want to emphasize that it is crucial for African American women in doctoral programs to understand not only the conventions of disciplinary discourse but also its cultural, political, and rhetorical dimensions. I wouldn't have been able to publish this essay if I hadn't taken these things into consideration. However, it is also crucial for Black women to understand how these considerations might interface with the conventions, cultural positions, political agenda, and rhetorical power of the other discourses they wish to bring to bear in their lives after graduation. *I believe that graduate programs owe their students specific education in understanding and exploiting that interface.* As I have tried to show, by telling stories about myself and my sister graduate students, our personal and professional lives are vitally dependent on such knowledge and insight. I am inspired in this endeavor by remarks from Joy James and Ruth Farmer in an eloquently titled book, *Spirit, Space, and Survival: African American Women in (White) Academe:*

> We write because unless we as African American women shape a reality, and make a space for ourselves to creatively share our stories, education remains an elitist, White and/or male domain. Writing by, and not simply about, African American women is part of taking our space to challenge a stultifying hegemony and work to develop academe. (1993, 3)

I see two areas that faculty in English graduate programs would do well to consider as they open their doors ever more widely to students from a diversity of cultures: (1) how they equip students to contend with the grounding assumptions of academic discourses, and (2) how the particular discourses that define English studies—those of literature, rhetoric, composition and pedagogy, folklore, critical theory, creative writing, and so forth—are constructed so as to facilitate or inhibit the ability of these students to make meaningful contributions to those disciplinary communities.

On the consideration of academic discourse generally, it is important for graduate faculty to appreciate the continual negotiations that students must undertake in order to navigate the social and intellectual territory that discourse conventions map out for them. Patricia Bizzell raises some important points in this regard:

> Some of the conventions that enable academic discourse to generate and test knowledge through consensus and debate are: agreement on a standard language, Standard English, as the medium of discourse; familiarity with "common knowledge," or a standard range of literary and historical allusions, terms that have transcended their disciplines, and so on; employment of specialized vocabulary specific to the kind of problem addressed (disciplinary vocabulary); employment of a method for defining the problem to be addressed, a method predetermined by disciplinary practice; employment of a predetermined method for generating and applying evidence; employment of a predetermined method for judging the plausibility of the argument advanced. Members of the academic community win their intellectual freedom by submitting to discourses conventions. The community is continually straining its own bonds of unity by encouraging debate, but its members' training in certain conventions of debate helps in turn to reestablish those bonds. (1992, 140)

I consider these points to be sites of resistance for those who seek enfranchisement in a given disciplinary community. Such conventions are problematic for those who have been considered outsiders because in certain respects these conventions have been developed without significant input from the range of cultures that are now claiming enfranchisement in the academy. African American women in doctoral programs are intelligent and savvy enough to seriously question the notion of "common" knowledge, the de facto restrictions on the range of literary and historical allusions presented to them, the implications of the specialized vocabulary, methods, lines of reasoning, and evidence that work well for some audiences and some topics, but not for others. They see a need to challenge the very *predetermination* of these factors because they can easily envision the danger of being co-opted into a hegemonic institution before they ever get a chance to become agents for dismantling that hegemony. I'm reminded here of an old saying: *It's not that we want a larger piece of the pie; we want to change the recipe for pie.*

Much of what I've interpreted over the last few years as academic "debate" involving scholars of color has been manifested in the selection and validation of one or two nonmainstream voices in journals, at conferences, as faculty hires, to represent a presumably univocal "minority" perspective that can be "handled" by the mainstream without significantly disrupting the status quo. Meanwhile, I see that a range of diverse subjectivities is continually waiting in the wings for a chance to be recognized. I propose that, to a large degree, conformance to predetermined (ask: By whom?) academic conventions has served a gatekeeping function, screening out those whose writing betrays them as "outsiders"—unrefined, lacking in rigor, "angry," undisciplined (in both senses: untrained and rebellious). While the personal narrative has become somewhat more common in recent years, a personal stake in a subject under discussion translates, for the establishment, into the failure to be "objective." The extensive use of narrative as a framework for building a case is branded as the inability to construct a "rational" argument. The insertion of words, phrases, and sentence structures borrowed from nonacademic discourses is decried as corruption of "Standard English."

Bizzell further states that community members' training in the conventions of debate helps in turn to reestablish community bonds. What must be recognized and interrogated is how those conventions are the constructions of certain cultural and political perspectives but not others—how those bonds might keep the community from extending itself to welcome people with divergent views. Given that the terms of debate have been defined by generations of academics who have objectified, marginalized, and in many cases excluded non-White, nonmale perspectives, Black women who aspire to become full-fledged members of the academy have to decide whether to accept the terms of the debate and, by doing so, risk becoming bonded to the source of their oppression. If they choose to accept the challenge of entering the debate, they must then consider which strategies would enable them to productively engage in those debates without feeling that they are selling themselves out.

Narrowing this general discussion to the particular context of English studies, I turn to Bizzell once again. She asserts that "by entering a discipline, one commits oneself to looking at experience in the particular way established by that discipline" (1992, 149). However, students and faculty must be aware that uncritical acceptance of a discipline's vision may actually put these women at a disadvantage, if that positioning forces students to assume roles that trivialize their own vested interests with regard to their scholarship, teaching, and community activism. I think that many Black women are drawn to the disciplines of English studies because they can see the potential of these disciplines as sites of empowerment for themselves and for those to whom they will ultimately reach out. They recognize important opportunities for interrogating and reenvisioning the canon, critical perspectives, rhetorical theory, writing pedagogy, language development, and so forth. At the graduate school level, as I have said earlier, these opportunities reside in interactions with faculty, in coursework, exams, and dissertations, as well as in invitations to publish and to make conference presentations.

This brings me, finally, to the challenge I see facing English graduate programs which welcome African American women into their scholarly community. That challenge is to invest equally with these women in the agendas which bring them to these programs in the first place. In order for students to feel confident about using all of the discursive resources at their command, they need the assurance that their professors are cognizant and appreciative of the alternative ways of knowing and being which they bring to their acts of composing. Further, engendering these students' trust also means developing strategies for helping them as writers to exploit effectively their culturally rich resources in composing texts designed for academically oriented purposes and audiences. In sum, faculty readers should prepare themselves to encounter the texts of their doctoral students in ways that make it more likely that genuine communication is taking place between culturally different but equally enfranchised people. It is a matter of reading to understand the writer as well as the text.

Works Cited

Belanoff, Pat. 1993. "Language: Closings and Openings." Pp. 251–75 in *Working-Class Women in the Academy: Laborers in the Knowledge Factory*, ed. Michelle M. Tokarczyk and Elisabeth A. Fay. Amherst, Mass.: University of Massachusetts Press.

Bizzell, Patricia. 1992. "Academic Discourse and Critical Consciousness: An Application of Paulo Freire." Pp. 129–52 in *Academic Discourse and Critical Consciousness*. Pittsburgh, Pa.: University of Pittsburgh Press.

Bowser, Benjamin P., Gale S. Auletta, and Terry Jones. 1993. *Confronting Diversity Issues on Campus*. Newbury Park, Calif.: Sage.

Collins, Patricia Hill. 1991. *Black Feminist Thought: Knowledge, Consciousness, and the Politics of Empowerment*. New York: Routledge.

De Veaux, Alexis. 1995. "The Third Degree: Storming the Ivory Tower." *Essence* 25.12 (April): 68+.

Henderson, Mae. 1994. "What It Means to Teach the Other When the Other Is the Self." *Callaloo* 17.2: 432–38.

Holloway, Karla, and Stephanie Demetrakopoulos. 1986. "Remembering Our Foremothers: Older Black Women, Politics of Age, Politics of Survival as Embodied in the Novels of Toni Morrison." *Women and Politics* 6 (Summer): 13–34.

hooks, bell, and Cornell West. 1991. *Breaking Bread: Insurgent Black Intellectual Life*. Boston: South End.

James, Joy, and Ruth Farmer. 1993. *Spirit, Space, and Survival: African American Women in (White) Academe*. New York: Routledge.

Smithson, Isaiah. 1994. "Introduction: Institutionalizing Culture Studies." Pp. 1–22 in *English Studies/Culture Studies: Institutionalizing Dissent*, ed. Isaiah Smithson and Nancy Ruff. Urbana, Ill.: University of Illinois Press.

Literacy, Classrooms, and Students' Lives

PATRICIA SHELLEY FOX
DONALD L. TINNEY
CRISTINA KIRKLIGHTER
KATHLEEN R. CHENEY
SARAH ROBBINS
JUANITA RODGERS COMFORT

Patricia Shelley Fox

I suspect that each of us in the profession has shared a version of this familiar experience: One is introduced, on some social occasion, as a teacher of English to someone who—eyes widening as he sees that he has an "expert" in his grasp—asks, through pursed, what-is-the-world-coming-to lips, the question that is not a question: "Do they still teach . . . grammar? . . . spelling? . . . sentence diagramming? . . . Shakespeare? . . . all or any of the above?"

At such moments I often find myself tempted to respond with the line that a priest friend reports his spiritual advisor delivered to him in his early days as a seminarian. The young man, in his fervor and eagerness to get all things theological correct and clear in his mind, came to see his advisor on this particular day full of pointed and earnest questions. After entertaining the first few, the advisor stopped him on the next, in mid-question, with a simple caution: "Your God is too small," he warned. And I find myself wanting to say precisely this to my new acquaintance, to say, "Your vision of our work is too narrow."

As Bob Dylan reminds us, you've "gotta serve somebody." And so the question arises, in our profession as English teachers:

Who or what is it that we serve by the particular version of English we teach? Are we experts in linguistic etiquette? Gatekeepers? Technicians? High priests and priestesses of the canon? Is our purpose to clean students up? To hold them back? To get them ready? To fill them up? Or is our purpose none of the above, all of the above, or something else altogether? Do we serve institutions or individuals? Neither or both in turn?

When Kathleen R. Cheney hopes "to encourage reading, analysis, discussion, and writing that [will transfer] to the experience outside the classroom"; when Donald L. Tinney—believing that to "define the mission of [his] work" is "to declare the meaning of [his] life"—sees his English class as a community in which "the poem can be written or discovered . . . the raging heart can be released in prose . . . students can see themselves as learners, as readers, as writers, as storytellers, as citizens . . . as human beings"; when Sarah Robbins invites us to consider "making English studies relevant by linking curriculum development to a proactive brand of personal and communal literacy"; when Cristina Kirklighter urges us to designate our classrooms as spaces "that allow students to play out the relationships between concepts they confront in academia and the experiences that shape their lives"; when Juanita Rodgers Comfort asserts that "many black women are drawn to the disciplines of English studies because they can see the potential of these disciplines as sites of empowerment for themselves and for those to whom they will ultimately reach out"; I am struck by the sense we share of the depth and breadth of our common mission.

It seems to me that the stories of teaching that we tell illustrate that what each of us serves is an idea of literacy in action, of language as an instrument not only of self-creation and community creation but also of social transformation. Each of us sees the teaching of English as a progressive, liberatory project and defines a common need to serve students by engaging ourselves and them in acts of critical literacy. In turn, what each of us seems to be resisting is an idea of English that is too small, while at the same time we are all grappling earnestly with the question of who or what it is we serve, a version of which Robbins insists we continually pose in an exercise of Freirean praxis, reflection upon action: Why are we doing this?

While our inquisitors, both publicly and privately, often seem to yearn for us to serve a small god, as English teachers we resist such reductive urges. We know that language as a basic instrument of human communication is irreducible, and each of us reckons that we have larger moral, ethical, and intellectual responsibilities to ourselves, to our students, and to the world we share. Such responsibilities require a measure of discomfort, of uncertainty, on our parts, along with a willingness to engage in dialogue with our students and to see our roles broadly as partners in meaning making rather than narrowly as arbiters/experts of linguistic etiquette or as guardians of a particular canon. Seeing the relevance of our work in expansive rather than myopic terms, we all recognize that we meet our students on what Dewey calls "the experiential continuum"; our work with them at any given moment is informed by our sense of both our individual and our collective pasts, as well as by our visions of the future. And because we have a sense of language as instrumental in shaping the outcome and the quality of human lives, we have visions of literacies put to the service of both our individual students and the communities in which we all live.

Donald L. Tinney

As writers in this particular collection of chapters, we share a strong commitment to creating opportunities for our students to develop the skills and strategies necessary to become participants in the larger community. While our approaches may vary, I believe we have properly emphasized the need for leading our students to become active citizens. Without an active citizenry, democracy will die. Kathleen R. Cheney defines this underpinning of English studies when she points out that her students "need to learn how to learn; they need skills that allow them to access ways to be informed, to support their development as participatory citizens empowered to act through their ability to use language as a connection to community." To be participants in democracy, our students need to find their voices and generate their own authority, enabling them to discover their own powerful selves. Citizens in a true democracy do not wait for permission to act.

In describing her student Fran's experience, Patricia Shelley Fox sees Fran's bold moves of studying her own story alongside other feminist texts as "a measure of her having gone beyond silence, beyond received knowledge from appointed experts, to become an expert in her own right, a connected knower able to affirm her own voice among many as one who has light to shed on a complex situation, but finally, no easy answers." Is this not our common goal for all students? I want all of my students to tell and study their own stories alongside those written by published authors. How else will they affirm their own voices? Each one of our students has light to shed on complex situations. As teachers of English, we must take the responsibility for learning what each and every student needs to know to become what Adrienne Rich calls a "self-conscious, self-defining human being." If students cannot see the connection between their stories and the stories of other people, other cultures, and other times, how will they ever be able to make the necessary connections between their own lives and the lives of other people in their community and across the planet?

In this section, we have all emphasized the importance of valuing our students' stories along with stories from the canon and elsewhere. This blend contributes to the relevance of English, for it allows students to grow and expand their self-definitions. Patricia Shelley Fox presents evidence from her students that further articulates this point:

> It is students like Fran and Margaret, Willa and Karly, students I never expected to find, who, because of their rich, complex, and often contradictory life experiences, enrich our work and the conversations in our classrooms. Their voices, both written and oral, tell the stories of their encounters with ideas and texts that, often for the first time, offer them (and those of us who work with them) ways of seeing and naming women's lives that allow them to make sense, to lay claim, and to move forward.

Can we afford to doubt the relevance of English studies when English teachers are engaged in work that allows their students "to make sense, to lay claim, and to move forward"? Sarah Robbins and her colleagues encourage their students to move forward by linking their curriculum development to a proactive brand of personal and communal literacy:

> By linking our students' initial efforts to identify *what* they wanted to research with an exploration of the multiple ways others in the larger culture were already examining those issues, we hoped to help class members being to see that literacy acquisition involves more than learning facts, that is also requires learning socially constructed methods for using language to communicate and to foster change.

We need to be sure that our approaches to teaching enable students to learn how to communicate and how to foster change. We need to see our own responsibility in being part of the larger community, ensuring our own relevance.

English curricula and English classrooms will continue to change in the new century, for we will continue to redefine literacy, along with its related standards, and we will continue to attempt to meet the needs of a diverse and growing population. The social, political, and economic tensions will not disappear, but will instead probably grow more intense and more complicated as our population increases. What will remain constant? What piece of English studies must remain relevant? Cristina Kirklighter explores this question in her chapter. She writes,

> With all the distant battle cries about standards, literacy, and pedagogical reforms, where, in this turbulent stew of national politics, is there room to test what is "good and clean" at the bottom of our English studies pot?

At the bottom of the pot is a simple truth: teaching is an act of pure, unselfish love.

When Cristina Kirklighter explains that "the powers in the act of love come when we can relinquish a part of our agendas so others can be heard," she articulates what all of us have discussed in our chapters about allowing students to discover their own voices, their own authority, their own stories—the same kind of "genuine communication" Juanita Rodgers Comfort calls for among graduate students and their teachers. Kirklighter wonders what others in academe might say if she uses the act of love as the center of her pedagogical scholarship. I believe that we must have the courage to allow our students to love us. If we are more committed to our own comfort than to our students, then we will not risk loving them and will simply train them to analyze literature and train them to score well on the next standardized examination.

Our communities face too many challenges today to allow the next generation to grow up feeling disconnected and powerless. They need to believe that they are important to their families, to their communities, and to their world. If they don't see themselves as agents of change, as gifts and contributions to the world, then all the information from the Internet and elsewhere and all the high-tech literacy skills will be nothing more than a combination of amusement and consumption.

The relevance of English is up to us.

Cristina Kirklighter

In Donald L. Tinney's essay "The High School English Teacher: A Relevant Member in a Good Tribe," he calls upon English teachers to emphasize stories as a way to connect with the lives of their students. In the spirit of Tinney's request, I must respond to his essay by telling a story.

Once upon a time not so long ago, I remember, as a student, taking a class on Emily Dickinson. In previous semesters at another school, I took several classes revolving around Victorian women and feminist theories, so I was anxious to share my knowledge and stories with this professor. I diligently studied her poems, carefully weaving in my personal experiences and academic knowledge. I came prepared to share my genuine narrative interpretations. I came equipped to participate in a tribe valuing communal student-teacher knowledge such as Donald Tinney describes in his essay. However, I soon realized, after a few classes, that not everyone belongs to the same tribe. My professor belonged to another tribe that believed in one interpretation of a text, and this interpretation came from him. As the semester progressed, the once eager student slowly lost her enthusiasm to share her thoughts concerning this nineteenth-century writer. Emily Dickinson became a lifeless literary form that held little meaning for me in the classroom. Instead, she and I shared our private thoughts in the quiet chamber of my mind. I gradually withdrew from actively participating and watched passively as the professor shared his one-way love of this great poet. Tinney seems to know such a professor when he says, "Far too many adults today do not read, simply because literature was ruined for them in the high school or university English class." Love for literature is not a one-way street that moves from the professor to the student but a two-way street where both students and teachers can share in this love of storytelling.

Tinney speaks about those in communities who fear this storytelling, who believe that children and adolescents have no right to define themselves in relation to what they read in class. I must tell Tinney that there is a community of English professors who carry this belief to the university level as well when teaching adult students. These professors are afraid to love and to be loved. Somehow they learned from their predecessors that professors were the knowledge makers and students were the recipients of that knowledge. Unfortunately, this mind-set eventually created arrogant and insecure professors who teach under the delusion of superiority. This unhealthy mind-set can often extend beyond the classroom and harm their relationships with colleagues, family, and friends. Like Tinney, I often wonder why and how teachers could lead such self-centered and detrimental lives in and out of the classroom. As I watched certain professors, I always vowed that I would not carry this burden of consuming authority. I vowed to create a healthy teaching environment not only for my students but for myself as well. Oftentimes, I hear those who promote a healthy environment of shared classroom knowledge and stories say that they create such a classroom for their students. I cannot profess to be so benevolent. Just as my students want to be loved, I want to be loved in return. I want my students to share with me this love of teaching. Love is indeed a two-way street.

Although I felt unloved in the Emily Dickinson class, she came back to visit me via one of my students in a first-year writing class. I noticed that this particular student, Arthur, never said much in this particularly lively class of students. The class and I more or less accepted Arthur for his quiet demeanor and one-word responses. For most of his life, he was a loner, and he shared his past solitary existence with me through his papers. In his writings, Arthur was ambivalent about both his experiences in solitude and his shared life with a significant other. Both had their positive aspects and drawbacks. It came as no surprise to me when he asked to write a research paper on solitude. This is the story that Arthur knew best. Just as Tinney's student needed to write about her experiences with foster homes, Arthur needed to write about solitude. Drawing on the personal was, in Tinney's phrase, their shared "extraordinary source of personal power." After class one day, Arthur and I talked about possible literary figures who would complement his topic. I mentioned Emily Dickinson, and Arthur's eyes lit up with recognition. Arthur had an "extraordinary source of personal power" that could knowingly speak about Dickinson's poems of solitude. I would never deprive him of sharing such a personal knowledge with me, and I looked forward to gaining his insight on her. In the conclusion of his paper, Arthur came to a realization that he could never return to his solitary life and feel quite the same about it. He missed sharing his love with another. Before I read his writings about solitude, I often wondered why a loner would sign up twice for a class like mine that so obviously engaged students in collaborative activities and discussions. Could it be that not many of us want to teach or learn in isolation? Could it be that even loners like Arthur realize this in their passage to adulthood?

Arthur, in some ways, redeemed the loneliness I experienced as a student in the Emily Dickinson class. The anger that I felt towards the professors who plunged me into solitude subsided into sadness for what was lost in those classrooms. The sadness is alleviated, however, every time I enter a classroom where students and teachers lovingly share the stories that mean the most to them. This is the happiness that comes with love.

Kathleen R. Cheney

A recent issue of *College English* included an article that focused on the dilemmas faced by instructors when students submit personal writing (Dan Morgan, "Ethical Issues Raised by Students' Personal Writing," *College English* 60.3 [1998]: 318–25). In particular, the author discussed student writing that is confessional in nature and, therefore, creates complex problems: how to respond to the students' experiences, how to present effective feedback about the quality of the writing, and how to promote critical thinking so that the writing helps the students make sense of the world. Of course, these concerns are usually part of the challenge of teaching composition, but they become more complicated when the focus of the writing is of a personal nature, is self-disclosing. Yet I believe that facing this complication is worth the struggle. I am not arguing for confessional writing. My classroom is an English classroom, not a guidance office. However, I do think that writing which comes from, focuses on, or intersects with the students' lives plays a critical role in my teaching.

Therein lies a connection with the chapters in this section. Although the writers' ideas are framed differently, each author expresses a deep concern for and an active engagement in empowering students. We seek to validate our students by creating learning environments that invite connections—between students, between teacher and students, between students and communities, and between the particulars of students' experiences and the abstract ideas that the academic world explores.

Our chapters emphasize the powerful role personal lives play in the learning process. We write about "celebrating the diversity of our students' interests, needs, and abilities" (Robbins). We speak of creating opportunities for them "to recall moments in school and out of school that tell their stories as people who live with and through language" (Fox). We explain how we invite them to learn "how to become storytellers" so that "their stories will enable them to define their own lives" (Tinney). We promote a human pedagogy that seeks to "understand the writer as well as the text" (Comfort). And we identify our need to promote literacy in ways in which "our personal experiences are never far from our research and teaching practices" (Kirklighter).

How many more students might I help if I recognize more effective ways to bring their life stories into the classroom? I am reminded of Charlie, a nontraditional student I met in my early years of teaching. He was returning to school to gain a career direction after several years of prison life. In his composition course I had selected gender issues as a theme, with the readings, discussions, and writing assignments focused on it. Around the third week of the semester, that theme and my invitations to explore the numerous aspects of it became for Charlie a site of increasing frustration rather than a site for learning. We were discussing paper drafts when Charlie's frustration turned to blatant hostility and anger. He exploded. Grabbing his backpack with its weighty contents of books, he threw it over the heads of fellow students and out the door, all the while shouting at all of us and especially at me. Hurling expletives at me, he indicated that he didn't need the "damn course!" He raged out of the room. Several days later, under conditions required by the dean of students, he apologized to me and returned to class only to drift away from all courses within three weeks.

Compared to the events of late in our schools, Charlie's outburst was mild. No one was hurt, the semester continued, and at least some students in that course improved as writers. But then there's Charlie. Did Charlie fail, or did I fail Charlie? He represents a disturbing and growing problem in our educational institutions. Increasing numbers of students bring to our classrooms a sense of alienation. They feel marginalized, as revealed in their passivity or their hostility. How do we connect with them? How do we create ways for them to connect to the world? How do we nurture their sense of empowerment? How would I handle that situation today?

Rather than my imposed focus, I would invite Charlie to select his own from the complex material of his life. I'm sure he had a life full of stories, rich and raw. The challenge would have been to get him to respond to an invitation to write from these resources. Carefully selected reading material could have contributed to his thinking and enabled him to choose an appropriate and useful focus for his writing. Suitable essays and the stories of others could have diminished his sense of isolation and feelings of being different, making it safer for him to share. I would encourage him to reflect and to sort out, to make sense of the conditions of his life. Perhaps the most challenging approach would have been to encourage Charlie to write, not just record, and to affirm his life in ways that reflect and critically evaluate not only his personal experiences but also the society in which those experiences happened. These personal narratives would give testimony to his life and create a text through which his voice could be heard.

My struggle and my joy is to have my teaching be personal—to create a learning community in which our messy, complex, often unsorted lives rich in raw material can be molded and shaped by us, composed into experiences, thoughts, opinions, and understandings that validate, invigorate, and empower.

Sarah Robbins

At the beginning of a recent academic year, as faculty and students across the University of Georgia system were just returning to classrooms, our chancellor was being interviewed by a reporter about essential instructional goals at the turn into a new millennium. In response to a question frequently asked in our state, a question about the "relevance" of university study for career preparation, the chancellor made a joke (at least, he swore later that it was a joke) about the *ir*relevance of subjects like "English" in a region known recently for stressing "jobs skills development" in institutions ranging from college on down to pre-kindergarten. The response of English teachers who wrote to chastise the newspaper's report, who joked in faculty gatherings about the "irrelevance" of their work, or who chose to shrug off the snafu entirely, was most notable, I think, for its lack of intensity and commitment. Even those who rose to the defense of "English" seemed to settle for trotting out familiar platitudes about the relevance of our field in terms of such "life skills" as "critical thinking."

Certainly, I agree that English can promote critical thinking, and I likewise affirm the benefits of connecting our discipline to the very practical/instrumental tasks of "real life." But more particularly, reading the stirring collection of pieces in this cluster of our anthology has underscored for me that we who "do" English, as well as the students and educational decision makers who guide our work, could profit from hearing more stories like these—stories that argue for honoring the personal as a step toward creating and sustaining the communal, both in the classroom and in the larger society.

I would call these essays themselves "personal *and* communal" because one of the strands running through them is a simultaneous insistence on valuing individual students (their diverse, particular needs, interests, expertise) and on valuing community building in the classroom. As is too seldom the case when we talk about curricular goals, the writers of these essays bravely wear their beliefs on their sleeves; specifically, they take the risk of implicitly defining "English" as "different" from other subject areas because of its dedication to acknowledging and developing *feelings*—a messy business indeed, in these days of quantitative "accountability" models.

Cristina Kirklighter, for instance, boldly asserts "that the personal represents the heart of Freire's teachings and writings," and her construction of "democratic goals" for the classroom places more emphasis on "an act of love" performed by teachers and students than on the more instrumentally political ends we often hear discussed by educators drawing on other elements of Freire's oeuvre than the hopeful, caring pieces Kirklighter chooses. Toward that end, Kirklighter is more than ready to hold back from defining specific "concepts" for her students to master academically so that she can instead leave "spaces" for their "testimony." The testimonies they share are not simple exercises in self-absorption; these teaching/learning moments are even more important for the way they highlight possible connections, opening up "the way for classroom humanity" based on community building.

The need for "establishing connections," in fact, is at the heart of both the philosophy and the practice guiding Kathleen R. Cheney's efforts to give new meaning to the "community" of "community college" as an English learning site. Cheney recognizes the practical motivation that brings most of her students to college: "believing that a college degree . . . will open doors otherwise closed to them," they come to Cheney's English classroom seeing a "college education" as their pathway into "a better life . . . in some yet unknown *field of work*" (emphasis added). For Cheney herself, however, this "better life" will be achieved not simply by getting a job, but also by becoming "informed partici-patory citizens," by learning "how to learn," and by "establish-ing connections." Seeing her classroom as a microcosmic space where students learn "to speak up, challenge, and in general take risks that will allow their voices to be heard," Cheney clearly hopes that these experiences will make the classroom an "envi-ronment in which there is . . . human connection," a harbinger for similar communal interaction when students have completed her English class yet not left its lessons behind.

Similarly, Patricia Shelley Fox, writing about the particular needs of one group of nontraditional university learners—return-ing women students—calls for making their English course learn-ing relevant by supporting their development of both personal and professional literacies. Telling stories of two particular stu-dents, Margaret and Fran, Fox shows how both are eventually able to make more sense of their lives in part because their learn-ing of English invites them to weave personal experience, response, and reflection into new ways of reading their world—ways that highlight new possibilities without sugar-coating the challenges. For Fox (and for Margaret and Fran), "to make sense, to lay claim, and to move forward" involves learning in an English class-room that is open to sharing of individuals' "rich and complex life experiences" in ways that generate shared understandings about ourselves and our relations with others.

So what is the role of the English teacher in such a class-room? Certainly not simply to teach pragmatic skills, nor even to promote more complex analytical abilities. It is also (and most crucially), as high school English teacher Donald L. Tinney as-serts, parental. Tinney unabashedly declares that the construc-tive social responsibilities of English teaching are the most important, and that carrying out those duties requires an empha-sis on communal caring—providing the "support and assistance" students need in order "to feel loved and accepted" so that they too can become proactive members of "the tribe."

Unfortunately, as Juanita Rodgers Comfort's moving essay illustrates, students do not always find such nurturing "support and assistance" in English studies classrooms. Comfort's inter-views with graduate students, alongside her own reflections on personal experiences in graduate courses, are synthesized into a compelling story about the challenges African American women can face in classes where the professor is not committed to "helping them as writers to exploit effectively their culturally rich resources in composing texts" and/or is not "cognizant and appreciative of the alternative ways of knowing and being which they bring to their acts of composing." To emphasize the culturally productive systems of value, belief, and practice which the students she interviewed brought to their graduate English programs, Comfort juxtaposes their "vital spiritual lives" and their commitment to social activism with the more limited vision of literacy learning represented in academic documents like a red-pen-marked paper and a syllabus whose purportedly inclusive moves smacked of tokenism. Calling for an English studies that would welcome the relevance of African American women in the university and the larger society, Comfort affirms the quest to help students "develop rhetorically useful identities"—a sense of self that would not force individuals from diverse backgrounds "to leave one community in order to enter another," but instead allow them "to reposition themselves in relation to several overlapping and often conflicting communities." If the painful experiences Comfort describes make us doubt that we will ever be able to guarantee that all students feel welcomed and nurtured in English studies classrooms, we can at least celebrate the fact that the women she writes about are themselves educators for the future—in colleges and in the community.

Taken together, the personal visions of English teaching delineated in this cluster of chapters brim with a self-confidence and commitment sometimes lacking among teachers in our field these days. They inspire us with their willingness to center "English" as much in shared feeling as in the acquisition of skills, and they challenge us with their promise to value those aspects in our work that are as difficult to measure quantitatively as they are essential to living in a genuinely communal "tribe."

Juanita Rodgers Comfort

Periodically, I teach an upper-division composition pedagogy course that is part of our department's teacher preparation curriculum. I also facilitate a graduate colloquium for teachers of college-level composition. At the beginning of every semester, I ask all my students the same fundamental questions: Why do you want to teach English? Why invest *your* professional and intellectual energies in this endeavor, especially at a time when (English) teachers are some of our most underpaid and underappreciated professionals? Almost without fail, whether undergraduates or graduates, most will dance around these questions. Their first, most facile, and most impersonal, response is usually "because students need 'English' in order to 'succeed' in life outside of school." To which I always respond, "Why—why do people need to study this subject called 'English' in order to 'succeed' in life? Just what does it mean to 'succeed'? And why do you *personally* feel inspired to teach this subject? What will make *your* acts of teaching matter?" Here many students get stuck, and, even for me, with teaching experience that spans almost fifteen years, the answers aren't always easy.

In my experience, so many preservice teachers and graduate teaching assistants, and even a few inservice teachers and college professors, approach literature, composition, language studies, creative writing, and so forth with the rather simplistic idea that these areas of study are "gifts" that teachers bestow upon students. As the recipients of these gifts, students are supposedly well equipped to master life's challenges. But in my view, literacy education is *negotiated,* not bestowed, public school teachers and college professors are not the only ones who shape the content and method of English studies, and students deserve a rightful, respectful place as co-constructors of their own learning. This stance, of course, resonates strongly with the spirit of "the profound liberatory experience of encouraging all participants in the pedagogical dialogue to share their lives of studies in relation to the world" to which Cristina Kirklighter makes reference in her chapter on the relevance of Freire.

Reading through all the chapters in this section, I was of course struck by both the distinctive and the resonant ways in which the authors attend to the question of why English studies is or should be relevant. But the authors, both individually and collectively, also address, albeit perhaps a bit more obliquely, a question that I had posed in my own chapter: *What is the relevance of our students to English studies?* Put another way, in what ways might the groups of students represented by these chapters make significant contributions to the scope, function, and influence of English studies? Our stories focus on a broad range of students and classroom situations:

- eighth graders in a middle school,

- students in high school English classes,

- students in a basic skills program at a community college,

- nontraditional women students in first-year composition,

- international students in a literature class,

- Black women pursuing doctoral degrees in English.

My reading of these stories suggests that, by asserting their needs and expectations, their experiences, values, and imaginations, their frustrations and at times their rebelliousness, students at all levels of education challenge us to reexamine and reconfigure our theoretical underpinnings, our canon, our interpretive schemes, and our instructional methods. Each group of students, in its own way, gives teachers and scholars the impetus and direction for reconceptualizing English studies in light of our present society's social, political, and cultural diversity. Patricia Shelley Fox asserts, for instance, that returning women in first-year English bring "a new kind of text and a new kind of reader into our classrooms, one who comes poised . . . to do the real intellectual work of the academy, and who in many cases has already begun to do so." She further points out that "[b]y challenging our inherited cultural narratives—of schooling, of domesticity, of womanhood, of individual freedom—they work within and among the competing discourses in their lives to offer us an oppositional world view." Certainly, the extent to which we teachers and scholars are responsive to such contributions from students helps to determine the shape that English studies takes. Donald R. Tinney taps this very concept of responsiveness when he invokes the value of literature as a heuristic for self-discovery. "[Students] also need to learn how to tell their own stories, how to become storytellers," Tinney asserts. "They need to find their own voices and they need to be heard. Their stories will enable them to define their own lives. They need to be able to say, 'This is who I am.'"

As a result of our collaboration with students, it is they, ultimately, who decide what, and how, English studies mean, as they apply the fruits of their literacy negotiation in their daily lives. I can think of numerous instances in which people extend critical reading, writing, and speaking, as well as appreciation of texts, well beyond the classroom walls. Many look forward to sharing meaningful works in reading groups. They purchase (or borrow from libraries) a wide variety of fiction and nonfiction works, and they support their favorite authors by attending readings at local booksellers. Quite a few write memoirs, family histories, letters, and creative works. In the workplace, they compose or supervise the composition of numerous corporate and public documents. As citizens and consumers, they write to legislators, corporations, and newspaper editors. As parents, they pass along their appreciation for literacy to their own children, reading to their toddlers, giving older children books as birthday and holiday presents, teaching them how to write thank-you notes, and practicing any number of other kinds of literacy.

Those of us who go on to become teachers of English will contribute even more directly to English studies by bringing those same kinds of sensibilities to bear on the legitimization, discussion, and production of texts in our classrooms. We are inspired to rethink our teaching philosophies and classroom practices as we grow more responsive to student perspectives. Those of us who also become scholars launch critical inquiries into the production and consumption of diverse texts. We then incorporate our insights into the scholarly conversations generated in the pages of our professional journals and essay collections like this one. We read our colleagues' work and respond with even more sophisticated work that eventually constitutes the framework of our discipline.

This brings my remarks full circle. One possible way to follow up the question I posed at the start of this response—"Why invest in teaching English?"—may be to ask pedagogy students to read these chapters and consider how involving themselves along with their students in negotiating the terms of their studies might be worthy of a personal stake in being a teacher of English. The stories told by my fellow contributors do more than address the relevance of English studies for their students; I sense that the teachers who have told these stories have, in collaboration with their students, substantially reshaped the field itself.

PART III

FUTURES: ENGLISH STUDIES FOR THE NEW MILLENNIUM

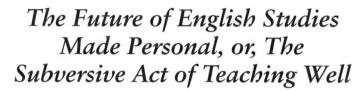

The Future of English Studies Made Personal, or, The Subversive Act of Teaching Well

VALERIE HARDIN DRYE

Concord High School, Concord, North Carolina

As April pushes up new life again, dotting the trees along my drive to work with more shades of green than even my box of sixty-four crayons could reproduce, I am reflecting on the new life I have chosen at the not-so-spring-like age of forty-five: I am an English teacher, nearing completion of my first year. For me, April has always been my true New Year's month; January may bring imperceptible increases in daylight, but the cold, dreary days of midwinter do little to lift my spirits. Now, I feel myself surging forward, as restless as my students who, prematurely sporting tank tops and shorts, shiver in the early morning air before the first bell. Yet even as we rush to get to that last bell on that last day, I shiver with the uncertainty of what the last bell will bring. Yes, I'm finishing my first year. But do I want to come back in the fall? Is there a future in this profession for me? Is there even a future in English studies as I've come to understand it? Answering these kinds of questions is never easy, but given how far I've come to get to this point, the very fact that I can ask them at all is troubling. Perhaps if I better understood why I am here, the answers would become clearer.

As the mists of the April morning burn off to reveal a cloudless sky, I am reminded of my first teacher, my father. This April marks the sixty-sixth anniversary of his birth—and the fifth anniversary of his death. From him, I learned lessons to last a lifetime. Sitting warm and safe, wrapped in his arms as we watched thunderstorms crash across the valley, his voice murmuring both mythology and meteorology, I learned the awesome power and beauty of deadly forces—and how stories could enhance perception and understanding. Walking mountain trails, my short legs struggling to keep up with his long strides, or scaling the sides of water falls behind him, terrified that I would slip and fall, I learned to take wider steps and to risk dangling over chasms—both literal and metaphorical. I also learned to trust the guidance of those more experienced, to rely on a calm voice, a steady hand, encouraging words.

If my father had not taught me to open my eyes and see the world around me, I would have missed the sparkle of mica-studded pebbles in a rocky stream, the mystery of caddis fly larvae hidden beneath river rocks, the subtle glide of a snake whose sunbath we'd disturbed, the smell of sweet brush, the taste of sassafras. No matter where we went, my father taught me to respect the natural order—and care for it. Toting a garbage bag, we'd pick up trash others left behind. Blaming others was pointless: if something needed to be done, you did it. Cleaning and repairing the rental homes we lived in or fishing broken bottles out of the streambed—both summed up one of his most important lessons: Leave the world a better place than when you found it.

Alongside the lessons, there were always his stories. And books! He loved to read, both silently and aloud to his children. Often, he couldn't resist reading a passage from one of the many books he read for his own pleasure. Over the years, as he shared his books and stories, his rich bass voice wrapped around words as luscious as cold plums, he gave me a world beyond the confines of the western North Carolina mountains where we'd both been born.

Today, as I think back on my early apprenticeship, I'm surprised I did not come to this place in my life sooner. But in the smug self-assurance of adolescence, I thought I knew what I wanted. Believing I had endured enough of school to last a lifetime, I told myself that the academic route suggested by all my teachers was definitely *not* for me. Instead, I started down the marriage/motherhood/work-at-minimum-wage-jobs path. It didn't take long to realize my mistake. Deciding what I didn't want—to be someone's secretary for the rest of my working life—was easy. Searching for the more positive "What do I *want* to be when I grow up?" (not to mention solving the "How do I get there?" dilemma) has proven to be more difficult.

I knew I was being tugged gently toward the things I loved the most—whatever I chose, it would involve reading and writing. My favorite teachers, after my father, were my English teachers and the one math teacher who let us work in cooperative groups (before that label was used) and *write* about math in our notebooks. *(Julia Lappin, Sharon Shaw, Betsy Copollillo—if you are reading this, then know that you have my eternal gratitude for giving me the tools to live life more fully and bring myself to this point today.)* Reading and writing have been keys that unlocked countless doors in my own imagination. Magic carpet rides to treasure islands, adventures down rabbit holes and through Orc-infested tunnels, glimpses of worlds beneath the sea and beyond the stars, voyages back to the dawn of humankind or forward to our future—I boldly went where so few of my students now dare to go. Writing has given me the means to reflect on my own thoughts, to literally write myself out of confusion and into new insights, to turn my own daydreaming into stories I can share with others. For ten years, as I worked full-time doing the clerical work I despised, I plugged away at a bachelor's degree in English—one course at a time. Although I still didn't know I'd be teaching high school, I knew I'd find a way to use what I was being taught. If anyone had asked me then if there was a future in English studies, my answer would have been, "Absolutely!"

When, finally, I walked down the aisle clutching my diploma, I knew I would be moving on to master's work. Choosing between the Unitarian Universalist ministry and teaching wasn't easy, but once I'd made the choice I realized that the two careers aren't so far apart. Both are calls to serve, both require a sense of mission. As I progressed through my master's program in writing and rhetoric as a graduate teaching assistant, I grew more and more excited. In addition, I began the secondary licensure process. All my classes introduced the latest in teaching and writing theory. All the texts spoke of successful teaching practices. The journals I subscribed to, the conventions I attended, the other students I spoke with—all painted the picture I wanted to believe: Not only was there a future in English studies, but the future of our students, life, civilization, and the world as we know it *depended* on dedicated English teachers wielding the best that educational research has to offer, i.e., on *me!*

I wasn't totally naive (so I thought). After all, I had teenagers at home (although, since I'd read to them since they were babies, they'd continued the family habit of voracious reading—not exactly a representative sample of the teenagers I was preparing to work with). I'd listened to them speak negatively about their teachers and sighed as grade after dismal grade turned up. Later, as I began taking education courses, I did some observations that caused my belly to flutter in a burst of anxiety: How was I going to handle *that?!* Yet I was still confident. I can do this. I can learn. They will learn. They *need* what I and English studies have to offer. This will work.

Mine wasn't the only voice of reassurance or inspiration:

> The vision guiding [the NCTE/IRA] standards is that all students must have the opportunity and resources to develop the language skills they need to pursue life's goals and to participate fully as informed, productive members of society. These standards assume that literacy growth begins before children enter school as they experience and experiment with literacy activities—reading and writing, and associating spoken words with graphic representations. Recognizing this fact, these standards encourage the development of curriculum and instruction that makes productive use of the emerging literacy abilities that children bring to school. Furthermore, the standards provide ample room for the innovation and creativity essential to teaching and learning. They are not prescriptions for particular curriculum or instruction. (Smagorinsky 1996, viii)

Key to this passage for me was the "ample room for . . . innovation and creativity" and the reassurance that the standards are not intended as "prescriptions." I have always been the kind of person who cringed at the words, "But that's the way we *always* do it." I look at a task and see endless possibilities (some more—or less—practical than others, admittedly). The teaching profession seemed tailor-made for me, particularly English, with its emphasis on process and individual ways of knowing and creating. NCTE again stressed teachers' prerogatives in selecting what works best for their classrooms, their students, in the Standards

Consensus Series volume *Teaching the Writing Process in High School*:

> The day of know-all, tell-all books is past. Student populations differ; cookie cutter activities simply don't work in every classroom environment. Most significant, teachers know their own students and have sound intuitions about the kinds of ideas and materials that are and are not appropriate in their classrooms. From this solid collection of materials, teachers are invited to select, discard, amplify, adapt, and integrate ideas in light of the students they work with and know. (National Council of Teachers of English 1995, viii)

In addition to the view of teachers as informed professionals, capable of exercising their "sound intuitions," what appealed to me as much—if not more—was the notion that kids *need* the literacy skills I can help them acquire. They "*must* have the opportunity and resources to develop the language skills they need to pursue life's goals and to participate fully as informed, productive members of society" (Smagorinsky 1996, viii; emphasis mine). I spoke earlier of wanting that sense of mission, to quite literally change the world for the better, to do as my father taught me: "Leave the world a cleaner, better place than when you found it." However, I wasn't content that I should be the only custodian here—I wanted my students to pitch in as well. Other English teachers shared my fervor. One in particular, Randy Bomer, provided the headnote for my teaching portfolio:

> Students' memories are the raw material from which they make meaning. By bringing experience to their reading and writing, they can forge a deeper and more precise understanding of themselves and their social and natural world and then take that deeper understanding with them, away from the text and the classroom, to help them live more thoughtful, examined lives. I can't enter the realm of language and meaning and remain value-neutral; my project is to collaborate with my students to make them and me better people in a better world. If that's idealism, well, something has to get me up in the morning and make me aspire to be good at my life's work. (Bomer 1995, 15)

My exuberant response to Bomer's words: "I want to be like that when I grow up!" I, too, wanted something to "get me up in the morning." I wanted more than just a job; I wanted a "life's work."

So I got one—a life's work, that is. Or, perhaps, it's gotten me. I have struggled through my first year as a lateral-entry teacher of tenth-grade English. Lateral-entry: Trial by fire. Sink or swim. High wire without a net. Pick your own metaphor. I walked into my first classroom in August with no teaching experience at the secondary level. No student teaching. No supervising teacher. I wanted to save the world (or at least clean it up a bit) and inspire my students to do the same, but what I got was sixty-five to seventy fifteen- and sixteen-year-olds for four and a half months (twice), few of whom seemed interested in anything I had to say. As if that wasn't scary enough, I was supposed to present them with World Literature (you mean the one literature class I *didn't* take?), and—more importantly—prepare them to take the North Carolina Tenth Grade Writing Test. It took a few months for me to realize that, with six sections of tenth graders, I was personally responsible for close to *50 percent* of the school's writing test scores—one of several measures that were taken into consideration by the North Carolina Department of Public Instruction's Office of Accountability and the ABCs, which, taken together, constitute a school's "report card."

Now, in case I'm losing sight of my original mission here—to answer the question "Is there a future (for me) in English Studies?" —let me invoke Randy Bomer once more. In part, his words, which I discovered in the heady days of my participation in the University Writing Project's Invitational Institute, inspired my vision of how my own future classroom might work. Yet, even as I'd read of his successes, I'd also gotten to the part where he walks away from teaching high school and returns to the world of the university. He left because teachers were being "stripped of autonomy and thus of purpose in their work with students," because the administration's push for a uniform curriculum made

> every classroom look like every other. Every teacher's desk was piled high with binders articulating objectives, units, formative and summative evaluations, and other papers no one read, leaving formerly strong-willed educators dazed and baffled. . . . Student's faces were erased. Teacher's names were erased. Student's

names, if they ever had been written, were erased. This was not why I went into teaching. I left to avoid erasure. (Bomer 1995, 221)

Bomer quit teaching kids and moved to Teacher's College, where he works with their Writing Project, teaching and consulting with other teachers. His vision hadn't worked in his district, yet here he was sharing it with other teachers (including me). Before my first year of teaching at the secondary level, I downplayed the significance of his retreat. Now, I'm not so sure.

I look at the bookshelf here next to my computer, and I see a binder labeled "North Carolina's Standard Course of Study" next to other binders containing unit plans I've created, all tied neatly to those state standards. Next to the bookshelf are two file boxes filled with Tenth Grade Writing Test stuff: prompts, matrices, scoring guides, planning sheets, and boxy layouts for the "five-paragraph theme" (the one I'd worked so hard to move my first-year college students away from in the comp class I'd taught!). As I think back over my first year, I remember my pacing guide, the one that looked so much like the other tenth-grade teachers' pacing guides. To my jaundiced eye, the memory looks pretty grim. An essay a week for twelve weeks until they took the test. We stayed away from any other (substantial) kind of writing (frills) until after the test. With one exception in one honors class, we read only those works proven for their ability to provide fodder for a variety of writing prompts. There wasn't time to worry too much about history or culture or diversity or multiethnic voices or *anything that smacked of being authentic or meaningful;* I just made sure that enough of them could follow the format so that a high enough percentage were at or above grade level and our school would not only meet its required growth expectations but might also be labeled *"Exemplary"!* I helped keep the vultures from the Office of Accountability off our backs for one more year. Maybe we'll earn a little extra money to compensate us for the fact that we're already miserably underpaid as it is.

At our New Teacher's Orientation, when I first heard what I was expected to do as a tenth-grade English teacher, I panicked. I'm afraid I also made a few comments about the "dreaded five-paragraph theme" that would have been better left unsaid. Who was I, anyway, an upstart, lateral-entry type who hadn't even paid her student-teaching dues, to be criticizing what the more experienced teachers had created in their best attempt to raise test scores? *I* hadn't been sweating the low scores, the "report card" in the local papers, and the very real threat to the teachers and administrators that poor performance constitutes. No, *I* had come from that false reality, the world of academia, where college professors feed us the stuff of theory and fantasy. College professors who either never taught in a *real* classroom or, if they did, had lost touch with what it's like to be *out here in the trenches.*

I bridled at the comments, biting my tongue *most* of the time. Yet as I frantically moved from day to confusing day, trying desperately to figure out "What do I do now?" I found myself questioning the value of much that I'd gone through at both the undergraduate and graduate levels, even while I questioned the value of what I was putting my own students through. Here I was, the product of today's English studies, ready to pass on the torch to the youth of the world. And I couldn't be sure if the flame remained bright enough to chase away the encroaching darkness.

My students reflected my uncertainty. "I don't mean no disrespect," one young man began early in the fall semester as I went over the writing test format for the umpteenth time, "but when am I ever gonna need this stuff?" *You? Probably never,* I thought, but hastened to list all the benefits of being able to organize and use examples to support a claim. He was one of several boys in my class who had already failed tenth-grade English once. Raised by a single mother doing her best, he came from a poor, rural culture that taught him to settle his differences with his fists, never to show weakness, and to hold school and teachers suspect. I wish I could say I'd been able to turn him around, but his behavior swung between lethargy and open defiance. His attendance was sporadic. He came by my office a few times to seek help (a rare occurrence!), made an effort for a couple of classes after each visit, and then disappeared for days.

What I had to offer this student was not what he needed. Once, early on, when I'd put up some kind of focus prompt about our reading that was designed to get us into another five-paragraph essay, he ignored the prompt and just began writing. I'd taken the risk of sitting down in the middle of this rather difficult and boisterous class to write and, for once, this helped to settle everyone—including him—for a few minutes. This is part of what he wrote:

> I don't know what's wrong with me lately. My mom's worried and I guess she has a right to be. Ever since the wreck I can't seem to keep my mind on anything. I thought I was gonna die and now I hurt so bad all the time I keep missing school its like I can't sit still for too long or something. Its not something I can talk about to anybody, especially my mom. But that wreck did something to me. I know I'm not stupid but I just can't seem to get it together. I don't want to hurt my mom so I guess I got to try harder. Sometimes, though, I get to feeling like I'm about to bust and I want to hit something. It helps to get all this down—makes me feel a little better.

Of course, I realize that this young man needed counseling and drug treatment—measures beyond the scope of my classroom (he *was* referred for more help). The tools I *could* have offered him—more opportunities to write about things important to his life, reading at a more appropriate level about a character with whom he might have identified—were denied to me, because I had to teach to a test.

This boy was one of the lost ones, those few who seemed hell-bent on failing regardless of how many chances I gave them to pull themselves out of the holes they dug for themselves. I suppose I could write off his resistance to that unavoidable low end of the curve, but even my best students were frustrated. Jennifer, who routinely received the highest scores on her practice essays, loved to write—and she loved me: seeking me out in the halls or at lunch to chat, giving me a hug when I was down one day, politely hounding me until I made the time to sign her annual, confiding both her fears and dreams to me. She was my staunchest supporter in a large, highly verbal, sometimes rebellious honors class. Yet one day she asked, "Mrs. Drye, why is it when I write about something I really care about and spend a lot of time on, I get a lower grade than on these other essays? I don't even know why I'm getting better grades! I mean, I'm following the format and doing what you told us to do, but I don't like any of what I'm writing. I don't think it's very good."

She was right. I was using the state's scoring guide and pushing them all to churn out five-paragraph essays—with all the requisite parts—that were just under two pages. It was on-demand writing that didn't allow much time or room for creativity or depth or practicing the recursive process supposedly valued by our curriculum. I had a room full of bright, talented young people, many of whom enjoyed some other forms of writing. They did need to learn expository writing, because all of them planned on going to college. However, based on my college experiences as student and as teacher, I knew that the times they'd be asked to write a five-paragraph theme in one hundred minutes would be limited to essay tests (rarer now with larger classes and the use of Scantron sheets) and that some poor first-year comp instructor would have to spend half a semester moving them beyond the rigid format I'd just drilled into them. I kept thinking there had to be a better way to teach this, a way that made sense to my students (and me!), that was more than teaching them to "fill in the blanks," as my own son described the process after he'd taken the Tenth-Grade Writing Test (and made a "6," the highest possible score).

In addition to the format, which unfortunately does encourage most students to fill in the blanks rather than think about how their essays should connect logically, the prompts ask questions that I'm not sure my students are developmentally capable of answering. No matter how much we talked about how to answer questions like, "What is the impact of x on the overall work?", most of my students could not see the "work," the story, as an abstract idea made concrete by an author's choices. Authorial intentions, to their still egocentric way of looking at the world, were beyond most of their grasps. It was as if the story world was still "real" in their minds and things happened in the story because of the characters'—not the author's—actions. And in perhaps another indication of a worldview still very much centered on their own experiences, most of my students chose texts they had liked (therefore remembered) to use on the test, regardless of the texts' suitability for the prompt.

Consider the Spring 1999 prompt:

> Authors often use settings and details to create a dominant mood
> or atmosphere (overall emotional effect of the piece) in a work of
> literature. Identify the dominant mood and explain how the set-
> ting and details establish this mood, affect the characters, and
> impact the overall work.

If we teachers had done a good job and discussed the *mood* of at
least one of the works we'd read, our students should be set. (We
won't even get into the fact that our faculty's unofficial analysis
of the last several prompts showed that the state seemed to be
moving away from focusing on purely literary terms, and, as a
result, we had decided to spend less time focusing on them.) When
I saw the prompt after the test began, I cringed. Yes, I'd discussed
mood, but not as intensely as I knew many of my regular students would have needed to remember enough to respond to this
prompt. Even after our discussions, most students still confused
the mood an author tried to establish with the moods of the characters.

I'd been rather more pointed with my honors class during
our reading of Erich Maria Remarque's *All Quiet on the Western
Front* and, later, as we reviewed the day before the test. Several
of my students had not liked this book (finding it a difficult read)
and commented that they certainly wouldn't use it on the essay.
Reminding them of our earlier discussions about how the author
used his descriptions of setting to establish the horrific mood of
the novel, I cautioned them not to rule out anything until they
saw the prompt. Even with that prophetic statement (and I swear
I hadn't seen the prompt!), most of these same students chose to
use another work; only eight out of twenty-five students used
Remarque's novel.

The same thing had happened in the fall. When I read that
prompt, which asked, "How does the desire for power or wealth
affect the characters, action, and overall work?" I was ecstatic,
knowing that my students couldn't help but use Anton Chekhov's
short story "The Bet," which we'd read in *all* three classes. Many
had neither liked nor understood it very well, but it was perfect!
So why did half of them refuse to use it, making garbled messes
of their essays in attempts to use other, more favored works?

One can tell from reading my students' responses to the mood
question that the notion of how a particular device affects the

overall work is still foreign to many of them. One such response: "The mood [of hope] is important to the overall work because if Gerda had not thought about what her parents told her, she would have drank the poison and died." A similar inability to step back from the story world is evident in this response: "The [sad and dreadful] mood affects the overall work greatly. Without this mood to keep Ilse and Gerda going, they might have died, or committed suicide, along with many others." Still others reflect an attempt to parrot back *something*, if only to show they'd seen the prompt: "The dominant mood of the work kind of makes the novel. The mood is very important to the overall work because if the depressing and sad parts of the novel weren't there then the novel wouldn't exist."

Granted, I'm touching on some of the more problematic responses. Several of the essays, particularly from my honors class, reveal thoughtful application of the format, understanding of the text, and appropriate response to the prompt. Others, from both honors and regular classes, reveal acceptable responses to at least parts of the prompt. All essays, even the three that simply summarized the plot, showed that I'd managed to teach them the format well enough for them to show they'd seen the prompt and were at least making an attempt to organize a five-paragraph expository essay. By all accounts, the increases in my students' test scores from my first to second semesters show that I was getting a feel for how to prepare my students to take the test. But what else was I teaching? What else were they learning? And was this what I'd amassed a yearly income's worth of student loans to do?

During the spring semester, as I watched the students struggle with that "impact [on] the overall work" concept, I reflected that one of the reasons my students weren't understanding authorial intent was that they'd had too little opportunity to be authors of their own creative work. Most kids (and adults) learn best by doing. I, and a handful of the more insightful students, can talk all day about why an author wrote these particular words in this particular way, but to the majority of my students the information either doesn't make much sense or must be memorized for later (possible) use on a test. I harkened back to my desire to include a writing workshop, with authentic writing opportunities, in my classroom and wondered if that would help prepare my students for the test better than this endless stream of responding to canned prompts.

When I approached my principal about trying this out, her first response was that I should wait until after the test. When I pointed out that I believed such a move might increase their test scores, she cautiously approved my idea. Now, I must ask this question: All you advocates of accountability, standardized curriculum, and standardized assessment, please tell me how we can continue to support a system where the criteria for whether or not I do something in my classroom is whether it will improve their test scores and not whether it will improve my students' ability to learn and understand what it is to be a reader and a writer.

Unfortunately, I did not have time, as late as it was, to implement my ideas until after the test. I decided to use the final five weeks as a trial run for the next time I taught tenth-grade English. During those final weeks, I developed a genre study that, ideally, would have students both reading *and writing* short fiction, poetry, and memoir. I had them each begin a writer's notebook and offered them a variety of suggestions on how to use it that encouraged them to be observers of themselves and their world, to record their observations and reflect on them. I tried to offer them more choice in their reading selections and prompted them to begin looking at their reading as writers, not as test takers. They developed their own characters, settings, and plot (limited by the too-short time span) and experimented with several poetic forms. Working in groups, students selected a poem to use in a Microsoft PowerPoint presentation, explored how to convey the word images using visual images, and researched the author's life and times for a research report.

The project was much too ambitious for the last five weeks of school. Following the intense preparations for the writing test, we all were tired and suffering from spring fever. Spring break came two days after the test. Who of us really wanted to expend that much energy when the end was so near, especially following a whole week away from school? But I still had twenty-five more days of ninety-minute classes to get through, and I wanted my students (and myself) to come away from our semester together with something more than five-paragraph essays to show for it. So I made some adjustments to the work requirements—and my own expectations. At times it was chaotic, because I was learning how to do this even more than my students were. Except for moments of supreme frustration, I was having fun, and, when they weren't too frustrated and bewildered, so were (most of) my students! Even more important, they were learning some of what I wanted them to learn—and some things I hadn't even planned on.

Josh benefited from the freedom to choose his reading material. He commented on the short story "The Devil and Daniel Webster" by Stephen Vincent Benét: "It's been awhile since I've read anything outside of school, and I must say that I liked it." Not having to match his insights to what he thought I or my teacher's edition would test him on, he felt free to express his own opinions. "I believe Benet could've made his story a little more interesting if he would've thrown more detail into the trial. He [sic] use of specific arguments or anything used, he just kind of summed the whole thing up (basically putting the smallest amount of detail into what seemed to me to be the most important part of the story)." Josh used his writer's notebook frequently as a journal, often writing at length, and often quite eloquently. Although he may have had some difficulty expressing what mood or metaphor a given story expressed, he demonstrated his own understanding of those concepts in an entry about a rainy day:

> It's raining outside. I really love the rain. It's so soothing for me to just drop what I'm doing for a couple of minutes and just sit still or lay down and listen to the rain falling. I always prefer a rainy day over a sunny day. Rain just seems to fit my personality more. I'm usually laid back and easy going. I have a large amount of patience, and I'm usually pretty soft spoken, though I can be firm and fierce at times just like the rain! . . .
>
> I think it's odd how often in horror movies they use rain as an effect. They'll use it to add horror or suspense. Maybe when most people think of rain, that's what they relate to and envision . . . but not me! . . .
>
> I couldn't imagine living in a place where there was hardly no rain at all! Rain seems to wash bad times away. So . . . I see it not only as a way to benefit the earth, but as a kind of therapy or replenishment for the creatures which live on it as well.

Had he written this earlier, before the test, I could have used this as a perfect "teachable moment" not only for Josh but for his classmates as well. As it was, I didn't see it until the end of the semester.

There were other entries I wish I could have read much earlier. It amazes me what students will write, when given the opportunity. Many of my students opened themselves up to me in ways they never would have done in front of their peers or in conversation. One girl who'd flatly stated the uselessness of the reading and writing we were doing also used her writer's notebook as a journal. A couple of her entries refer to the time she'd gotten pregnant, then lost the baby in a miscarriage. The character she'd created in her short story shared this experience; I'd wondered, when I read earlier drafts of the story, if she'd had firsthand knowledge of this situation. Now I knew.

Another entry speaks of her father's angry yelling and about how her mother tells her to "just let her father get everything out. See the only thing bad about that is I can't just listen to somebody yell at me when I haven't done anything or I'm right." She goes on to describe how much it meant to go out to eat with her family one night when "we actually put everything behind us and talked. It made me feel good for a change that my dad wasn't yelling at me or putting me down." Although she's tightly wrapped up in her own experience, she adds a valuable insight: "Looks can be deceiving and a lot of people think my life is all hunkie-doorie but behind closed doors it's really not everything everybody makes it out to be."

Soon, this student may be ready to see that this same insight can be applied to other people, even her angry father. And in the context of the short story she was developing, these entries provide rich material for talking about the pros and cons of using autobiographical material, considering the difference between fiction and memoir, exploring point of view, characterization, motivation, effective use of dialogue—and the list goes on. She, like any author, possesses experiences that can bring life and shape to her characters. And once she begins to sort out the difference between putting something down because "This is the way it happened" and doing so because "This is the way *I* want to tell the story," she will be much more capable of understanding the impulses behind another author's work. Again, just as with Josh, the material, the revelations, the keys that might have broken through some of that tough, disdainful exterior came too late for me to do anything but sigh over missed opportunities.

Of course, not every student bought into my enthusiastic, end-of-the-semester project. Joe's final reflection is, if anything, honest:

> In January I didn't like reading nor writing and I still don't like reading nor writing. This English class is the most boringnest class I ever have took. I hope English next year will be better. I would change everything because I did not like this project. My blank verse poem was my best because its about a farmer. I learned that writing is very boring and I don't want to be a writer.

Well, the world needs farmers just as much as it needs writers— maybe even more. I wish I'd had longer to work with Joe on the value of using writing as a way to think and express ideas—even if only for oneself. The poem he mentions *is* his best work. Titled "A Farmer's Day," it touches on images of worth to him:

> Dust from the hay balers fills the
> air on a hot summer's day.
> The beaming hot sun bears down on us
> farmers as we walk through the field
> picking up hay.
> At the end of the day, we are wore
> out from a hard day's work.
> We look forward to a hot shower,
> and a big home cooked meal.
> Then we have to rest up because
> there's another long day that's
> waiting for us.

I didn't see it until a few days before the final version was due and, by then, revision was the last thing he wanted to hear. Given an expanse of weeks instead of days, I would have encouraged him to add the visual images, the sounds and the smells locked up inside his head. I would have tried, at least, to show him that he doesn't have to be "a writer" in order to write about things he

cares about in a way that he can point to with pride in acknowledging his authorship.

Another boy in Joe's class, who would never have considered
himself a writer or poet—ever—nevertheless crafted a poem similar to Joe's. Josh surprised me with his poem "Country Boy Can
Survive" when, based on his previous in-class performance, I had
been sure he would turn nothing in:

> I see the dust from the plows
> Stirring up a hot summer's day.
> As the farmers are wore out from
> A hard day's work, the kids still
> Run, jump, and play.
> Through this day so much sweat
> Has come and gone, but the farmers
> Always work from dusk till dawn.
> I look back in the distance to see
> My house on the hill top, to smell
> Country ham and cornbread which
> Only we have on Sundays.

Now, I suppose this poem would never be published anywhere
but on these pages, but there's a certain simple beauty about some
of the lines, and there's the potential for adding details in the
missed opportunity for revision that could have transformed the
rest of it. Even without the revision, however, Josh was transformed by the act of writing it. I could see it in his face, when he
asked me to look at his (late) work. "Did you see my poem?
Ain't it good?" he asked. Yes, Josh, it certainly is.

Despite the stumblings and grumblings of those last five
weeks, I believe many of my students will remember the work
they did then far longer than the twelve-week grind leading up to
the test. Because I didn't get the completed portfolios until the
end of the grading period, I was unable to return them by the
time students left for the summer. Many wanted to make sure
they could pick up their material in the fall. The only question I
got about the essays, in contrast, was "Can we throw these away
now?" Did the students learn more in the last five weeks? I think
so, but I can't quantify that; we simply ran out of time. My vision needed a whole semester to grow and develop. Next year, I

decided, I'd combine the genre project with the essay work, allowing them time to revise fewer essays while learning something more about the craft of writing and *being* a writer. I'd start with the writer's notebook and use them to develop a better understanding of my students as individuals. I'd . . .

But I'm not teaching tenth grade next year. I've taken a position in another school district closer to home, as a ninth-grade teacher. Kids a year younger, different texts, different end-of-course test. Yes, a North Carolina, state-mandated, standardized test. Part of the ABCs. In this new job, I haven't been given *the* suggested way to run the class or been given the freedom to select my texts and shape my own pacing guide. No. It's worse. I have been presented with a departmental pacing guide which was created expressly to cover the material students need for the test. I must use *Romeo and Juliet* and *Night*. I do have the latitude to select another novel as well as the short stories and poetry I will use in those specified units. Again, I have to ask myself: Do I really want to keep doing this? Is there a future for me in English studies, given the trend of accountability and standardized testing?

If mine were the sole voice of discontent, I'd have to say "I quit!" But it isn't. In the July 1999 *English Journal,* the issue of standardized testing's chilling effect on the ability of teachers to make professional decisions in their classrooms is discussed in three separate articles. Robert Scholes's (didn't he write one of those hard-to-wade-through, full-of-theory textbooks I'd used in one of my college classes?) speech to the NCTE Spring Conference Secondary Section Luncheon is reprinted in that issue. He, in fact, mentions North Carolina as one of the states being held up by Diane Ravitch as a shining example of improved test scores because, Ravitch says, we identify "'what is to be taught and tested in each grade'" (qtd. in Scholes 1999, 30). Scholes's response sent me on a mad scamper through several drawers to find a functioning highlighter:

> If you announce what will be on the test, and teachers then teach to the test, you can get better scores. But what has this got to do with whether students are actually learning anything more than how to get a good score on this particular test? (30)

Indeed.

Scholes goes on to warn about how the use of a *required* text "forces that text into the realm of commodities—and also into the realm of the detested" (31). He likens standardized testing to sausage making,

> that is, they don't bear much looking into if you want to go on consuming the product. But what die in the slaughterhouse of academic testers are not hogs but works of literature. . . . In sausage-making, it is what goes in that is worrisome, of course, but in testing, the problem is what is left out. (31–32)

This may sound corny, but the more I read (and highlighted in bright yellow), the more excited I grew. I even found myself on the verge of tears as I read the words of a person I'd thought was one of "them" (that is, too academic to be of help in my real world). He spoke of how we needed to find ways to speak and write about literature that were "less artificial, closer to the lives of our students and ourselves, and just less phony" (34).

On the dangers of viewing literature through the screen of literary terms, Scholes warns that we are "turn[ing] the poor student off and driv[ing] many of the others to find the answers in Cliffs Notes, whether online or in books, instead of reading the work and trying to discover what it may have to say to them as human beings" (34). By playing it "safe" in our world of literary terms and devices, he continues,

> we are losing the game. The great works of literature are worthy of our attention only if they speak to our concerns as human beings, and these must take precedence over the artificial concerns of symbol, tone, and irony. [These], after all, are only devices, or ways of talking about technique. We need, and shall have to find, better ways of talking about what these works mean and how they connect to our lives. (35)

How wonderful it is to find other, weightier voices speaking the same language!

I won't go into the other two articles at length; rather, I will offer a gem from each to tantalize you into delving more deeply on your own. Joan Naomi Steiner, a past president of NCTE, writes of the value of the decisions we teachers make in our class-rooms and of the dangers we face as standardized curricula and assessment curtail our ability to make those decisions. She asks the same questions I'm asking: "I ask," she concludes, "that you put yourself in the place of your students. Look at your class-room. Look at your teaching. See what your students see. Are we doing what we can to promote learning, or have we succumbed to a test-prep curriculum?" (Steiner 1999, 40).

As if in answer to Steiner, Sue Ellen Bridgers (1999) follows with an article about "the value of story" and finding "meaning in the world through language" (42). As an author of what we call "young adult fiction" (as opposed to *real* literature—the kind they test you on), Bridgers stresses the value of creating young male and female characters who are authentic and who will in-spire their readers to a richer existence. "Times are changing," she states. Now that we're in the new millennium, we teachers need to remind ourselves that the students who pass in and out of our classrooms are literally *our* future. She continues:

> In a time when the earth's resources are so fragile and our legacy of care for each other feels so inadequate, we can encourage our young people to tell their own stories. We can help them find mindful stillness. Their gifts are not meager ones. Their hearts are open. I hope the work we do reflects our confidence in them. Who knows but that when we help one, we are helping many. (47)

Amen. There's that sense of mission I want, that life's work Randy Bomer speaks of. The potential, it seems, is still there—to do something worthwhile, to make a difference. Not just in the lives of my students, but in my own life as well. I still want that. The threat to *my* vision of the future of English studies, however, looms as dark and ominous as a heavy thunderhead on the hori-zon. The evidence is there, in conference topics and journal ar-ticles: a major storm is brewing between the forces of accountability and standardization and those of us who believe that the teaching and *doing* of reading and writing must con-tinue to be a creative, collaborative act between teachers and teachers, teachers and students, students and students.

Wistfully, I find myself longing for the little-girl comfort of my father's voice as I begin another year of blundering through a new curriculum and trying to make sense of something that just doesn't make much sense. At times, I come close to identifying with Bomer's fear of erasure and wonder how long it will be before I, too, flee the halls of secondary education. But I've got this stubborn streak. I'm not going to let the state's Office of Accountability or the growing stacks of binders surrounding my computer keep me from pursuing my dream. There's got to be a way I can play the game, get my kids over the testing hump *and* do something worthwhile with them—while I work with others to change the system.

It may take some time for me to learn about teaching English what all good writers know about writing: learn the rules, and then *break them!* The way I see it, teaching well in the midst of a testing frenzy is a subversive, radical, rebellious act. I will neither walk away nor let the focus on accountability force me to kill the life that English studies can offer my students. I just have to stick around and keep getting better at what I want to do. That will be my revenge.

Works Cited

Bomer, Randy. 1995. *Time for Meaning: Crafting Literate Lives in Middle and High School.* Portsmouth, NH: Heinemann.

Bridgers, Sue Ellen. 1999. "Notes from a Guerrilla." *English Journal* 88.6: 41–47.

National Council of Teachers of English. 1995. *Teaching the Writing Process in High School.* Standards Consensus Series. Urbana, Ill.: National Council of Teachers of English.

Scholes, Robert. 1999. "Mission Impossible." *English Journal* 88.6: 28–35.

Smagorinsky, Peter. 1996. *Standards in Practice, Grades 9–12.* Urbana, Ill.: National Council of Teachers of English.

Steiner, Joan Naomi. 1999. "From Sense to Soul." *English Journal* 88.6: 36–40.

CHAPTER THIRTEEN

Cybrarians and Scholars in the New English Classroom

TED NELLEN

Alternative High Schools Superintendency, New York City

When I ask a question in my class, everyone provides an answer. All of my scholars are fully engaged for the entire class. I call my scholars *scholars* because I want to instill in them that high ideal of scholarship. The word *scholar* connotes high expectations, great intellectual capacity, and respect. It shows that I respect them and expect great things from them. They interact with each other on a scholarly level. They think about the work they are doing in my class, even when they aren't in the class. My scholars stay up late because they can't go to sleep, and they wake up early because they have to engage a thought. My scholars are so happy to be in my class that they don't leave when the bell rings.

"Ted, Ted! Wake up! You've overslept! You're going to be late to school, and it's the first day of school. Get up! Get up!" coaxed my wife, as I slowly opened my eyes.

"Oh shit!" I grunted as I realized the gravity of her words. Teacher dreams always end so abruptly. What were those images that were flashing before my eyes? Were they just part of a dream, a fancy? "Gosh, were it possible," I contemplate as I roll out of bed with a yawn.

"And turn off the alarm," begged my wife, as she left the room.

Late on the first day of my second year in this new school. "Great! This is just great!" I muttered as I stumbled to the shower.

"What a beautiful dream I was having," I thought as the water beat against my face and I slowly gathered my faculties and prepared for this first day.

"Bye, Daddy, I'm off to school," groaned my daughter from somewhere inside the fog. "You better hurry up, you don't want to be late."

"Yeah, yeah, thanks, sweetheart. Have a good first day of school," I answered.

"Dad, that's a good oxymoron," she responded.

"Love you, smarty pants," I retorted.

The door slammed. I shaved, lathered up, rinsed, and I was out of there. Thank goodness I laid out my clothes last night: right now I couldn't make any decisions like what to wear.

"You're not wearing that tie, are you?" queried my wife.

"No, I just wanted to see if it might work," I countered.

"Oh, well, it doesn't. Let me help you," she said as she went into my closet and found a better tie. "Here, try this one." She handed me a better tie.

I was not late to school, but I didn't have time to say many hellos as I arrived at the first bell. This was the first day of the 1984 school year. My supervisor met me as I entered the English Department office and handed me my schedule, saying, "Ted, I want to show you your new classroom."

"What's this?!" I exclaimed, as I stared at a room filled with computers.

"We've been given this computer room, and the principal and I decided we wanted you to use this room."

"But I don't know how to use a computer. I don't want to use computers. How can an English teacher use a computer anyway?" I stuttered.

"You will. You have to. You'll learn," she replied and left.

I sat down in one of the chairs. I wanted to cry. I wanted to quit. I wanted to wake up. As I sat there, I thought about why I even wanted to teach.

I became a teacher because I had had a terrible education. I had more teachers who hurt me than helped me. My worst experience was in third grade when I was publicly humiliated by my teacher. My fourth-grade teacher was gentler and kinder. Middle school was a nightmare. For high school my parents sent me to a New England prep school. I developed into a jock and that was what got me through. Although I graduated last in the class of 125 scholars, I was still admitted to college. Instead, I enlisted in the army in September 1968. I did this because I would have flunked out of college and would have been drafted. It was at this point that I took control of my life. While in the army and in Vietnam, I read everything I could find. I fell in love with Shakespeare. I read *Troilus and Cressida,* and I was hooked. I read more Shakespeare and much of the American literature canon, it seemed. I reread stuff I must have read in school but didn't remember. I took some correspondence courses. When I entered college, I was ready. I completed the first year at the top of the class and transferred to another college. Then I decided to be a teacher of English.

While I was in college, our school instituted a January intersession. During one of these intersessions, I took a course that was to change my life and my thinking about teaching forever. It was a bookbinding course. We made a book of poetry. I chose to write five haiku. We then went through the process of printing the work onto handmade paper, using inks we had made and a hand printing press. Next, we took the printed paper and bound it into handmade books, hand-sewn with handmade covers. Upon completion of our half dozen tomes, we hand-delivered them to a local bookshop, where we left them for the spring semester. At the end of the spring semester we went to the bookstore to retrieve our unsold copies. I recovered only two books and about $10, my pay for the sold books. This experience brought an epiphany that was crucial in the work I was to do in my career. I had been in total control of my work from the conception of the haiku to the delivery to the bookstore. It was a complete process, in which I did everything I could to create myself in another form, the book. That someone else bought the book was amazing. I had an audience of someone other than my teacher. So it has become my quest to provide for my scholars that same opportunity.

I began teaching in 1974 in a New England prep school. I eventually ended up teaching at my alma mater. Even though I was a traditionalist and very conventional, I used performance, oral presentations, group work and murals, and multimedia activities—photography, art, music—in combination with the obligatory paper to let my scholars submit their work. I left the prep schools to teach in a New York City public school. Now, as

I stared at these computers, the reasons for changing my environment were not important. I felt I was about to lose all of those possibilities and uses of multimedia I had been developing over the past ten years. Visions of Ned Ludd flooded my brain as I wanted to lash out. The bell to start class brought me out of my trance.

I spent the first day in a stupor as five classes came and went. I explained to the students that we were going to be using these computers in our English class this year. Thank goodness these classes were only twenty minutes long. I had only enough time to take attendance and didn't have time to explain how we were going to do this. I couldn't explain how. I wasn't ready for this.

I had spent the summer contemplating the inefficiency of the traditional classroom and preparing to make for a more efficient classroom. I hadn't even considered the effect computers would have on learning. I had read in my graduate classes that scholars learned best by doing and by teaching others, while listening to lectures, which, ironically, was how most information was delivered in my graduate classes, was the least effective means of promoting student learning. My goal was to create a classroom in which all of the scholars *did*. Computers, however, didn't fit into this scenario—not yet, anyway.

Looking to the Past

I see the traditional classroom and most schools geared for the status quo by teaching to the middle. Top students are bored and become listless, as they always have to wait for "the class" to catch up or finish the work before "the class" can move on to the next assignment. These students are often lamented over later as having such great potential that is wasted by their dropping out or just never quite achieving what they might have. In addition, the students at the bottom of the range are also lost, in this case for the sake of the class's "moving on." These students are in a constant state of frustration, taking up most of the teacher's time and creating the most distractions in the class. Thus the traditional class allows for the loss of those at the top and bottom of the range of student abilities, all for the sake of teaching to the middle.

Perhaps the greatest problem with the traditional class is that not everyone participates or learns in this teacher-dominated, sit-in-rows kind of classroom. As an example, let me use our typical New York City public high school class—one which is probably reflective of many classes across the country. We have forty-minute classes with no more than thirty-four scholars per class. When I do the math, I see each scholar getting about one minute of instruction each day in each class. I arrived at that number after considering the six to eight minutes it takes to set up and to break down: taking of attendance, setting the lesson, and giving homework. In the remaining thirty-seven to thirty-nine minutes, the teacher has to ask the question and get a response from each scholar without incident, prompting, or other distraction. The problem is that scholars don't respond in succinct answers, they don't hear or understand the question all the time, and they don't all participate; they need coaxing. Consequently, not all scholars are actively involved in their own instruction. They can find a way to hide behind the high-performance scholars, and eventually a handful of scholars become the major respondents and participants in the class because the teacher has been programmed by the "scholars" to rely on the handful of active scholars so as to get through the class and to look good—especially when an outsider like a supervisor or principal enters the classroom. Just walk the halls of any school or sit in any class in any high school, and you will see or hear this. The traditional classroom is not efficient or conducive to effective education for all. It serves the status quo, however, very well.

The above scenario was my experience when I entered a New York City public high school English class. Trying to hear from those who never spoke or participated, and trying to ignore those who moaned and frantically waved their hands, I was frustrated by how programmed these scholars had become. I had to find a way to alter this state of affairs. The first thing I tried was to break the large class up into smaller classes. So I created four groups. Doing that became a science unto itself. Using any kind of alphabetical arrangement, or letting friends form, or using any lottery system just didn't work: the same malady of the large group always befell the small groups. Then one day when I entered class, two girls in one group were reading the paper and doing their horoscopes. In the exchange, they discovered they had the same sign and explained how cool that was and how that must have explained why they worked so well together. A third girl from the same group entered and asked about her horoscope. Upon learning the third girl's sign, the first two exclaimed almost in unison, "No wonder you always disagree with our interpretations, we aren't compatible!" Out of the mouths of children, the ray of truth and understanding hit me square in the head. That day I collected the birth signs from every scholar, and that afternoon I arranged the classes into groups based on the elements earth, water, air, and fire, which are the group headings for their astrological signs:

fire = Aries, Leo, Sagittarius
air = Gemini, Libra, Aquarius
water = Cancer, Pisces, Scorpio
earth = Taurus, Virgo, Capricorn

From this point on, the groups worked more efficiently. It may have been that the students responded to my use of something—astrology—that they had fun with outside of school. And since we were also dealing with "the stars" in our mythology course as well as in the Shakespeare play we were reading, astrology was already a part of our classroom conversations. Whatever the reason, these groups seemed to work better than the groups I had previously organized. As I moved about from group to group, I saw more scholars engaged and more scholars involved in the discussions. I still didn't have 100 percent participation, and I still hadn't eliminated the dominance of the top scholars, but I had achieved a higher percentage of participation for more time in the class. Somehow, though, I had to find some way to involve all of the scholars every day for the entire class in order for their educational experience to be worthwhile within the confines of the given structure and design of our classrooms and the class day. I knew schools were inefficient, but I just couldn't find the method to fix that until the fall of 1984, when I was introduced to my new classroom.

That year I learned that computers allowed me to utilize the ideas I was learning from the National Writing Project as it was being instituted in our school. The computer allowed me to integrate the timed aspects of writing more effectively as well as the peer review components of the writing project. During parts of the timed writing, I had the scholars turn off the monitors so they would not be overwhelmed by making corrections as they wrote. Editing was much better since scholars were able to use spell-check and the thesaurus function as well as other nifty editing tools like block-and-move, search-and-replace, and more. These tools aided weak writers and inspired strong writers. One of the most powerful uses of the computers was for peer review. For this activity, I incorporated the broadcast feature of the computers into my lab. While working in the computer lab, I could view all the scholars as they worked. Broadcast allowed me to display a scholar's work on everyone's screen to watch a scholar write and edit and then return them all to their own work with two simple computer commands. I was also able to begin the process of peer review in a more efficient manner. At any point in the class, I would have the scholars stop working. They would save their work, put a piece of paper next to their computer, and then get up. They would all move a certain number of chairs to the left or right. At the new computer they would sit down, read the work in front of them, and, using the sheet of paper next to the computer, do their peer review. They would then get up, move to the next computer, and repeat this process three or four or more times. In this way I slowly learned how to make for a more efficient classroom, which would eventually be the foundation upon which I would understand how to use the Internet classroom.

How to Get Over to the Future

Now that I have had time to learn more and to practice the theories, I have come to the conclusion that the traditional classroom must be razed and replaced with classrooms that intensively use computers and the Internet. The space must be redesigned and reorganized to be learner-centered. The space must be used for the construction of projects that demonstrate the scholar's learning. (Keep in mind the data of the learning activity retention chart.)

Names will change, too. The school is to be a *learning community*. The classroom is to be a *learning center*. The teacher morphs into a *cybrarian*. The student evolves into a *scholar*. The new scenario would go something like this: The scholars enter the learning center and settle each into his or her individual space. Using their laptops, the scholars log on and begin their day of study. They are tapping into the messages from their cybrarians, telementors, and peers. Cybrarians enter in groups, ready to provide some guidance for the day's study. Telementors interact with the scholars via the Internet. Peer review, from within and from without, is crucial. Scholars are reading e-mail, selecting books, loading Web pages, and preparing to take notes and construct their Web pages or Microsoft PowerPoint or multimedia presentations of their study, all of which becomes part of a Web folio. This scholarship is done in groups. Community-raising the learner is the ideal: the classic belief that it takes a village to raise a child. Rather than have the scholars moving from class to class every fifty or so minutes all day long, all week, all year, leave them at a desk or learning space and have the cybrarians move about the learning spaces providing direction, assessment, guidance. The scholars are not only studying with the cybrarians; they are also interfacing with many others via digital communications. Their scholarship is displayed via their Web folios. This multidimensional environment will promote learning for all because all learners will be doing the work and will be interacting globally. The cybercommunity will enhance learning.

The juxtaposition between this new classroom and the traditional classroom is immediately obvious as we consider how it is and how it could be. Instead of the teacher being unaware of what each student is doing in his or her work and thinking in the traditional class, the cybrarian is able to monitor each step of scholarship by the scholar. When the student passes in an essay after working on it privately for a couple of days or weeks only to find it is inadequate, she or he becomes discouraged. Not so with the scholar whose work is constantly being evaluated from conception through construction. Teachers are too often bored with the same essay from all of their students. In the project-based classroom, the scholars customize their work, and no two projects can or will be the same. The teacher is usually alone in his or her workings in the classroom, whereas the cybrarian works as a team member and models collaboration for the scholars.

These are just a few comparisons of the obvious differences between the traditional classroom and the learning community. And this is a vision of the future relevance of English—a vision already becoming reality.

CHAPTER FOURTEEN

The Past and Future of (Two-Year) College English Studies

MARK REYNOLDS
Jefferson Davis Community College

Background

Two-year colleges enroll over fifty percent of all entering college students. They are the only segment of higher education to show consistent growth over the last two decades, and all indicators suggest their continued growth well into the twenty-first century. Historically, these institutions have operated under policies of open admissions, admitting all who apply with a high school diploma or the equivalent. Comprehensive community colleges—the majority of these institutions—have traditionally fulfilled four functions: collegiate, career, developmental, and continuing education.

The collegiate function consists of offering the first two years of college courses for students who then transfer to a four-year college or university to complete a bachelor's degree. The career function provides degrees and programs in technical fields such as automotive mechanics, cosmetology, computer drafting, dental hygiene, nursing, masonry, welding, and many others—courses of study that prepare students for a specific job in the workforce. Developmental programs serve students needing remedial preparation in basic literacy and mathematical skills. Continuing education offerings provide specially designed short courses for a particular group, as well as programs of interest to those desiring enrichment or leisure activities. Students in any of these program areas usually attend part-time; many have jobs, working from ten to forty or more hours a week. Few enroll full-time or pursue a consistent, straight-line approach to complete a program or degree. The students may "stop out" because of a job, family problems, or a number of other valid reasons. They are almost exclusively commuter students, because few two-year colleges offer campus housing or residence life. The average age is 29 (Griffith and Connor 1994, 2).

English programs within two-year colleges have played an integral and vital role in helping their institutions fulfill the above functions. A number of factors related to these functions and to the nature of two-year colleges have influenced English studies at these institutions: open admissions, the large number of nontraditional students, the many adult students, the large number of immigrants, the many technical students wanting only a year or two of training before seeking full-time employment, and the presence of workers desiring to update workforce skills or effect a career change, community members wanting leisure activities or enrichment, and traditional college students whose ultimate goal is to obtain bachelor's degrees. Such a diverse student body, with many different needs, goals, and levels of ability, has created quite varied English offerings, and, over the years, English studies in individual colleges has evolved in response to the diverse needs of particular student populations.

In most two-year colleges, one finds various levels of basic writing or developmental courses; first-year college composition (from one to three courses); technical writing; business writing; creative writing; advanced composition; ESL courses; introduction to literature; surveys of British, American, and World literature; and, often, specialized courses in women's literature or other literatures important to a local area, such as Hispanic, Native American, New England, or Southern. Sometimes one finds journalism, classical mythology, speech, study skills, or library orientation courses in two-year English departments. Such courses as these may be taught by English faculty or adjuncts, or they may be grouped with English but taught by various faculty in related disciplines, either within the English program or in another institutional unit.

In addition to being responsive to their communities, two-year college English faculty frequently offer various short courses, such as life writing or resume writing, in settings as diverse as nursing homes, shopping malls, or local banks. They also frequently develop programs of workforce training by going into local businesses or industries to teach courses to targeted workers, or they design special courses tailored to a particular audience—for example, business letter formats for secretaries in a bank or medical report writing for health workers in a medical center. For those institutions with technical programs, additional attention may be given to specific kinds of vocational writing: lab reports or patient workups for nurses, technical writing for computer systems students, business letter and report writing for office assistants, and many others. Such writing is taught as a part of the college's regular schedule, but this instruction may also be transported to the workplace for workers to receive before, during, or after their normal work period.

Most often, it is technical students not interested in collegiate work, students admitted only through an open admissions policy, or recent immigrants who challenge even the best instructors to develop innovative methods of instruction that include heavy use of media, tutorials, discussion and demonstration (in lieu of lectures), multiple and varied collaborative activities, and computer-assisted instruction. Such students force teachers daily to make education accessible, meaningful, and, above all, utilitarian. These challenges are the very ones that make two-year colleges unique in American higher education (see Griffith and Connor 1994). The success of these institutions in meeting these challenges has been fundamental to the democratization of higher education in this country during the past century.

The Two-Year English Department

English departments in two-year colleges can be as distinct as the institutions that house them. English departments may function as individual entities, but most are located within some larger structure, often a humanities division or another similar unit (Raines 1990, 154). As a result, some do not operate independently of a larger unit, which means that the person who directs the overall program labeled "English" may be a music, art, speech, drama, or foreign language discipline member. On many larger campuses, separate English departments do exist, with a chair and various major components, such as developmental studies, technical writing, or English as a Second Language. Even on smaller campuses where English is subsumed under a larger division, however, English faculty usually unite informally to accomplish disciplinary goals, and more often than not refer to themselves collectively as a department, which I shall do in this discussion.

Most two-year colleges do not have traditional academic rank, terming all faculty *instructors*. Minimum preparation is a master's degree with eighteen graduate hours in the teaching discipline. The majority of faculty have a master of arts degree with at least thirty semester-hours in English. Many have a Ph.D. or doctor of arts in English; some hold an Ed.D. in English education. Promotion and tenure at most two-year colleges can be achieved after three or four years of successful teaching and campus service. Evidence of publication and research is seldom required to achieve tenure or gain promotion.

Due to the nature of the students, English studies at two-year colleges has focused most often on literacy—teaching reading and writing—through various levels of composition. Because of open admissions, two-year colleges have found themselves dealing with basic skills in a number of remedial or developmental courses. Many departments also deal with nonnative speakers in ESL classes. In addition, many departments staff writing centers or tutorial labs, where, again, the focus is on literacy skills. Some departments include reading courses within their offerings. Again, most of these courses are remedial. Such requirements become essential for institutions which admit many nontraditional students and adults who either have had little formal education or have been away from it for a number of years. One may even find adult basic education programs attached to two-year college English departments. These programs prepare students to take the General Equivalency Development (GED) examination in order to achieve the equivalent of a high school diploma. Most students receiving their GED certificates subsequently enroll at two-year colleges.

Because of such varied students and courses, the English instructor in a two-year college who teaches British Romantics at

8 A.M. to bachelor's degree seekers may also be the instructor who teaches memo writing or technical report writing to air-conditioning and refrigeration students at 10 A.M., creative writing to residents of a local nursing home at 3 P.M., and basic writing in a campus computer lab to college hopefuls at 6 P.M. Such is life in the two-year college English department, where generalism is the norm for faculty members, and diversity of teaching assignments usually matches diversity of student body. Specialization often comes in the expertise it takes to deal with different student populations and in the ability to move easily among a variety of teaching assignments under a very large English studies umbrella. Much of the preparation for teaching involves determining the best methods for translating complex course materials into manageable and comprehensible segments for the various student populations. While two-year college faculty may spend some time each day dealing with students who need basic skills instruction, most also teach transfer students, who are often as capable as those found on any university campus. This large group includes the vast numbers of adults who may have delayed their college education for any number of reasons. Many two-year colleges also have well-developed honors programs that attract highly capable students. These programs often involve English faculty, who either administer them or develop specific honors courses which they teach.

Faculty normally consider themselves specialists in the teaching of writing because they teach more writing courses than any other. While some faculty primarily teach basic writing or college-level composition or technical writing, few teach only those courses. Although the major focus is on teaching writing, most two-year faculty also teach at least one literature course. Such courses typically include introduction to literature; American, British, or world literature surveys; and other courses related to a particular interest such as women writers, Caribbean writers, or science fiction. For many, the variety of courses available within two-year English studies and the opportunity to teach in varied settings to diverse populations are part of the profession's appeal (see Starr 1994).

The number of courses taught is frequently great—too great. Most faculty teach four or five courses each term. The enrollment in these courses, especially writing courses, is usually large. Such course and student loads unfortunately are common in two-year colleges, where large enrollments and lack of financial resources often create problems. The solution most turned to by administrators has been the overuse of part-time faculty. The widespread use of adjunct instructors creates additional difficulties for two-year English departments, difficulties that have been well documented over the past few years: adjuncts only teach—they do not serve on committees or assist with other departmental work; most do not have offices or keep regular office hours; they do not help advise or counsel students; they do not routinely attend departmental meetings and thus do not always know or follow departmental procedures or protocol despite written instructions or special meetings; although given departmental syllabi to follow, some insist on teaching their special interests regardless of departmental requirements; and many lack an understanding of or concern for a local college's culture because they are busy attending as well to part-time positions on other campuses, both two- and four-year.

The Curriculum

To deal with the diversity of students with varied needs has meant a constantly changing curriculum, and two-year English studies has been at the forefront of curriculum change in order to serve new populations. Two-year colleges were instrumental in creating courses for basic writers during the 1970s throughout the period when massive numbers of open-enrollment students, particularly military veterans, flocked to two-year campuses. At the same time, and continuing into the 1990s, these institutions developed English as a Second Language programs (see Kasper 1995, 1996). In the 1980s, many embraced writing across the curriculum and established successful programs (see Stanley and Ambron 1991). Also in the 1980s, two-year colleges began to incorporate technology on a large scale as they turned to computer-assisted instruction. In the 1990s, many two-year institutions again revamped curricula by taking on major curriculum transformation projects in order to update course offerings to assure that issues of gender, race, ethnicity, and class received appropriate attention. Large-scale transformation projects in states like Maryland and New Jersey have allowed two-year colleges to join forces to update and create new curriculum that takes into account the new and diverse student populations and developments in critical thinking, critical pedagogy, and multiculturalism (see Barrett and Wootten 1994; Davis and Silverberg 1994; Goldenberg and Stout 1994).

While many of their colleagues at universities may have engaged in theory debates, culture wars, canon revolutions, and controversies over the place of composition and literature within English studies, two-year faculty have primarily remained on the sidelines of these developments, maintaining their focus on students. Most two-year faculty have read and kept up with the new developments in theory, but they have examined and mined them for what they could contribute to their pedagogy. Two-year faculty have been most ready to adapt those new developments in composition and literature that could be of immediate value in the classroom. They found the process approach to teaching writing appropriate to their composition work on all levels. Reader-response theory proved especially helpful in their literature classrooms. Many embraced the theory of collaboration and social constructionism in both writing and literature classrooms, finding peer editing groups helpful to students and finding their students willing to collaborate with peers on writing and reading assignments. Faculty welcomed discussions of multiculturalism and integrated new literature selections into their already multicultural classrooms. They found much of value in critical pedagogy, especially in the work of Paulo Freire and Ira Shor, since so many of their students represent the "other," the historically oppressed and underrepresented: women, minorities, immigrants, displaced workers. They have welcomed the developments in ethnographic research which have confirmed what they have known: that classrooms are rich sources for research, that firsthand observation and case studies of students and classroom behavior yield valuable and worthwhile information (see Wilson 1994, 1997). They have been particularly receptive to discussions of classroom research that have shown it to be valid and worthy of pursuit. No group represents better than do two-year college teachers that vast category of practitioners that Stephen North (1987) labels as "lore-makers." Much two-year teacher lore has become and is becoming valuable knowledge. More and more, faculty are attempting serious and sophisticated reflection and analysis of practice so that it does not remain mere lore but has value to others throughout the profession (see Hamilton-Johnson 1997; Ott 1997; Tinberg 1997; Wilson 1994, 1997).

Because they teach only the first two years of college courses (usually surveys or introductory courses); because of the nature of their students (often nontraditional students or those in need of basic skills); and because their classes are often scheduled in locales other than a campus classroom, two-year college faculty have normally been heavily involved with issues of pedagogy. They see themselves almost exclusively as teachers, not as researchers or as scholars in the traditional academic sense. Nevertheless, two-year college research and scholarship often involve classroom activity, pedagogical investigations, ethnographic studies of types of students, or studies of teaching methods. Reports of such work appear regularly in the journals *Teaching English in the Two-Year College, inside english,* and other Two-Year College English Association regional publications. In other instances, individual two-year colleges or state community college systems publish the results of their faculty's efforts. *Pedagogy Journal,* published annually for the past four years by the New Hampshire Community Technical Colleges, is an excellent example of the kinds of teaching activity across the disciplines that goes on regularly in two-year colleges. (Representative articles from recent issues include Dick Conway's "Integrating Music into Your Classroom," Nancy Marashio's "Students as Assessors," and Doyle Davis's "Teaching with Interactive Multimedia Technologies.") Unfortunately, such efforts do not receive much attention beyond their local areas.

Teachers concern themselves a great deal with various methods of presenting material in ways other than through traditional lectures, with how to translate the complex and esoteric into manageable language and understandable concepts for varied student populations, with developing supplemental materials beyond the usual course textbooks, with authoring textbooks aimed at two-year college students, and with analyzing the various student populations on their campuses in attempts to discover how better to teach their diverse students.

When I became frustrated some years ago because students were having trouble reading and were even resisting reading for literature classes, I undertook a close examination of the students and the types of assignments I was using. Simply assigning the reading of a poem or a short story, offering comments on it in class, trying to elicit student discussion about the work, and then asking for a written assignment of literary analysis were not achieving the desired results. In an effort to do a better job and engage students more actively in literature classes, I spent a good deal of time adapting and integrating both journal writing activities and reader-response theory into literature classes. I developed a number of prereading/prewriting and postreading/postwriting activities paired with the assigned literary works to engage students actively with their reading. Those activities proved more successful than what I had been doing, making for more engaged and happier students and a more satisfying classroom experience for us all (see Reynolds 1986, 1990, 1991, 1993). To continue trying to enhance the classroom experience for students and engage them in literature, I have been experimenting recently with activities that require students to "play" with required reading assignments in literature. I have been adapting some of the textual intervention activities developed by Rob Pope (1995), and I've gone further than Pope by encouraging students to manipulate texts on computers. I ask them to use different font sizes and styles to present text visually in order to suggest a particular interpretation of lines or passages from poetry or short fiction. I have also been encouraging the use of computer graphics to visually represent meaning in literary passages. In addition, I am working to incorporate various performance activities into literature classes, such as having student groups create dialogues, pantomimes, or "scenes" that interpret literary passages or whole works. These experiments in literature classes parallel efforts I have been making to engage students more actively with computer graphics and performance activities as aids to invention in writing classes. All of this is experimental, but such work is not uncommon in two-year college classrooms.

These pedagogical foci, because they are not traditional academic studies, are often misunderstood or undervalued by colleagues in universities. Two-year faculties most commonly want the time to teach and the opportunity to develop new materials and techniques related to their teaching. The majority are content with success in the classroom—success that is too often only a private, personal success. Some publish the results of their work; many do not. Some present papers at professional conferences; most do not. More and more, however, are authoring textbooks and articles that contain the results of their pedagogical success. Peter Dow Adams, Diana Hacker, John Langan, Sylvia Holladay, Audrey Roth, Marilyn Smith, Rod Keller, John Lovas, Robert Dees, Nell Ann Pickett, Frank Madden, Lynn Troyka, Judith Lambert, and Jane Peterson are among a growing number of successful two-year college textbook authors who are making public the work of two-year English studies.

The Future

With recent efforts on the national scene to encourage, through financial incentives, the completion of the first two years of college, two-year institutions can expect to see their enrollments increase, perhaps dramatically. Much of the population targeted for this education is the very population historically served by two-year colleges. This population of minorities, immigrants, displaced workers, underprepared academic students, adult women—those formerly labeled "other"—will become the majority: these "others" will become the central focus of higher education in the very near future. This new group of students will create new demands on all segments of higher education, including two-year colleges:

> By virtue of rapidly changing demographics, we as educators can expect to participate to an even higher degree in what is termed "basic writing" or remediation. An increasing pool of non-traditional students, and a shrinking pool of traditional ones, urges teachers, administrators, and writing-center directors to attempt more creative pedagogies to teach and retain college students who will graduate in or after the year 2000. The margin has

become the center. Today's classrooms are tomorrow's America. (Kells 1997)

All indications are that the country's basic workforce must become a much more educated one, not only to keep up with technology, but also to possess the critical thinking skills necessary to adapt to the rapid changes brought on by new technology. In the past and currently, the two-year college has trained the majority of the workforce population that has received any formal training beyond the secondary level. It is the only institution with a proven record of success in workforce training. It will be called on even more to expand such training in the future. Job training has been encouraged by recent efforts in federal welfare reform that limit welfare benefits and shift responsibility for aid for families with dependent children from the federal government to the states. As more states seek ways to move recipients off welfare and into productive positions in society, additional "others" will turn to community colleges for remediation, job training, and the skills essential for success. Two-year colleges are the only currently operational institutions in society with the staff, the facilities, and the knowledge to take on this major task of improving the productivity and the lives of millions of unskilled citizens.

A number of other focuses will also occupy community colleges and their English faculties in the first decade of the twenty-first century. With the spread of distance education and the ongoing development of new technology, colleges will be called on to deliver education twenty-four hours a day, year-round. For English studies, this will require developing new methods of delivering and presenting material. Courses will have to be developed on interactive software, especially in CD-ROM and video formats. For faculty who are used to live interaction with students when they teach writing and share the belletristic features of literature in classroom settings, such developments will require major transitions. Faculty may communicate with students via computers more often than in person; computers currently in development that will allow video contact between student and instructor may ease the transition for those who are used to classroom settings. More and more, faculty will be called on to support alternative learning modes adjusted to students' learning styles and to students' time schedules. After years of predictions of the demise of the traditional four-walled classroom, the early twenty-first century will see that demise. Faculty will then become managers of information dissemination as well as innovators in translating information into new electronic forms. Along with these changes will come new demands to individualize and customize learning, to provide self-paced instruction. Again, to meet these needs, English faculty will be called on to produce electronic texts in multiple versions and multiple modes. The *Interactive English* writing software recently developed by Academic Systems Corporation of Mountain View, California, and authored by a two-year college English teacher is an excellent example of these new methods of delivering information. Such technology should free teachers for more individualized instruction, giving them the opportunity to adjust teaching to individual learning styles.

Technology will also allow faculty to be networked within departments, across campuses—indeed, with institutions around the world. These electronic networks will allow for greater interdisciplinarity, for electronically team-taught courses, and for courses taught by experts a world away. All of these possibilities offer exciting prospects for two-year English studies to continue evolving to meet changing needs. Increasingly, two-year institutions will use data from demographic, economic, and employment research for long-range planning of instructional programs. Curricula will have to adapt to changing needs within communities. Two-year colleges are used to such changes and to rapid response. When Germany's Daimler-Benz corporation decided to locate a new Mercedes automotive plant in Alabama to produce its first sports utility vehicle, part of its decision was based on the proximity of the site to a local community college. It was to the community college that the state turned first to provide job training for much of this plant's new workforce.

In addition to a heavy and continuing emphasis on meeting local economic needs, two-year institutions will continue to be centers of learning for their local communities. As in the past, most two-year colleges will be responsive to that large and increasing number of students who are beginning their baccalaureate training. This will mean new articulation agreements with four-year institutions. Two-year colleges will continue to provide the first two years of undergraduate training in writing and literature in response to the needs and requirements of the four-year institutions to which their students transfer to complete their college degrees. This should mean a continued emphasis in English studies on the teaching of composition and literature. In addition, two-year institutions will increase offerings in literature and enrichment courses with a literary focus for an expanding number of retirees and senior citizens desiring leisure activities. Continuing response to local needs will be required in areas like creative writing, and new courses will be created for particular audiences in focused literatures like African American women writers, South Georgia folklore, Illinois writers, or Colorado ghost stories. For English studies, all of these needs will mean a continuing focus on the needs of transfer students for English courses appropriate for baccalaureate programs at four-year institutions, continuing attention to the economic and employment needs of local communities, and a response to cultural and aesthetic requirements of local citizens. If English studies in universities gives way to something more akin to cultural studies, as some critics like Michael Bérubé (1996) have suggested, or even becomes institutionally irrelevant as departments of classics have become (since English departments met the popular demand for literature in the vernacular toward the end of the nineteenth century), as Harold Bloom (1994, 17) has suggested, it is possible that English studies as it has been traditionally known, especially the belles lettres emphasis, will be found flourishing in two-year college English departments and smaller four-year institutions much more so than in traditional research universities.

Conclusion

Tuition in community colleges remains significantly lower than in four-year colleges and universities. This economic factor alone will keep enrollment high at the nation's two-year colleges. The recent national initiatives to offer tax incentives for the first two college years will also increase enrollments. Given that the children of baby boomers are now reaching college age and that predictions indicate the number of eighteen- and nineteen-year-olds will exceed nine million by 2010, two-year colleges will continue to see a substantial number of students enrolling.

Two-year college student populations are highly reflective of society at large, much more so than those of most universities. Because their students are so representative of society and because their focus has always been and will remain on the local communities they serve, two-year colleges fill a crucial role in society and in higher education. They are responsive to local communities in vital ways, whether offering essential training to support a new industry or providing ESL training to a new group of immigrants. Whenever societal, cultural, political, economic, or technological changes occur in an area served by a two-year college, that institution will reflect and respond to those changes. When required, English studies within those institutions, because of its flexibility and its generalist nature, will also adapt to changing needs to teach reading and writing, both the practical and the belletristic. The two-year college will continue to bridge the gap between the often disparate worlds of academe and external society.

As more and more states develop articulation agreements between their community colleges and their four-year institutions, easing the transition between these institutions, students will continue to attend the colleges closest to home that are the most economical. Therefore, two-year college English departments will continue to see large enrollments. Even though a number of states are debating who is responsible for remedial programs—the secondary schools, the two-year colleges, or the universities—in most states, it is the community colleges that have been fulfilling the remedial function since their inceptions. It is likely that when final decisions are reached about who will provide remedial training in all areas of literacy skills, it will remain the two-year colleges that most effectively and efficiently handle this essential area of education. As more and more immigrants seek entry into the American mainstream, it is likely, too, that the majority will find their way into community college classrooms, initially for ESL work, but later for workforce training. As technology and a global economy create rapid and constant changes in the world's work environment, the need for training and retraining of workers should make the two-year college a major and important segment of higher education throughout the first half of the twenty-first century. Increased numbers of students beginning their baccalaureate training, along with a growing number of retirees, should ensure that two-year English studies continue an emphasis on a variety of literature courses. The traditional humanizing argument for literary study as a counter to technology's dehumanizing tendency will grow more significant in the next century. Although literature may be delivered electronically, such delivery will enhance its meaning to new generations.

For all these reasons and more, English studies in two-year colleges will remain essential and vibrant, becoming even more relevant to the highly varied constituencies it will serve. Course work may become more technologically oriented and focused, but the teaching of reading and writing will continue to flourish in these institutions. They will continue to be student-oriented, to focus on pedagogy, to respond to the needs of their communities, and to be a major factor in training American workers.

Works Cited

Barrett, Claudia M., and Judith A. Wootten. 1994. "Today for Tomorrow: Program and Pedagogy for 21st-Century College Students." Pp. 85–93 in *Two-Year College English: Essays for a New Century,* ed. Mark Reynolds. Urbana, Ill.: National Council of Teachers of English.

Bérubé, Michael. 1996. Address. National Council of Teachers of English Annual Convention. Chicago, Illinois. 21 November.

Bloom, Harold. 1994. *The Western Canon: The Books and School of the Ages.* New York: Harcourt.

Conway, Dick. 1996. "Integrating Music into Your Classroom." *Pedagogy Journal* 3.1: 51–54.

Davis, Doyle V. 1995. "Teaching with Interactive Multimedia Technologies." *Pedagogy Journal* 2.1: 39–45.

Davis, Judith Rae, and Sandra S. Silverberg. 1994. "The Integration Project: A Model for Curriculum Transformation." Pp. 108–19 in

Two-Year College English: Essays for a New Century, ed. Mark Reynolds. Urbana, Ill.: National Council of Teachers of English.

Goldenberg, Myrna, and Barbara Stout. 1994. "Writing Everybody In." Pp. 94–107 in *Two-Year College English: Essays for a New Century*, ed. Mark Reynolds. Urbana, Ill.: National Council of Teachers of English.

Griffith, Marlene, and Ann Connor. 1994. *Democracy's Open Door: The Community College in America's Future*. Portsmouth, NH: Boynton/Cook.

Hamilton-Johnson, Lisa. 1997. "A New Kind of Research Paper: Bridging the Gap between Reader Response and Formal Critical Analysis." *Teaching English in the Two-Year College* 24.1: 14–26.

Kasper, Loretta Frances. 1995. "Discipline-Oriented ESL Reading Instruction." *Teaching English in the Two-Year College* 22.1: 45–53.

———. 1996. "Writing to Read: Enhancing ESL Students' Reading Proficiency through Written Response to Text." *Teaching English in the Two-Year College* 23.1: 25–33.

Kells, Michelle Hall. 1997. Call for Papers for *Composition/2000: Negotiating the Margins*. Texas A&M University–Kingsville.

Marashio, Nancy. 1995. "Students as Assessors." *Pedagogy Journal* 2.1: 121–30.

National Center for Educational Statistics. 1995. *Trends among High School Seniors, 1972–1992*. U.S. Department of Education. Washington, D.C.: Government Printing Office.

North, Stephen M. 1987. *The Making of Knowledge in Composition: Portrait of an Emerging Field*. Upper Montclair, N.J.: Boynton/Cook.

Ott, C. Ann. 1997. "Collective Research at an Urban Community College." *Teaching English in the Two-Year College* 24.1: 7–13.

Pope, Rob. 1995. *Textual Intervention: Critical and Creative Strategies for Literary Studies*. London: Routledge.

Raines, Helon. 1990. "Is There a Writing Program in This College? Two Hundred and Thirty-Six Two-Year Schools Respond." *College Composition and Communication* 41.2: 151–65.

Reynolds, Mark. 1986. "Pre- and Post-Reading Activities for Selected Wordsworth Poems." Pp. 47–50 in *Approaches to Teaching*

Wordsworth's Poetry, ed. Spencer Hall and Jonathan Ramsey. New York: Modern Language Association.

———. 1990. "Teaching the Metaphysical Poets in a Two-Year College." Pp. 107–14 in *Approaches to Teaching the Metaphysical Poets,* ed. Sidney Gottlieb. New York: Modern Language Association.

———. 1991. "Using a Reader's Journal to Teach Byron's Poetry." Pp. 50–54 in *Approaches to Teaching Byron's Poetry,* ed. Frederick W. Shilstone. New York: Modern Language Association.

———. 1993. "Writing to Read Poetry: Teaching Blake's *Songs of Innocence and Experience.*" *Alabama English* (Spring/Fall): 21–29.

Stanley, Linda, and Joanna Ambron. 1991. *Writing across the Curriculum in Community Colleges.* New Directions for Community Colleges, No. 73. San Francisco: Jossey-Bass.

Starr, Al. 1994. "Community College Teaching: Endless Possibilities." Pp. 165–74 in *Two-Year College English: Essays for a New Century,* ed. Mark Reynolds. Urbana, Ill.: National Council of Teachers of English.

Tinberg, Howard B. 1997. *Border Talk: Writing and Knowing in the Two-Year College.* Urbana, Ill.: National Council of Teachers of English.

Wilson, Smokey. 1994. "What Happened to Darleen? Reconstructing the Life and Schooling of an Underprepared Learner." Pp. 37–53 in *Two-Year College English: Essays for a New Century,* ed. Mark Reynolds. Urbana, Ill.: National Council of Teachers of English.

———. 1997. "Acts of Defiance (and Other Mixed Messages): Taking Up Space in a Nontransfer Course." *Teaching English in the Two-Year College* 24.4: 291–303.

CHAPTER FIFTEEN

Enacting Cultures: The Practice of Comparative Cultural Study

PAULA MATHIEU
Boston College

JAMES J. SOSNOSKI
University of Illinois at Chicago

At a time when the academic "field" of English Studies is undergoing profound redefinition, this collection poses the central question, "In what ways are the various pedagogies, contents, and curricular structures associated with the academic study of English in secondary schools, colleges, and universities, relevant (or irrelevant) to students in an increasingly complex and interconnected world?"

ROBERT P. YAGELSKI

Introduction

In a review of several books loosely related to cultural studies, entitled "Out of the Fashion Industry: From Cultural Studies to the Anthropology of Knowledge," Kurt Spellmeyer writes:

> It would be pleasant to think that professors of English, concerned as they are with both language and style, might be able to see through the ruse of fashion, but no: for us, in fact, fashion is nearly everything. As our profession's first century comes to a close, what do we really have to show for it all, other than a sad parade of styles, beginning with philology and ending, for today, with the movement known as "cultural studies"? (1996, 425)

Spellmeyer equates current interest in cultural studies to the period in the '60s and '70s when literary theory was in vogue, remarking that "even the defenders of cultural studies understand that it looks today the way French theory did thirty years ago" (425). Having construed cultural studies as yet another imported theory—this time from England—he goes on to complain that cultural studies is a fashionable jargon, implying that there is no theoretical substance to the movement.

That an English professor might complain about jargon is hardly a surprise. Every theory that has challenged traditional modes of "close reading" has been greeted with similar accusations. That a leading journal publishes such an attack may be more significant because it might signal a willingness on the part of the professoriate to abandon a theory that had gained a foothold in the academy. By itself this symptom of declining interest would not be fatal. However, the malady may be serious and a portent of the demise of cultural studies.

In the history of literary and rhetorical theory, arguments about the validity of a theory are less significant indices of its viability than are its pedagogical successes. Close reading (whether understood as New Criticism, a traditional version of historical formalism, or simply a mode of analysis) is still a widely successful practice in literature classrooms. Students feel that they can understand poems and stories better after being schooled in close reading. As a result, despite the continuous challenges to its popularity, it survives in countless textbooks and remains the most widely accepted critical practice. Thus, for advocates of cultural studies such as ourselves, the lack of pedagogical success enjoyed by cultural studies is a more alarming symptom of its possible demise than an attack on it in a leading journal.

The complaints about cultural studies are various, but we wish to focus on one in particular: its reliance on "cultural critique" as a pedagogical technique. Most teachers of literature and rhetoric advocate some form of criticism as a teaching practice. For example, many writing instructors encourage students to be critical of their own prose. When it comes time to study argument, teachers usually try to get their students to read arguments critically and to be self-critical about their own. Similarly, most literature teachers inculcate critical habits of reading in their students. Critique, however, is a special brand of criticism as it is advocated in the textbooks about cultural studies, one that begins with political theory, which students "apply" to their life experiences. This can be a distancing approach, rather than a more organic one that places criticism within students' life experiences.

We believe that to teach is to persuade someone else to do or think in a manner different from the one to which they are accustomed. If you teach someone how to play tennis, for example, you show them a different way of holding the racket, moving their feet, or turning their elbows from the way to which they have grown accustomed. Teaching implies that many cultural practices (e.g., writing, reading) that are habitual have to be changed in order to accomplish a different aim. Close reading, in most instances, is a different way of reading from the one acquired while growing up. Teaching students how to read more closely asks them to change the way they read. Getting persons to change their habitual way of doing things is always a difficult task.

Teachers of rhetoric and literature schooled in the traditional criticism tend to see texts as separable from their social and cultural contexts. Criticism, thus, is limited in that it focuses only on textual matters and does not extend to social and cultural issues. As we begin the twenty-first century, many teachers like ourselves welcome a view of criticism that sees texts embedded in social and cultural contexts. However, the mode of cultural critique advocated in textbooks often implies or presumes social, political, and cultural systems as a metacritical vantage point that sometimes appears to students as a moral imperative. Our view is that this technique of "cultural critique" is often not an effective one rhetorically.

The Rhetorical Limits of "Critique"

The cultural critique "method" of doing cultural studies is a legacy of the movement's roots in the publications of the Birmingham Centre for Contemporary Cultural Studies. An example of this "method" adapted to the composition classroom can be found in the work and writings of James Berlin (see Berlin 1996; Berlin and Vivion 1992). For Berlin, the purpose of teaching composition is to "make students aware of the cultural codes—the various competing discourses—that attempt to influence who they are . . . and to encourage [them] to resist and negotiate these codes—these hegemonic discourses—in order to bring about more personally humane and socially equitable economic and political arrangements" (Berlin 1991, 50).

While we are sympathetic to Berlin's teaching aims, there is evidence that this sort of technique is often not successful. Composition teachers trained by Berlin who are advocates of cultural studies have expressed some difficulties with this approach (see Downing and Sosnoski 1997). Libby Miles, for example, describes her class as follows:

> We learned ways to teach students how to critique using binaries to decode the dominant reading. My students dutifully learned to identify and decode. Their papers were formulaic and flat. There was little interesting reading in these papers; students spent a paragraph each on a type of code (race, class, gender, sexual orientation, education, religion, age, etc.), and they all concluded that advertising was bad because it perpetuates these images. The life and individuality and creativity and critique that was in their impromptu writing was missing from these papers that they spent weeks on—under my instruction. (Miles 1997, 241)

Miles stresses that she still respects the motives behind this pedagogy but admits that it no longer occupies a central role in her teaching.

The problems with this pedagogy, we would argue, are complex. Some relate to the distance students feel when being asked to interact with abstract theory that seems remote from their lives and to apply that theory to a practice with which they are familiar. Another problem is more rhetorical in nature, based on the expectations of the students in the classes. Many students come into our classroom predetermined to resist or refuse any teaching they find "political," "feminist," or promoting what often gets misnamed "reverse racism." We would argue that such resistance isn't necessarily the product of students who are inherently conservative or hostile to ideas of human rights or political freedom. Rather the dominant culture, driven by the corporate-controlled media and bombarded with "studies" by right-wing scholars, constructs a conversation that labels pedagogies that ask students to be critical of social and cultural practices as merely code words of the plotting advocates of political correctness.

In *Critical Teaching and the Idea of Literacy*, C. H. Knoblauch and Lil Brannon (1993) provide an excellent analysis of the ways the media and conservative scholars are shaping public discussions by distorting and misrepresenting efforts to democratize education. They pay particular attention to the ways this prevailing cultural opinion determines what they call "conventional school reality" which has the power "to shape or restrict the possibilities of critical teaching" (72). In other words, while the case against critical teaching is often based on spurious evidence, the rhetorical effects it has on students are real. These resistances, which Jim Berlin argues are actually positive signs of a student's assertion of initiative, can nevertheless seriously undermine critical goals in a classroom.

If we view "critique," as it seems many students do, as the process by which one must abnegate their entire way of life and existing cultural practices, then we can begin to understand why this teaching technique is resisted as a moral imperative taking the form of "political correctness." We use the word "abnegate" with all its religious reverberations to refer to the imperative of renunciation or self-denial that students perceive, implying that they should give up the practice under scrutiny. Students feel as if they are being given a moral imperative (don't do "x") rather than being asked to choose the cultural practices that benefit them.

Given the difficult constraints that teachers who want to practice cultural studies or a critically oriented pedagogy face, can we "re-rhetoricize" our methods to make them more successful? This is not to ask us to conceal our goals or misrepresent our actions. Rather, we would like to seek methods that introduce students to a form of cultural criticism that makes productive use of students' everyday experiences and critical abilities rather than merely inspiring their ire.

Miles offers what we feel is a good starting place for an answer. Instead of asking students to critique using theory, she said, she likes to start with asking students to "articulate how and where they already critique" (1997, 241). Similarly Lisa

Langstraat, responding to Miles, concurs that Berlin's pedagogy is groundbreaking, but that it's not a useful starting place for students:

> For me, helping students start thinking about "what isn't there" in a text is a way of getting them used to denaturalizing that which seems so familiar that it does, indeed, become ideologically naturalized, to be expected, etc. Students' own experiences, perceptions and affective states inevitably become a central part of this process of "denaturalizing," and I encourage them to start there, to start with the dissonance they feel about a text and their own experiences with it. (Langstraat 1997, 260)

Concerns about the problem of the rhetorical effectiveness of cultural critique (as abnegation) and alternatives to it became the research problematic of a seminar taught at the University of Illinois at Chicago (UIC).

The "Teaching of Reading and Writing as Cultural Studies" Seminar

In the second semester of 1996, Jim Sosnoski led a seminar that addressed various problems concerning the historical development of cultural studies (CS). The seminar began and ended by asking the question, "Why was CS necessary in the 1990s?" The aim of the seminar was to collaboratively design a cultural studies–oriented first-year writing course. As the seminar progressed, our efforts in designing a viable cultural studies writing course intensified. When we considered assignments and readings, the problematic of the rhetorical ineffectiveness of cultural critique became a focal concern.

We agreed that a cultural studies orientation was necessary in 1996 because our culture was a multimedia one with the explosion of interest in the World Wide Web that expanded our conception of "texts" and required attention to their cultural and political contexts. A traditional historical-formalism did not fit the bill. Further, we agreed that cultural studies was not a discipline in the classic sense. It is a postdisciplinary endeavor.

Correlatively, we assumed that the authorities in CS were not restricted to cultural "theorists." Members of the culture were its best "authorities," the implication being that students were better "authorities" on their cultures than were their teachers. Their voices needed to be heard. Jim Berlin's key role in bringing CS into composition studies became the focus of our discussions. We unanimously agreed that writing (and reading) should be taught as a study of culture, and thus a key question arose: "If writing is taught as a study of culture, is this form of pedagogy cultural critique?" This question focused the issues we had been discussing because it forced us to think about them in the context of our teaching practices. Considering student responses to the CS elements in courses we had already taught, we formed the resolve to bring rhetoric into the picture. Although the "re-rhetoricization" of "critique" did not play a major role in the seminar discussions, it did have an impact on the Enacting Cultures course that was taught in the fall of 1996.

The re-rhetoricizing of critique that began in the seminar led to the comparison of cultural practices, a tactic that became a key pedagogical practice. This practice has two correlative aspects:

1. It focuses on comparing cultural sites or practices so that the advantages and disadvantages to their practitioners become apparent. In this tactic, the criticism of one practice or site is implicit in its comparison to another. However, the rhetoric of comparison has a positive valence since it does not restrict itself to negating one site or practice without offering an alternative to it.

2. It anticipates the building of a new site or the development of a new practice or the remodeling of one. The rhetorical effect here is also positive rather than negative. It makes students aware that they are potential agents of culture rather than mere passive recipients.

Similar to the practices described by Miles (1997) and Langstraat (1997), this pedagogy allowed us to respond to the problem of "critique" by proposing a different view of cultural criticism, one that begins not with established theory but with the lives and cultural practices of students.

The Practice of Comparative Cultural Criticism

Reading, Writing, and Enacting Cultures, a pilot composition course that involved students in reshaping specific, local, cultural practices in which they were positioned as subjects, was designed by Paula Mathieu along with Jennifer Cohen, a member of UIC's Cultural Studies Collective. Before discussing this course, however, we would like to provide some background about the campus where we teach. The University of Illinois at Chicago is a large urban university[1] whose mission, according to the UIC Undergraduate Handbook, is, in part, to serve students "for whom a university education is not a long-standing family tradition and who must surmount economic, social, and educational barriers to achieve academic success."[2] UIC has traditionally attracted an ethnically and linguistically diverse population of students from the city's high schools and surrounding suburbs. The majority of students are additionally employed outside of the university, many of them full-time.[3] This is a mostly commuter school where students spend little time on campus before or after classes. The student retention rate is poor, especially among African Americans.[4] Survey statistics show that retention is higher among students who take their composition classes in their first year.

Because of the many obstacles UIC students must face, the English composition program places a high priority on classes that invite students into the university as participants and promote interaction among students to help build community. Many courses designed and taught by teaching assistants and instructors at UIC seek innovative ways to allow students to engage their own experiences as integral to the process of academic inquiry. Reading, Writing, and Enacting Cultures is just one example of the many courses that share these goals.

We hesitate, in writing this essay, to claim that this course and these assignments are "successful" and thus should be replicated wholesale by other instructors. Judging the success of one's teaching always seems elusive at best, and at worst dangerous. As with any teaching endeavor, there were interesting and successful moments as well as disappointments and unexpected problems. Rather than seeing this course as a model to be emulated, we refer to it here merely as an illustrative example of a comparative and action-centered course influenced by cultural studies.

The course, taught by Paula Mathieu for two consecutive semesters, examines university culture by focusing specifically on UIC's culture and its electronic presence. After a four-week introduction in which students wrote essays about a personal learning experience and read about education from the points of view of a number of theorists, activists, and reporters, we turned to an exploration of UIC. This exploration took the form of two comparative assignments, one concrete and one imaginary.

The concrete comparison assignment asked students to generate a question, problem, or issue related to UIC about which they would like to find more information. Topics that students chose covered a wide range, from day-care on campus to the (lack of) quality of teaching and professor-student interaction; from university policies, such as adding and dropping courses, to parties and the lack of an active student culture on campus. Once students or student groups selected a topic, they were asked to investigate the university's Web pages to see if and how well their issue had been addressed there. (They were given a questionnaire to answer about the Web page.) After completing this search, they were asked to select the Web page of another university and explore the same issue there. Some students picked the pages of schools they had considered attending, some chose schools from their native countries (Mexico, Greece, Guatemala, Russia, Ghana), and still others picked those "impossible-to-get-into" schools such as Harvard and MIT.

During the first semester in which Paula taught this class, most students were appalled to find that the UIC Web pages contained no heading for "students" and that there was relatively little information of interest to students (there were headings for administrators, the classroom, the library, the computer, etc.). Most had trouble finding information on their topic at UIC, and the other schools they investigated almost always did a better job. During the second semester the course was taught, the university updated its Web pages while we were in the middle of our research. As a result, some students in the second semester did their comparison as a before-and-after study using only UIC's pages, while others started over in the middle of evaluating their issue. (We had no idea when we started that the pages were about to be updated, which would have been useful information.) After the revisions, the analyses of the students were mixed. Many found adequate discussion of their topic, while others found little to nothing or were hopelessly lost in the search. One student, who was researching questions related to UIC's budget, found that his link to the fiscal breakdown of yearly spending had disappeared from the Web page. The comparisons with other universities seemed more mixed than the almost entirely negative evaluations from the first semester. Some students, for example, expressed real pleasure in seeing that Harvard's pages had even less information than UIC's.

In the written analyses of this assignment, students were asked to evaluate the Web entries and discuss how useful UIC's site was for students. Significantly, the students seemed better able to be critical and confident in their assertions than if they had not done the comparative work. For example, when a student researching day care found no information on UIC's Web page, she seemed a bit frustrated, but when she found ample detailed information about the day-care center at the University of Michigan, she was able to label UIC's lack of information as a university problem. Also, the collective nature of the search gave students more confidence in their findings. When several students, for example, were unable to find any information about what they perceived as a lack of quality teaching on campus, they shared those findings and developed a mutual desire to take action about it. In addition to the creation of an alternative Web page (described below), the first-semester class sent an e-mail message to UIC's Webspinner expressing their dissatisfaction with the current set up. We don't know, however, whether or not the first-semester critiques played a role in the revision made to the Web pages during the second semester.

Asking students to perform this concrete comparison allowed them to begin criticism at a place of their own interest and choosing. Also, rather than asking them to "critique" by using an existing theoretical model, their criticism was derived from comparing one cultural site to another. Rhetorically, comparison allows students to look critically at a practice without forcing them into an impossibly negative space, which often results in resistance or cynicism. Relying solely on comparisons, however, would limit the scope of such criticism to the best that the world currently offers. For example, the current disregard for funding education at adequate levels by state and national governments means that "good" educational models for comparison are often hard to come by (for example, it would be difficult to argue for free unlimited access to education for all citizens, based on current global educational systems). Comparative criticism, however, is not restricted to existing conditions; it can turn to the past or, even better, to the not-yet future, found currently in imagination.

An assignment involving an "imaginative" comparison asked students to write a detailed essay describing the workings of their ideal university. Two parameters were given for this assignment: (1) One could not describe only results without indicating the material conditions that brought them about. (For example, one could not say, "Teachers here really care about students," without showing how the ideal system solved a problem that previously kept teachers from caring about students, such as class size, research demands, or the like.) (2) One had to stipulate the conditions of the possibility of an ideal school. (For example, for all students to attend her ideal university for free, one writer levied high taxes on corporations.)

The goal of this assignment was to invite students to escape the purely negative space of critique by asking them to imagine better ways to teach and learn. One of the anticipated effects of this assignment was that these writers' visions of their ideal university became implicit indictments of the institutional problems at UIC. For example, many students' ideal university offered a free education to any who sought it or to any who maintained a certain grade point average. Class sizes were small, and students and teachers could regularly interact. One student focused on an intensive training program for teaching professors how to teach, while several others discussed expanding the curriculum to include more works by women, U.S. ethnic, and international writers. One woman's ideal university included a uniformed security guard posted at every door, while another's included security lights and emergency-phone boxes that work consistently. Even in these positive expressions, it is clear that students were making tacit critiques of the high cost of U.S. education, as well as UIC's large classes, often-restrictive curriculum, and lack of security. In other papers, students explicitly compared their ideal university to UIC and designed their ideal space as one that would remedy the problems that UIC currently faces. We would argue that these critical elements are inherent in comparison, especially imaginary or utopian comparisons which implicitly ask students to think of the "not-yet" in relation to "what is."

Instead of using our own evaluation of whether and how well these assignments worked, we report how students felt about this work and their perceptions of UIC and of the possibility of social change. What follows are excerpts from course evaluations:

> I liked writing the paper about the Ideal University. It made me look to see what things I would like to see happen at UIC, or any other universities I attend during my academic years.

> I know the assignment made me look at the UIC in a different way because before I was just going to class and not really caring what was going on at UIC and now I see all the problems that we have here.

> It actually let me see the different wants and needs of other students and myself. . . . The students really spoke up about how they feel toward UIC and how colleges should be.

> It helped me to evaluate the aspects of UIC I like and the areas that could use a little more improvement.

> I was able to express my feelings and display my dream on paper. . . . When I was done with my paper I realized how UIC needs major work in many things.

> It was a way to create and expand my thoughts of school. It has really changed the way I look at school, now I wonder how school would be if some things were different.

While we can't generalize the significance or gauge the sincerity of the students' comments, we would like to suggest what they say to us. These responses tend to emphasize that students developed their desires and critiques through the process of writing. The act of comparison, either concrete or "utopian," became a process of critical creation, through which students were able to form and test critiques in the light of their desires for a better place to live and work. While students had strong responses to the assignment, not all were unequivocally positive:

> It made me realize that the whole school system would never be changed. And that our ideas might be heard but never put in process. I discovered the things that I actually want for me to feel comfortable in a school.

> Like I said in my paper it might sound good on paper and not work at all.

These comments seem to indicate that the students are skeptical of the idea of creating a blueprint for social change. We believe this caution is well-founded, for students and teachers alike. The political value of any course is difficult to gauge. What Margaret Whitford suggests about utopian writing, we would argue remains true for comparative practices: "the value . . . is not to programme the future but to help change the present" (Whitford 1991, 17). She argues that a genuinely different future cannot be entirely foreseen, and certainly not predicted. The purpose, therefore, of utopian writing and for comparative criticism is not the product—one won't ever create the perfect blueprint for the future—but the process one goes through. When one names an ideal world, desires and critiques are formed. And while not all of these ideal worlds necessarily stand in opposition to the capitalist, patriarchal status quo, we feel that helping students articulate desires for a better world and to initiate discussion about different views of the ideal is a worthwhile political and pedagogical goal.

Don't Stop at Criticism: Enacting Culture

An important assertion by Marx that cultural studies theorists of the Birmingham School brought to teaching was that culture is dynamic and changeable and that people bring about cultural change. Writing pedagogies that have emerged from cultural studies theory, however, often underplay the dynamic nature of culture, casting students merely as analysts. In this vein, Alan France (1993) writes critically of textbooks that encourage students merely to analyze the culture around them as a sort of cultural critic by closely examining and picking apart texts. France fears this practice encourages a word-world split, which leaves students in an analytical, yet passive, position.

Our course tried to embrace the resistance inherent in culture by asking students to respond to the UIC culture and cultural problems their analyses turned up by changing it in some way. Paula gave students a choice in deciding how their work would take on a public voice but encouraged students to create Web pages to publish their views. All but one student decided to create a Web page that responded to and filled in some of the gaps of UIC's official Web page.[5] They called the pages "The Missing Links," and the resulting Web site includes their essays on UIC's services, its teaching, and its support for students. The "Missing Links" Web site differs from the strictly informational university Web site in that its essays are a mixture of information, analysis, and critique, written by students, and intended for other students. (It is linked to the English department page, so UIC students do have access to it.) For example, one student wrote about the add/drop procedure and included an interview with a university administrator who detailed the policy on dropping a course late. The student supplemented description of the official policy with interviews with students who demonstrated that the policy is implemented in an inconsistent and fickle manner; she also included a beautifully illustrated, six-panel cartoon detailing one student's "drop dilemma."

Another student provided the missing information about the university day-care center, but mixed it with her analysis of the problem of day care at UIC. She did this by detailing the center's invisibility on campus, its mysterious fee scale and waiting list, and its policy of granting first priority to faculty, then to graduate students, and finally to undergraduates if spaces are available. At the same time, this writer described the effects this policy had on students and provided examples of the lengths they must go in order to attend school while caring for their kids:

Another student I interviewed is . . . an undergraduate with a three year old son and has recently gotten married. Therefore, he is "very tight on cash." He and his wife signed up early enough to get their son into the [university day care] center. But they only kept him in there for a short while because they could not afford it. . . . What they are doing now, since they are both attending UIC, is to switch off days taking their son with them to classes, "unless we absolutely cannot bring him to a class like a lab or an exam day or something. It's hard at times, but we work it out." John has attended every single one of my math lectures and discussion classes, sitting in the back with his dad, coloring in his books, and playing with his cars. I have never once heard a sound out of him. Because they have a good child, that works for them, but what are people with "real" kids supposed to do?

In the second semester that Paula taught this course, students chose to add to the Missing Links pages, although the focus of their work was somewhat different. Some students wanted to publish their ideal university essays, while several others wanted to focus on how their previous cultural experiences often made life difficult at UIC. One student, for example, wrote an entry entitled "My Latino Experience at UIC," which included the following text:

It was bad news all around for me. My eagerness regarding school was replaced with the pessimistic wondering on "Who will die next month?" What made it worse is that some professors did not understand that I lived in two worlds. Not only do I have to watch my back in school and be prepared for pop quizzes and the likes, but I also had to watch my back on the streets and be prepared for ANYTHING on the streets. Unfortunately, this is the reality for many Latino students.

Needless to say, I am on probation because I missed a lot of school last semester. I missed a lot of school this spring semester, too, also because there was yet another death in the family, my cousin Armando. No matter what teachers believe and no matter how many times a person experiences this, there is no getting used to it. My current English teacher, Paula, commented, after missing several weeks of her class because the death of Armando, that it seemed that I didn't want to participate in her class. She even stated, "I don't even know why you are here."

This is also a hard reality that I had to face. Most teachers will not know what it is like to live in "two worlds". The people who do know what it is like can only tell you to hang on. At this point in the semester I am hanging on to a thread. This is my Latino experience in the University.

We include this entry because of the explicit critique it makes of the teaching of the course. While I (Paula) am saddened to realize that I was grouped among the teachers who didn't understand this student's experience, and space does not allow me to examine the larger issues related to this, I felt pleased that the student felt able to articulate his view of the situation, which differed from my own. I felt that after he had missed three weeks of class, I was very fair in setting up a program for him to complete and pass the course on time, which included regular attendance in class. After he missed an additional week, I asked him why he had been away. He provided no answer. Then I asked him why he had returned to class. My attempt to get information and communicate a necessity for his being in class was interpreted by this student as an evaluation of his worthiness to be in college. As it turns out, he did remain in the course and pass it.

Whether or not these entries actually change the culture at UIC is difficult to answer. In some ways, it seems unlikely, in that Web access is still a problem for many students, and even if people do read the essays, there are no easy or immediate actions requested that would make the effects tangible. On the other hand, we have been changed by this writing, as have some of the students. For us, these essays act as a continual reminder of the complexities of the lives of UIC's students and call us to constantly and vigilantly evaluate our own responses to them. As for the students, these Web entries were many different things, as their course evaluations attest. Many felt enthusiastic about having learned to navigate in electronic settings and about their public contribution to the Web, while a few remained skeptical about or frustrated with the Web:

> Being a part of our web page really made me happy. I can have my work displayed to the whole world, or anybody who wants to see it.

> I wasn't sure that I would be able to produce an effective contribution to the web. But as I looked into my topic I saw that I had a legitimate problem. I knew that if I put it in the right words, it

would definitely be effective. Hopefully some action will be taken to make professors more available for their student needs.

Technology is definitely not the answer to all of the worlds problems, but it does have many benefits.

The final project is interesting, but I am not in complete awe. I think that after we actually have completed it, it would be thrilling to realize that so many people will read this and take our ideas and findings into consideration.

I don't really like the final project. It's difficult to get the truth from anyone on this campus so I'm having trouble getting good research information. I really hate it here already and this project does seem to throw it in my face when I'm trying to concentrate on not hating it here so that I can make it through without going completely insane. I also think that the web page isn't really going to be that helpful for the people that we're trying to design it for. Not everyone has a computer and a lot of beginning students here don't know about the web pages.

I am excited about the final project because this way people will be able to see that they're not alone about what they're thinking or how they're feeling. It will let other people know what UIC is lacking and give you a better outlook of what your next four years are like.

It has helped me voice my opinion and understand that I am not alone in my opinion that many people feel the same and want to do something about it.

It would be a big gratitude to know that the web page can help other students with their problems about the University.

I believe that some of the problems that I have been experiencing many other students have too. If through my research I could help other students I say why not? I think they should be posted on a web page because I believe everyone in this class has something different to say.

My contribution to the web page was as important as any other contribution because it dealt with real problems which students may find themselves in at one time or another. I provided information that can help students avoid certain hazards while finding out about their financial aid.

> I have only been familiar with computers for 3 months and I already contributed to a web page. That is kind of fast don't you think?

While these evaluations offer some encouragement, several problems with the use of technology in our "comparing cultures" approach remained unsolved. Students with computer access at home and those who are most fluent in both speaking and writing had an advantage in this class—as seems to be the case in many classes—over students struggling with English or learning how to type or use a computer. Although Paula tried to make allowances for these obstacles, her efforts were not completely successful. Additionally, we realized that student retention is a complicated issue that often goes well beyond the scope of what a single course can do. For example, in the first semester, four of the twenty-two students told the class that they would not be back the following semester. For two, the reasons were purely material: lack of money and lack of transportation. For the other two, profound frustration with problems outside of this course (inattentive professors, huge lecture classes, unfulfilled promises by their college) prompted them to look elsewhere. Perhaps one useful lesson learned about the political effectiveness of this course is that its reach is certainly limited.

This essay is not intended as a repudiation of critique. Rather it is an effort to present the idea of cultural criticism to students in a way that is more organic and more rhetorically palatable than traditional methods. Our goal remains allied with cultural studies' aims to help students see themselves as cultural critics as well as active producers of culture.

Notes

1. The university's overall enrollment is more than 25,000, with approximately 17,000 undergraduates. Composition courses can serve more than 3,000 students per semester.

2. There are indications that the university's mission may be changing in order to attract more students with histories of academic success. UIC continues to make efforts to redefine itself and attract various types of students, in order to rival the University of Illinois's flagship campus

at Urbana-Champaign. Major cosmetic renovations have been performed, including tearing down old structures, building new dormitories, and landscaping, in an attempt to change UIC's image as a walled-in, concrete, commuter campus. The university is also raising admission standards. It recently announced programs to offer scholarships to top students from high schools in Chicago and throughout Illinois.

3. Based on preliminary data from a survey taken in spring 1995 of 1,254 students enrolled in the second of two required composition courses, 67 percent of students were employed in addition to going to school, and 48 percent worked more than fifteen hours per week. Nearly 39 percent of students surveyed indicated that they speak a language other than English at home. (This preliminary data has been compiled by Ann Feldman, Director of Composition, UIC Department of English.)

4. Only 37 percent of students who enroll at UIC graduate within six years (only 35 percent based on students beginning in 1988). This figure is as much as five percentage points below the national mean, and it ranks UIC as fifth-worst among thirteen surveyed urban universities (see Blum 1995). Thirty percent of new first-year students do not return for a second year; only 53 percent are enrolled in clear academic standing at the end of the first year. Seventy percent of students will be on probation at some time during their academic career. These statistics are even worse for African American students: only 29 percent will graduate within six years. (Data compiled by Julie Smith, UIC Data Resources Department for Institutional Analysis.)

5. The one demurring student, however, felt that no one reads Web pages. Instead of contributing to the page, she sent a letter to the editor of the school paper detailing the problems she had had at UIC that were causing her to go to another school.

Works Cited

Berlin, James A. 1991. "Composition and Cultural Studies." Pp. 47–55 in *Composition and Resistance,* ed. C. Mark Hurlbert and Michael Blitz. Portsmouth, N.H.: Boynton/Cook, Heinemann.

———. 1996. *Rhetorics, Poetics, and Cultures: Refiguring College English Studies.* Urbana, Ill.: National Council of Teachers of English.

Berlin, James A., and Michael Vivion, eds. 1992. *Cultural Studies in the English Classroom.* Portsmouth, N.H.: Boynton/Cook, Heinemann.

Blum, Debra E. 1995. "Academics and Athletics." *Chronicle of Higher Education,* 7 July: A34–A36.

Downing, David, and James Sosnoski, eds. 1997. "Conversations in Honor of James Berlin: A Special Issue of *Works and Days.*" *Works and Days* 27/28 (Fall).

France, Alan W. 1993. "Assigning Places: The Function of Introductory Composition as a Cultural Discourse." *College English* 55 (October): 593–609.

Knoblauch, C. H., and Lil Brannon. 1993. *Critical Teaching and the Idea of Literacy.* Portsmouth, N.H.: Boynton/Cook.

Langstraat, Lisa. 1997. "Discussion." *Works and Days* 27/28 (Fall): 259–60.

Miles, Libby. 1997. "Lingering Questions and Mingling Voices: Continuing Conversations with Jim Berlin." *Works and Days* 27/28 (Fall): 239–44.

Spellmeyer, Kurt. 1996. "Out of the Fashion Industry: From Cultural Studies to the Anthropology of Knowledge." *College Composition and Communication* 47.3: 424–36.

Whitford, Margaret. 1991. *Luce Irigaray: Philosophy in the Feminine.* London: Routledge.

CHAPTER SIXTEEN

Critical Technological Literacy and English Studies: Teaching, Learning, and Action

RICHARD J. SELFE
Michigan Technological University

CYNTHIA L. SELFE
Michigan Technological University

E nglish teachers—many of whom, two decades ago, deplored the antihumanistic effects of technology—are now some of the strongest proponents of computer use. Indeed, as the twenty-first century begins, it is difficult to find an English studies or literacy program in the United States that does not make significant use of computers and of technology-rich communication facilities in a range of teaching and learning situations. And although such computer-supported programs and sites have provided some English departments with a productive opportunity to reconsider and revise their curricula in light of changing cultural and communication contexts, they may also have generated some less productive secondary effects that our profession must both recognize and work to address.

Specifically, given the number of collegiate-level writing programs now operating with computer support, English composition teachers may be inadvertently involved in pedagogical programs that educate students to become technology-dependent consumers—without also helping them learn how to become critical thinkers about technology. When faculty require students to use computers in completing a range of English studies assignments—without also providing them the time and opportunity to explore the complex issues that surround technology and technology use in our culture in substantive ways—we may, without realizing it, be contributing to the education of citizens habituated to technology use but with little critical awareness about, or understanding of, the complex relationships between humans, machines, and cultural contexts. Composition teachers and scholars need to recognize that the relevance of technology in the English studies disciplines is not simply a matter of helping students work effectively with communication software and hardware, but also a matter of helping them understand and be able to assess the social, economic, and pedagogical implications of new communication technologies and technological initiatives affecting their lives.

This approach—which recognizes the complex links that now exist between literacy and technology at the beginning of the twenty-first century—we refer to as *critical technological literacy*. And given the ubiquity of computer use in schools, homes, and workplaces, we recognize this phenomenon as one that is overdetermined at the level of larger cultural formations. Operating from this understanding, the critical technological literacy practices we outline in later sections of this chapter are meant to help English studies (ES) teachers—those teaching composition, literature, and technical communication courses—provide a context for understanding the literacy-technology link both within the classroom and beyond it.

Some Assumptions That Shape This Chapter

The assumptions that shape this chapter are predicated on expectations of an increasingly technological culture, but also one in which the gap between technological haves and have-nots will continue to widen, both in this country and around the globe.

As this new century unfolds, for example, we expect that many citizens in this country and other countries will find their personal lives challenged on a daily basis by changing communicative technologies—among them, sophisticated extensions and adaptations of e-mail, video- and voice-conferencing systems, and pagers—that function around the clock to connect them to job and avocational interests. Given such an environment of change, educational systems will be designed, in part, to educate citizens about how to deal effectively with such technologies—not only how to use them, but also how to understand their uses and limitations, and how to design and manufacture even more sophisticated versions of these tools.

Within this context, students who attend schools having the resources to succeed at these tasks—schools that have adequate funding and well-prepared teachers, that operate in areas with healthy tax bases, that serve populations with incomes above the poverty level—will have an edge over students who attend schools that cannot offer adequate exposure to electronic environments for practicing literacy. Similarly, students from families with adequate resources—with incomes that allow the purchase of home computers and software, of subscriptions to online access providers, and of additional instruction in technology use—will have more exposure to electronic environments, more opportunity to practice literacy in such environments, and more experience with the literacy activities that go on within such environments (Coley, Cradler, and Engel 1997, 3).

Graduating students will find that high-paying jobs will require increasing amounts of, and ranges of, computer literacy as the ubiquity of computers—and the networks that connect them—affects all aspects of manufacturing and service industries within this country and others. And in this increasingly wired social context, electronic networks and communication devices will influence not only the people with whom most citizens work, but also the environments within which they interact. Such environments will become the basis for national and international connections that relay digitized text, image, and sound; expand the amount and kind of information to which many individuals and groups have access; and modify the fundamental structures of the "post-bureaucratic organizations" in which people work (Heckscher and Donnellon 1994). Those citizens who do not have access to such environments will, nonetheless, find themselves influenced by the demands of technological contexts (e.g., changing conceptions of privacy, changing criteria for advancement on the job, changing understanding of communicative effectiveness), often without the opportunity to partake fully of the benefits or the opportunities available therein (e.g., access to an expanded array of information sources; additional audiences and contacts; tools for composing, manipulating, and exchanging information).

The students taught by English composition teachers today, we believe, will become the designers and users of these complex digital, networked environments in the next decade. And given the challenges inherent in the environments we have described, students must develop technical literacy practices that go well beyond the conventional conception of literacy education. Their reading activities need to include not only strategies for navigating, interpreting, and using traditional print sources, but also techniques for understanding what it means to author, design, and construct texts from information in online databases and libraries, interactive CD-ROMs, e-mail, newsgroups, World Wide Web (WWW) chat systems, video libraries, animation clips, graphic image files, electronic group decision-making systems, and other forms of media-based information. Citizens' increased access to a range of primary sources will also require a broad understanding of ethics and privacy concerns as these concepts intersect with specific cultural expectations, as well as an increased willingness to analyze the quality of information and to decide which information warrants construction in rhetorically useful forms.

The implications of the technological world we describe are enormous—not only because our cultural understandings of such concepts as authorship, ownership, reading, designing, literacy, and text will continue to change dramatically, but also because our understanding of where, when, how, and with whom citizens work and play will be affected in fundamental ways. For many people, an increasingly cyborg lifestyle will be marked by a continuing lack of stability as the availability of information and the many forms in which it is distributed undergo radical change. A citizenry educated to cope effectively and responsibly with such change—one that has a hope of influencing the design and use of such systems with an eye toward humanist values—will require a complex understanding of the interrelated social and technological systems within which individuals live and function. Further, such citizens will require an understanding of technological activism and a keen sense of social agency. These elements are part of the critical technological literacy that we suggest both teachers and students should work to develop, since, not surprisingly, many adult educators are as challenged by this range of literacy practices as are our students.

Deciding how to provide an education in critical technological literacy raises key questions for teachers of English composition: What have we, as a profession, learned from our experience with technology during these past two decades, and what do we now see as productive ways of dealing with technology in English studies and literacy programs? What are our responsibilities for educating students about technology and the complex issues associated with technology, especially as these issues relate to the practice of literacy in this country and in other places around the world? In what specific sites can this education best take place? What are our roles for teaching students how to think about and respond to technology as it continues to shape our lives and as we continue to affect its design and use in society?

Some Background: Ideological Roots of Technology Use and Technological Literacy

In many ways, the recent expansion of technology within English studies and literacy programs should not be at all surprising to teachers of composition. It grows out of the same complex, overdetermined set of social formations that have so vigorously shaped this country's attitude toward technology in general. And the stable foundation for these formations is America's broad historical and economic investment in the related projects of science and technology. The potent cultural narratives generated by this articulation of social and cultural forces ensure that English teachers, like most other citizens of this country, see and understand social progress primarily in terms of technological progress, and that we perceive both of these projects as being fueled, necessarily, by a capitalistic economy and taking place within the framework of an openly democratic society. These beliefs have, in turn, shaped our basic understanding of technology's role in education.

Simply put, these representations tell us that computers in the hands of right-minded citizens working within a fair and democratic system can help us make the world a better place in which to live—especially when this technology is refined in its design by knowledgeable scientists and engineers committed to making technology serve the needs of human beings and when it is carefully legislated by a democratic federal government, committed to looking after the best interests of citizens. According to this narrative, American technological know-how, fostered and encouraged within our current system of education, has helped us develop the knowledge and skills needed to create a global information infrastructure that links people around the country—and the world—in productive ways, and, generally speaking, without regard for race, class, gender, or national origin.

This infrastructure, commonly referred to as the Internet or the World Wide Web (really a hypertext-based subset of the Internet), supports ongoing and much-needed research on health, scientific puzzles, national defense projects, and international environmental problems. We also believe that this infrastructure, as it develops, will continue to support the vital and democratic involvement of all citizens in decisions of national importance (cf. *Getting America's Students Ready* 1996; *Global Information Infrastructure* 1995; *The National Information Infrastructure* 1993).

The linkage of computers with these related social formations—science, social progress, economic prosperity, education, capitalism, and democracy—lends this cultural narrative a potent cumulative power. Within this representational framework, computers come to be understood as the latest discovery in a long line of discoveries that will contribute to making the world a better place, in part by extending the reach and the control of humankind, most specifically the reach of Americans and our particular brand of free-market capitalism and democracy. We come to expect, for instance, that technology will help us unravel the mystery of human genes and thus help us find the cure for diseases that have plagued humankind for centuries; that it will help us travel to far-off planets and map the floor of the oceans and thus ensure an improved understanding of the natural world; that it will help us solve the mysteries of natural events like hurricanes, tornadoes, earthquakes, and volcanoes and thus predict and avoid the danger posed by such phenomena; and that it will help us make education more effective and efficient and thus will help us prepare citizens who are capable of increased democratic involvement.

This extensive web of cultural understandings, then, influences the way we think about the education of Americans in public schools and universities. As a society, we have generally come to believe that—in order to prepare students to assume their roles as productive and literate citizens of the twenty-first century, individuals who can make their own contributions to the project of scientific advancement and social progress—the American education system must expose students early and often to technology and train them in its efficient design and innovative use. In this context, we have also come to understand the American system of schooling as the official venue for a technological education and for an education in technological literacy (*Getting America's Students Ready* 1996).

By the term *technological literacy*, we are not referring to what is often called "computer literacy"—that is, individuals' understanding of what computers are and how they are used, or their basic familiarity with the mechanical skills of keyboarding, storing information, and retrieving it. Rather, technological literacy is based on our ability to "read" our technocentric culture. It refers to the direct linking of technology and literacy at a fundamental level of both conception and practice—so that technological contexts for communication become an *essential part* of our cultural understanding of what it means to be literate and to practice literate behaviors, the reading and writing and exchange of texts of various kinds. Within this definition, we refer to both literacy "events" and literacy "practices" (Street 1995, 2).

At the level of literacy *events*, the term *technological literacy* refers to the tasks associated with reading, writing, and communicating within computer-based environments: among them, understanding the uses and functions of common computer applications for generating, organizing, manipulating, researching, producing, and distributing information, discourse, and texts (print, still graphics, audio, moving images) using such tools as databases, word-processing packages, multimedia production packages, e-mail, listserv software, bulletin boards, and graphics packages. At this level, *technological literacy* also refers to the skills involved in navigating and constructing online communication environments, via the WWW or other components of the Internet, by using browsers and search engines in order to locate, obtain, and use information within contexts involving writing, reading, and the exchange of texts.

At the level of literacy *practices,* these events are influenced by a common set of cultural beliefs: among them, the belief that public education will introduce all students to new communication technologies and provide them with access to the available technologies; the belief that students exposed to these new communication technologies will be able to function more effectively as competitively literate citizens in a global and increasingly technological marketplace; the belief that technology will help students learn more efficiently and effectively; and the belief that learning to use technology will allow students to take advantage of increased opportunities for economic advancement, both domestically and abroad. As we have noted, these beliefs—based on the commonsense assumption that success in educational settings will lead to success in professional settings—help establish a strong cultural association between the project of technological advancement and the projects of improving public education, increasing economic opportunity, and contributing to social progress.

Technological Literacy in English Studies Curricula

In business and professional arenas, in the private sector, and in our education system, this complex set of cultural beliefs about technology and literacy practices has come to serve as the basis on which our culture formulates its thinking about computers. And if the ideological context often serves to mask the larger picture of technological literacy in our culture as a whole, it also functions to naturalize such relations in college-level writing programs.

Most English departments, for instance, invest in the increased use of computers in an effort to prepare students more effectively for employment after graduation. Within this context, faculty are encouraged to introduce computers into various curricula because they know that students will be expected to use these communication devices when they graduate. If students hope to compete successfully for jobs upon graduation, faculty reason, they will have to display some expertise as computer-based communicators. Using this reasoning, most first-year English programs, and many basic writing programs, now teach or are planning to teach students such things as how to compose and revise using word-processing packages, to create computer-generated graphics, and to conduct research on the World Wide Web. This rationale is given additional credence within technical writing programs in which students are trained in the use of advanced communication technologies and software, such as page layout and design programs, multimedia software, digital photography, and video production systems.

Faculty also integrate computers into curricula in an effort to make English studies more relevant to students' interests. Such efforts recognize that students in more traditionally configured English programs often find it difficult to make meaningful connections between conventional literary studies and the problems that they now encounter on a daily basis: pervasive drug use, the continuing destruction of global ecosystems, the epidemic spread of AIDS and other diseases, terrorism, war, racism, homophobia, the impotence of political leaders, and the apparent irrelevance of their parties. Teachers who recognize this disjuncture often turn to computers because they offer environments within which students can work on real-world communication projects in conjunction with individuals from other countries or cultures— for example, students studying French culture in the United States having conversations with students living in Francophone countries, or students from urban cultures engaging in collaborative projects with students from rural cultures (cf. Branscomb 1998; Condon and Butler 1997; Reiss, Selfe, and Young 1998).

English composition teachers have also discovered a great deal of value in using technology to enact more vividly and concretely certain kinds of theoretical and philosophical approaches to language study and use. Word-processing programs, for example, have proven a tremendous boon to teachers who want to demonstrate and encourage process-based approaches to the teaching of composition. Similarly, computer networks have been employed by teachers who take a collaborative approach to composition. In addition, other teachers have used hypertext to demonstrate how the conventional distinctions between author and reader collapse in poststructuralist and postmodern contexts (cf. Condon and Butler 1997; Miller and Knowles 1997; Rodrigues 1997).

Finally, English composition teachers have introduced computers into English classrooms because these devices can support written exchanges with a wider range of interested readers, thus supporting authentic writing practice in ways that traditional academic assignments and environments do not. English teachers are increasingly mindful, for instance, of the fact that the Internet is the fastest-growing self-sponsored literacy forum in the world. For this reason, many teachers have begun to design assignments that take advantage of students' personal interest in MOOs and MUDs (i.e., multi-user domains), listservs, and the World Wide Web (cf. Miller and Knowles 1997; Rodrigues 1997; Reiss, Selfe, and Young 1998).

If our increasing use of technology has been well intentioned, however, it has also been less than complete. Each of the uses of technology we have mentioned—while potentially valuable at the local level of a particular classroom, teacher, and student—is nested within the set of broader cultural and social beliefs, and the very real material conditions, that we outlined earlier. Hence, it is not simply the *use* of computers that constitutes a robust literacy education in a technological world; rather, the benefits of literacy—to an individual, to a society—also depend on *a critical understanding of the contexts out of which literacy values emerge and the conditions within which literacy practices are enacted.*

English composition teachers (ourselves included), however, are just beginning to take on the attendant responsibility of educating students critically about the contexts that underlie and surround their technology practices (what we define later in this chapter as a "critical technological literacy"). In addition, we have failed to involve students in making decisions about everyday technology practices that would force them to think critically about these assumptions. The upshot of our efforts—as Richard Ohmann (1985), C. Paul Olson (1987), and Michael

Apple (1986) long ago noted—is that we have contributed to educating a generation of consumers who are dependent on computers for their communication needs, but who are also too frequently unaware of the microeconomic and social implications of such use, the underlying cultural formations that shape this use, and the global conditions that constrain such use.

Some Truth Telling: An Additional Perspective

Given the potency of the ideological system we have described, it is seldom examined critically—indeed, seldom even identified at all in connection with the increasing use of technology in English classrooms. However, it is this very understanding of the cultural consequences and implications of technological literacy events, practices, and values—and the need to come to terms with technology as it actually functions in social, political, economic, and cultural contexts—that we refer to when we talk about *critical* technological literacy.

What English studies faculty are not, generally, helping students understand—through our use of computer-enriched assignments—is that technology is an artifact of our culture and that it is closely and complexly aligned with other social formations that characterize our culture—among them, racism, sexism, and classism. Thus, we do not, generally, help students understand that, although Americans have looked to technology as an ally in preparing all citizens for the twenty-first century and providing all students in our schools with equal opportunity for learning and advancement, we now have a great deal of evidence that such beliefs are unfounded, that technology may, indeed, exacerbate rather than address some of the larger social problems that currently plague our culture.

A brief historical examination of educational computer use, followed by a snapshot of our current educational situation, can provide additional perspective on this claim. The first fully assembled microcomputers started entering American classrooms in 1980, and during these early days, the enthusiasm for these machines ran high. One of the major hopes that educators had for computers was that they could, somehow, help democratize

American classrooms. As the culturally informed reasoning went in the early 1980s, if the nation could put enough computers into enough schools, then all students—regardless of socioeconomic status, race, or gender—would have access to technology and thus to success through the technologically supported power structures of our culture.

Impetus for the movement to integrate computers into the schools was prompted by at least two important cultural realizations: first, that our society would be increasingly dependent on technology, and second, that we were not providing equitable educational opportunities to all students within the existing system. As Wheelock and Dorman (1989) pointed out in their report for the Massachusetts Advocacy Commission, of those students who enrolled in secondary schools in 1980, 12 percent of White students dropped out of secondary schools, while 17 percent of African American students, 18 percent of Hispanic students, and 29 percent of Native American students did so.

When computers were introduced into schools during the succeeding decade of the eighties, however, the expected changes turned out to be only partial, and the resulting reforms no more than minimal. In fact, by the end of the eighties, a number of educators (e.g., Cole and Griffin 1987; Sheingold, Martin, and Endreweit 1987) were noting alarming trends in connection with race and poverty associated with computers. Mary Louise Gomez (1991) summarizes Cole and Griffin (1987):

- more computers are being placed in the hands of middle- and upper-class children than poor children;

- when computers are placed in the schools of poor children, they are used for rote drill and practice instead of the "cognitive enrichment" that they provide for middle- and upper-class students;

- female students have less involvement than male students with computers in schools, irrespective of class and ethnicity. (Gomez 1991, 321)

By the end of the eighties, as this information suggests, computers were indeed present in many schools, but they were being used in ways that sustained rather than changed the existing educational trends.

According to Gomez, while teachers perceived a range of benefits from computer-assisted instruction, poor and non-White students, who, generally, most needed the benefits of enhanced educational opportunities and of improved literacy programs, were not getting them in terms of computer-supported education. She explained this trend in the following terms, observing that literacy programs were operating on an unexamined set of assumptions about the education of

> poor children and nonwhite children, and these groups' perceived abilities to learn with and about computers, [that] replicates existing models of teaching and learning with traditional resources .... [It] perpetuates stereotypic assumptions regarding the superior abilities and greater interests in technology ... of ... whites, and students of higher socio-economic status. These assumptions guide teachers' expectations of students. In turn, teachers' assumptions about learners' abilities and interests guide the development of activities for students. (Gomez 1991, 322)

A similar pattern was also certainly true in terms of a continuing gender bias. As Emily Jessup pointed out in 1991, the "gender gap" (338) in educational computing had—and continues to have—both a qualitative and a quantitative side. Citing numerous research projects (c.f. Gerver 1989; Hawkins 1985; Becker 1987), Jessup noted that in programs depending on computer support,

> at all levels of learning about computers—in school, in higher education, in further education, in training, in adult education classes, and in independent learning—women tend to be strongly underrepresented. The extent of their underrepresentation varies from sector to sector and to some extent from country to country, but the fact of it is so ubiquitous that the evidence tends to become monotonous. (Jessup 1991, 336)

Have we made progress, then, with current efforts? The most recent national project to fund technology in the public schools was undertaken by the Clinton Administration and outlined in *Getting American Schools Ready for the 21st Century: Meeting the Technology Literacy Challenge,* a document issued by the Department of Education in 1996. Estimates associated with this national effort to fund technology use in schools range from $10 billion (Rothstein 1997), at the low end, to $100 billion (Oppenheimer 1997). And as Todd Oppenheimer has noted, these costs may seem even more staggering at state or local levels. California's Pete Wilson has committed to spending $500 million on technology over the next five years (Banks and Renwick 1997), while New Jersey cut state aid to several districts in order to muster $10 million for classroom computers last academic year (Oppenheimer 1997, 46). Union City in California recently allocated $27 million to wire eleven schools (Oppenheimer 1997, 46), and Los Angeles "spent more than $8.5 million on technology in the 1995–96 school year" only to reach the conclusion that "many of its campuses are still saddled with outdated equipment" (Banks and Renwick 1997, A1).

Data about how this money is being used and what kinds of changes technology has helped us effect are disturbing. In May 1997, for example, the Policy Information Center of the Education Testing Service issued a policy report entitled *Computers and Classrooms: The Status of Technology in U.S. Schools* (Coley, Cradler, and Engel 1997). This report indicated more computers are going into schools and being made accessible to students—4.4 million with the "typical school owning between 21 and 50" (11). The report also indicated that "students with the most need get the least access" to computers (11). Among additional findings from this report are the following:

◆ Ninety-eight percent of all schools own computers. The current student-to-computer ratio of ten to one represents an all-time low ratio.

◆ While 85 percent of U.S. schools have multimedia computers, the average ratio of students to this type of computer is twenty-four to one, nearly five times the ratio recommended by the U.S. Department of Education. . . . Students attending poor and high-minority schools have less access than students attending other schools.

◆ Sixty-four percent of U.S. schools have access to the Internet, up from 35 percent in 1994 and 50 percent in 1995. In Delaware, Hawaii, New Mexico, and South Carolina, all schools are connected. . . . Students attending poor and high-minority schools are less likely to have Internet access than other students.

◆ Thirty-eight percent of our schools are using local area networks (LANs) for student instruction. . . . Students attending poor and high-minority schools have less access to LANs than students attending other schools. (Coley, Cradler, and Engel 1997, 3)

This report also provided other indications that the success of the project has been mixed. For instance, although computer access is increasing in schools, technology continues to be differentially distributed according to both race and socioeconomic status:

> The ratio of students to computers decreases as grade level increases. Elementary schools have a ratio of 11 to one; middle/junior highs have a ratio of 9.7 to one; and senior highs have a ratio of 8.4 to one.
>   . . . [S]chools with large proportions of minority students . . . have the highest ratios. While schools with less than 25 percent of such students have a student to computer ratio of about 10 to one, students in schools with 90 percent or more of minority students have a ratio of 17.4 to one.
>   High-spending districts [districts that are able to spend a high percentage of instructional monies—not salaries—on technology] have an average of 9.7 students per computer, compared to 10.2 students per computer for medium-spending districts, and 10.6 students per computer for low-spending districts. (Coley, Cradler, and Engel 1997, 11)

The report comments further on the unequal distribution of technology:

> While Title I funding is designed to help poor schools, these targeted resources are apparently ineffective in getting schools up to par technologically with other schools. Since much of the technology that currently resides in poor schools is probably due to Title I funds, it is hard to imagine what the technology level in these schools would be like without this federal funding. (Coley, Cradler, and Engel 1997, 12)

In sum, although American citizens and educators have great faith in technology as an ally in addressing some of our persistent social problems, this faith may not be borne out in fact. Given this situation, we might benefit more from the strategy of taking a critical perspective on technology use within the context of our common social goals—especially in educational settings.

In the remainder of this chapter, we will examine the reasons that English studies teachers need to assume an expanded responsibility for providing relevant and responsive technological education and suggest some routes for doing so in the classroom, in the technology-rich environments that we build and use, and by connecting ourselves with those outside our own institutions.

Is There Hope?

In his book, *The Gutenberg Elegies* (1994), Sven Birkerts offers a dark vision of computers as literacy tools. His reaction to new communication technologies—shaped by his lived experience as a literary scholar, a former rare-book dealer, an English teacher, a parent, and an essayist—leads him to this simple conclusion, "From deep in the heart I hear the voice that says, 'Refuse it'" (229). Birkerts hopes that a significant number of people will "refuse" technology because he sees little evidence that we gain much from our involvement with it, and he imagines that we have a great deal to lose.

Most English teachers, however, do not see this path as an option within their current working and living environments. There is very little doubt that students must be prepared to work in and understand electronic literacy environments if they hope to succeed in the increasingly technological cultures of the twenty-first century—and if they hope to understand the changes that such environments will generate within our culture and others. For many teachers, refusing technology means refusing access to a range of effective scholarly tools and professional support systems. And the investment of schools in technology is sustained and reproduced by the investment of the culture at large: workplaces in which approximately 70 percent of jobs requiring a bachelor's degree or an advanced college degree now require the use of computers (*Digest of Education Statistics* 1996, 458); a corporate sector focused on exploiting the 89 percent of "teachers and the public" who believe that the Internet adds value to teaching and learning specifically because it "reduces the costs teachers spend on classroom activities" (MCI Nationwide Poll 1998); schools in which 87 percent of high school students are now writing on computers by grade 11 (Coley, Cradler, and Engel 1997, 27); and homes in which 86 percent of parents are convinced that a computer is *the* one "most beneficial and effective product that they can buy to expand their children's opportunities" for education, future success, and economic prosperity (*Getting America's Students Ready* 1996, x).

Given this context, allowing ourselves the luxury of simply "refusing" technology seems not only misguided but dangerously shortsighted. We are all—each of us—now teaching students who *must* know how to communicate as informed thinkers and citizens in an increasingly technological world. Importantly, we know that these students must come to terms in increasingly intelligent and humane ways with technology as it really functions in social, political, economic, and cultural contexts. They must, in other words, not only learn how to *use* technology, but also how to develop a *critical* technological literacy; they must learn how to *think critically* about and *pay attention to* what they and others are doing in connection with technology.

For humanist scholars, perhaps the most direct case for engaging technology issues head-on comes from Martin Heidegger. In *The Question Concerning Technology* (1977), Heidegger reminds us that the danger we face from technology does not involve the machines themselves, but, rather, the relationship we maintain with technology (and with each other and with the natural world around us) as human beings. Heidegger maintains that we *must* take the time to question technology—and our relationship to it—if we hope to understand it. More importantly, however, Heidegger notes that how we think about technology, how we question it and approach the social issues connected to it, also limits and extends our understanding of the *human* condition in a technological age.

According to Heidegger, it is the questioning relationship we establish in connection with technology, not the technology itself, that is so vitally important to our understanding of human beings and the human condition. If our only approaches to, and practices within, technological systems are unconscious and unquestioning, we run the risk of developing a "technological understanding of the world." This way of understanding the world is engendered by our culture's habitual dependency on techno-logical solutions and can come to enframe our practices complete-ly, instilling in us the intellectual habit of turning to technology, and technological practices, as the solutions for all problems.

In English studies classrooms, in other words, the habitual use of technology—especially when it is untempered by the criti-cal examination of humans' relationships to technology—may serve as the immediate means to solve communication problems efficiently (e.g., to get an assignment done, to add graphics to a technical communication report, to provide an online collabora-tive experience for students, to distribute an assignment to the members of a class via the World Wide Web), but it may do so at the expense of our "unrevealing" a more important underlying relationship between humans and technology within the world. Hence, the practice of turning to technology to support assign-ments within our classroom—the use of word-processing in as-signments for papers, the use of computer networks for collaborative responses, the use of the World Wide Web for re-search papers—while admirable, can quickly become a habit that encourages another, and another, and another computer-assisted assignment. At some point, we and our students come to know only one way of communicating effectively—that of turning to computers as tools and environments within which to write, read, and exchange documents.

It is in this way, then, that we can easily fall into the trap of educating students and ourselves to be consumers of technology and to take up what Heidegger would call a technological under-standing of the world and our relationship to it. When we estab-lish such a pattern, the use of technology becomes naturalized, invisible—the stuff of common sense. We assume—and students assume—that all assignments should be completed on comput-ers because that seems like the most efficient or commonsensical approach. Within such contexts, however, the actual literacy prac-tices in computer-supported communication classrooms can eas-ily become disassociated from the larger educational goals of those classes and, in turn, from the very real experiences that students may bring to our classes—those based on their race, their mate-rial conditions, their gender, their home circumstances.

Equally or more problematic, perhaps, is the fact that a technological understanding of the world encourages the intellectual habit of perceiving everything around us—including the natural world—as a "standing reserve" (Heidegger 1977, 17) of resources that can be used to create, design, and manufacture technologies. Heidegger notes further that as we develop these two related intellectual habits—a technological understanding of the world and an understanding of the world's resources as a standing reserve, ready to hand for our own use—we enter into a process of "ordering" the world and everything in it in the service of technology. Through this process of ordering the world, "man . . . ensnares nature as an area of his own conceiving" and as an "object of research." (19) This mind-set blinds humans to a full understanding of the natural world as well as to a full understanding of their relationship to this world and to the technology they have created. This way of understanding, or enframing, the world—our technological understanding of the world—becomes dangerous when it serves to reduce our repertoire of human response to a "single way" (32) of understanding and, as a result, our other ways of understanding and dealing with the world atrophy and disappear. In addition, Heidegger points out, when humans fall into a habit of ordering the world's resources into a standing reserve that they put at their own disposal, they come, without realizing it, "to the very brink" of seeing other humans as part of this standing reserve, as objects to be put to the service of technology. In this sense, a person "fails to see himself [or herself] as the one spoken to" (27) by his or her limited understanding of technology and his or her relationship to it.

From this perspective, by relying simply on the *use* of technology in English studies classrooms—unconsciously and in unexamined ways—as a habitual means of solving communication and literacy problems, we encourage ourselves and students to understand the resources that go into such a system (to name just a few of them: the machines themselves, the computer-supported communication facilities maintained by a department or university, the training and educational efforts that make such a system possible, the factories and chemical processes required to manufacture computers, the computer and software industries, the efforts of programmers and designers and technicians, the efforts of teachers and students) in a similar fashion, as ready-to-hand materials that can be used to solve the communication problem that we deal with in classes and that students will deal with when they graduate. Moreover, within the context of such computer-rich English classrooms, the habit of understanding the world as a standing reserve may encourage us and students to lose sight of the real social costs and implications of the technology we are using—to ignore the realities of its uneven distribution along the related axes of race and poverty on our campus, the surrounding community, throughout America, or around the globe; to lose sight of the conditions in which technology support staff, factory workers, and microchip assemblers must work in order to make such facilities ready for our use; or to ignore the hard educational decisions that must be made in order to fund technology in a limited number of elite schools (Coley, Cradler, and Engel 1997; Selfe and Selfe 1994).

In such a context, without some substantive discussion of the real costs—such as a substantial proportion of American taxes and corporate investment; at least two decades of military research; between $40 billion and $100 billion in government funding for educational efforts; the professional education of American teachers (Oppenheimer 1997)—or without discussion of implications of this network of computers—especially in terms of America's hypercompetitive efforts to establish a global information infrastructure (C. Selfe 1996)—an English studies teacher who encourages students to use the World Wide Web for research assignments may in fact encourage students to adopt a technological understanding of the world. In addition—because the lack of critical approaches to technology serves to naturalize computer use by divorcing it from the complex social issues surrounding technology—we may also be encouraging students to think of the World Wide Web as a real global network rather than a limited network of individuals and countries and organizations who can afford technological infrastructure within the contexts of their lives.

Heidegger is also, of course, committed to seeing through this problematic enframing that characterizes a technological mind-set. Quoting the poet Norbert von Hellingrath, Heidegger (1977) claims, "But where danger is, grows/The saving power also" (42). He notes that it does us no good to avoid the dangers associated with technology and maintains that we must work through a systematic questioning of—confronting of—technological issues in order to understand how very limiting our current view of the world can be. There is no retreat as we face this dilemma.

How one makes this switch in attitude or approach is difficult to describe. Michael Heim, in *The Metaphysics of Virtual Reality* (1993), concludes his discussion of Heidegger this way:

> Because it accepts historical drift, [Heidegger's] existential criticism [of technology] proceeds without possessing a total picture of the whither and wherefore, without accepting the picture promoted by either technological utopians or dystopians. There is no need to enforce closure of pro or con, wholesale acceptance or rejection. While recognizing the computer as a component in our knowledge process, we can attend to what happens to us as we collaborate with technology. Because human history is a path to self-awareness, as we deepen our understanding of computer interaction, we will also increase our self-understanding. (Heim 1993, 70)

In more concrete terms, we can also find in Heidegger a suggestion about how to help English studies teachers and students break out of a technological understanding of the world—a suggestion that involves them in coming together expressly for the purpose of questioning technology and the social practices surrounding technology, directing their questioning through the lens of humanistic values rather than technological values. When we actively create and re-create humanistic communities that value questioning as a way of knowing, we can resist the enframing that Heidegger describes. The "saving power" of such approaches, as Heidegger describes it in *The Question Concerning Technology,* can be found in "insignificant things" or unanticipated events (Dreyfus 1995, 105). These events, or what Michel de Certeau (1984) might call "small potent gestures," provide English studies professionals and students with moments of agency in a world of technological change.

Strategies and Sites for Developing Critical Technological Literacy and Agency

If the need for students to develop critical technological literacy is clear, the way to go about giving them opportunities to do so in English studies programs is less obvious. In addition, the role of English teachers in this effort also remains undetermined. In this final section, we explore the shape of the literacy practices described above from the perspective of teachers of English studies and offer several strategies and sites within which English teachers might think about working with students to develop critical technological literacy.

Critical Technological Literacy

In the context of the current discussion, we want to continue to differentiate the term *critical technological literacy* from what is commonly referred to as "computer literacy." Computer literacy refers to individuals' understanding of what computers are and how they are used, or their basic familiarity with the mechanical skills of keyboarding, storing information, and retrieving it. Although such *technological* skills are obviously part of the literacy we are discussing, critical technological literacy focuses more specifically on the literacy *practices,* as well as skills (Street 1995)—that is, the discursive and communicative acts—undertaken in and around electronic environments. Critical technological literacy also encompasses the cultural and historical attitudes, values, and conditions that shape and influence these practices. The term "practices," in this context, also refers to the linkages between technology and literacy at a fundamental level of both conception and cultural practice, so that the technological and social contexts for discourse and communication, as well as the products and practices of communication, become essential parts of our cultural and historical understanding of what it means to be technologically literate: for instance, social, cultural, and historically informed understandings of how values are designed into computers as manufactured artifacts; who has and does not have access to electronic environments; how technology relates to and helps shape the cultural formations of science, education, poverty, racism, sexism; how the skills of technological literacy are taught and learned in this country; how access to and use of technology benefit citizens differentially according to power, race, gender, and socioeconomic status; and why technological systems are constructed as they are and distributed as they are within this country and around the world.

When we study practices of technological literacy critically, we see that to some extent they are influenced by the official venues of technological literacy education—the schools and the educational systems within which official literacy instruction takes place and official literacy values are inculcated. But a critical and cultural approach to understanding technological literacy practices also traces those influences introduced by a range of unofficial values: deeply sedimented cultural practices that influence why our culture considers some technological literacy activities to be officially useful and appropriate (e.g., using the WWW to do research for an officially sponsored project, using an e-mail list to communicate with people from other cultures or to practice another language, using a graphics package to add explanatory illustrations to a formal written report), and why the culture identifies other technological literacy activities to be either problematic (e.g., frequenting WWW chat rooms predominated by marginal social groups, cruising the Web for pornographic pictures, using the Internet to find recipes for designer drugs, using a Web site to join a cult) or outside the official realm of technological literacy altogether (e.g., using an ATM machine, playing a handheld video game, programming a VCR). An understanding of electronic communication practices from the perspective of critical technological literacy, for example, might recognize several, complexly related formations and institutions that shape both technological environments and the reading and writing activities that take place within these environments. Among these, for example, might be the government, which has constructed a National Information Infrastructure (NII) for supporting, first, government-sponsored military research and, later, corporate research and communication, educational activities, the distribution of information to citizens, and the provision of citizen-based input to elected officials. Similarly, companies, corporations, and nonprofits play a role in shaping online literacy practices and values—for example, by encouraging employees to use computer environments for reading and writing texts such as e-mail messages in an effort to increase communication within and among organizations. Private-sector entities also encourage technological literacy practices (the use of databases, computer-generated and archived reports, hypertext, computer-supported group decision making, etc.) to increase efficiency, improve performance, and reduce costs (cf. Duin and Hansen 1996; Johnson-Eilola and Selber 1996; Zuboff 1988).

Finally, a critical perspective on technological literacy might also recognize the influences of nonofficial, but nonetheless authoritative, sources in individuals' lives. Literacy values and practices at home, for example, may influence whether computers are used to find practical information on such topics as golf lessons, the raising of guppies, the calculation of taxes, and homeopathic remedies, among many others. Or such practices may influence a family to set up a "school work" priority on their computer, which gives school-age children first crack at the use of technology before other family members. To complicate matters, within a family each member has his or her own complex set of values that informs technological literacy practices: one adult family member may use the computer very little, perceiving it as a tool for communication only for the children; another adult may use the computer at home to catch up on work-related tasks, to stay informed about church activities, to communicate with family members in other geographical locations, or to support a hobby; one child may use the computer at home both for school-related work and for cruising chat rooms while posing as an adult. Similarly, technological literacy practices influence, and are influenced by, the values of various formal and informal social groups—gay teens, religious orders, professional groups, and drug dealers, among others—that are bound together by their use of listservs, chat rooms, bulletin boards, and Web sites.

The Role of English Studies Teachers: Strategies for Action, Sites of Agency

Given the breadth and complexity of the definition we have just sketched, there is a range of activities that English studies teachers can engage in as they attempt to help students develop critical technological literacy, and the sites within which these activities can be undertaken also varies widely. For example, while many of these activities include practicing literacy in electronic environments—that is, using computers in computer-supported writing or multimedia facilities—others, clearly, can take place in traditional classrooms with the help of print resources or in community venues where technology is distributed unevenly along existing axes of race, socioeconomic status, age, and gender, among other factors.

At Michigan Tech, for example, using Gail E. Hawisher's and Cynthia Selfe's *Literacy, Technology, and Society* (1997), we engage students in some first-year composition and third-year technical communication classes in reading about and responding to literature, provocative essays, and technology-laden images that deal with the use of technology in our culture. In particular, Hawisher and Selfe's text offers readings in five topic areas that bear broadly on technological literacy practices and values: social issues and technology, education and technology, ethics and law and technology, gender and technology, and government and technology. Within these topic areas, teachers use a range of perspectives and genres for fostering a critical perspective on technological literacy practices and values. Students read and discuss, for example, technology scholarship and criticism such as Kenneth Gergen's "Social Saturation and the Populated Self," Langdon Winner's "Mythinformation," Alvin Weinberg's "Can Technology Replace Social Engineering?" and Lee Sproull and Sara Kiesler's "Computers, Networks and Work," (all in Hawisher and Selfe 1997). This academic or scholarly perspective on technology is balanced, in part, by readings on technology from popular sources such as *Wired, Time, Utne Reader, Vogue,* the *New Yorker,* and the *Washington Post.* A critical perspective is also fostered through the inclusion of fictional readings on technology from various historical perspectives: among them, Franz Kafka's *The Penal Colony* (1948), William Gibson's "Johnny Mnemonic" (1986), and James Tiptree Jr.'s (i.e., Alice B. Sheldon's) "The Girl Who Was Plugged In" (1973). Finally, students are asked to both "read" and develop a critical understanding of technology by analyzing commercial images in which the complex social relationships of humans and computers figure prominently.

Using "Reading and Rereading" questions attached to each contribution in this collection, students can be asked to identify—and gain a critical perspective on—the cultural contexts that are revealed in connection with technology, the belief and value systems that function to influence and shape the literacy practices associated with technological environments, and the ways in which the interests and tendencies of various cultural formations (e.g., education, science, poverty, race, gender, government, business) intersect with those of technology and literacy. Finally, writing assignments associated with each contribution and section of the collection ask students to conduct their own observations of literacy practices and values within technological environments, analyze the data from these observations, and report on them to a range of audiences. One writing assignment, for example, asks students to do original research on attitudes toward technology and technology use (or non-use) in various sectors of the community within which they live and in their family. Other assignments ask students—individually or in groups— to investigate patterns of computer use for literacy activities in a local school district or a single school building; to write a proposal for a community free-net and anticipate arguments against such a proposal; to investigate the percentage of women and men using a campus computer network and report on the findings to network administrators and to the student body at large; to draft or revise a policy of sexual harassment in online environments for their campus; to write an editorial on calls for "universal" access to the Internet; or to conduct historically based research on popular-press claims for the telegraph, television, and the computer as literacy tools.

Other assignments ask students to conduct systematic examinations of contemporary commercial images that focus on technology (e.g., from *Wired*, from *Newsweek*, from television commercials) and tease out the cultural values that underlie these representations; to try living without access to electronic technology for a single day while keeping notes of the changes such a lifestyle necessitates; to craft arguments in response to essays by authors who are uncritically enthusiastic about technology (e.g., addressing claims such as those of Jon Weiner who notes, "No one is excluded [from the Internet] because of race, ethnicity, or gender") and those who are less than realistic in their advice to reject technology (e.g., addressing the advice of Sven Birkerts to "Refuse it!"); and to write letters to grade-school students about how to "stay safe" as they cruise the WWW and the Internet.

In Classes with Access to Technology-Rich Environments

In those classes that are conducted in computer-supported environments, English studies teachers can focus on building in moments of critical reflection on specific technology uses—e-mail, chat systems, the World Wide Web, MOOs and MUDs, scanners, or image manipulation software, and the like—that influence the communication projects of that course. Indeed, when we choose to teach with a specific communication technology, we might also make it a point to encourage students to think critically about the implications of such technologies on the practices and values associated with literacy. For instance, if we use e-mail, we might consider having students analyze transcripts of the flame wars or uncivil arguments that often erupt in virtual discussions and then have those students develop guidelines for civil and productive conversation in electronic environments. (For a thoroughly developed example of a process like this, see Chadwick and Dorbolo [1998].) Similarly, when we ask students to use synchronous chat environments, we need to plan time for reflection on and discussion of the material costs of real-time Internet interactions—the costs associated with computers, software, network costs, and connection fees that clearly come at the expense of other educational efforts and initiatives. We might also engage students in a discussion of how restricted some students' access is to MOOs and MUDs on many campuses, given the gaming tradition out of which those systems were developed, or how the ASCII code on which these systems are based discourages the use of languages other than English.

When English studies teachers make use of the WWW, scanners, and image manipulation software, the time is ripe for discussions of intellectual property law and policy. Classroom discussions could center on specific issues that teachers and students will encounter with increasing frequency when they operate within electronic environments and use digital materials. These issues might include digital forgery and our changing notions of plagiarism, fair use practices for educational and not-for-profit publications, or national legislation that might restrict or enhance online publishing efforts.

English faculty seeking a guide to resources in these areas can turn to the Special Intellectual Property Issue of *Computers and Composition* (August 1998). In this issue, a collection of scholars provide critically informed discussions of digital issues that both teachers and students will find valuable. These articles can be used as supplemental readings for students to inform their own in-class discussions on computer-based assignments and as starters for written reflections that are completed out of class in asynchronous, online conferencing environments. They might also be useful as the foci for lessons on such topics as the citation of online materials, the changing nature of authorship and ownership in digital environments, or new definitions of "composition" that include video images, sound, and animation as well as written text. The point here, of course, is that each time we provide reflective opportunities of this type, we encourage critical technological literacy practices in our students and in ourselves.

In Computer-Supported Communication Facilities

One site in which English studies teachers can encourage constructive and critical thinking about technologically based literacy practices and values is, ironically, in the computer-supported communication facilities themselves—technology-rich classrooms, labs, centers, and online environments. These facilities can serve not only as teaching environments for students completing literacy assignments—as sites within which both faculty and students can develop a critical understanding about the linkages between technology and literacy and critical perspective on their own and others' technology use—but also as sites within which students and faculty can formulate guidelines and policies for critically informed practices that put these understandings to work in complicated social situations. In other words, although the management and running of technology-rich sites is not often considered part of most college curricula, they offer us, in fact, one of the richest sites for the critical assessment of educational technology to be found in postsecondary education.

Andrew Feenberg's (1995) concept of underdetermination in technological systems can help us further conceptualize these facilities as sites for work. In *Alternative Modernity,* Feenberg offers the possibility of considering such sites in terms of their underdetermined potential, which can be exploited by interested agents determined to make a difference in their own lives. We know, for example, that the technology-rich communication facilities associated with English studies programs are already replete with such interested agents—the English teachers who are involved in designing and teaching within them, the students who are involved in using them and learning within these sites, the staff members (often students) who are responsible for keeping them operational, and the administrators who help to fund them.

As Feenberg notes, the potential of such agents to enact meaningful change lies in their ability to exert influence over the actions of others in contexts that involve technology. In technology-rich communication facilities, students and teachers can develop a more critically informed sense of technology by actively confronting and addressing technology issues in contexts that matter—contexts involving real people (e.g., peers, faculty, community members, staff members) engaged in a range of daily practices (e.g., making decisions about software and hardware purchases, hiring individuals who can help teachers and students deal more effectively with technology, setting lab fee levels for students, deciding on etiquette and use guidelines, identifying access problems) within their various lived experiences and in light of their own goals. When confronted and addressed in these complicated and often contradictory contexts, technology and technological issues become immediately connected with social issues, human values, and material conditions—rather than naturalized and separated from such experiences.

These and other sets of issues are all part of the process of managing technology-rich environments, and each is a component of the critical technological literacy we believe students and teachers must develop to become effective social agents and citizens in the twenty-first century. Our culture will need these activists in school board and PTO meetings when enthusiastic and reluctant committee members struggle with technology initiatives. We will need critically literate activists in small businesses, on corporate boards, and government agencies, where decisions about communication technologies will influence the personal and professional lives of citizens.

In the humanities department at Michigan Technological University, students are encouraged to consult in departmental computer-based communication environments in support of those who learn, teach, and work there. Within the context of these consultant positions, for example, students help decide how to spend a $120,000 technology budget each year. They also learn directly about the literacy needs of fellow students and about the complex technology infrastructure needed to meet such needs. They debate the pedagogical and economic value of software and hardware and they make decisions about purchasing, installing, debugging, maintaining, and documenting our system components. They also determine which students and teachers will have access to computers and at what level. Similarly, we ask both students and teachers to be involved with departmental and university committees and task forces that help determine long-range plans for technology development and use within our institution. These sites attract active technological agents who, with some direction, form communities dedicated to supporting communicative activities across the disciplines—activities that are vocational, avocational, or purely intellectual in nature. The relevance to students and teachers of that sort of community formation can't be over emphasized in an era of increasingly disparate learning and working environments.[1]

In Local Communities and in K–12 Classrooms

A final set of productive venues for developing and exploring critical perspectives on technological literacy can be found outside the walls of colleges and universities. We can identify several reasons for looking beyond our own classrooms as part of an effort to help students think critically about communication technologies.

First, we know that students and teachers develop more robust understandings of technological literacy practices by attending to audiences who face different sets of constraints than college students and teachers may encounter in their postsecondary institutions. For example, students and teachers working on in-class assignments or service-learning projects can benefit from becoming increasingly knowledgeable about how technology initiatives influence local libraries, school districts, and technical communication efforts in business and industry.

Reporting on such initiatives to various audiences in ways that avoid the simplistic representation of technology and technology-based literacy is a challenging and useful task and one that is rhetorically complex. Writing assignments of this sort—whether they are journalistic pieces, literary nonfiction, or fictional narratives—must be an activity that is rhetorically situated between a public hungry for thoughtful analyses of how new communication systems influence the humans who use them (citizens, students, teachers, and workers) and institutional representatives of libraries, schools, organizations, and businesses who are sensitive to the fiscal trade-offs that must be made in order to sustain technology initiatives. For many English studies classes (i.e., composition, technical communication, and even some literature courses), K–12 and community projects of this sort can engage students in rich, motivating, communicative projects that provide them the opportunity to think critically, thoughtfully, and in complex ways about literacy practices as they are influenced by communication technologies.

An additional reason to undertake such technological literacy initiatives outside postsecondary institutions has to do with our responsibility to attend to the future, and, in particular, to future students and future job environments. Such projects fulfill this academic responsibility in two ways. First, K–12 communities link English studies professionals with the students who will soon inhabit our classes. And, of course, local businesses, professionals, and community organizations put our current students (as well as ourselves) into contact with the technologically mediated literacy environments into which they will soon graduate. By engaging in such projects, we build our own knowledge base and, to some degree, influence our future classroom communities.

Finally, such projects may be productive because they provide authentic venues for the examination of technologically based literacy activities and values. If, as Donna Haraway suggests, "[t]he only way to find a larger vision [in this case, of critical technological literacy practices] is to be somewhere in particular" (1995, 187), technology-mediated contacts outside our classrooms provide spaces within which the "particular" and local of literacy practices and values can be examined critically in terms of broader patterns of national and global technology issues. The discussions generated by such outward-looking projects, and the understandings developed out of them, can—in turn—open up debates about appropriate technological practices that are informed by a much wider set of human, economic, and institutional issues than students might encounter in most English studies classrooms. And, in some cases, those debates can be used to influence micro- and macropolitical decisions (e.g., developing recommendations about whether or how to network an elementary school in the community; composing guidelines for collaborative cybereducation for parents and children; writing letters of opposition to or support for local, state, and federal technological literacy initiatives).

Identifying specific sites for such literacy projects and connecting to these sites is not difficult. Composition teachers will find it a relatively simple technological task, for example, to connect students in their college classrooms with K–12 students via e-mail, Web pages, or WWW chat systems. Technical communication instructors can easily find business and community organization professionals willing to act as online resource people for student projects. Though such projects can have their own complications, not so much in terms of technology as in terms of human interaction, literature faculty will find it increasingly possible to introduce published authors and critics to their students in online environments.

What is often difficult to imagine is how to embed a critical technological learning component into these exciting educational events. Ideally, in such communication projects, students will be asked to reflect on how the technologically mediated literacy practices they observe, and participate in, affect individuals and groups in the organizational and social environments of public schools, individual authors, businesses, community organizations, and their own postsecondary institutions.

Some Concluding Thoughts

We began this chapter by posing a number of questions. We might now be able to offer some brief, if necessarily incomplete, responses.

What have we, as a profession, learned from our experience during these past two decades and how do we now see the role of technology within English studies and literacy programs? We have learned how inextricably bound we are to the complex human, economic, and institutional infrastructures associated with technology use in our classrooms. Avoiding or refusing involvement with technology is not only impossible, but it also places our departments and programs at the mercy of other social agents and formations that are remarkably influential within our institutions and our culture. Such a stance also avoids our disciplinary responsibility to students who will continue to face technological challenges upon graduation and who will need critical perspectives in order to respond humanely.

What are our responsibilities for educating students about technology, especially as these issues relate to the practice of literacy in this country and in other places around the world? In what specific sites can this education best take place? We have a responsibility to involve students in the study of technology by introducing it as a related subject when we talk about literacy, explore literacy values, and engage in literacy practices. We have a responsibility to provide opportunities and encouragement for students to reflect critically on literacy practices within a range of technological and nontechnological environments and on the cultural values associated with these specific practices and sites. Encouraging students to reflect critically on literacy activities in a range of sites both inside and outside the university provides them (and us) with places "in particular" (Haraway 1995) from which to develop a larger vision of their own and others' language use.

What are our roles for teaching students how to think about and respond to technology as it continues to shape our lives and as we continue to affect its design and use in society? Our obligations as humanists and teachers suggest that we must continue to learn with students about our humanistic responsibilities in a technological age, continue to insist on developing informed and critical perspectives on technology and technological literacy issues, and continue to insist on our roles as social agents in determining appropriate and productive uses of technology.

English studies professionals—despite the humanist traditions that encourage them to locate technology in the background of their professional lives—must do a better job of taking advantage of these sites. We cannot simply use technology, nor can we afford to ignore it. We are, in sum, suggesting that most environments in which students, faculty, and staff work, write, learn, and act are already technologically mediated and are potential sites for developing the critical technological literacy practices essential to a generation of proactive, literate citizens. Taking advantage of such sites in English studies programs requires faculty who are willing to engage in careful thinking, planning, and education about literacy and technology as they are now linked in our culture, and thus to bring humanistic studies and technology studies together in responsible ways.

Note

1. However, the complexity of creating and sustaining technology-rich sites for critical technological literacy shouldn't be underestimated. Certainly, a description of that complexity is beyond the scope of this chapter. In his dissertation, Richard Selfe (1997) has developed a systematic

approach to the many social, financial, institutional, pedagogical, and technological issues influencing technology-rich environments.

Works Cited

Apple, Michael W. 1986. *Teachers and Texts: A Political Economy of Class and Gender Relations in Higher Education.* New York: Routledge and Kegan Paul.

Banks, S., and L. Renwick. 1997. Classroom Computers: A Progress Report, Part 1. *Los Angeles Times,* 8 June: A1.

Becker, Henry J. 1987. "Using Computers for Instruction." *BYTE* 12.2: 149–62.

Birkerts, Sven. 1994. *The Gutenberg Elegies: The Fate of Reading in an Electronic Age.* Boston: Faber and Faber.

Branscomb, H. Eric. 1998. *Casting Your Net: A Student's Guide to Research on the Internet.* Boston: Allyn and Bacon.

Certeau, Michel de. 1984. *The Practice of Everyday Life.* Translated by Steven Randall. Berkeley, CA: University of California Press.

Chadwick, Scott A., and Jon Dorbolo. 1998. InterQuest: Designing a Communication-Intensive Web-Based Course. Pp. 117–28 in *Electronic Communication Across the Curriculum,* ed. Donna Reiss, Dickie Selfe, and Art Young. Urbana, Ill.: National Council of Teachers of English.

Cole, Michael, and Peg Griffin, eds. 1987. *Contextual Factors in Education: Improving Science and Mathematics Education for Minorities and Women.* Madison: Wisconsin Center for Education Research, School of Education, University of Wisconsin–Madison.

Coley, Richard J., John Cradler, and Penelope K. Engel. 1997. *Computers and Classrooms: The Status of Technology in U.S. Schools.* Princeton, N.J.: Educational Testing Service, Policy Information Center.

Condon, William, and Wayne Butler. 1997. *Writing the Information Superhighway.* Boston: Allyn and Bacon.

Digest of Education Statistics, 1996. 1996. Washington, D.C.: U.S. Department of Education.

Dreyfus, Hubert L. 1995. "Heidegger on Gaining a Free Relation to Technology." Pp. 97–107 in *Technology and the Politics of Knowledge*, ed. Andrew Feenberg and Alastair Hannay. Bloomington: Indiana University Press.

Duin, Ann Hill, and Craig J. Hansen. 1996. *Nonacademic Writing: Social Theory and Technology*. Mahwah, N.J.: Lawrence Erlbaum Associates.

Feenberg, Andrew. 1995. *Alternative Modernity: The Technical Turn in Philosophy and Social Theory*. Berkeley: University of California Press.

Gerver, E. 1989. "Computers and Gender." Pp. 481–501 in *Computers in the Human Context: Information Technology, Productivity, and People*, ed. Tom Forester. Cambridge, Mass.: MIT Press.

Getting America's Students Ready for the 21st Century: Meeting the Technology Literacy Challenge. 1996. U.S. Department of Education. Washington, D.C.

Gibson, William. 1986. "Johnny Mnemonic." *Burning Chrome*. New York: Arbor House.

Global Information Infrastructure: Agenda for Cooperation. 1995. U.S. Department of Commerce. Washington, D.C.

Gomez, Mary Louise. 1991. "The Equitable Teaching of Composition with Computers: A Case for Change." Pp. 318–35 in *Evolving Perspectives on Computers and Composition Studies,* ed. Gail E. Hawisher and Cynthia L. Selfe. Urbana, Ill., and Houghton, Mich.: National Council of Teachers of English and Computers and Composition Press.

Haraway, Donna. 1995. "Situated Knowledges: The Science Question in Feminism and the Privilege of Partial Perspective." Pp. 175–94 in *Technology and the Politics of Knowledge,* ed. Andrew Feenberg and Alastair Hannay. Bloomington: Indiana University Press.

Hawisher, Gail E., and Cynthia L. Selfe. 1997. *Literacy, Technology, and Society: Confronting the Issues*. Upper Saddle River, N.J.: Prentice Hall.

Hawkins, Jan. 1985. "Computers and Girls: Rethinking the Issues." *Sex Roles* 13.3–4: 165–80.

Heckscher, Charles C., and Anne Donnellon, eds. 1994. *The Post-Bureaucratic Organization: New Perspectives on Organizational Change*. Thousand Oaks, Calif.: Sage.

Heidegger, Martin. 1977. *The Question Concerning Technology and Other Essays.* Trans. William Lovitt. New York: Harper & Row.

Heim, Michael. 1993. *The Metaphysics of Virtual Reality.* New York: Oxford University Press.

Jessup, Emily. 1991. "Feminism and Computers in Composition Instruction." Pp. 336–55 in *Evolving Perspectives on Computers and Composition Studies,* ed. Gail E. Hawisher and Cynthia L. Selfe. Urbana, Ill., and Houghton, Mich.: National Council of Teachers of English and Computers and Composition Press.

Johnson-Eilola, Johndan, and Stuart A. Selber. 1996. "After Automation: Hypertext and Corporate Structures." Pp. 115–41 in *Electronic Literacies in the Workplace: Technologies of Writing,* ed. Patricia Sullivan and Jennie Dautermann. Urbana, Ill.: National Council of Teachers of English.

Kafka, Franz. 1948. *The Penal Colony.* Trans. Willa and Edwin Muir. New York: Schocken Books.

MCI Nationwide Poll on Internet in Education. 1998. Washington, D.C.: MCI.

Miller, Susan, and Kyle Knowles. 1997. *New Ways of Writing: A Handbook for Writing with Computers.* Upper Saddle River, N.J.: Prentice Hall.

The National Information Infrastructure: Agenda for Action. 1993. U.S. Department of Commerce. Washington, D.C.

Ohmann, Richard. 1985. "Literacy, Technology, and Monopoly Capital. *College English* 47.7: 675–89.

Olson, C. Paul. 1987. "Who Computes?" Pp. 179–204 in *Critical Pedagogy and Cultural Power,* ed. David W. Livingstone. South Hadley, Mass.: Bergin & Garvey.

Oppenheimer, Todd. 1997. "The Computer Delusion." *Atlantic Monthly* 280.1: 45–62.

Reiss, Donna, Dickie Selfe, and Art Young. 1998. *Electronic Communication Across the Curriculum.* Urbana, Ill.: National Council of Teachers of English.

Rodrigues, Dawn. 1997. *The Research Paper and the World Wide Web.* Upper Saddle River, N.J.: Prentice Hall.

Rothstein, E. 1997. "Technology: Connections." *New York Times,* 7 July: D3.

Selfe, Cynthia L. 1996. "Theorizing E-Mail for the Practice, Instruction, and Study of Literacy." Pp. 255–93 in *Electronic Literacies in the Workplace: Technologies of Writing,* ed. Patricia Sullivan and Jennie Dautermann. Urbana, Ill., and Houghton, Mich.: National Council of Teachers of English and Computers and Composition Press.

Selfe, Cynthia L., and Richard J. Selfe Jr. 1994. "The Politics of the Interface: Power and Its Exercise in Electronic Contact Zones." *College Composition and Communication* 45.4: 480–504.

Selfe, Richard J., Jr. 1997. *Critical Technical Literacy Practices in and around Technology-Rich Communication Facilities.* Doctoral Dissertation, Michigan Technological University: UMI Microforms #9810904.

Sheingold, Karen, L. M. Martin, and M. W. Endreweit. 1987. "Preparing Urban Teachers for the Technological Future." Pp. 67–85 in *Mirrors of the Mind: Patterns of Experience in Educational Computing,* ed. Roy D. Pea and Karen Sheingold. Norwood, N.J.: Ablex.

Street, Brian V. 1995. *Social Literacies: Critical Approaches to Literacy in Development, Ethnography, and Education.* New York: Longman.

Tiptree, James, Jr. 1990. "The Girl Who Was Plugged In." *Her Smoke Rose Up Forever.* Sauk City, Wisc.: Arkham House.

Wheelock, Anne, and Gail Dorman. 1989. *Before It's Too Late: Dropout Prevention in the Middle Grades.* Boston: Massachusetts Advocacy Center.

Zuboff, Shoshanna. 1988. *In the Age of the Smart Machine: The Future of Work and Power.* New York: Basic Books.

CHAPTER SEVENTEEN

The Plural Commons: Meeting the Future of English Studies

KATHLEEN BLAKE YANCEY
Clemson University

I never think of the future. It comes soon enough.
Albert Einstein

In May 1997 I traveled to Bethel, Alaska—a community of about two thousand people, located about fifty miles inland from the Bering Sea, about three hundred miles west of Anchorage—a place that sits on the tundra: a place with, as they say, no roads. Home to the Yupik tribe, Bethel has attracted a diverse population: Russians and Chinese and Koreans as well as older and younger American men and women hailing from the "Lower 48." My purpose in traveling to Bethel was to work with the American and Yupik teachers who teach the children in this district.[1] More specifically, I was to continue the development of a bilingual portfolio responsive to the two majority communities: the Alaskan American English and the Alaskan American Yupik. The value of such a portfolio is that it allows students to inhabit both linguistic worlds: that of the Lower 48 and that of their own village.

As part of this project, we weighed the merits of several alternatives:

◆ local portfolios developed by each school, or a districtwide portfolio;

◆ two separate portfolios, one for English and another for Yupik, or a hybrid portfolio including both languages and cultures;

◆ different scoring guides for different age groups (elementary, middle school), or a generalized scoring guide that could transcend different contexts and showcase development.

Over and over again, as we considered alternatives and purposes and effects, we bumped up against the same issues: identity and difference; community and the individual; textuality and its power to shape as well as represent.

As I reflect on this trip now, I become aware that embedded in this work are the central issues that will define the future of English studies. I know such a claim will surprise some, confound others. To claim that the future of English studies is centrally concerned with issues like identity and difference makes me sound like Rip Van Winkle's cousin. Haven't we already looked at, dissected, and incorporated these issues into both life and school (if not, in fact, ground them into lifelessness)? Put alternatively, where are the real issues, like the effects of media transformations (e.g., the Web and MTV) and their relationship to thinking? What about ethnocentric curricula? Collaborative learning? And writing process—will it be postprocess, antiprocess, or none of the above? (In electronic text, is process recovered to the point where it is the point? Is process once again everything? Or: Is process as we once knew it even possible anymore?)

Good questions, but they all operate *within* at least one overriding context, that of democracy. Historically, English studies in this country has not focused on technology or types of curricula or process/product distinctions. It has, however, consistently focused on identity formation (Berlin 1984; Faigley 1989). Schools have dedicated themselves to producing certain kinds of students, and we English teachers have been among the most influential agents effecting that aim. Our aim, in turn, has been located within—and sometimes positioned against—the prevailing American ideology of capitalism and individualism. Consequently, identity and difference, both national and individual, provide one theme that will mark our future. The role of *story* in forming identity is likewise relevant, particularly given our focus in English studies on storymakers and storymaking. Key to all three concerns—identity, difference, and story—is the relationship between and among community, the individual, and textuality.

Over four thousand miles from Bethel, Alaska, a forty-eight-acre plot of land provides an early vantage point for understanding the larger context in which English studies functions. In 1634, four years after the Puritans landed in what they called the New World, the immigrants imagined a common meeting place. William Braxton, the owner of a parcel of land stretching from the current Beacon Hill to the then-marshes of the Back Bay, was ready to move on, and the Boston townspeople saw in his land a chance to replicate something they had valued in England: the village institution of the common land, or "'common,' a tract set aside from royal or manorial lands for the use of the townspeople," according to a brochure available at Boston Commons. The Boston townspeople contracted with Braxton to buy his property. Each householder was assessed six shillings to underwrite the purchase, which became newly named: Boston Commons, a place for cattle as for children, for citizens as well as for visitors. A common place for commoners.

Since that time, the Commons has witnessed many major events in American history: the encampment of British troops in the Revolutionary War and Union soldiers in the Civil War; the speeches of abolitionists in the nineteenth century and civil rights marchers in the twentieth; the play of children and the Mass of a Pope; the daily exchanges of people of all colors and shapes, all sizes and ethnicities. *It is a plural commons: a singular, enduring place where multiplicity is possible.* It continues to represent, I think, what is possible in this country, though not yet realized: a pluralism composed of different peoples coming together and interacting as one without being assimilated or absorbed or oppressed.

About 150 years after the founding of Boston Commons, the country itself was established, and key to that establishment was another idea radical for the times, the Jeffersonian ideal of an educated electorate, an informed citizenry that through wise decision making could lead its own country. This notion of informed citizenry is, like the Commons, still vital today, as James Berlin (1994) suggests. Like many others (e.g., McComiskey 1999; Yagelski 2000), he argues that capable decision making in a democracy derives precisely from an individual's discursive multiplicity:

> The point of education in a democracy is to discover as many
> ways of seeing as possible, not to rest secure in the perspective
> we find easiest and most comfortable or the perspective of those
> currently in power. (Berlin 1994, 66)

Or, as Linda Kerber puts it in articulating the constricting and
destructive role that master narratives have played in the history
of this country, "The promise of democracy is that we always
seek more stories to tell" (1997, 13).

If we expect to create such a democracy, such an education,
we must, I think, find ways to practice these ideals.

The notion of multiplicity within a unity, especially as represented
both in the physical place of Boston Commons and in the educational spaces we call schools, might be seen as an icon for one
version of the American promise; I'm certainly invoking it that
way here. Even without F. Scott Fitzgerald's critique, however,
we know that the dream is exactly that, more potential than reality—and a return to the other side of the continent and the country, to Alaska, makes that point all too clearly.

In Alaska, there was neither a physical commons nor a theoretical commons to bring people together as equals.[2] A polyglot
mix of the individualism of the so-called frontier and the communal of the indigenous peoples, Alaska at the time of its purchase by William Seward in the later nineteenth century didn't
inherit an ideology calling for such a commons—or the pluralistic engagement that such a commons might produce. Nor did the
more communal ideology of the native peoples prevail. Regardless of where one landed in Alaska, the populace was neatly divided between the indigenous peoples—many different Native
American tribes—and the nonindigenous peoples, principally the
Russians and North American Whites from the Lower 48. What
brought the peoples together was the schools, although the schools
were explicitly ideological agents.

In early Alaska, schools operated under a charter established
by the U.S. Congress. As explained to its members by Sheldon
Jackson in 1892, the multiple purposes of the schools coalesced
in a singular purpose and effect: eradicating any semblance of
multiplicity:

It was to establish English schools among a people the larger portion of whom do not speak or understand the English language. . . .

It was to instruct a people, the greatest portion of whom are uncivilized, who need to be taught sanitary regulations, the laws of health, improvement of dwellings, better methods of housekeeping, cooking and dressing, more remunerative forms of labor, honesty, chastity, the sacredness of the marriage relation, and everything that elevates man. So that, side by side with the usual school drill in reading, writing and arithmetic, there is a need of instruction for the girls in housekeeping, cooking, and gardening, in cutting, sewing and mending; and for the boys in carpentering and other forms of wood working, boot and shoe making, and the various trades of civilization.

It was to furnish educational advantages to a people, large classes of whom are too ignorant to appreciate them, and who require some form of pressure to oblige them to keep their children in school regularly. It was a system of schools among a people who, while in the main only partially civilized, yet have a future among them as American citizens. (qtd. in Breece 1997, 23)

The overriding purpose of these schools was, then, to "Americanize" the children completely and uniformly; initially, this purpose was carried out by teachers who often doubled as missionaries. Like Hannah Breece—whose account, *A Schoolteacher in Old Alaska* (1997), is illustrative—they played multiple roles: teacher, minister, friend.

The first White woman to teach in Alaska, Hannah Breece arrived in Kodiak in 1904, then cheerfully migrated from one community in one year to another in the next year. Because her stay in each community was short, she developed a pedagogy not unknown to the rest of us in the later years of *this* century: a peer tutoring that could sustain continued learning in teacherless classrooms. As her historian niece Jane Jacobs explains, Hannah Breece was inventive with teaching methods and projects. She had to be; often enough, when pupils entered school, she and they had no language in common. Sometimes pupils' opportunities for schooling were so short that at the same time she was teaching them, she was devising ways for them to continue by teaching each other (Breece 1997, x). Like others of her time—and like others of our own time—Breece could be, as her niece notes, racist, imperialist, and chauvinist. Unlike others of her time, however, she began to interrogate her faith in the civilization she was "delivering," particularly as she witnessed the prostitution and alcoholism introduced and funded by the "civilizers," that is, the miners, saloon keepers, and traders of the Yukon. Through the power of personal experience, she began to understand that the Americanizing of the natives could work for bad as for good, that there might be another American story to write here, one quite different from the one she had originally projected.

The very idea of alternate American stories continues to provoke dispute, though at least we are beginning to consider the question as a public issue. Until fairly recently, as the debate about the National History Standards has demonstrated, the American story was assumed to be both stable and monological. Insofar as it still exists, it includes certain unquestioned key ideas—for instance, that

> the Progressive Era was a time of great political innovation; Washington, Lincoln, and FDR were the "great" presidents; the League of Nations failed, and the United Nations succeeded; matters related to women are less important than matters related to men. . . . [Other] false certainties are the assumption that immigrants have been, compared with native-born people, insignificant historical actors, and that enslaved people had no agency in their own emancipation.[3] (Kerber 1997, 9–10)

But as Kerber goes on to explain, the truisms that have defined the American story are grounded in a false universal that fails to account for other perspectives and/or that contradicts the experiences of various groups. As she points out,

> When lynching is taken seriously, then the nation that served as a haven for immigrants in the Progressive Era was simultaneously a polity that colluded in terrorizing a large proportion of native born citizens. Indeed, from the African American perspective, the Progressive Era requires a quite different name. (11)

As a nation, we are still coming to terms with the idea that the national story is plural; whose stories, after all, will count? Moreover, questions like these cannot simply be assigned to those whose explicit work is in history: one premise of democracy is that we the people are the history. It's a responsibility that belongs to all of us.

More to the point here, perhaps, it is also the case that these three constructs—America, American democracy, and the role that education plays in both—are central to English studies specifically, and not only as a kind of theoretical and intellectual backdrop. Taking the question "What is the American story?" and pluralizing it more than transforms it (though it does that). It also provides a means of inviting the silenced to participate in the storymaking of America, at the same time that, in doing so, we demonstrate the influence and the power of storymaking.

More specifically, we in English studies can appropriately practice such American storymaking in at least three ways:

◆ First, we can acquaint ourselves with the canonical stories that do exist—oral stories and written stories, fictional stories and nonfictional ones, reviewing these stories with our students, critiquing them, discussing them in terms of genre and gender and ethnicity and voice and culture.

◆ Second, we can collect and create and tell and share "other" American stories—as exercises in storymaking of various kinds, as exercises in Americana.

◆ Third, we can reexamine and restory our own work in English classrooms.

For assistance with this last task, we might turn to Beverly Moss and Joseph Harris: located in different perspectives, they speak in common about the need for all of us in English studies not only to separate and outline and understand, but also to negotiate.

As an African American faculty member teaching White middle-class students, Beverly Moss (1994) is acutely aware of the "problem" that the combination of commonality and diversity can engender. She first encountered it in her own research on African American religious tradition. Although she had expected to find some diversity within the tradition, Moss was surprised both at the variations within it and at the role they play in maintaining the tradition. "I had to listen to these voices within the community," she says, "to understand that the diversity that exists within the tradition is what keeps the tradition going" (79). It's not either/or, but both/and. The same principle obtains in our work with students; we need, Moss argues, both difference and unity, a plural commons. As she explains,

> We get this "common culture, common literacy" approach; or a multicultural literacy, multicultural classroom model, in which "only the differences count." What seems missing in both approaches is that sameness/diversity perspective. We're either focusing too much on how we are all the same—which usually translates into all of us being held up to one single standard held by a group in a power position—or we focus on how we are different. There never seems to be a sense that we need to do both. (85)

How to do both is the question Joseph Harris (1997) takes up, and, like Moss, he focuses on how differences require more than identification and analysis: they have to be brought into "meaningful interchange" (117) so that they "intersect and inform each other" (119). Borrowing from Mary Louise Pratt's discussion of "contact zones"—"spaces where cultures meet, clash, and grapple with each, often in contexts of highly symmetrical relations of power, such as colonialism, slavery, or their aftermaths as they are lived out in many parts of the world today" (Pratt 1991, 34)—Harris argues for and against the contact zone as a way of apprehending difference within the classroom. On the one hand, such a concept helps us see the classroom "as a contested space where many discourses and cultures may meet and struggle with each other" (Harris 1997, 117). On the other hand, without a way of bringing the contested together, no change is effected.

To "deepen" our understanding of the contact zone, Harris turns to Richard Miller, who imagines the contact zone not as a space which one can form simply by bringing differing groups and views together, but as a forum that one can keep going only through a constant series of local negotiations, interventions, and compromises. The contact zone thus becomes something more like a process or event than a physical space—and it thus needs to be theorized, as Miller suggests, as a local and shifting series of interactions among perspectives and individuals (Harris 1997, 122). Ultimately, what Harris calls for is a "new rhetoric of court-ship or identification (a sense of 'common ground,' as Kurt Spellmeyer would have it)" that would invite writers to "imagine new public spheres which they'd like to have a hand in making" (Harris 1997, 124). In sum, we see the classroom as a place for creating a new rhetoric of identification that is itself a rhetoric for public life.

In sum, *the classroom as plural commons.*

Community is composed by individuals, the very people who tend to get lost in our rush to embrace postmodernist notions of social constructionism, a postmodernism which is often perceived to be at odds with individual agency. Ironically, one promise of postmodernism lies in its complex understanding of the individual: a human being engaging, knowing, and believing not in a unified way but complexly, largely as a function of being multiply situated, of being a self-in-relation-to-one-another. As Kenneth Gergen (1991) explains it,

> The postmodern turn . . . not only de-objectifies the individual self but points the way to a new vocabulary of being. . . . If individuals are by definition elements within relationships, they can neither stand apart from the social world nor be pushed and pulled by it, any more than the movements of a wave can be separated from or determined by the ocean. The sense of being threatened by the oppressive group becomes not a case of "me against the group," but of the conflict between one form of relat-edness and another.[4] (242)

In English studies, this notion of individual-in-relatedness plays itself out in two sites: text and student.

To understand the first, the textual individual, I want to cite a work that has been used in many English classes almost since its first publication: *The Diary of Anne Frank.* The reasons for using this text with students are numerous: text as means of Burkean identity between (student) author and (student) reader; the effect of the Holocaust as narrated by one individual; the role that ethnicity plays in identity politics; and more. In other words, the motives we might ascribe to the use of Anne Frank in the classroom are many and often worthy. But as Cynthia Ozick (1997) points out in "Who Owns Anne Frank?," even good motives can be thwarted, and they can be thwarted particularly when we reduce the individual to a type, when we, like the characters in Carson McCullers's *The Heart Is a Lonely Hunter,* project our (universal) needs onto that figure.[5]

Ozick makes this point by citing correspondence between an American student, Cara Wilson (nee Weiss), and Otto Frank, Anne's father. Wilson's identification with Anne derives from her reading of *Diary,* and, as she makes clear, such a reading is permeated (indeed determined) by the tropes of American affluent youth:

> I was miserable being me. . . . I was on the brink of that awful abyss of teenagedom and I, too, needed someone to talk to. . . . Dad's whole life was a series of meetings. At home, he was too tired or frustrated to unload on. I had something else in common with Anne. We both had to share with sisters who were smarter and prettier than we were. . . . (qtd. in Ozick 1997, 79).

Ozick's objection to such reader-projection into *Diary* stems primarily from her sense of how it dilutes history: "any projection of Anne Frank as a contemporary figure is an unholy speculation: it tampers with history, with reality, with deadly truth" (76). As a teacher, I'd locate my objection to it in at least one other place as well: in the equivalence of situation assumed by Wilson.

Still other lessons obtain for those of us in English studies, among them how we enact textual identification when it comes to locating an individual writer and the individual reader.[6] Kenneth Burke's point regarding rhetorical identification between reader and writer isn't intended to promote co-identity or certainty, but to understand how identification, ambiguity, and division work together within a text: "The thing's identity," he says, "would here be its uniqueness as an entity in itself and by itself, a demarcated unit having its own particular structure" (1969, 20). Of course an individual writer benefits from the Bakhtinian heteroglossia that has come before, and to that extent all writing entails a collaborative dimension, it's true. But it's also true that, textually, the writer is what he or she has made of that heteroglossia. What, we might ask, did Anne Frank make of hers?

In other words, Anne Frank is—and the *Diary* is—more than a type, more than a universal, more than someone else's projection, be that someone else the teacher or the student. Frank is a self-in-relation, an author-in-relation, and we readers are likewise in-relation: we are a plural finding ourselves in the commons of the text. Maintaining that plurality is key to sustaining the commonality of the text. This understanding, it seems to me, is a necessary starting place for reading activities in English studies, and if so, then we have other kinds of questions we need to put to our classroom practice. When we choose texts, for instance, do we consider both how they will be read and what kind of projections they lend themselves to? How do we situate readings—by means of other readings, related writing assignments, activities like readers' theater, films, discussions, and so on? Do such situatings limit if not preclude the kind of projection we see in Wilson? Are there, then, commonplace ways of situating texts so that the likelihood of (false) projection is lessened? And what can students tell us about this: how might they help us in this project?

To put my own point in yet another context, I think it's true that students do read more literature than they did when basal texts dominated educational institutions, and this change has come about partly in response to the whole language movement and partly due to state testing agencies' inclusion of "literature" in state assessments. This is to the good. Unless: the literature becomes nothing more than a mirror to play back to a reader his or her own version of reality. When that happens, reading becomes merely an exercise in solipsism, and, as Ozick's analysis attests, all of humanity—each one of us—is cheapened.

I indicated earlier that we might ask students to help us understand how they read—not under the guise of a formal research project, but routinely, as readers from whom we could learn something. Such a concept isn't new, but it is radical, and, in general, it isn't what we see in schools today. Again, Kenneth Gergen (1991) outlines the kind of coming paradigmatic shift that I refer to here:

> Traditional educational practices are built around improving the minds of single individuals. Sustained by modernist assumptions, teachers and professors take the role of authorities in a given subject, their task to fill the students' minds with knowledge of their specialty. The postmodernist, however, would view academic subjects as forms of discourse peculiar to communities (biologists, economists, etc.) engaged in different activities. Students themselves are experts within the discourses of their own particular subcultures—languages that help them to maintain their life-styles and adapt to the world as they construct it. Thus, education should not be a matter of replacing "poor" with "superior" knowledge, but should be a dialogue, in which all subcultures may benefit from the discourses of their neighbors. Teachers would invite students into modes of dialogue as participants rather than pawns, as collaborative interlocutors instead of slates to be filled. (250)

Specifically, I want to suggest three ways that students can collaborate with us. First, students can help us understand the texts that they write. Second, students can help us explore that over which we do not and cannot exert control: the understanding and interpretation of text. Third, students can work with us to develop new forms of textual production.

The idea that students work with us to help us understand and interpret their texts is not new: that, in part, is the intent of context-setting texts like Jeff Sommers's "The Writer's Memo" (1989), Sam Watson's "Letters on Writing" (1991), my own "Guide for Readers and Writers" (in Yancey 1998), and multiple versions of the now-ubiquitous reflective "Letter to the Reader" fronting writing portfolios. What these plural forms intend varies: Sommers wants a description of writing process, for instance, while reflective letters can include process descriptions, self-assessment, and relevant autobiographical information. What's becoming increasingly clear, however, is that we readers need the assistance in reading that these forms provide.

In 1994, Charles Schuster expressed his concerns about the value of such letters precisely because of the influence they can wield. When faced with such a reflective text, he says, we as readers have a "strong tendency to create a portrait of the writer" (319), a practice at odds with the (nonfictionalized) purpose of assessment:

> In effect, fictionalizing student authors moves readers away from normed criteria, replacing careful evaluation with reader response . . . . Presumptions concerning personality, intention, behavior and the like skew readings or turn assessment into novel reading . . . . Such fictionalizing serves a useful purpose within a classroom; by doing so, instructors individualize and humanize their students, or at the very least, create narrative explanations and justifications for student work. Writing assessment, however, demands that we exclusively evaluate what the student has produced on the page in the portfolio. Fictionalizing in this context can only obscure judgment. (Schuster 1994, 319)

Schuster focuses on the role that fictionalizing plays in reading portfolios when the "primary" texts are interpreted by the author in a reflective text. The assumption here, of course, is that when reading single texts, we don't so fictionalize. However, an increasing body of research—conducted by Francis Sullivan (1997) and by Lucille Schultz, Marjorie Roemer, and Russel Durst (1997)—suggests that fictionalizing is exactly what we do when we read student texts; or, put differently, when we read, we project into texts our own images—or not. When the images replicate ourselves, Sullivan (1997) finds, we evaluate the texts accordingly: beneficently. When we can create a sympathetic context for reading the text, we evaluate kindly. In other words, we don't read and evaluate independently—ever. Like our students reading Anne Frank, we project.

Call the tendency what you will—fictionalizing, narrativizing, or projecting—it's an impulse that calls for a correction. One means of "correction" is, as Wendy Bishop (1989) suggests, to "triangulate" the writer by reviewing different kinds of texts; such a collection makes it more difficult to project a unified self onto the texts. Another means of correction is to include various readers, both "insiders" and "outsiders." In this case, we are the outsiders; the students are the insiders. As insiders, they necessarily bring a different context—authoritative in its own right— to our reading, and in so doing, they enrich that reading. Because we speak with different authorities, we can have Gergen's dialogue: *the texts as commons, we as plural.*

Students can also help us interpret other texts, particularly when we locate them in a context we call literacy. If there were one truism about literacy about which we all might agree, it's that literacy changes. One group of actors engaged in changing it, as Gergen remarks, consists of students themselves. As I have argued elsewhere,[7] their literacy—a product of MTV as much as of Shakespeare, of the World Wide Web as much as of the Bible—isn't my mother's, nor, I should add, is it mine. The only way to understand what it *is* involves going to the source: to the students. As important, they frequently are more engaged in the technology that is changing the literacy I call upon to write this text. Students can speak to the methods of such technology, to the rhetorics and poetics and visuals of its texts, to the ways they understand them. They can speak to these issues, it should be emphasized, in ways that I as teacher *cannot*. We have much to teach each other.

And finally, we in English studies need to work with students to develop new textual production—and then we must value it. While in the last twenty-five years we have moved away from reading only canonical texts composed by "authors," as Susan Miller (1989) calls them,[8] most of us haven't budged when it comes to assigning and valuing anything other than canonical texts by students. The no-longer-recent debate between Elbow and Bartholomae, in this context, can be seen as merely a dispute about which canon will dominate.[9] But if, as Burke maintains, genre is a way of excluding—of not knowing—as well as of knowing, then it behooves us to assign not only the multiple writings that compose the postmodern self, but also multiple *kinds* of writings—everything from Winston Weathers's (1980) Grammar B to homepages for the Web, from MOO essays (i.e., essays in multi-user domains on the Internet) to Geoff Sirc's (1997) celebration of the Sex Pistols. As expressed by Derek Owens, such multiplicity provides the core of what we should be doing in English studies:

> We cannot on the one hand invite the students and colleagues of a linguistic community to think differently about a given philosophy or idea if at the same time we confine them to preselected, inflexible discourses hostile to changing ways of making knowledge with language. It's not a pejorative relativism we need to acknowledge, the dismissal of all ideology based on the fact that

none are superior or inferior to one another, but a constructive relativism, one tolerant of shifts, conflicting traditions, and opposing imaginations. (1994, 230–31)

What does this mean?

◆ That we ask students to work within poetics and rhetoric and expand them both and bring them back together.

◆ That we allow students to play with the texts produced and encoded by new technologies.

◆ That we ask students to represent and express the multiplicity that they are, in text.

In sum, that *we become a plural commons.*

While in Alaska, I worked with the teachers as planned. I understood myself as an outsider, the teachers and their students as the insiders, although I could map us differently, of course—the teachers *and* I as outsiders, the students as insiders; the Yupik (still) as insiders, the native English speakers as outsiders (yet). During our time together, I hoped, we would create a portfolio model together, one that was

stable enough to locate practice,

multiple enough to include diversity,

rich enough to honor texts and students.

To do *this* work, we quite literally had to create a language. We were bound to the standards for language arts used by the state: that was one linguistic context. We were bound to the practices within the schools: that was another context. We worked within a bilingual context that was heavily influenced by Yupik culture: that was a third. Within these contexts, we worked to create our own. Contextually, metaphorically, we were creating language, of course. We were in fact speaking in English, but we wanted what we had created to be rendered in *both* languages. Accordingly, we quite literally had to create the words in Yupik:

words like "reflection," criteria like "consults with elders." What we did was create (yet) another context for meaning to occur in.

After I left, what we had created—our model of portfolio contents and expectations—was reviewed and revised by a different group: team leaders, teachers, parents, community activists. What they created is now being interpreted and embodied (or not) by students and teachers. Next May, another group will gather to review what has been accomplished—and to learn about accomplishments and understandings that we could not have predicted.

Ultimately, this too is what English studies is about: learning.

The challenge for English studies is twofold: to honor the plural commons that we create and to practice it. Historically, that challenge has cut both ways. On the one hand, we have the commons of democracy, the promise that probably never will be realized but *that relates us all to each other.* On the other hand, we have understood a limited model of the commons all too well; have tended (more often than not) to enact the agenda of this limited commons; and, even if with good intentions, have engaged in practices whose primary effects have been to replicate ourselves.

But in this country, within the last decade particularly, we have begun to see things differently: to understand that the commons is plural, to appreciate that we need the diversity of pluralism at the same time that we are a common. We understand that contacts (and perhaps their zones) are necessary but not sufficient; we need to engage and negotiate and interact. We are beginning to understand literacy as generative and common, which means that all of us are participants as well as spectators; that students bring their own lived expertise to this topic. We are beginning to understand the powerful impulse to overgeneralize and universalize, and what the terrible costs of that impulse are. We're looking more at how we read and thus how we might read better, and, I hope, we're moving beyond the canon in writing.

The challenge and opportunity for English studies is to deliver on all these promises, to continue learning as we do, and to make new and humane use of that learning.

In sum, to embody ourselves as the plural commons.

Notes

1. The district itself is enormous geographically, but each village has its own multigrade school, and the first language for the majority of students is Yupik.

2. Of course, Boston Commons was suspect in this regard as well, although at first, Native Americans did participate in the Commons, and it's worth remembering, even without apologizing for Boston, that it provided the home for the abolitionist movement. Still, no analogous space was considered in Alaska, perhaps because of climate, its many inaccessible locations, or its division into two primary groups of people: the indigenous peoples, considered subhuman by many; and the settlers.

3. Interestingly, the original native-born people are not considered at all in this portrayal.

4. This kind of dichotomous thinking characterizes even those who argue in favor of a more multiple, postmodern approach: see McComiskey (1999) for a discussion of this problem.

5. For another example of this tendency, see "Visualizing 'The People': Individualism vs. Collectivism in *Let Us Now Praise Famous Men*" by John Louis Lucaites in the *Quarterly Journal of Speech* 83.3 (August 1997): 269–88.

6. See Mike Crang's *Cultural Geography* (1998) for a useful discussion of this point, especially Chapter 5.

7. See Chapter 8, "Literacy and the Curriculum," in my *Reflection in the Writing Classroom* (1998).

8. See Susan Miller's (1989) distinction between authors and writers, for example.

9. An interesting instance of this debate occurs periodically on the electronic listserv WPA-L, where debates flourish regarding criteria for writing-intensive courses, with one side holding forth for rhetorical features, another for arhetorical features like number of pages—in print, of course. For the original texts of the debate between Elbow and Bartholomae, see Villanueva (1997), pages 479–510.

Works Cited

Berlin, James A. 1984. *Writing Instruction in Nineteenth-Century American Colleges*. Carbondale: Southern Illinois University Press.

—————. 1994. "The Subversions of the Portfolio." Pp. 56–69 in *New Directions in Portfolio Assessment: Reflective Practice, Critical Theory, and Large-Scale Scoring*, ed. Laurel Black, Donald A. Daiker, Jeffrey Sommers, and Gail Stygall. Portsmouth, N.H.: Boynton/Cook Heinemann.

Bishop, Wendy. 1989. "Qualitative Evaluation and the Conversational Writing Classroom." *Journal of Teaching Writing* (special issue): 267–85.

Breece, Hannah. 1997. *A Schoolteacher in Old Alaska: The Story of Hannah Breece*. Ed. Jane Jacobs. New York: Vintage.

Burke, Kenneth. 1969. *A Rhetoric of Motives*. Berkeley: University of California Press.

Crang, Mike. 1998. *Cultural Geography*. London: Routledge.

Faigley, Lester. 1989. "Judging Writing, Judging Selves." *College Composition and Communication* 40.4: 395–412.

Gergen, Kenneth J. 1991. *The Saturated Self: Dilemmas of Identity in Contemporary Life*. New York: HarperCollins.

Harris, Joseph. 1997. *A Teaching Subject: Composition since 1966*. Upper Saddle River, N.J.: Prentice Hall.

Kerber, Linda. 1997. "The Challenge of 'Opinionative Assurance.'" *National Forum* 77.3: 9–14.

McComiskey, Bruce. 2000. *Teaching Composition as a Social Process*. Logan: Utah State University Press.

Miller, Susan. 1989. *Rescuing the Subject: A Critical Introduction to Rhetoric and the Writer*. Carbondale: Southern Illinois University Press.

Moss, Beverly J., ed. 1994. *Literacy across Communities*. Cresskill, N.J.: Hampton Press.

Owens, Derek. 1994. *Resisting Writings (and the Boundaries of Composition)*. Dallas: Southern Methodist University Press.

Ozick, Cynthia. 1997. "Who Owns Anne Frank?" *New Yorker*, 6 October: 76–88.

Pratt, Mary Louise. 1991. "Arts of the Contact Zone." Pp. 33–40 in *Profession 91*. New York: MLA. (Originally presented as the keynote address at MLA's Responsibilities for Literacy conference in September 1990 in Pittsburgh.)

Schultz, Lucille, Marjorie Roemer, and Russell Durst. 1997. "Stories of Reading: Inside and Outside the Texts of Portfolios." *Assessing Writing* 4.2: 121–32.

Schuster, Charles. 1994. "Climbing the Slippery Slope of Writing Assessment: The Programmatic Use of Writing Portfolios." Pp. 314–25 in *New Directions in Portfolio Assessment: Reflective Practice, Critical Theory, and Large-Scale Scoring*, ed. Laurel Black, Donald A. Daiker, Jeffrey Sommers, and Gail Stygall. Portsmouth, N.H.: Boynton/Cook Heinemann.

Sirc, Geoffrey. 1997. "Never Mind the Tagmemics, Where's the Sex Pistols?" *College Composition and Communication* 48.1: 9–29.

Sommers, Jeffrey. 1989. "The Writer's Memo: Collaboration, Response, and Development." Pp. 174–86 in *Writing and Response*, ed. Chris M. Anson. Urbana, Ill.: National Council of Teachers of English.

Sullivan, Francis J., Jr. 1997. "Calling Writers' Bluffs: The Social Production of Writing Ability in University Placement-Testing." *Assessing Writing* 4.1: 53–81.

Villanueva, Victor, Jr., ed. 1997. *Cross-Talk in Comp Theory: A Reader*. Urbana, Ill.: National Council of Teachers of English.

Watson, Sam. 1991. "Letters on Writing—A Medium of Exchange with Students of Writing." Pp. 133–51 in *Teaching Advanced Composition: Why and How*, ed. Katherine H. Adams and John L. Adams. Portsmouth, N.H.: Boynton/Cook.

Weathers, Winston. 1980. *An Alternate Style: Options in Composition*. Rochelle Park, N.J.: Hayden Book Co.

Yagelski, Robert P. 2000. *Literacy Matters: Writing and Reading the Social Self*. New York: Teachers College Press.

Yancey, Kathleen Blake. 1998. *Reflection in the Writing Classroom*. Logan: Utah State University Press.

Language, Technology, and the Future of English Studies

VALERIE HARDIN DRYE
MARK REYNOLDS
PAULA MATHIEU
JAMES J. SOSNOSKI
RICHARD J. SELFE
KATHLEEN BLAKE YANCEY

MARK REYNOLDS: The essays in this section seem appropriate based on predictions about the future of higher education in the new millennium.

RICHARD J. SELFE: One theme that binds these chapters together is the increasing awareness of connectedness. The lives of each group of students and teachers are bound—through language use, language practices, languages values—to a much wider set of individuals and groups: through shared cultural formations, historically situated literary traditions, richly articulated cultural narratives, networked electronic environments, and common global patterns of war, poverty, hunger, and ecological or cultural degradation. In each chapter, there is a realization that teachers and students can no longer afford to work in isolated language contexts—that classroom language practices and literacy education must resonate with public and workplace demands, historical and cultural traditions, and changing electronic environments.

VALERIE HARDIN DRYE: Yet, as I read over the thoughtful and thought-provoking chapters contributed by my colleagues, I find myself wondering if we teachers of *English* aren't taking on more than most of us can handle—or should. Even as I recognize the need for inviting multiple cultures and languages into the classroom, questioning the dominant culture, and incorporating technology in my lessons, I look at my regular (or general) ninth graders and have to ask: Who is going to teach them how to read and write the *English* language? Yes, the dominant culture's the standard. The one that's used in most business discourse. The one in which text books, newspapers, junk mail, credit terms, contracts, technical manuals, and most reliable Web sources are written.

PAULA MATHIEU: Mark Reynolds makes me wonder about the fit of cultural studies in community college classes, where faculty teach so many classes and wear many hats. Reynolds writes, "While many of their colleagues at universities may have engaged in theory debates, culture wars, canon revolutions, and [other] controversies . . . , two-year faculty have primarily remained on the sidelines of these developments, maintaining their focus on students." Ultimately the stories of two-year faculty are vitally necessary to critique courses, like ours, as well the whole enterprise of cultural studies in composition.

JAMES J. SOSNOSKI: I agree. At the same time, I'm struck by the fact that, while Mark suggests that his colleagues rarely engage in theory debates, he invokes Steve North's conception of "lore" as the governing mode of pedagogical generalizations on two-year college campuses. If we take Patricia Harkin's glosses on North's use of the term "lore," then Reynolds's colleagues are *theorizing* rather than applying theory. In *Token Professionals,* I discuss Harkin's view of lore as "theorizing," arguing that it is a much more vital mode than the invocation and application of the theories of Master Critics. Most important, it is more likely to succeed in addressing the problems teachers face when helping students learn to learn. Many teachers want their students to adopt their views of the world and its cultures. The lore/theorizing that Reynolds speaks about might be a more productive form of cultural studies than the text-oriented version that has been promulgated in universities. I'm thinking specifically of the kinds of curricular adjustments Reynolds cites that are made on the two-year college campuses to accommodate their multicultural student populations.

VALERIE HARDIN DRYE: However, I'm not convinced that much of what is being proposed here should fall on the shoulders of English teachers, or at least those of us at the elementary and secondary levels. As Mark Reynolds pointed out, much of what the two-year colleges are doing is remediation and basic reading and writing. I have to wonder what happened at the elementary and secondary level that so many students need this kind of remediation. And I have to ask myself, as a teacher of

ninth graders, what my students *really* need from English studies professionals and what our future response should be. Communication skills in a common language are essential in a society
as complex as ours. Without that, do we not run the risk of a
modern-day Tower of Babel?

MARK REYNOLDS: I think Paula Mathieu and James Sosnoski's efforts to use cultural criticism united with students' experiences
offer a hopeful turn for pedagogy with future English students.
Having students expand their notion of texts and examine their
cultural and political contexts offers interesting classroom
possibilities for tomorrow's students. The population of students at the University of Illinois at Chicago sounds much like
many community college populations, with its diversity and
the amount of student employment. Such student populations
will only increase on college campuses in the future. Moreover,
such students respond best to course content that holds personal interests, connection, or involvement, such as that
Mathieu offers to her students. The use of student-created Web
pages that result from course work also suggests a way to enhance students' interest and engage them in course content.
The goal of getting students to be critical observers and thinkers about culture rather than mere producers or consumers is
admirable.

PAULA MATHIEU: Richard and Cynthia Selfe caused me to immediately and completely rethink my "well-intentioned" teaching
relationship to technology. I've thought and written about critical approaches to technology and sincerely want our Enacting
Cultures course to help students take a critical stance toward
technology. In reality, though, the Selfes' article makes me wonder how well I've done. They write, "English composition teachers may be inadvertently involved in pedagogical programs that
educate students to become technology-dependent consumers
without also helping them learn how to become critical thinkers about technology." Is my comparative Web assignment an
effort to get students to think critically about technology, or
am I just encouraging more choosey shoppers? The consumer
subject position is so powerful that, as teachers, we really need
to think through how to engage students in other roles as well.

JAMES J. SOSNOSKI: I think "more choosey shoppers" is another way
of saying "more critical shoppers." Putting an end to a consumer society seems an unrealistic goal. If educational priorities are emphasized, then helping persons who use technology

become more "choosey" about what technologies they are choosing seems to me a more realistic goal.

If the Selfes' first "assumption" (that the gap between onliners and offliners will increase) is on target—and I believe it is—then English teachers like ourselves are implicated because we are engaged in the "business" of "computer literacy." We need to undertake this task with a critical attitude toward technology, because we are simultaneously engaged in the education of citizens whose "technological literacy" will become the basis of our democracy. Hence the need for "technological literacy." I'm thoroughly in agreement with this point. A key issue is the one you (Paula) have identified: To what extent are we complicit in the ideology of consumerism (which is corollary to the assumption that technological advances are forms of cultural progress) when we attempt to teach "literacy practices"? Richard and Cynthia Selfe note that "it is not simply the *use* of computers that constitutes a robust literacy education in a technological world; rather, the benefits of literacy— to an individual, to a society—also depend on *a critical understanding of the contexts out of which literacy values emerge and the conditions within which literacy practices are enacted*" (emphasis in original). I would use their thesis to argue that Enacting Cultures uses technology to promote values that benefit the students who are learning how to use the technology. I'll be interested to see if the Selfes believe that we are promoting "technological literacy" or simply being complicit in prevailing economies.

MARK REYNOLDS: Selfe and Selfe's chapter problematizes many areas of concern regarding the current tidal wave of technology engulfing all of higher education, most importantly the dehumanizing possibilities inherent in technology use and abuse. Faculty everywhere are being pressured to become users of technology, to incorporate it into their classrooms, and to create Web pages for their courses, departments, and professional selves without being given the essential time for critical reflection on the implications of such technology. Selfe and Selfe worry about the technology-dependent students who have not been taught to think critically about technology—a major and justifiable worry. I worry, too, about the faculty I see rushing to use technology almost with no thought about their actions or the implications. We are blinded by the speed and the daily newness of electronic gadgetry.

RICHARD J. SELFE: So what is the future of English studies according to the chapters contained within this section? A robust modern and postmodern mix of multiplied challenges and multiplied possibilities. Textured by an underlying sense of the importance of language as a crucial means for political agency, the future of English(es) studies is characterized by these authors as a multiplied set of discursive environments for productive social action—part MTV, part *Canterbury Tales,* part radical cyborg hangout, a digitized landscape within which new primary identities are created, based on a blend of cultural narratives, oral histories, and public exchange. And this expanded set of literacy studies is self-reflexive—about the limitations of its own discursive identities; about the forms of language and the sources from whence they came; about the power that accrues to language use and literacy education; about the effects of various language technologies and their distribution (or lack thereof) around the world; about the relationship between language and existing social/cultural formations like race, socioeconomic status, geography, and technology.

JAMES J. SOSNOSKI: In the "contact zone" we call a classroom, personal histories (and hence identifications) merge into more general histories and those into even more general histories of classrooms, and so on. I would hope that the "democratization" of the storytelling about learning and teaching how to read and write in English in America(s) will provide us with a rereading of the *his*-stories of English studies. And one function of a "contact zone" must be to enable student storytelling in a way that allows their stories to be an "identification" with the general history of English studies rather than an alienating encounter with the Master Teacher's story. I think Yancey is on target when she suggests that a "multiplicity" of multiform retellings in the present contact zones—even in Alaska—anticipate what the future history of English studies can be.

RICHARD J. SELFE: And if this circus of language teaching and learning sometimes seems daunting or confusing to those of us raised within the safer confines of a more coherent modernist perspective—a current-traditional understanding of English studies—it can also be exciting in its multiplied possibilities for discursive agency. We look forward to exciting times.

The Future of English Studies Redux: Teaching and Learning as Rhetorical Acts

KATHLEEN BLAKE YANCEY

> Narrative, for Burke, is not story so much as it is contextuality. Contextuality embeds ideas and identity alike in the particular and dynamic complexities that develop in relational life, and it denies them any possibility of their anonymity or autonomy. (Clark 1997)

It's a Thursday morning in the upstate, the dogwoods' heart-shaped green leaves find their edges tinged with a reddish purple, and we're in the MATRF—Clemson's "Multi Authored Teaching and Research Facility." That place, it's *almost exactly* what it sounds like: a clean, almost sunny, softly carpeted room, PC workstations interspersed with mice and scanners, table tops matched up with light gray upholstered easy chairs on wheels, the space overseen by a fixed projection system that broadcasts the central screen.

It doesn't feel like a classroom.

No, go further: it doesn't **feel** like a school.

In teams, the first-year comp students take up a three-part task: they are to submit a single document in which they

- give an account of World War II;
- find some information on the Web that contributes to this account, and some that doesn't;
- find a visual to include in the account.

Drew, the cynical frat pledge who missed class (apologetically, of course) last time, looks for his team, finds them, and goes for visuals. Nick searches for government documents that will confirm what he believes about the war. Sarah finds "The History

Place" on the Web, looks for facts, can't verify that they are accurate, but sends them to the printer anyway, while James embodies disengagement: he sits silently aside. Across the room, Pamela sits, too, but points now and again at something on the screen where Michael almost single-mindedly drafts their account. In Katie's team, she and another James talk their draft through together as she keyboards their words; their colleagues Brett and Jessica talk at each other as they compose the second half of the team doc. Ty watches Ben click from one visual to the next.

The printer alternately spits and hums.

With or without technology, they don't quite have collaborating figured out yet.
Or: rhetoric.

> Rhetoric's primary function, Gregory Clark
> suggests, is to provide *a means to the end of*
> *bringing people together.*

What role will technology play in this?

* * *

Sometimes, we in English studies say that our focus is literacy: it's a claim made in this book. When asked how she is literate, Jessica replies:

> My literacy exhibit is a personal pan pizza
> box from Pizza Hut. My reasoning behind bring-
> ing a pizza box is that in elementary school it
> acted as a bribe to read books. It wasn't just
> my parents trying to get me to read. It was
> also the elementary school and Pizza Hut who
> were trying to encourage literacy. . . . It
> ended up being a competition between the stu-
> dents to see who could get the most blue dots.

I juxtapose this account of literacy with the version a friend and I coauthored this summer.

> Humans attempt to make meaning in many different ways: and that's what reading is, making meaning. We attempt to comprehend what is written. We attempt to make sense of what is being said in light of our own experiences and reading practices. We hope that what is being said connects with us intellectually as well as emotionally, spiritually. (Vielstimmig 2000)

In one case, we're connecting dots; in the other, we're connecting humans. What does this juxtaposition tell us about literacy?

***

Two years ago (was it?), I opened this essay saying that I wasn't going to focus on what I thought most readers might expect, given my topic—the future of English studies. I wasn't going to talk about "the effects of media transformations (e.g., the Web and MTV) and their relationship to thinking." And I wasn't going to talk about "ethnocentric curricula" or "writing process," although I found writing process questions pretty interesting: "Will it be postprocess, antiprocess, or none of the above? (In electronic text, is process recovered to the point where it is the point? Is process once again everything? Or: Is process as we once knew it even possible anymore?)"

I was going to tell a narrative that I thought was instructive.

> Narrative, for Burke, is not story so much as it is contextuality. Contextuality embeds ideas and identity alike in the particular and dynamic complexities that develop in relational life, and it denies them any possibility of their anonymity or autonomy. (Clark 1997)

It's two years (and a lifetime or two) later, but my sense of this issue is the same:

"The future of English studies is centrally concerned with issues
like identity and difference."

Yeah, well, so: there it is: Identity and difference.
As English teachers, we create the rhetorical situation of the
classroom
where issues of identity and difference can be
textually expressed, represented, negotiated, and revised
as we work toward a plural commons.

Technology is part of this work;
it is not, I think, *the* work.

* * *

Literally, I am in a different place today than I was when I
wrote my chapter, and while location may not be completely de-
terministic, it can be defining. At UNC Charlotte, I'd used technology in my teaching for some time, but in the summer of 1999,
I moved to Clemson University. Before my classes and I met here,
the students were automatically enrolled in our class listservs; I
could greet them electronically before I saw their faces. Once
we'd started meeting, we used the CLE, the Collaborative Learning Environment, for bulletin boards, for shared folders, for class
readings . . . you name it. All of which is to say: yes, my teaching
is changing, too.

The students like the new teaching. It's a residential campus,
so we're all in one place; the weather is sunny, the campus beautiful, so it's pleasant to go outside, but given a choice between a
face-to-face appointment and an email appointment, *over half
the students choose e-mail.* Another way of saying: yes, my
teaching's changing, too.

I said above,
Technology is part of this work;
it is not, I think, *the* work.

Which begs the question, What *is* the work, Yancey?

* * *

My father went to elementary school in San Francisco in the 1930s. He was a good student. He was left-handed, and that handedness served him well in every dimension of his life save one: *writing*. He was forced, as were all lefties of the time, to write right-handed. (The technology constructed him; he did not construct it.)

Is there a lesson here?

* * *

Teaching and learning are rhetorical acts: that's what my title claims. What that means, to me, is that in the classroom we make knowledge and represent knowledge within the rhetorical situation of the human relationship: that's the purpose of English studies yesterday and today and tomorrow. That was the story of Hannah Breece in Alaska, the story of the teacher who intended to instruct and enlighten, who found herself instructed and enlightened by those she taught; that is the story—the hope—of the authors here.

How we forge that human relationship is technologically informed, of course, and always was. There is no learning, no communicating, no teaching without technology of some sort. Who controls it, how it constructs us, what it enables us to do—
> to emphasize production of knowledge as well as
> consumption;
> to include design as well as critique;
> to move across media in new ways so as to communi-
> cate with new peoples in unfamiliar ways—
all this offers potential—for good and for ill, as Kenneth Burke reminds us.

With current technologies, some of us move to widen and complicate and underwrite (old, linear) process—with notions like materiality and composition and space and page design and Web text. Others use *the same technology* to distribute the same standardized tests to sort the same students in the same ways for the same ends.

It's not clear, to me at least, that technology is on the side of the angels.

And: at the end of the day, technology and new languages and new curricula and new educational structures all go to one end: the development of human relations through communication, a development that always circles back to the place where we are and are not, that place where you and I talk and read and write and think and become as one as we are not,

> the place where rhetoric provides
> *a means to the end of bringing people together.*

Or:

the place to which we bring our identity, you and I our difference,
the place we call a plural commons.

Works Cited

Clark, Gregory. 1997. "Genre as Relation: On Writing and Reading as Ethical Interaction." Pp. 125–35 in *Genre and Writing: Issues, Arguments, Alternatives,* ed. Wendy Bishop and Hans Ostrom. Portsmouth, N.H.: Boynton/Cook Heinemann.

Vielstimmig, Myka. 2000. "Reading and the Art of Berry Picking." Pp. 177–91 in *The Subject Is Reading: Essays by Teachers and Students,* ed. Wendy Bishop. Portsmouth, N.H.: Heinemann.

AFTERWORD

RICHARD M. OHMANN
Wesleyan University

R obert Yagelski opens his introduction to this volume with
mention of J. Mitchell Morse's 1972 book *The Irrelevant
English Teacher,* which argues against any demand that literature be "relevant" to our present condition, and in favor of appreciative, formalist teaching of acknowledged great works. I
remember the argument well. As editor of *College English,* I published two or three of Morse's essays, including "The Case for
Irrelevance" (December 1968), which launched this crusade. The
essay signaled its commitments straight off: Morse was a liberal,
concerned about Vietnam and civil rights, but he did not want
literature or its study drafted into political service, however desperate the political times. The best an English teacher could do
for peace and justice was promise the pleasure of art.

This claim was central not only to the New Criticism that
Morse and the rest of us practiced, but also to preprofessional
ideologies of literature at least from Sir Philip Sidney to Walter
Pater. That Morse chose to defend poetry under the banner of
"irrelevance" may seem odd now. Then it did not, because the
call for relevance was urgently in the air. It came first from the
students.[1] It was lightly theorized, and vague, but expressed fa-
tigue or moral disgust with courses and subject matters that
seemed abstract, purely academic, out of touch with students'
concerns, and mute in the face of crisis or suffering. Relevant
literature would be contemporary, or at least legible in reference
to current issues. It and the teaching of it would have personal
meaning for students. Courses across the liberal arts were measured by this standard: the judgment of humanities courses was
especially demanding, perhaps because they could not offer even

indirect access to socially remedial work, as could economics and political science and sociology. And the call for relevance sounded loudest at elite colleges and universities, where students had the class privilege to expect that they might conjoin work and personal growth and social service, not just train for jobs.

The student power movement met English at a critical point in the latter's development. Before the Second World War its practitioners had, through historical and philological research, won for it a place in the array of legitimate academic disciplines. But its presentation to undergraduates was still laced with tacit or explicit values of linguistic propriety and upper-class taste. In the postwar period, English grew along with the whole Cold War university system; democratized itself with the aid of the GI Bill and the New Criticism; and presented itself to undergraduates more as a professional field of study than as a place to acquire the cultural capital of gentlemen and ladies. An introductory course in literary study became like one in economics: we were showing the uninitiated our theoretical framework and bag of professional tools, and inviting the interested and talented to follow in our career path.[2] The demand for relevance around 1965 was in part a refusal of such invitations, a wish for a curriculum to be more than a sampling of academic specialties, or more deeply, a distrust of the professions and of schooling itself. I think Yagelski captures this opposition well in framing the present volume, speaking of a concern "that English as a discipline (indeed, institutionalized education in general) has not adequately responded to our students' needs" in hectic times. Gerald Graff remarks on a "gulf" between the culture of students and that of teachers. And all but two or three of the contributors cast the issues of relevance in terms of students' valid desires and needs. Evidently, this book inherits and carries forward the revolt of the young that drew Mitchell Morse into combat thirty years ago.

Now here is something to ponder: during those thirty years, English has in fact changed dramatically in several of the ways that sixties rebels wanted. Now, college instructors teach Tillie Olsen, Zora Neale Hurston, Richard Wright, and a hundred U.S. writers that were well outside the 1965 canon. In Massachusetts, at least, many K–12 teachers do, too: indeed, the canon enforced by our curriculum "frameworks" and high-stakes tests is far more like the one sixties radicals imagined than the one against which they rebelled—to the extent that a major charge of the Right against English is its supposedly having abandoned Shakespeare and most Great Authors in favor of the trendy, contemporary, multicultural, and correct. In colleges we also teach about movies, television, advertising, and so on; and Massachusetts has installed a parallel requirement of something like literacy in commercial culture for those who would graduate from high school. Finally, composition—now highly professionalized—has scrapped the five-paragraph theme[3] and valorized personal writing in a way that might almost satisfy the 1960s critics of academic distance and "objectivity."

I know what Yagelski is getting at when he says the English curriculum hasn't changed much in a hundred years (ix), and what Scott Leonard means in saying that our profession circles around the same old issues, never making permanent gains as does a scientific discipline. I propose nonetheless that "relevance" has won vast tracts of ground in English since 1965. It's easy to see how that happened. Among other things, activists from sixties movements came into university and even into middle and high school English in large numbers. That migration included many who had championed relevance from the beginning, or who were so influenced by them as to take relevance for granted as a goal. The causes of racial equality, women's liberation, gay rights, ethnic diversity, and so on manifested themselves in a curriculum sensitive to difference and committed, however idealistically, to the kind of society imagined by sixties activists. In my view, that change will not easily be reversed in traditional universities, since it is built into the culture and structure of our discipline and rests on a liberal ideology of respect for difference that pervades many campuses in spite of the Right's objections.

So why does "relevance" still trouble the sleep of English teachers? Perhaps in part because these changes—driven by sixties discontent with Cold War complacency and the megaversity and the impersonal high school—are now out of synch with the conditions that have succeeded postwar boom and sixties rebellions. The "commodity model of education" that Scott Leonard neatly analyzes is dissonant not only with "the nineteenth-century liberal arts model" but also with its late-twentieth-century socially engaged incarnation. Now, insistent voices and forces press education at all levels to earn its keep by bluntly economic criteria: turn out an up-to-date workforce, help increase productivity, keep the United States competitive in overheated global markets. Universities look for ways to commodify the knowledge produced in their labs and the "courseware" of their faculty members. Administrators learn, perforce, to run them like businesses, with "brands" and market niches, benchmarking and best practices, Coke and Nike contracts, venture capital offices that seem to "partner" with businesses, outsourcing and subcontracting and engaging in the degrading labor practices of which Stephen North reminds us. Privatization has not yet altered K–12 schooling so dramatically, but it is more than nibbling at the edges. For-profit companies look to enter this multi-billion-dollar "business." Voucher schemes invite their entry. In many states, charter school legislation puts public education on the defensive. High schools, like universities, must grab at Coke and Nike contracts and such partnerships with businesses as Channel One. Finally, it seems probable that high-stakes testing will facilitate a more brutal adjustment of schools to a more unequal job market.

Education in this country is a complex system, and some of its sectors remain partially immune to these commercializing forces. In elite private schools and colleges, for instance, such as the ones where I taught and the ones where Gerald Graff taught until recently, many students enjoy, by birth or meritocratic striving, the class privilege to pursue relevance in the form of personal growth or the quest for social justice, without worrying too much too soon about the job market. These institutions are barely represented in this volume, which brings news from across a spectrum that ranges through large state universities like Albany and Washington State, to more peripheral branches of public education and community colleges where older women return for a second chance (see the articles by Patricia Shelley Fox and Kathleen Cheney), to public high schools, all the way to a middle school for delinquent wards of the state (see Margaret Finders's article).

Now, many of these writers acknowledge the importance to their students of knowledge and skills that will translate into decent jobs, and some writers locate relevance squarely in that sort of economic credentialing. But almost all want something less immediately practical for their students, too. One cluster of goals includes creativity, pleasure in language, the ability to go on learning, conscious production of culture, human growth, purpose in life, self-understanding, validation of the self, or a new and fuller self—in short, versions of personal fulfillment. Another cluster of goals includes effective social agency, active citizenship, democratic collaboration, critical or subversive awareness, radical utopian hope. The two clusters are compatible. Individual and social empowerment can be mutually reinforcing, and I suspect that most of the authors do want both. For that matter, both are theoretically compatible with having a good job and furthering the economic competitiveness of our society in the global marketplace. But for many of these authors, economically pragmatic relevance sits uncomfortably with other kinds. The paradigm case may be that of Valerie Drye, whose calling is to teach creatively, personally, subversively, and for human betterment, but who can't use what she knows to help students address crises in their lives by writing about "things important" to them, because "I [have] to teach to a test." The college and university teachers probably don't experience the contradictions of relevance in just this way, but many, perhaps all, have similar concerns.

Maybe that's because powerful agents and forces outside education are trying to set terms of relevance that are at odds with what committed professionals think is most needed for their students. Certainly, our national leaders have long since decided to give schooling high or low marks as they see it fostering or impeding the growth of the American economy and the international dominance of American capital. Other influentials want more or less traditional literacy—verbal propriety and high culture—without, so far as I can see, a clear idea how achieving those goals would expand the gross domestic product. More oddly still, this liberal arts goal guides some of the more draconian high-stakes testing schemes for high schools, as in Massachusetts (where I serve on a regional school board). Should its plan "work," the dropout rate will rise steeply, few inner-city kids, or kids in special education, will get diplomas, and the same will be true of students at vocational schools, which were becoming a kind of elite, highly selective stratum because of the demonstrable economic value of their credential. This exquisite contradiction is a reminder that the most influential force of all is the economy itself—which "wants" cheap labor, not cultivated and critically thinking youth, for the millions of alienating jobs out there; which "wants," through privatization, to draw education into the increasingly universal market; and which "wants" to reproduce or deepen social inequality. All our schools and colleges are, on this view, parts of a smoothly functioning system: how could it be otherwise, with the economy booming? And if by the time this book sees print the economy is *not* booming, well, the reserve army of the unemployed will only prove that the system is smoothly correcting its excesses.

Understandably, many students—especially those trying to hoist themselves out of poverty—have a hard time looking beyond what the economy "wants" to other ideals for their education. Against their economically driven idea of relevance, the humane ideals of many who work in English studies may seem a distraction or worse. On the other hand, the essays in this collection offer abundant evidence of students who yearn to read and write about what is important, in some less instrumental way, who would like richer lives and even a more democratic society in which to live those lives. I take it as a good sign for our disorganized profession that many of its practitioners want the same things.

Notes

1. And out of the "student power" movement. Interesting that it has virtually dropped off the standard list of 1960s movements. I suppose the grievances of chiefly upper-middle-class students lost force in the turmoil of 1968 and after; also, student power was strenuously enacted through most of the other movements.

2. Composition was different: it was what we did as a "service," often reluctantly or contemptuously. The field had barely begun to professionalize. Those teaching the first-year course did not hope to lure promising students into apprenticeship.

3. K–12 may lag behind in this: cf. Valerie Hardin Drye's disheartening article in this volume.

Work Cited

Morse, J. Mitchell. "The Case for Irrelevance." *College English* 30.3 (1968): 201–11.

———. 1972. *The Irrelevant English Teacher.* Philadelphia: Temple University Press.

INDEX

research vs. teaching, 108–12
tuition as resource, 108
See also English studies
English Journal, 294
English majors, 116
English-only laws, 40, 43
English Ph.D., 69, 79n. 11, 112–13,
117
gender issues, 131, 235–56
graduate school writing,
235–56
English studies
definitions and concepts of, 152
diverse purposes of, 257–59
origins in German university
system, 106–10
"plural commons" concept,
382–400
reshaping, 270–74, 316–21
economic issues and, 13–14,
52–81, 127–28
business of English Studies,
105–26
commodity model, 52–81,
415–16
politics and, 2–4, 127–40,
135–40
schools
community college, 204–20,
307–23
high school, 143–56, 277–97
honors programs, 311
middle school, 157–82
teaching
authorial experience, 289–94
authorial intention, 286–88
composition, 4, 418n. 2
critical technological literacy
and, 368–78
first meeting of class, 212
remedial writing, 4, 309, 311,
402
See also Classroom issues;
Curriculum; Pedagogy;
Technology issues
Erickson, Frederick, 87, 91

ESL. *See* English as a second
language
Ethnicity, terminology of, 38–51
Ethnography, 98, 313
Ethos, 243

Faculty
adjunct and non-tenure-track,
312
ambivalence of roles, 26–27
discounting, 110–12, 115,
121–22, 124
elitism issues, 61
exploitation, 137
generalism vs. specialization,
311
nonfaculty employees, 115, 121
part-time, 117–19, 121, 312
proactive role, 15
professional pluralism, 16
ratio between full- and part-time,
119
stereotypes of, 65–66
tenure, 310
Faigley, Lester, 383
Fairbanks, Colleen, 163
Fanon, Frantz, 36, 43, 45, 132
Farmer, Ruth, 251–52
Feenberg, Andrew, 372
Fetterley, Judith, 194
Finders, Margaret J., 10, 127–29,
130–31, 416, 426
Fish, Stanley, 62
Fitzgerald, F. Scott, 385
Flynn, Elizabeth, 187
Fordham, Signithia, 94
Foucault, Michel, 86, 90
Fox, Patricia Shelley, 12, 183,
257–59, 260, 265, 269,
272, 416, 426
France, Alan, 337
Frank, Otto, 391
Franklin, Phyllis, 119–21
Freedman, Sarah Warshauer, 83
Freire, Paulo, 11, 12, 136–39,

EDITORS

Robert P. Yagelski is associate professor of English education at the University at Albany, State University of New York, where he teaches courses in writing, literacy, pedagogy, and rhetoric. Previously, he co-directed the English education program at Purdue University and chaired the English department at Vermont Academy, an independent high school. He is the author of *Literacy Matters: Writing and Reading the Social Self* (2000) and of numerous articles and essays about teaching writing that have appeared in *College Composition and Communication, Research in the Teaching of English, English Education,* and *Journal of Teaching Writing,* among other publications.

Scott A. Leonard is associate professor of English at Youngstown State University, where he wears many hats. Currently, he directs the composition program and teaches composition, mythology, British Romantic literature, and critical theory. An alumnus of Ohio State University, he has published and is conducting ongoing research in collaborative writing and Victorian travel writers. Lately, he has been developing a project that considers mythology as episteme.

CONTRIBUTORS

Kathleen R. Cheney is associate professor of English at Adirondack Community College in upstate New York. She teaches courses in composition, journal writing, literature of social movements, and autobiography and memoir. She is also a frequent faculty tutor in the college's Center for Reading and Writing. In addition to teaching regular English courses, she team-teaches in the College Survival/Developmental Studies program designed for underprepared and at-risk students.

Juanita Rodgers Comfort teaches courses in composition and rhetoric at West Chester University of Pennsylvania. She has recently published "Becoming a Writerly Self: College Writers Engaging Black Feminist Essays" in *College Composition and Communication* and "African American Women's Rhetorics and the Culture of Eurocentric Scholarly Discourse" in *Contrastive Rhetoric Revisited and Redefined* (2001).

Beth Davis teaches at Simpson Middle School in Marietta, Georgia.

Valerie Hardin Drye, a native of Western North Carolina, currently resides with her husband, two cats, and an assortment of teddy bears in Mount Pleasant, North Carolina. In 2001, after two years of lateral-entry "trail by fire," she is finally fully licensed and nearing her first year of the tenure process with Cabarrus County Schools (N.C.) at Concord High School. A teacher of ninth- and tenth-grade English, she still wrestles with her state's continuing preoccupation with standardized assessment as she works to prepare her students to pass their state-mandated Eighth Grade Reading Competency Test, English 1 End of Course Test, English 2 Writing Test, Tenth Grade Reading and Math Competency Test, and the field testing for the state's newest: an exit exam that all students must pass to graduate. And now the state's leaders are talking about teacher competency tests. "The jury's still out," she says, "on whether this is something I want to keep doing. Do you suppose we can require competency testing for all politicians seeking office?"

Margaret J. Finders is associate professor of education and director of teacher education at Washington University in St. Louis, where she teaches courses in literacy and teacher preparation. Her research interests focus on early adolescence and sociopolitical dimensions of literacy learning.

Patricia Shelley Fox is assistant professor of English and director of the Coastal Georgia Writing Project at Armstrong Atlantic State University in Savannah, Georgia. A member of the editorial review board for the *Journal of Teaching Writing,* her research interests include discursive practice, the politics of literacy, women's studies, and the work of nontraditional students in the academy.

Gerald Graff is associate dean of curriculum and instruction and professor of English and education at the University of Illinois at Chicago. He is finishing a book entitled *Clueless in Academe: How Schooling Obscures the Life of the Mind.*

Cristina Kirklighter is assistant professor at the University of Tampa. She is coeditor with Cloe Vincent of *Voices and Visions: Refiguring Ethnography in Composition* (1997) and is currently working on a book entitled *Traversing the Democratic Borders of the Essay in Western Europe, Latin America, and the U.S.* She has given numerous conference papers and published several essays, book reviews, and chapters on personal narrative.

Paula Mathieu received her doctorate in Language, Literacy and Rhetoric from the University of Illinois at Chicago and is currently assistant professor of English at Boston College. She is coeditor with David B. Downing and Claude Mark Hurlbert of *Beyond English, Inc.* (2002) and has written articles for *Rhetoric Review, Works and Days,* and other essay collections.

Mary Miesiaszek teaches at Simpson Elementary School in Norcross, Georgia.

Ted Nellen, cybrarian, educational consultant, staff developer, adjunct professor at Fordham University and New School University, as well as guide and TA for Classroom Connect University, is a full-time teacher and staff developer for the Alternative High Schools of New York City, working currently at Bronx Tech. He began teaching high school English in 1974. He began using computers in his NYC public high school Cyber English class in 1983, using the Internet in 1985, and using the World Wide Web in 1993. He is a Shakespeare scholar, a Carnegie scholar, a doctoral candidate, a conference speaker, and a published author, and he has been named

teacher of the year twice in NYC public schools. He is actively
engaged on many foundation educational advisory boards and on
NCTE technology assemblies, commissions, and committees.

Stephen M. North is professor of English at the University at Albany,
State University of New York, where he has directed both the writing center and the writing program. He is the author of *The Making of Knowledge in Composition: Portrait of an Emerging Field*
(1987) and, with a group of contributors, of *Refiguring the Ph.D.
in English Studies* (2000). He is the founding editor of NCTE's
Refiguring English Studies series and is founding coeditor of *The
Writing Center Journal*. His writings have appeared in *College English*, *CCC*, *Rhetoric Review*, *Writing on the Edge*, and a variety of
other venues.

Richard M. Ohmann taught at Wesleyan University for thirty-five years,
edited *College English* for twelve, and currently serves on the board
of *Radical Teacher*, which he helped found in 1975. His book *English in America: A Radical View of the Profession*, published in
1976, is widely considered a classic analysis of the discipline of
English studies. His latest book is *Selling Culture: Magazines, Markets, and Class at the Turn of the Century.*

Mark Reynolds is instructor of English at Jefferson Davis Community
College in Brewton, Alabama, where he also chairs the humanities
division. He has recently completed a seven-year term as editor of
Teaching English in the Two-Year College. He is the editor of *Two-
Year College English: Essays for a New Century* and the author of
articles on professional issues and the teaching of writing and literature.

Sarah Robbins is director of the National Writing Project's site at
Kennesaw State University in Georgia. She is currently collaborating with teachers across Georgia and around the country on a
multiyear curriculum development project funded by the National
Endowment for the Humanities called Keeping and Creating American Communities. Project teachers and their students are using inquiry-based and writing-centered approaches for studying their own
community's place in American culture.

Cynthia L. Selfe is professor of humanities in the humanities department at Michigan Technological University. She has served as chair
of the Conference on College Composition and Communication
and as chair of the College Section of the National Council of Teachers of English. Selfe's work appears, among other places, in the
following volumes: *Technology and Literacy in the Twenty-First*

Century: The Importance of Paying Attention (1999); *Passions, Pedagogies, and 21st Century Technologies* (coedited with Gail E. Hawisher, 1999); *Global Literacies and the World-Wide Web* (coedited with Hawisher, 2000); and *Computers and the Teaching of Writing in American Higher Education, 1979–1994: A History* (coauthored with Hawisher, Paul LeBlanc, and Charles Moran, 1996). Selfe is coeditor (with Gail Hawisher) of *Computers and Composition,* an international journal for teachers of composition who use technology, and founder (along with Hawisher) of Computers and Composition Press. In 1996, Selfe was recognized as an EDUCOM Medal Award winner for innovative computer use in higher education—the first woman and the first English teacher to receive this award.

Richard J. (Dickie) Selfe is director of computer-based instruction in the humanities department at Michigan Technological University and directs the Center for Computer-Assisted Language Instruction, a technical communication–oriented computer facility. He teaches a range of computer-intensive technical communication and graduate computer studies courses. His professional interests include technology-rich communication pedagogy as well as the social and institutional influences of electronic media on educational institutions.

James J. Sosnoski is professor of English at the University of Illinois at Chicago. He is the author of *Token Professionals and Master Critics: A Critique of Orthodoxy in Literary Studies* and *Modern Skeletons in Postmodern Closets: A Cultural Studies Alternative,* as well as various essays on literary and pedagogical theory, computer-assisted pedagogy, and online collaboration. With David Downing, he coedited "The Geography of Cyberspace," "Conversations in Honor of James Berlin," and "The TicToc Conversations"—all special issues of the journal *Works and Days.* He has served as executive director of the Society for Critical Exchange (1982–86), director of the Group for Research into the Institutionalization and Professionalization of Literary Studies (1982–84) and the TicToc project (1996–97), a collaborative effort to bring together experts in technology and members of the English department at UIC to develop an online work environment. He has been a member of MLA's Delegate Assembly, Ethics Committee, and Emerging Technologies Committee. He is collaborating with David Downing on *Living on Borrowed Terms,* a study of the use of terminology in literary and rhetorical studies. He is also currently coordinating the Virtual Harlem, an instructional technology project using virtual reality scenarios, and working on *Configuring,* a study of analogous understanding.

Donald L. Tinney, a graduate of the University of Vermont, served as president of the Vermont Council of Teachers of English for four years. He has taught English and reading in both private and public schools for the last sixteen years. His first book, *Vermonters,* was published in 1985.

Victor Villanueva is professor and chair of the English department at Washington State University, where he also teaches rhetoric and composition studies. He is author of *Bootstraps: From an American Academic of Color,* for which he has won national awards, and editor of *Cross-Talk in Comp Theory: A Reader.* A prolific writer of articles and a frequent speaker at professional conventions, he was declared the Rhetorician of the Year for 1999 by the Young Rhetoricians Conference. He is also the former head of the Conference on College Composition and Communication, has chaired its national conference, and has twice co-chaired its Winter Workshop. His concern is always with racism and with the political more generally as embodied in rhetoric and literacy.

Kathleen Blake Yancey is Pearce Professor of Professional Communication and director of the Roy and Marnie Pearce Center for Professional Communication at Clemson University. She is author of *Reflection in the Writing Classroom* (1998) and of many articles on teaching and assessing writing. She is also editor of *Portfolios in the Writing Classroom* (1992) and *Voices on Voice* (1994) and co-editor (with Brian Huot) of *Assessing Writing Across the Curriculum* (1997), (with Irwin Weiser) of *Situating Portfolios* (1997), and (with Jane Bowman) of *Self-Assessment and Development in Writing* (2000).

This book was typeset in Sabon by Electronic Imaging.
Typefaces used on the cover were Eras, Frutiger, and Officina Sans.
The book was printed on 50-lb. Husky Offset
by IPC Communication Services.

1657

AEE-8230